The Power of God

The Power of God

BY THOMAS AQUINAS

Translated by

RICHARD J. REGAN

OXFORD
UNIVERSITY PRESS

OXFORD
UNIVERSITY PRESS

Oxford University Press, Inc., publishes works that further
Oxford University's objective of excellence
in research, scholarship, and education.

Oxford   New York
Auckland   Cape Town   Dar es Salaam   Hong Kong   Karachi
Kuala Lumpur   Madrid   Melbourne   Mexico City   Nairobi
New Delhi   Shanghai   Taipei   Toronto

With offices in
Argentina   Austria   Brazil   Chile   Czech Republic   France   Greece
Guatemala   Hungary   Italy   Japan   Poland   Portugal   Singapore
South Korea   Switzerland   Thailand   Turkey   Ukraine   Vietnam

Published by Oxford University Press, Inc.
198 Madison Avenue, New York, New York 10016

www.oup.com

Library of Congress Cataloging-in-Publication Data
Thomas, Aquinas, Saint, 1225?–1274.
[Quaestiones disputatae de potentia Dei. English]
The power of God / by Thomas Aquinas ; translated by Richard J. Regan.
p. cm.
Includes bibliographical references (p.   ) and index.
ISBN 978-0-19-991462-3—ISBN 978-0-19-991439-5
1. God (Christianity)—Omnipotence—Early works to 1800. I. Regan, Richard J. II. Title.
BT133.T52Q34713   2012
231'.4—dc23   2011037886

Contents

Preface   xi

Biblical Abbreviations   xiii

Other Abbreviations   xv

Introduction   xvii

Question 1: *The Power of God Absolutely*   3

    Articles

       1. Is There Power in God?   3

       2. Is God's Power Infinite?   6

       3. Are Things Impossible for Nature Possible for God?   9

       4. Should We Judge Something to Be Possible or
         Impossible by Lower or Higher Causes?   12

       5. Can God Cause Things That He Does Not Cause and Abandon
         Things That He Causes?   14

       6. Can God Do Things Possible for Others, Such as Sinning,
         Walking, and the Like?   17

       7. Why Do We Call God Almighty?   19

Question 2: *The Power in the Godhead to Generate*   21

    Articles

       1. Is There a Power in the Godhead to Generate?   21

       2. Do We Speak of the Generative Power in God Essentially or
         Notionally?   25

3. Does the Generative Power Proceed to the Act of Generation at the Will's Command? 27

4. Can There Be Several Sons in God? 30

5. Is the Power to Generate Included in Omnipotence? 32

6. Are the Power to Generate and the Power to Create the Same? 34

Question 3: *Creation, the First Effect of Divine Power* 36

Articles

1. Can God create Something Out of Nothing? 36

2. Is Creation a Change? 39

3. Is Creation Something Really in a Creature, or If It Is, What Is It? 41

4. Is the Power to Create or the Act of Creation Communicable to a Creature? 43

5. Can There Be Anything That God Did Not Create? 48

6. Is There Only One Source of Creation? 50

7. Is God Active in the Actions of Nature? 54

8. Does God Act in Nature by Creating, That Is, Is Creation Involved in Nature's Action? 59

9. Does Creation Bring the Rational Soul into Existence, or Does the Transmission of Semen? 62

10. Is the Rational Soul Created in the Body or outside It? 68

11. Does Semen Create or Transmit the Sensory and Vegetative Souls? 71

12. Is a Sensory or Vegetative Soul in the Semen at the Moment of Its Emission? 74

13. Can Any Being from Another Being Be Eternal? 76

14. Can What Essentially Differs from God Have Always Existed? 79

15. Did Things Proceed from God by a Natural Necessity or by a Decision of His Will? 81

16. Can Multiplicity Proceed from One First Thing? 84

17. Has the World Always Existed? 89

18. Were the Angels Created before the Visible World? 94

19. Could the Angels Have Existed before the Visible World? 98

Question 4: *The Creation of Unformed Matter* 100

    Articles

      1. Did the Creation of Unformed Matter Precede in Time the Creation of Things? 100

      2. Was the Formation of Matter All at Once or Successively? 109

Question 5: *The Preservation of Things in Existence by God* 132

    Articles

      1. Does God Preserve Things in Existence, or Do They Remain in Existence Intrinsically, with All God's Action Circumscribed? 132

      2. Can God Communicate to a Creature to Be Intrinsically Preserved in Existing without God? 137

      3. Can God Annihilate a Creature? 138

      4. Should a Creature Be Annihilated, or Is Any? 141

      5. Does Heavenly Motion at Some Time Cease? 144

      6. Can a Human Being Know When the Heavenly Motion Ends? 149

      7. Do the Elements Remain When Heavenly Motion Ceases? 151

      8. Do Action and Being Acted Upon Remain When Heavenly Motion Ceases? 154

      9. Do Plants, Irrational Animals, and Minerals Remain after the World's End? 156

      10. Do Human Bodies Remain When Heavenly Motion Ceases? 158

Question 6: *Miracles* 161

    Articles

      1. Can God Do Anything in Created Things Outside Natural Causes, Whether Contrary to Nature or Contrary to the Course of Nature? 161

      2. Can We Call All the Things God Does without Natural Causes or Contrary to the Course of Nature Miracles? 165

      3. Can Spiritual Creatures by Their Natural Powers Cause Miracles? 167

      4. Can Good Angels and Human Beings Work Miracles by a Gift of Grace? 172

5. Do Devils Also Act to Work Miracles? 174

6. Do Angels and Devils Have Bodies by Nature United to Them? 176

7. Can Angels or Devils Assume Bodies? 182

8. Can an Angel or Devil with an Assumed Body Perform the Actions of a Living Body? 185

9. Should We Attribute Miraculous Activity to Faith? 187

10. Do Certain Sensibly Perceptible and Material Things, Deeds, or Words Force Devils to Work the Miracles that Magical Skills Seem to Cause? 189

Question 7: *The Simplicity of the Divine Essence* 193

Articles

1. Is God Simple? 193

2. Is the Essence or Substance in God the Same as His Existing? 196

3. Is God in a Genus? 200

4. Do We Predicate *Good, Wise, Just* of God as Accidents? 202

5. Do the Aforementioned Terms Signify the Divine Substance? 205

6. Are These Terms Synonymous? 210

7. Do We Predicate Such Terms of God and Creatures Univocally or Equivocally? 213

8. Is There a Relation between God and a Creature? 216

9. Do Such Relations between Creatures and God Really Exist in Creatures Themselves? 219

10. Is God Really Related to a Creature, So That the Relation Is Something in God? 222

11. Are These Temporal Relations in God Conceptually? 225

Question 8: *The Things That We Predicate of God Eternally* 227

Articles

1. Are the Relations Predicated of God Eternally, Which the Terms *Father* and *Son* Signify, Real or Purely Conceptual Relations? 227

2. Is Relation in God His Substance? 231

3. Do the Relations Constitute and Distinguish the Persons or
Hypostases? 234

4. Does a Hypostasis Remain When We Exclude a Relation
Conceptually? 238

Question 9: *The Divine Persons* 242

Articles

1. How Is Person Related to Essence, Subsistence,
and Hypostasis? 242

2. What Is a Person? 244

3. Can There Be Personhood in God? 248

4. Does the Word *Person* Signify Something Relative to Something
Absolute in the Godhead? 250

5. Are There Several Persons in the Godhead? 254

6. Can We Properly Predicate the Word *Person* in the Plural in the
Godhead? 259

7. How Do We Predicate Numerical Terms of Divine Persons,
Namely, Whether Positively or Only Negatively? 260

8. Is There Any Diversity in God? 266

9. Are There Three, or More or Less, Persons in the Godhead? 268

Question 10: *The Procession of the Divine Persons* 276

Articles

1. Is There Procession in the Divine Persons? 276

2. Are There One or More Processions in the Godhead? 280

3. What Is the Order of Procession to Relation in the Godhead? 286

4. Does the Holy Spirit Proceed from the Son? 288

5. Would the Holy Spirit Still Be from the Son if He Were Not to
Proceed from Him? 296

Notes 305

Bibliography 319

Index 321

Preface

THE DOMINICAN FATHERS have not yet completed editing the Leonine text of Thomas Aquinas's Disputed Questions on the Power of God, nor are they expected to do so any time soon. One Dominican Father before his death had completed editing Q. 3, on creation, but the text has not yet been published. Susan C. Selner-Wright had access to the text and translated it, with commentary (see Bibliography). My translation of the entire treatise is based on the best text currently available: Thomas Aquinas, *Quaestiones Disputatae*, II:7–276 (Turin: Marietti, 1949). That text, however, has a few typographical errors (e.g., *causale* for *casuale* in connection with Democritus, famous for attributing the motion of matter to chance [*casus*]. Such typos are fortunately easy to spot.

I have taken the liberty of transforming the text's format in one respect. I first relate the question-and-answer of each article and then list objections and replies. I include those objections that elicited the longest replies, sometimes several pages long, as well as a sample of other objections and replies. Professional academicians may understandably wish that all the objections and replies be included, but I think that one can very well comprehend the basic questions and answers without reference to every objection and reply. There is also a consideration of economy. Were I to include all of the objections and replies, the text would be twice its present extensive size. The present text should suffice for the use of most students and readers. For study of the objections and replies not included in this book, specialists and students can consult Lawrence Shapcote, *On the Power of God*, 3 vols. (London: Burns, Oates, and Washbourne, 1934).

I have provided the notes given in the Marietti text. The notes, however, are frequently incomplete, and there are many places where there should be notes. Scholars will have to await publication of the authoritative Leonine text. I have used the Latin titles of texts of Aristotle where that titling is in general usage (e.g., the *De anima*). For other authors, I have used the English titles of works when the English titles are commonplace and readily recognizable but have retained Latin or Greek titles where an English translation might not be recognizable (e.g., the *Hexameron*). I add a comment on my translation of the Latin word *suppositum*, which features prominently in Thomas' discussion of the Persons in the Trinity. Most translators leave the Latin word in place, as Shapcote does, or use the equivalent but unfamiliar English word *supposit*. There is no need to do so. The *Index Thomisticus* cites several places where Thomas defines *suppositum* as *existing individual*, and the unabridged English dictionary gives the same definition of the English equivalent.

I have provided an Introduction that chiefly summarizes Thomas' theses and arguments, and a Bibliography that refers the reader to a comprehensive compilation by Brian Davies, to which I have added a list of more recent notable works.

Richard J. Regan
Bronx, N.Y.

Biblical Abbreviations

Col.	Colossians
Cor.	Corinthians
Eccl	Ecclesiastes
Ex.	Exodus
Ez.	Ezekiel
Gal.	Galatians
Gen.	Genesis
Hebr.	Hebrews
Hos.	Hosea
Is.	Isaiah
Jn.	John
Jon.	Jonah
Jos.	Josiah
Kgs.	Kings
Lk.	Luke
Mt.	Matthew
Prov.	Proverbs
Ps.	Psalm
Rev.	Revelation
Rom.	Romans
Sam.	Samuel
Sir.	Sirach
Thess.	Thessalonians
Tim.	Timothy
Tob.	Tobias
Zcch.	Zechariah

Other Abbreviations

A., AA.	article, articles
Comm.	comment
Counterobj(s).	Counterobjection(s).
CT	Thomas Aquinas, *Compendium of Theology*
Dist.	distinction
Hom.	homily
n., nn.	number(s)
Obj(s).	objection(s)
Prop(s).	proposition(s)
Q., QQ.	question, questions
SCG	Thomas Aquinas, *Summary against the Pagans*
ST	Thomas Aquinas, *Summary of Theology*

Introduction

THE PHILOSOPHER-THEOLOGIAN Thomas Aquinas (A.D. 1224/1225–1274) composed three comprehensive treatises on God, human beings, and the universe: the *ST*, the *SCG*, and the *CT*. Earlier, he also wrote an extensive *Commentary on the Sentences* of Peter Lombard, a standard practice of the masters of theology at the University of Paris. In addition, he composed treatises on particular topics, the Disputed Questions, one of which is on the power of God (the *De potentia*).

During the academic year, masters at the University of Paris were required to conduct frequent public disputations on theological topics. These disputations were an integral part of a theological program of studies. Thomas did so with great frequency, especially in the three years of his first professorship at Paris (1256–1259), when he held one every other week during term. The Disputed Questions of Thomas consist of a systematic series of discussions on the questions. Two mornings were normally set aside for a public disputation, during which lectures by the faculty were suspended.

On the first morning, an audience of masters, bachelors, students, and attendants attacked a thesis chosen by a master and announced beforehand. A bachelor, directed by the master, defended the thesis. The master presided and controlled the discussion and gave his resolution. On the next scheduled morning, the master briefly summarized in order the points raised and briefly responded by citing rational arguments and biblical and ecclesiastical authority. Then he gave a detailed explanation and proof of the thesis, followed by specific replies to the objections. The master or a reporter under his direction recorded the disputations. Each article in the Disputed Questions reports a disputation, and the articles in the longest series of disputations were grouped into questions.

Thomas returned to Italy in 1259 and was an advisor to the papal court and regent master of Dominicans in their course of studies until 1267. As master of Dominicans in studies there, Thomas conducted disputations like those in

Paris, one of which was the *De potentia*. While scholars agree that he compiled the latter during this period, the place and exact date are disputed. According to Pierre Mandonnet, the disputations were written during Thomas' stay at Anagni (1259–1261), but according to Martin Grabmann, they were written at Rome when Thomas was regent of studies at the Priory of Santa Sabina (1265–1267).

The Disputed Questions on the Power of God

Like all Thomas' other works, the *De potentia* is a theological treatise. He speculated on the tenets of the Christian faith, using rational arguments to support theses but always from a theological perspective.

Question 1 considers God's power in general. As God is pure actuality and perfect, his power is necessarily infinite, that is, unlimited (AA. 1 and 2), and can do more than nature can (A. 3). He distinguishes things possible by lower causes, that is, nature, and things possible by higher causes, that is, spiritual creatures and God (A. 4). God can cause other things than those he does, and he can annihilate creatures, although it would be contrary to his wisdom to do so (A. 5). God cannot do contradictory things, things contrary to his goodness, such as sin, or his essence, such as walking (A. 6). God is almighty in this sense (A. 7). Thomas bases these positions on arguments from natural reason.

In Question 2, Thomas moves from considering the power of God to cause external things in the world to considering the power in the Godhead to generate naturally, that is, the Son within the Trinity. As an orthodox Christian, he accepts on faith that there is a power to generate the Son (A. 1). Unlike the power to create external things, the power in the Godhead to generate the Son is essential to the Godhead, but the common divine nature, because it needs to be the source of an action of generation that befits only the Father, needs to be the source insofar as it belongs to the Father as a personal property (A. 2). As in the case of our intellect conceiving a word, that is, the form of what it understands, God's will is in no way the source of the divine generation. Although the Godhead wills the Son and the generation of the Son, God's will does not freely decide whether to generate the Son, something possible only regarding the creation of creatures (A. 3). There is only one Son, since only the relation of sonship can distinguish the Son from the other Persons of the Trinity, and that relation constitutes the Person of the Son (A. 4). The power to generate the Son belongs to the omnipotence of God but only as that power belongs to the Father (A.5). The power to generate the Son and the power to create external things regard different kinds of action, although the powers as power are the same (A. 6). Note that Thomas is not concerned with demonstrating from Scripture that the Father does generate the Son but rather aims to connect the generation of the Son to God's power.

In Question 3, Thomas returns to rational analysis of creation. It is the most extensive development of any question in the *De potentia* and one of the fullest in any of his works. Creation causes being from nothing, that is, no preexisting matter (A. 1), and he thereby distinguishes it from natural change, that is, causing something to exist from something else (A. 2). Creation, considered passively in a creature, is a real relation to its active cause, God (A. 3). The act of creation, since it causes the very existing of a creature, cannot be communicated to another creature (A. 4). God creates everything in the universe (A. 5), and he is the only source of everything (A. 6).

He is also active in the actions of nature (A. 7), but his action consists of being the primary cause of the actions of nature in conjunction with secondary natural causes, not creating the effects from nothing (A. 8). One part of nature, however, is an exception. The rational soul, although it is the form of the human body, is intrinsically immaterial because of its immaterial activities of understanding and reason. Therefore, God necessarily creates it out of nothing (A. 9) and in the body of each human being (A. 10). The sensory and vegetative souls are not created, but as the natural generative act by semen produces the body, so does it produce the sensory and vegetative souls in human beings (A. 11). Those souls are not in semen at the moment of its emission, but rather semen contains an active power derived from the begetter's soul to produce them in the begotten (A. 12).

The Son by nature proceeds eternally from the Father, since the Son could not be in a different way from the Father (A. 13). We cannot say that something essentially different from God, that is, something created, could not always exist by his will. Nonetheless, the tenets of the Catholic faith hold that no creature always existed (A. 14). Creatures proceed from God by his free will, not any natural necessity (A. 15). The multiplicity and diversity of creatures proceed directly from the first thing, God, not by a series of processions, and the multiplicity and diversity of creatures are required for the perfection of the universe (A. 16). As the Catholic faith holds, the world has not always existed, and no demonstration by reason can prove that it did. Time exists in the world, and God allots as much time to it as he wills (A. 17). Catholic teachers agree that the angels were created at the same time as the material world (A. 18), although they could have existed before it (A. 19).

Question 4 attempts to reconcile the rational analysis of the creation of the world, the rational soul, and angels in Question 3 with the first chapter of the Book of Genesis. First, Thomas opposed two approaches: one that would presume that Scripture contains false propositions and things contrary to the Catholic faith; the other that would presume that the text prescribes a particular interpretation when Catholic teachers are divided about interpreting the text. As to the first, Thomas forthrightly declares that absolutely formless matter, that is, prime matter, is impossible, and nothing prevents us from understanding the formlessness of matter described in the text before the advent of form by the order of nature or origin, not in a temporal sense (A. 1). Then, in the lengthy A. 2, Thomas explains the two lines of interpreting the six days of creation and their morning and evenings. According to Augustine, the days indicate the successive production of forms in the mornings according to the order of nature, not temporally. Other saints interpret the six days of creation to indicate both the successive production of forms according to the order of nature and the temporal order. Thomas concludes that either interpretation is compatible with the Catholic faith and the context, although the second is more compatible with the words of the text. Thomas is not a biblical exegete in the modern sense, but neither is he a William Jennings Bryan fundamentalist.

Question 5 takes up the power of God in the preservation of things. In the first part (AA. 1–4), Thomas argues from reason that creatures always depend on God for their existing, with their every action prescribed by him, and that nothing created remains in existence by reason of itself (A. 1). God cannot communicate to a creature to be intrinsically preserved in existence apart from his power any more than he can communicate to a creature the power to create (A. 2). God could annihilate a creature (A. 3), but this would be contrary to his providence (A. 4). In the second part of this question (AA. 5–10), Thomas considers what will happen at the consummation of the world. Heavenly motion, no longer serving any function in the universe, will cease, and heavenly bodies will remain in stationary positions and beautify the cosmos (A. 5). No human being can know when this will occur (A. 6). The elements, namely, earth, fire, water, and air, will abide in their natural qualities (A. 7). Action and being acted upon will cease (A. 8). Other than the human body, material substances of mixed elements, namely, plants, irrational animals, and minerals will not remain, among other reasons because they will no longer be needed to satisfy human needs (A. 9). But human bodies will, since the immortal rational soul is their form, and are with the soul part of the perfection of the universe (A. 10).

In Question 6, Thomas considers the power to work miracles. Contrary to such Enlightenment thinkers as John Locke and David Hume, he argues that God as the cause of things existing can do things contrary to nature or the course of nature (A. 1). Thomas adopts Augustine's definition of a miracle as "something different and unusual above the capacity of nature and apparently beyond the expectation of the one wondering about it" (A. 2). (The reader may note that a miracle so defined requires that God's action *transcend* the action of natural things and the course of nature, although many or most Catholic theologians today hold that events involving an extraordinary and unusual concatenation of natural causes could qualify as a miracle.)

In addition to direct action by God, faith judges that spiritual creatures, namely, angels, can at his command cause the motion of the heavenly bodies and lower material substances. Angels produce certain wondrous effects on earth by their skill but do not work miracles by their natural spiritual power, contrary to the position of some philosophers (A. 3). Good angels can instrumentally work true miracles by a gift of grace, and so can good human beings (A. 4). Like good angels, devils have the power to move external material things and images in the imagination of human beings. They have the power to produce wondrous effects by their skill but none above their natural spiritual power (A. 5).

Article 6 considers whether angels and devils have bodies attached to them by nature. Some philosophers thought that all substances are material, and other philosophers thought that some substances are immaterial, but that they were always united to bodies as their form. Plato held that some immaterial substances are joined to airy bodies, and others to earthly bodies. But Aristotle denied the union of intellectual substances with airy bodies and posited some immaterial substances not united to a body. Thomas holds that, according to the true faith, angels and devils do not have bodies united to them by nature. Angels and devils can assume a human form in apparitions (A. 7), but they cannot with an assumed body perform the actions of a living one, such as speaking and eating (A. 8).

Saints rightly disposed can also instrumentally work miracles by their prayers and power, and even faith without charity congruously merits that one's petition for a miracle be heard, although charity is the foundation of meriting (A. 9). Devils work their wondrous effects by magical skills. God, angels, or human beings can compel them to refrain from doing such things, higher devils can compel lower ones to perform works, and material things can in various ways entice devils (A. 10).

Question 7 examines what philosophical reason can say about the divine essence itself, matter also treated in *ST* 1, Q. 3. God, as the first actuality, is simple, that is, pure actuality without any mixture of potentiality (A. 1). As uncreated, his essence or substance is his existing, and he does not share in existing (A. 2). Thus he does not belong to any genus of things (A. 3). Affirmative, nonmetaphorical predicates about God, such as good, wise, and just, are not accidents in God (A. 4). Rather, such predicates signify the divine essence itself, although defectively and imperfectly from the perfections of creatures (A. 5). Such predicates, however, are not synonymous, since our intellect conceives the divine essence by many deficient likenesses in creatures, as if reflections in a mirror (A. 6). We predicate the terms analogously, that is, in a sense partly the same and partly different, not univocally or purely equivocally (A. 7). There are relations between God and creatures (A. 8), the one of the creature really existing in the creature (A. 9) and the one of God to a creature being only conceptually in God (AA. 10 and 11).

The last three questions examine predication about God from eternity (Q. 8), the divine Persons (Q. 9) and the processions of the Son and the Holy Spirit (Q. 10). The examination is speculative theology, that is, rational speculation about the Trinity. In Q. 8, Thomas explains that the personal relations, such as Father and Son, that we predicate about God signify real, not purely conceptual, relations, and the Persons differ by relations, not anything absolute (A. 1). By analogy to the human intellect conceiving the word of what it understands but without the limitations of that process, the Father can originate the Son without prejudice to the unity of the divine essence. Since there is no composition in God, the internal relations in the Godhead are the divine substance itself but have a way of predication different from the substantial way we predicate things such as simplicity about God (A. 2). God the Father, as Father, is distinct from the other Persons, a hypothesis, that is, an existing individual, and his paternity constitutes him a hypostasis and distinguishes him from the other Persons (A. 3). When we conceptually exclude consideration of the internal relations in the Godhead, the Persons do not remain, and so neither do the hypostases, since what constitutes a hypostasis cannot remain when one excludes what constitutes it (A. 4).

Question 9 considers the notion of person, its relation to essence, subsistence, and hypostasis, and its presence in the Godhead. A substance as subject does not exist in another but subsists of itself. As such, the Greeks call a person a hypostasis. In immaterial things, there is no difference between essence and substance as existing individual, but there is in material things, since matter individuates the essence of such things. Person adds rational nature to hypostasis (A. 1). A person is an individual substance, or hypostasis, of a rational nature (A. 2). We can attribute personhood to God, since a person's way of existing is intellectual, namely, one who exists intrinsically (A. 3). The word *person* has something in common with the name predicated of God absolutely and something in common with the name we predicate to signify the internal relations in the Godhead. Divine Person formally signifies a distinct subsistent thing in the divine nature, and since such a Person can only be a relation or something relative, it materially signifies the relation or relative thing and so a substance or hypostasis, not an essence. The signified relation of fatherhood, for example, is included in the meaning of a divine Person, the Father, who is something subsisting in the divine nature and distinguished by the relation (A. 4).

The plurality of Persons in the Godhead concerns matters subject to faith, and we cannot adequately understand it, but we can by analogy to our intellect clarify it. It belongs to the nature of understanding that there is the one who understands and the thing understood. Unlike our intellect, God conceives only one Word, which perfectly represents him and all things, and which has the same essence and nature of the intellect conceiving it. The remaining difference after we exclude the differences between our intellect and the divine intellect consists of our word proceeding from something other and the divine Word proceeding from something the same. Therefore, since differences cause number, the plurality in God consists only of the subsistent relations, and so there is a plurality of divine Persons (A. 5).

We properly predicate the word *person* in the Godhead in the plural, since there are plural properties in it, just as we predicate the word of human beings in the plural because of their individuating sources (A. 6). We predicate unity and the corresponding multiplicity in the Godhead compatible with a being, not what belongs to the genus of quantity. The unity of a being adds only the negation or lack of division, but insofar as unity and multiplicity include the meaning of the things of which we predicate them, we understand them positively (A. 7). We should speak about the Godhead in such a way that we do not occasion the errors of Arius and Sabellius, namely, the error of Arius that denied the essential unity of the Trinity and the error of Sabellius that denied the plurality of Persons. Thomas enumerates expressions to avoid regarding each error (A. 8). The Catholic faith maintains the unity of the divine essence in three really distinct Persons, no more and no less. There are only two kinds of intellectual action, namely, understanding and willing. By understanding his essence, God understands himself and all things, and by willing his goodness, he loves himself and all the things he wills. Therefore, since there is only one understanding and one willing in God, there is in the Godhead only one product of God's understanding, the Word, and one product of his Love, the Holy Spirit (A. 9).

The last question, Question 10, continues discussion of the divine Persons regarding the processions of the Son and the Holy Spirit. Processions from God come about in two ways, transitively in the creation of external things and immanently within the Godhead. In the second kind of action, there is the procession of the Word, the Son, and that of Love, the Holy Spirit (A. 1). The origins of the processions multiply and distinguish them. The first procession in the Godhead, that of the Word, the Son, presupposes no other procession, and the second, that of Love, the Holy Spirit, presupposes the procession of the Word, since the love of anything can proceed from the will only if an understood good, the word, is the object of the will (A. 2). There is one way of understanding a relation in the Godhead, as constituting a divine Person, and another way of understanding a relation as such. Therefore, if one should consider a divine relation as such, it presupposes an understanding of procession. But if we consider the relation as constituting the Person, then the relation that constitutes the Person from whom there is a procession is conceptually prior to the procession, although the relation that constitutes the Person proceeding, even as such, is conceptually subsequent to procession (A. 3).

The last two articles of Question 10 consider in considerable depth the procession of the Holy Spirit from the Son, in conjunction with the Father. Thomas gives a number of rational arguments for this position, the first of which echoes A. 2 and asserts that there can be processions in the Godhead only in a successive order in which the second Person proceeding is from the first Person proceeding. To this and other rational arguments, Thomas adds brief scriptural ones. It is not enough to say, as the Greek Church does, that the Holy Spirit proceeds through the Son but not from him, since that whereby something is produced is always the source of what is produced. There is one and the same power in the Father and the Son in the procession of the Holy Spirit (A. 4). Thomas expands the argument against the position of the Greek Church on the procession of the Holy Spirit. From many considerations, Thomas concludes that the Holy Spirit would not differ from the Son if the Spirit were not to proceed from the Son, nor would the origination of the Spirit be different from generation (A. 5).

The *De potentia* is a theological work, chiefly about the Trinity. The principal patristic authority cited in the work is Augustine, the Church Father most highly regarded by Western medieval theologians. Nonetheless, the work contains much material that should be of interest to students of philosophy. For example, Thomas devotes extensive attention to the subject of creation, especially in Q. 3. He summarily explains the analogy of being, a central element of his philosophical analysis, in Q. 7, A. 7, and gives the classic example of predicating *healthy* of urine and medicine in Reply Counterobj. 2. And he explains the transcendental predication of *one* in Q. 7, A. 7. The principal philosophical authority cited in the work is Aristotle.

The Power of God

Question 1

THE POWER OF GOD ABSOLUTELY

Article 1

Is There Power in God?

To clarify the point of this question, we should note that we speak of power in relation to actuality. But actuality is twofold, namely, the first actuality, which is the form, and the second actuality, which is activity. And as we see from the common understanding of human beings, they first attributed actuality to activity and, second, transferred actuality to the form, inasmuch as form is the source and end of activity.

And so power is likewise twofold: one, active power, to which an act corresponds, and the word *power* seems to have been first attributed in relation to action; the second, passive power, to which the first actuality, that is, the form, corresponds, and the word *power* seems likewise to have been secondarily applied to the form. And as nothing undergoes anything except by reason of passive power, so nothing acts except by reason of the first actuality, that is, the form. For I have said that the word *actuality* was initially applied to the first actuality from its relation to activity. But it belongs to God to be the pure and first actuality. And so acting and pouring out his likeness to other things belongs especially to him. And so also active power especially belongs to him, since we call power active insofar as it is the source of activity.

But we should also note that our intellect strives to express God as the most perfect thing. And because it can come to him only from the likeness of his effects and does not find in creatures anything so supremely perfect as to altogether exclude imperfection, it strives to designate him from the various perfections found in creatures, although all those perfections lack something. Nonetheless, our intellect does this in such a way that whatever imperfection is connected with any of them is completely removed from God. For example, existing signifies something complete and simple but not subsistent, and substance signifies something subsistent but the subject of something else.

Therefore, we posit in God substance and existing, but substance by reason of subsistence, not by reason of underlying accidents, and existing by reason of simplicity and fullness, not by reason of inherence, whereby something inheres in something else. Likewise, we attribute activity to God by reason of his ultimate fullness, not by reason of the object into which his activity goes. And we attribute power to him by reason of what permanently abides and is the source of power, not by reason of what his activity accomplishes.

Obj. 1. Power is the source of action. But God's action, that is, his essence, has no source, since it is neither produced nor proceeding. Therefore, there is no power in God.

Reply Obj. 1. We should say that power is both the source of action and the source of an effect. And so, if we posit power in God as the source of an effect, we do not need to posit power as the source of his essence, that is, his action. Or we should say, and say better, that there are two kinds of relation in God. One kind is real, namely, the kind that distinguishes the Persons, such as fatherhood and sonship. Otherwise, the divine Persons would be distinguished conceptually, as Sabellius said, not really distinguished. The second kind of relation is only conceptual and signified when we say that God's action is from his essence, or that God acts by his essence. For these propositions designate certain relationships, and this so happens because, when we attribute action to God by reason of its nature requiring a source, we also attribute to it the relation of being from a source. And so this relation is only conceptual. But it belongs to the nature of action, not the nature of essence, to have a source. And so, although the divine essence has no source, neither really nor conceptually, divine action has a source conceptually.

Obj. 5. We should not signify anything about God by what is taken away from his primacy and simplicity. But God, inasmuch as he is simple and the first active thing,[1] acts by his essence. Therefore, we ought not to signify him as acting by power, which, at least in our way of signifying, adds something to his essence.

Reply Obj. 5. We should say that it is impossible to hold that God acts by his essence, and that there is no power in God, since power is what is the source of action. And so, because we hold that God acts by his essence, we hold that there is power in God. And so the nature of power does not derogate from his simplicity or primacy, since we do not posit anything, so to speak, in addition to his essence.

Obj. 6. According to Aristotle,[2] there is no difference in everlasting things between actual existing and potential existing, and so far more in the case of God. And where there is the same thing, we should take the common name from the more excellent thing. But essence is more excellent than power, since power adds to essence. Therefore, we ought to name only essence about God, not power.

Reply Obj. 6. We should say that we understand the statement that there is no difference between actual existing and potential existing in everlasting things to refer to passive power, and so it has no bearing on the question at issue, since there is no such power in God. But since it is true that active power is the same thing in God as his essence, we should say that, although the divine essence and power are really the same thing in God, power requires a special name because it particularly adds a way of signifying. For names correspond to understandings, according to Aristotle.[3]

Obj. 8. Any power separated from its act is imperfect, and so, since nothing imperfect belongs to God, there can be no such power in God. Therefore, if there is power in God, it needs to be always united with an act, and so the power to create is always united with the act, and so it follows that he created things from eternity. But this is heretical.

Reply Obj. 8. We should say that God's power to create is always united with his act, that is, action, since action is the divine essence, but the effects follow according to the command of his will and the ordinance of his wisdom. And so his power to create does not need to be always united with its effect, just as creatures need not have existed from eternity.

Obj. 9. When something suffices for doing something, anything else is added superfluously. But God's essence suffices for God to do anything by it. Therefore, the power to do it is superfluously posited in him.

Reply Obj. 9. We should say that God's essence suffices for him to act by it, but his power is not superfluous, since we understand his power as if something added to his essence, but it adds in our way of understanding only the relation of source. For the essence itself, being the source of acting, has the aspect of power.

Obj. 10. But you will say that his power is different from his essence only according to our way of understanding, not really. On the contrary, every understanding to which nothing corresponds is empty and meaningless.

Reply Obj. 10. We should say that something in reality corresponds to understanding in two ways. It corresponds in one way directly, namely, when the intellect conceives the form of a thing existing outside the soul, as, for example, a human being or a stone. It corresponds in another way indirectly, namely, when something results from the act of understanding, and the intellect reflecting on itself considers it. And so a thing corresponds to the consideration by means of the intellect, that is, there is intelligence of the thing indirectly. For example, the intellect understands the nature of animal in a human being, in a horse, and many other species, and so it understands animal as a genus. To this understanding whereby the intellect understands genus, no thing that is a genus exists outside the mind and directly corresponds to it. Rather, something corresponds to the intelligence that results from the representation. It likewise concerns the relation of source that adds God's power to his essence, since something real corresponds indirectly, not directly, to it. For example, our intellect understands a creature with a relation to, and dependency on, the creator, and since the intellect cannot understand one thing related to another without, conversely, also understanding a reciprocal relation, it understands in God a relation of source, which results from our way of understanding. And so the relation of source is related to the thing indirectly.

Obj. 12. You will say that the power we attribute to God is his essence, not a quality, and that his power and essence differ only conceptually. On the contrary, either something really corresponds to this concept or nothing does. If nothing does, the concept is empty. And if something real corresponds to it, something in God is consequently power besides his essence, as the notion of power adds to the notion of essence.

Reply Obj. 12. Something in divinity, namely, something one and the same, corresponds to the different notions of attributes. Our intellect is compelled to represent the simplest thing (i.e., God) by different forms because of his incomprehensibility, and so those different forms that our intellect conceives about God are in God as the cause of truth, inasmuch as all these forms can represent the very thing that is God. Nevertheless, the forms reside in our intellect as their subject.

Obj. 13. According to Aristotle,[4] all power and every productive thing should choose for the sake of something else. But nothing such belongs to God, since he himself is not for the sake of something else. Therefore, power does not belong to him.

Reply Obj. 13. We should say that Aristotle is thinking about active powers, productive things, and the like, which concern the products of skills and human affairs. For not even regarding natural things is it true that active power is always for the sake of its effects, since it is silly, for example, to say that the power of the sun is for the sake of the worms produced by its power. Far less is divine power for the sake of its effects.

Article 2

Is God's Power Infinite?

We should say that we speak of the infinite in two ways: in one way, privatively, and then we call something infinite that is constituted by nature to have an end and does not have any, and such an infinite is only in quantities;

in the second way, negatively, that something does not have an end. Understood in the first way, infinite cannot belong to God, both because he is without quantity, and because all privation denotes imperfection, which is far from God.

But the infinite predicated negatively belongs to God regarding all the things that are in him, since nothing limits him, neither his essence, his wisdom, his power, or his goodness And so all the things in him are infinite. But we should especially note regarding the infinity of his power that, since active power results from actuality, the amount of power results from the amount of actuality. For the more actual each thing is, the more abundant its power.

God is infinite actuality, and this is evident because actuality is limited in only two ways: one regarding the active cause, as, the beauty of a house receives its size and dimensions from the will of the builder; the other regarding the recipient, as, for example, the heat in firewood is limited and receives its strength from the disposition of the firewood. But no active cause limits the divine actuality itself, since that actuality proceeds from himself, not anything else, nor does another, receiving thing limit him, since, inasmuch as there is no admixture of passive power in him, he himself is pure actuality, not received in something. For God is his very existing, received in nothing.

And so God is evidently infinite, and this can be shown as follows. The existing of a human being is limited to the species of human being, since the existing is received in the nature of the human species, and the same is true of the existing of a horse or any creature. But God's existing, since it is pure existing, not received in something, is not limited to a particular way of a perfection of existing but has the whole of existing in itself. And so, as existing, understood in a universal sense, can extend to infinite things, so is divine existing infinite. And so his excellence, that is, his active power, is infinite.

But we should note that, although his power by his essence has infinity, it receives a mode of infinity that its essence does not have, because we relate it to the things of which it is the source. For there are many things in the objects of power. There is also in activity an intensity regarding its efficacy, and so we can attribute a certain infinity to an active power by its conformity to the infinity of quantity, both continuous and discrete. It is conformed to the infinity of discrete quantity insofar as we note the quantity of power by many or few objects, and we call this extensive quantity. It is conformed to the infinity of continuous quantity insofar as we note the quantity of power insofar as it acts lightly or intensely, and we call this intensive quantity. The first quantity belongs to power regarding objects, and the second regarding the action, since active power is the source of both.

God's power is infinite in both of these ways, since he never causes so many effects without being able to cause more, nor does he ever act so intensely without being able to act more intensely. But we should not note the intensity of divine action as the action is in the active thing, so that it is always infinite, inasmuch as the action is the divine essence. Rather, we should note the intensity of divine action as it reaches to its effect, since God thus moves some things more efficaciously, others less.

Obj. 1. As the *Metaphysics* says,[5] an active power in nature to which no passive power were to correspond would be in vain. But no passive power in nature corresponds to God's infinite power. Therefore, God's infinite power would be in vain.

Reply Obj. 1. We should say that we can call nothing in God in vain, since something is in vain when it is the means to an end that it cannot attain, but God and the things in him is the end, not the means to an end. Or we should say that Aristotle is speaking about active natural power. For natural things and also all creatures are coordinated with one another. But God is outside this order, since he himself is the one for whom this whole order is ordained, as a good external to it, like an army is subordinate to its commander, according to Aristotle.[6] And so nothing in created things needs to correspond to what is in God.

Obj. 2. Aristotle proves that there is no infinite power of infinite magnitude, since it would consequently not act in time, inasmuch as a greater power acts in less time.[7] And so the greater the power is, the less the time. But there is no proportion of infinite power to finite power. Therefore, there is no proportion of the time in which infinite power acts to the time in which finite power acts. But there is a proportion between any time and any other time. Therefore, since finite power causes movement in time, infinite power will cause movement outside time. By the same reasoning, if God's power is infinite, it will always act outside time. But this is false.

Reply Obj. 2. We should say that, according to Averroes in his *Commentary on the Physics*,[8] demonstration about the proportion of time and the power of a cause of motion is valid regarding power infinite in magnitude. Such power is proportioned to an infinity of time, since both belong to a fixed genus, namely, continuous quantity, but this does not hold regarding an infinity without magnitude, one that is not proportioned to an infinity of time, being of a different nature. Or we should say, as touched upon in the objection, that God, because he acts by his will, measures his movement by what he moves, as he wills.

Obj. 7. Every distinct thing is finite. But God's power is distinct from other things. Therefore, it is finite.

Reply Obj. 7. We should say that something is distinct in two ways. It is in one way by something else connected to it, as we distinguish a human being from an ass by the specific difference of reason. And such a distinct thing needs to be finite, since the connected thing determines it to be something. Something is a distinct thing in a second way by itself, and God is distinct from all things in this way, since nothing can be added to him. And so he does not need to be finite, neither himself nor anything signified regarding him.

Obj. 9. If God's power is infinite, this can be only because it is the power to create infinite effects. But many other things have infinite effects potentially, such as the intellect, which can understand an infinite number of things potentially, and the sun, which can produce an infinite number of effects. Therefore, if we should call God's power infinite, by like reasoning many other powers will be infinite. But this is impossible.

Reply Obj. 9. We should say that, as in the case of quantities, one can consider the infinite by one dimension and not another, and also the infinite by every dimension, so also in the case of effects. For it is possible that a creature, inasmuch as it regards itself, can produce an infinite number of effects in a particular way, as regards number in the same species, and then the nature of all the effects is finite, as determined to one species, as if we should understand an infinite number of human beings or asses. But it impossible that a creature can produce an infinite number of effects in every way, both numerically, specifically, and generically. This belongs only to God, and so only his power is absolutely infinite.

Article 3

Are Things Impossible for Nature Possible for God?

We should say, as Aristotle says,[9] that we speak of possible and impossible in three ways. We speak of possible and impossible in one way as to a particular active or passive power, as we say that a human being can walk by the power to walk but not to fly. We speak of possible and impossible in a second way as to itself, not a particular power, as we call possible what is not impossible to exist, and impossible what necessarily does not exist. We speak of possible and impossible in a third way by the mathematical power in geometry, as we call a line potentially measurable, since its square is measurable. With the latter possibility omitted, let us consider the other two.

Therefore, we should note that we call something impossible as to itself, not as to a particular power, impossible by reason of the incompatibility of the terms, and every incompatibility of terms is in the nature of a contradiction.

Moreover, an affirmation and a negation are included in every contradiction, as Aristotle proves.[10] And so, in every such impossibility, a simultaneous affirmation and negation is signified. Such impossibility cannot be attributed to any active power, since every active power results from the actuality and entity of that to which it belongs.

And each active thing is by nature constituted to cause something like itself, and so the action of an active power terminates in existing. For, although action sometimes causes nonexisitng, as is evident in passing away, this is only inasmuch as the existing of one thing is incompatible with the existing of something else. For example, being hot is incompatible with being cold, and so heat by its chief striving makes something become hot and destroys the thing's coldness as a result. But what is a simultaneous affirmation and negation cannot have the nature of a being or nonbeing, since existing takes away nonexisting, and nonexisting takes away existing. And so it can neither chiefly nor consequentially be the terminus of any action of an active power.

But we can note in two ways what we call impossible regarding a particular power. We can in one way because of the deficiency of the power of itself, namely, that it cannot extend to the effect, as when a natural active thing cannot change a particular matter. We can in a second way from something external, as when the power of something is prevented or restricted. Therefore, we say that something is impossible in three ways. We call something impossible in one way because of the deficiency of the active power, whether in changing the matter or in anything else. We call something impossible in a second way because of something resisting or hindering. We call something impossible in a third way because what we say is impossible cannot be the terminus of action.

Therefore, God can cause things impossible in nature in the first or second way, since his power, inasmuch as it is infinite, suffers in no deficiency, nor is there any matter that he can not change at will, since there cannot be resistance to his power. But God cannot cause what we call impossible in the third way, since he is the greatest actuality and the chief being. And so his action can only be terminated chiefly in being, and in nonbeing consquentially. And so he cannot cause affirmation and negation to be simultaneously true, or any things in which this kind of impossibility is included. Nor do we say that he cannot cause this because of a deficiency of his power. Rather, we say that he cannot because of the lack of possibility, which lack is from the nature of the possible. Therefore, some say that God can do it, but it cannot be done.

Obj. 1. An ordinary gloss on Rom. 11:24 says that God, as the author of nature, cannot do anything contrary to nature. But things impossible for nature are contrary to nature. Therefore, God cannot do them.

Reply Obj. 1. We should say that we should not understand the words of Augustine in the gloss to mean that God cannot do otherwise than nature does, since he often acts contrary to the usual course of nature. But whatever he does regarding things is not contrary to nature and is nature for them, since he is the author and coordinator of nature. Thus we observe in natural things that when a higher body moves a material substance here below, the movement is natural for it, although it does not seem fitting for the movement that it has by nature from itself. For example, the moon causes the ebb and flow of the sea, and this movement is natural for the sea, as Averroes says,[11] although the natural movement of water as such is to be borne downward. And all creatures have in this way as quasi-natural what God causes in them. And so we distinguish in them two kinds of power: one natural for its own actions and movements, and the other the one that we call obediential, regarding things that they receive from God.

Obj. 9. What is intrinsically impossible is more impossible than what is impossible incidentally. But God cannot cause what is impossible by accident, namely, that what existed will not have existed, as Jerome,[12] who says that, although God can do other things, he cannot make a virgin of one who is not, makes clear, as do Augustine[13] and Aristotle.[14] Therefore, God cannot cause what is intrinsically impossible in nature.

Reply Obj. 9. We should say that we say that it is impossible by happenstance that Socrates did not run if he has, since that Socrates runs or doesn't, considered in itself, is contingent but becomes intrinsically impossible by implying that a past event did not exist. And so we call it impossible by accident, by something else adventitious to it, as it were. And this adventitious circumstance is impossible as such and obviously signifies a contradiction, since to say that something existed, and that it has not, are contradictory statements. And so the result is that a past event, were it to happen, will not have existed.

Counterobj. 1. Lk. 1:37 says: "No word will be impossible with God."

Reply Counterobj. 1. We should say that a word is not only uttered by the mouth but is also conceived in the mind. But the mind cannot conceive that an affirmation and a negation are simultaneously true, as the *Metaphysics* proves,[15] nor consequently any of the things in which this is included. For, inasmuch as contrary opinions are of contrary things, it would follow, according to Aristotle, that the same person holds contrary opinions at the same time. And so it is not contrary to the words of the angel if we should say that God cannot cause the aforementioned kind of impossibility.

Counterobj. 2. Every power that can do this and not that is limited power. Therefore, if God can do things possible in nature but not things impossible, or these impossible things but not those, it seems that God's power is limited, which is contrary to things determined before (A. 2). Therefore, nothing is impossible for God.

Reply Counterobj. 2. We should say that God's power cannot do the aforementioned kind of impossibility, since it lacks the nature of possibility. And so we cannot say that God's power is limited, although he cannot do this.

Counterobj. 4. Privations are not susceptible of more or less. But we call something impossible by reason of privation of power. Therefore, if there is one impossible thing that God can do (e.g., give sight to the blind), it seems, by like reasoning, that he can do all things.

Reply Counterobj. 4. We should say that privation as such does not receive more or less, but it can in relation to its cause, as, for example, we say that one who has lost an eye is more blind than one whose sight a clouding fluid in the eye prevents. Likewise, we say that what is intrinsically impossible is more impossible than what is merely impossible.

Counterobj. 8. If we suppose that something falling under the definition of something is removed from the definition, it follows that contrary things are asserted at the same time, as, for example, that a human being is not rational. But two end points are in the definition of a straight line. Therefore, if one should remove the end points from the straight line, it would follow that two contrary things are true at the same time. But God did this when he entered through closed doors to his disciples, since there were then two bodies at the same time, and so two lines terminated at only two points, and each line at two points. Therefore, God can cause affirmation and a negation be simultaneously true and so it follows that he can cause all impossible things.

Reply Counterobj. 8. We should say that when Christ entered through closed doors, and two bodies were present at the same time, nothing was done contrary to the principles of geometry, since two lines, not one, terminated at the two points of different bodies on one or the other side. For, although only place can distinguish two mathematical lines, so that we cannot understand two such lines to coincide, we distinguish two natural lines in their subject, so that, supposing that the two bodies exist at the same time, the result is that there are at the same time two lines, two points of each, and two surfaces.

Article 4

Should We Judge Something to Be Possible or Impossible by Lower or Higher Causes?

We should say that we can consider judgment about the possible and impossible in two ways: in one way, regarding those judging; in the second way, regarding the thing about which one is judging. Regarding the first, we should note that, if there are two sciences, one of which considers higher causes, and the other lesser causes, we should not undertake judgments in both in the same way. Rather, we shall make judgments by the causes that each considers, as, for example, is evident in the case of a doctor and an astrologer, the latter considering uppermost causes, and the doctor proximate causes. And so the doctor will make judgment about the health or death of a sick person by proximate causes, that is, the power of nature and the power of disease. But the astrologer will make judgment by remote causes, namely, the position of the stars.

It is the same way regarding the present question. For there are two kinds of wisdom, namely, worldly wisdom, called philosophy, which considers lower causes (i.e., caused causes) and judges by them; and divine wisdom, called theology, which considers higher causes (i.e., divine causes) and judges by them. And we call divine attributes, such as wisdom, goodness, the divine will, and the like, higher causes.

But we should note that it is useless to raise this question about effects that can only belong to higher causes, that is, those that only God can cause, since it is unfitting to call them possible or impossible by lower causes. Rather, one raises this question about those effects that belong to lower causes, since the effects belong to both lower and higher things. For then the question of possibility can be thrown into doubt. Likewise, the question concerns possible and impossible things in themselves, not regarding a particular power. And the theologian judges the effects of secondary causes, with which the question is concerned, to be possible or impossible by higher causes, and the philosopher judges them to be possible or impossible by lower causes.

And if one should consider the judgment regarding the nature of what one is judging about, then it is clear that one ought to judge the possibility of effects by proximate causes, since proximate causes determine the action of remote causes, which the effects chiefly resemble. And so we especially make judgment about effects by those causes. This is also clear by comparison with passive power. For we do not say, properly speaking, that remote matter is in potentiality to something, as, for example, the earth to a drinking cup. Rather, we say that proximate matter is able to become actual by the action of a cause, as Aristotle makes clear in the *Metaphysics*,[16] as, for example, gold is potentially a drinking cup only if a craftsman's skill brings it into actuality. Likewise, we call effects, inasmuch as they come from their nature, possible or impossible only in relation to proximate causes.

Obj. 5. The world could have come into existence before it did. But this was not possible by lower causes. Besides, we should judge a thing's impossibility by higher causes.

Reply Obj. 5. We should say that the world could have existed by higher causes. And so this does not pertain to the present question. Therefore, the statement that the world could have come into existence is possible not only by God's active power but also as such, since the terms are not inconsistent.

Counterobj. 2. What is possible by lower causes is also possible by higher causes, and so in every way. But what is possible in every way is absolutely possible. Therefore, we should judge something to be absolutely possible by lower causes.

Reply Counterobj. 2. We should say that, although what is possible by lower causes is also possible by higher causes, this is not the case regarding impossibility. Rather, the contrary is. And so we should not make a universal judgment, or judge universally, about possibility or impossibility regarding lower causes.

Counterobj. 3. Higher causes are necessary causes. Therefore, if we were to judge effects by them, all effects will be necessary. But this is impossible.

Reply Counterobj. 3. We should say that we judge some things impossible or possible by some causes because they are possible or impossible for the causes, not because they are like their causes in possibility or impossibility.

Article 5

Can God Cause Things That He Does Not Cause and Abandon Things That He Causes?

We should say that the error, namely, that God can cause only the things he causes, belonged to two groups. The first consisted of certain philosophers who said that God acts by a necessity of nature. If this were to be so, since his nature would be determined to one thing, his power could not reach to do other things than those he causes. The second was of certain theologians who, considering the order of divine justice and wisdom, in accord with which God causes things, said that God cannot go beyond that order and fell into saying that God can cause only the things he does. This error is imputed to Peter Almalar [Abelard?].

Let us inquire into the truth of these opinions, and first of the first opinion. For it is plain to see that God does not act out of a necessity of nature. Every active thing acts for the sake of an end, since all things desire good. And the action of an active thing, in order to befit the end, needs to be adapted and proportioned to the end, and only an intellect that knows the end, the nature of the end, and the relation of the end to the means, can do this. Otherwise, the fitness of the action for the end would be by chance. But the intellect preordaining means to an end is sometimes joined to the active thing or cause of motion, as in the case of a human being in acting, and is sometimes separate, as is clear in the case of an arrow, which aims at a target by the intellect of the archer aiming the arrow, not by an intellect joined to the arrow. But what acts by a necessity of nature cannot determine for itself the end. For anything such is acting of itself, and the thing acting or moved to act by itself has in itself the power to act or not to act, to be moved or not to be moved to act, as Aristotle says in the *Physics*.[17] This cannot belong to something necessarily moved, since it is then determined to one thing.

And so something intelligent needs to determine the end for everything that acts by a necessity of nature. Because of this, philosophers say that the work of nature is the work of intelligence. And so, if a natural material substance is sometimes joined to an intellect, as is evident in the case of a human being, nature obeys the will regarding those actions by which the intellect determines the end, as the locomotion of a human being makes clear. But regarding those actions in which the intellect does not determine the end, nature does not obey the will, as in the activity of nutrition and growth. Therefore, we conclude from these things that what acts out of natural necessity cannot be the active source, since something else determines the end for it. And so God obviously cannot act by a necessity of nature, and so the foundation of the first position is false.

Next, it remains to inquire about the second position. Regarding that position, we should note that we say in two ways that one is unable to do something. We say this in one way absolutely, namely, when one of the sources necessary for an action does not extend to the action, as, for example, a human being cannot walk if one's foot is fractured. We say it in a second way by supposition, since, supposing the contrary of an action, the action cannot be done, as, for example, I cannot walk while I am sitting. And since God is active by his will and intellect, as I have proved (A. 1), we need to consider three sources of action in him: first, intellect; second, will; and three, the power of nature. Therefore, the intellect directs the will, and the will commands the power that executes the will. But the intellect moves only inasmuch as it proposes to the will the will's own object as desirable. And so the whole movement understood by the intellect is in the will.

But we say in two ways that God absolutely cannot do something. We say this in one way when his power does not extend to it, as we say that God cannot cause an affirmation and a negation to be simultaneously true, as what I have said before makes clear (A. 3). And so one cannot say that God can cause only what he does, since it is evident that his power can extend to many other things.

We say in a second way that God cannot do something when his will cannot extend to it, since any will needs to have an end that it wishes by nature, and whose contrary it cannot will. For example, a human being by nature and necessarily wills happiness and cannot wish unhappiness. And along with the will willing necessarily its natural end, it also wills necessarily things without which it cannot have the end, if one should know them, and these things are commensurate with the end. For example, if I wish to live, I wish to eat food. But one does not necessarily will things that are not commensurate with the end.

Therefore, the divine will's natural end is the divine goodness, which it cannot not will. But creatures are not commensurate with this end, so that the divine goodness cannot be manifested without them, which manifestation by creatures God intends. For, as the things now existing and the order of these things manifests God's goodness, so also other creatures and creatures ordered in a different way can, and so the divine will, without prejudice to his goodness, justice, and wisdom, can extend to other things than the ones he makes. Those in error have been deceived in this, since they considered the order of creatures to be commensurate with divine goodness, as if divine goodness could not exist without that order.

Therefore, it is evident that God can make other things than he has made. But since he cannot make contradictory things to be simultaneously true, we can say by supposition that God cannot make other things than those he has made. For, supposing that he does not make other things, or that he knew beforehand that he will not make other things, he cannot make other things, so that we understand the statement along with supposition, not separately.

Obj. 1. God can do only what he foreknows he will do. But he foreknows that he will do only what he does. Therefore, God can do only what he does.

Reply Obj. 1. We should say that the statement that God can do only what he foreknows that he will do is twofold, since the negative can be related to the power that the word *can* signifies, or to the act that the word *do* signifies. If in the first way, the statement is false, since he can do many things other than those he will do, and the objection proceeds in this sequence. But if in the second way, the statement is true, the sense being that he cannot do something and not foreknow it. But this sense is not apposite.

Obj. 2. But you say in response that the objection proceeds about power in relation to foreknowledge. On the contrary, divine things are more unchangeable than human things. But with us, it is impossible that things that have existed not to have existed. Therefore, far less is it possible that God did not foreknow the things that he foreknew. But with his foreknowledge abiding, he cannot do otherwise. Therefore, God, absolutely speaking, cannot do otherwise than what he does.

Reply Obj. 2. The past and the future are not in God, but whatever is in him is entire in the present of eternity. Nor do we signify the past or future in him as an expression except in relation to us. And so the objection about the necessity of the past has no place here. Nevertheless, we should say that the objection is not to the point, since God's foreknowledge is commensurate with his action, as I have said, not with the power to act, with which the question is concerned.

Obj. 11. According to philosophers, natural thongs are in the first cause of motion, that is, God, as craft products are in a craftsman, and so God acts like a craftsman. But a craftsman does not act without a form or idea of his work. For example, the house in matter is from the house that is in the mind of the builder, according to Aristotle.[18] But God has ideas only of the things that he made or makes or will make. Therefore, God can do nothing besides this.

Reply Obj. 11. We should say that the question is whether there is in God an idea of the things that do not exist, will not exist, and have not existed, but which God can make. It seems that we should say that, if we should understand the idea by its complete nature, namely, insofar as the idea signifies a form of the craft, not only as conceived by the intellect but also by the will ordered to action, then the aforementioned things have no idea in God. But if we should understand the idea by its incomplete nature, namely, as it is only conceived in the intellect of a craftsman, then the aforementioned things have an idea in God. For it is clear in the case of a created craftsman that the craftsman conceives particular actions that he never intends to perform. And whatever God knows is in him as something conceived, since there is in him no difference between actual and habitual knowing. For he knows all of his power and whatever he can make, and so he has natures conceived, as it were, of all the things that he can make.

Article 6

Can God Do Things Possible for Others, Such as Sinning, Walking, and the Like?

We should say, as I have said before (A. 5), that God absolutely cannot do something in two ways: in one way, regarding his will; in a second way, regarding his power. Regarding his will, God cannot do what he cannot will. And since the will cannot will the contrary of what it wills by nature, as, for example, the will of a human being cannot will unhappiness, the divine will cannot will anything contrary to God's goodness, which it by nature wills. But sin is a falling away from divine goodness. And so we should absolutely grant that God cannot sin.

Regarding his power, we say in two ways that God cannot do something: in one way, by reason of his power itself; in a second way, by reason of the possible. His power considered in itself, since it is infinite, is lacking in nothing that belongs to power. But there are some things that nominally signify power but really lack power. For example, there are many negations that are included in affirmations, as, when one says that something can fail, the mode of speech seems to imply a certain power, although, to the contrary, a lack of power will be signified. And so Aristotle says in the *Metaphysics* that a power is perfect without being able to do such things.[19] For, as affirmations of lack of power really have the force of negations, so negations of power to do impossible things have the force of affirmations. For this reason, we say that God cannot fail and so cannot be moved, since movement and failing signify an imperfection, and so he cannot walk or perform other bodily acts, which are not performed without movement.

By reason of the possible, we say that God cannot do something because it signifies contradiction, as what I have said before (A. 5) makes clear. In this way, we say that God cannot make anything equal to himself, since it signifies a contradiction because what is made needs to be potential in some way, inasmuch as it receives existing from something else and so cannot be pure actuality, which is proper to God himself.

Obj. 4. Whoever consents to a mortal sin sins mortally. But whoever commands a mortal sin consents to the sin; in fact, he in a way chiefly commits it. Therefore, when God commanded the mortal sin of Abraham (Gen. 22:2), namely, to kill his innocent son, Hosea to take a fornicating wife and produce from her a son of the fornication (Hos. 1:2), and Shimei to curse David, as 2 Sam. 16:7 says, it seems that God himself sinned mortally. (Shimei evidently sinned, judging by the punishment inflicted on him [1 Kgs. 2:46]).

Reply Obj. 4. We should say that nothing prevents an act that would in itself be mortal sin becoming virtuous by an added circumstance. For example, killing a human being is absolutely a mortal sin, but if a judge's officer kills a human being for the sake of justice at the judge's command, it is an act of justice, not a sin. And as the ruler of a political community has the power to dispose human beings regarding life and death, and other things pertaining to the end of his governance, which is justice, so God has the power to direct all things in his disposition to the end of his governance, which is his goodness. And so, although killing a human being of itself can be a mortal sin, still, if this should be done at God's command because of the end that God foresaw and ordained, even if that end is not known to a human being, it is meritorious and not a sin. And we should also say the like about the fornication of Hosea, since God ordains all human generation, although some say that this happened in a prophetic vision, not in reality. And we should say otherwise about the command to Shimei. For we say that God commands in two ways. He commands in one way by speaking spiritually or materially through a created substance, and he commanded Abraham and the prophets in this way. He commands in a second way by inclination, as he is said to have commanded a worm to eat ivy (Jon. 4:7). And God commands Shimei in this way to curse David inasmuch as he inclines his heart, and this is the way we describe in the reply to the sixth objection.

Obj. 6. Augustine says that God acts in the hearts of human beings by inclining their wills to whatever he has willed, whether good or evil.[20] But to incline the will of a human being to evil is a sin. Therefore, God sins.

Reply Obj. 6. We should say that we do not say that God inclines the wills of human beings to evil by putting wickedness into their wills or moving them to wickedness, but by permitting or ordaining it, namely, as those who consent to exercise cruelty do so against those whom God judges deserving of it.

Obj. 7. Human beings were made in God's image, as Gen. 1:26 says, and what is in an image needs to be in its exemplar. But the will of a human being is open to alternatives. Therefore, the will of God is also, and so he can sin and not sin.

Reply Obj. 7. We should say that, although human beings are in the image of God, it is not necessary that everything in a human being be in God, and yet, to the point at issue, the will of God is open to alternatives, since it is not determined to one thing. For he can do or not do this, do this or that, but it does not follow that he can act wickedly, that is, to sin.

Article 7

Why Do We Call God Almighty?

We should say that some, wishing to assign the reason for God's omnipotence, took some things that do not belong to the reason for it but are rather its cause, or belong to the perfection of omnipotence, or the nature of his power, or to the way in which he has power.

Some called God almighty because he has infinite power. They assign the cause rather than the reason for his omnipotence, as, for example, the rational soul, not the definition of human being, causes a human being.

Some called God almighty because he cannot undergo or lack anything, nor can anything have power over him, and the like, all of which pertain to his power.

Also, some called him almighty because he can will anything, and he has this from and by himself. This pertains to the way in which he has power.

But all these explanations are inadequate because they omit the relations of actions to their objects, which omnipotence signifies. And so we should say that we should take one of the three ways advanced by way of objection and speak of the relation to objects.

Therefore, we should say, as I have said before (A. 5), that God's power, considered in itself, extends to all the objects that do not signify contradiction. Nor are even objections about things that signify defect or bodily movement valid, since the possibility of such things is impossible for God. But God cannot do things that signify contradiction, which are indeed impossible as such. Therefore, we conclude that God's power extends to things that are possible as such. But there are things that do not signify contradiction. Therefore, we evidently call God almighty because he can do all the things that are possible as such.

Obj. 1. As we call God almighty, so we call him all knowing. But we call him all knowing because he knows absolutely all things. Therefore, we call him almighty because he can do absolutely all things.

Reply Obj. 1. We should say that we call God all knowing because he knows all knowable things, but he does not know false things, which are unknowable. And impossible things as such are related to power as false things are to knowledge.

Obj. 5. Why do we call God almighty and all knowing but not all willing?

Reply Obj. 5. To this question, we should answer that, in things that the will does, as the *Metaphysics* says,[21] the will determines power and knowledge for action. And so we express knowledge and power in God as if universally unlimited, as when we call him all knowing and almighty, but the will that determines cannot be of all things but only of those that determine power and knowledge for action. And so God cannot be all willing.

Question 2

Article 1

Is There a Power in the Godhead to Generate?

We should say that the nature to which any action belongs communicates itself as much as it can. And so each active thing is active insofar as it is actual. But acting is nothing else but to communicate what actualizes the active thing as much as possible, and the divine nature is the supreme and purist actuality. And so also the divine nature communicates itself as much as it can. It communicates itself only by a creature's likeness to itself, as is obvious to everybody, since any creature is a being by likeness to it. But the Catholic faith also holds another way of the divine nature communicating itself, as it is communicated by a natural sharing, as it were, so that, as one to whom humanity is communicated is a human being, so the one to whom the Godhead is communicated is not only like God but truly is God.

About this, we need to note that the divine nature differs from material forms in two ways. The first is because material forms are not subsistent, and so the humanity in a human being is not the same as the human being who subsists, but the Godhead is the same as God, and so the divine nature itself is subsistent. The second is that no created form or nature is its own existing, but God's very existing is his nature or essence, and so his proper name is "He Who Is," as Ex. 3:14 makes clear, since he is so named as if by his own form.

Therefore, the form in the inferior things, since it does not subsist by itself, there needs to be in that to which it is communicated something else by which a form or nature receives subsistence, and this is matter, which subsists by material forms and natures. But because a material nature or form is not its own existing, it receives existing by being received in something else. And so, insofar as it exists in different things, it necessarily has a different existing. And so there is not one and the same humanity in Socrates and Plato regarding existing, although there is the same humanity regarding its own nature.

But in the communication that communicates the divine nature, since it is self-subsistent, nothing material is required by which it would receive subsistence. And so it is not received in something as in matter, so to speak, so that the one so begotten is composed of matter and form. And because, again, the essence itself is its existing, it does not receive existing by the existing individuals in which it exists, and so the one and same existing is in the one communicating and in the one who is communicated. And so it abides numerically the same in each one.

There is an example of this communication most fittingly in the activity of the intellect. For the divine essence itself is spiritual, and so spiritual examples better manifest it. When our intellect conceives the essence of something intrinsically subsisting outside the soul, there is a communication of the self-subsistent thing, as our intellect somehow receives from an external thing the thing's form, which intelligible form, existing in our intellect, proceeds somehow from the external thing. But because the external thing differs from the nature of the one understanding, the existing of the form understood by the intellect and the form of the self-subsistent thing are different.

But when our intellect conceives the essence of itself, both are preserved, namely, that the form itself understood by the intellect somehow comes into the intellect when the intellect forms it. And unity is preserved between a conceived form that proceeds into the intellect, and the thing from which it proceeds, since both, one the intellect and the other the intelligible form, which we call the word of the intellect, have intelligible existing, But because our intellect is not by its essence in the complete actuality of intellectuality, and the intellect of a human being is not the same as human nature, the aforementioned word, although it is in the intellect and somehow conformed to it, is not the same as the essence of the intellect but an expression of its likeness. Nor, again, is human nature communicated in the conception of this intelligible form, so that we can properly call it a generation that signifies communication of a nature.

As there is in our intellect understanding itself a word proceeding and bearing a likeness of that from which it proceeds, so also there is in the Godhead a Word having the likeness of him from whom the Word proceeds. The procession of this Word is superior to the procession of our word in two ways. First, the procession of the Word is superior in that our word is different from the essence of the intellect, as I have said, but the divine intellect, which is by its essence in perfect intellectual actuality, cannot receive any intelligible form that is not its essence. And so its Word is of one and the same essence with it, and also the divine nature itself is its intellectuality. And so the communication in an intelligible way is also communication by way of nature, so that we can call it a generation. Second, the Word of God surpasses our word in that respect. And Augustine assigns this way of generation in his book *Trinity.*[1]

But we are speaking about God according to our way, which way of knowing our intellect takes from inferior things, by which it takes in knowledge. Therefore, just as, to anything we assign an action in the case of lower things, we assign a source of the action and call it power, so also in the case of God, although there is in him no difference between the source and the action, as there is in the case of created things. For this reason, given generation in God, which we signify by way of action, we must grant to him the power to generate, that is, the generative power.

Obj. 2. According to Aristotle,[2] action belongs to what has power. But there is no generation in the Godhead. Therefore, neither is their generative power. The proof of the minor is as follows. There is a sharing and reception of a nature wherever there is generation. But since receiving belongs to matter or passive power, which are not in the Godhead, reception cannot belong to God. Therefore, there cannot be generation in the Godhead.

Reply Obj. 2. We should say that, although receiving terminates in having, as the end, we speak in two ways of receiving as well as two ways of having. For, in one way, matter has its form, and a subject an accident or anything howsoever possessed outside the subject's essence, and an existing individual has its nature in another way, as this human being has human nature, and the nature is not outside the essence of its possessor; indeed, it is the human being's essence. For example, Socrates is truly what a human being is. Therefore, the begotten even in humankind receives the form of the begetter as an existing individual, or hypostasis, has the specific nature, not as matter receives form, or a subject an accident. It is likewise in divinity. And so no matter or subject of the divine nature needs to be in God begotten. Rather, the begotten is the subsistent Son that has the divine nature.

Obj. 3. The begetter needs to be distinct from the begotten, but not by what the begetter communicates to the begotten, since they are rather in agreement in this respect. Therefore, there ought to be something in the begotten different from what is communicated to it by generation. And so everything begotten needs to be composed, as it seems. But there is no composition in divinity. Therefore, there can be no God begotten. And so there is no generation in the Godhead. And so there is no generative power in it.

Reply Obj. 3. We should say that God begotten is not distinguished from God begetting by an added essence, since, as I have said in the body of the article, no matter in which the divine nature is received is necessary. And there is a distinction by the very relation, which is to have one's nature from another, so that the very relation of sonship in the son takes the place of all the individuating sources in created things, because of which we call it a personal property, and the divine nature takes the place of a specific nature. And because the very relation does not really differ from the divine nature, there is no composition in it, as with us a certain composition results from the specific source and the things that individuate.

Obj. 10. Since God's power is infinite, it is not limited to an act or an object. But if there should be generative power in God, his act will be generation, and its effect a Son. Therefore, the power of the Father will not be disposed to begetting one Son but will extend to many sons, which is absurd.

Reply Obj. 10. We should say that the Son of God is not related to the generative power as its effect, since we profess him to be begotten, not made. But if the Son were to be an effect, the power of the one generating would not be limited to him even if the Father cannot beget another Son, since the Father is infinite. It happens to be the case that there can be no other son in divinity because sonship itself is the Son's personal property and that whereby he is individuated, so to say. But the individuating sources for each individual belong to that individual alone; otherwise, it would follow that a person or individual thing could be shared conceptually.

Obj. 14. A nature that is perpetually and perfectly in one existing individual is not communicated to another existing individual. But the divine nature is perfectly in the Father, and perpetually so, since he is indestructible. Therefore, it is not communicated to another existing individual. And so there is no generation in the nature.

Reply Obj. 14. We should say that creatures by sharing in their specific nature attain to a likeness to God. And so, in order that a created existing individual subsists in a created nature, it is ordered to another thing as its end. And so, if one individual sufficiently attains the end by a perfect and proper participating in a specific nature, it is not necessary that another individual subsist in that nature. But the divine nature is the end and not for the sake of another end. And it is in accord with the end that it be communicated in every possible way. And so, although it is perfectly and properly in one existing individual, nothing prevents it from also being in another.

Article 2

Do We Speak of the Generative Power in God Essentially or Notionally?

We should say that there are several opinions about this. Some predicate the power in the Godhead to generate in relation to something, and the following argument convinced them. A power is by its nature a source, and we predicate a source relatively. It is notional[3] if the source is relative to divine power and not to creatures.

But in this argument, two things seem to have misled them. First, although the nature of being a source, which is in the genus of relation, belongs to a power, the source of action or undergoing action is an absolute form, not a relation, and what is such is the essence of a power. And so Aristotle considers a power in the genus of quality, not one of relation, just as he considers knowledge, although a relation is incidental to both. Second, we predicate notionally things in the Godhead that we call a source with respect to what is the terminus of an action, not things that in it signify a source in respect to an action, since the source that we predicate notionally in God regards a subsistent person, but we do not signify the action as subsistent. And so things that have the nature of a source with respect to an action do not need to be predicated notionally in the Godhead. Otherwise, we would predicate will, knowledge, intellect, and the like notionally.

Although a power is sometimes the source of both an action and what an action produces, one is incidental to it, and the other belongs to it intrinsically. For an active power by its action does not always produce something that is the terminus of the action. There are indeed many actions that do not have a product, as Aristotle says in the *Ethics*[4] and *Metaphysics*,[5] as a power is always the source of action or activity. And so it is not necessary that we predicate power relatively in the Godhead because of the relation of it being a source, which the word *power* signifies.

This position also does not seem consonant with truth. If the thing that is a power is the very thing that is the source of an action, the divine nature needs to be the thing that is the source in the Godhead. For, since every active thing as such produces something like itself, the thing is the source of generation in the one generating insofar as the one generated is like the one generating. For example, a man by the power of his human nature begets a son, who is like the father in human nature. But God the Son is conformed to God the Father in divine nature. And so the divine nature is the source of generation, as the Father by its power generates, as Hilary says.[6]

For this reason, others said that the power of generating signifies only the divine essence. But that also seems inappropriate, since an action that something contained in a common nature does by the power of that nature takes on a mode from its proper sources. For example, the action due to an animal nature is in a human being insofar as it belongs to the sources of the human species. And so also a human being has more perfectly the act of the power of imagination than other animals do, insofar as it is proper to the human being's rationality. Likewise, the action of a human being is in this and that one insofar as it belongs to the individual sources of this or that one, whereby one human being may understand more clearly than another. And so, if the common nature needs to be the source of an action that befits only the Father, it needs to be the source insofar as it belongs to the Father as a personal property. And so paternity is somehow included in the nature of power, even regarding what is the source of generation.

For this reason, we should say with others that the power of generating signifies both the divine essence and the notion of paternity.

Obj. 3. The source in the Godhead is distinguished from the thing of which it is the source. But we ought not to distinguish the essence. Therefore, the nature of being a source does not belong to the essence. And so power, which includes the nature of being a source, does not signify the essence.

Reply Obj. 3. We should say that the source of generation in created things is two fold, namely, the one generating and the means whereby the generator generates. But the begetter by generating is distinguished from the begotten, since nothing generates itself, and the means of generation that generates is not distinct but common to both, as I have said in the body of the article. And so we do not need to distinguish the divine nature as generative power, since the power is the source as the means whereby the begetter generates the begotten.

Obj. 5. The source of a proper action is the thing's proper, not common, form. For example, a human being understands by the intellect, since this action is proper to the human being in contrast to other animals, just as the rational, or intellectual, form is. But generation is the proper action of the Father. Therefore, its source is fatherhood, which is the proper form of the Father, and not the Godhead, which is the common form. But we speak of fatherhood in relation to something. Therefore, we speak of the power of generating, both regarding the nature of source and regarding the thing that is the source, in relation to something.

Reply Obj. 5. We should say that, in any generation, the source of generation is chiefly the form that belongs to a specific nature, not an individual form. Likewise, the begotten needs to be like the begetter regarding the begetter's specific nature, not his individual conditions. But fatherhood is in the

Father, so to speak, as the source of his individuality, since it is a personal property, not by way of a specific form, as human nature is in a human being, since the divine nature is in the Father. And so fatherhood need not be chiefly the source of generation but is somehow something understood with it for the reason just given. Otherwise, it would follow that the Father by generating would communicate both the Godhead and fatherhood, which is improper.

Article 3

Does the Generative Power Proceed to the Act of Generation at the Will's Command?

We should say that the generation of the Son can be related to the will as its object. For the Father willed both the Son and the generation of the Son from eternity, but the will can in no way be the source of divine generation. This is made clear as follows. The will, as such, since it is free, is disposed in alternative ways, since the will can act or not act, act thus or otherwise, will or not will. And if, with respect to something, this disposition should not belong to the will, it will not happen to the will inasmuch as it is the will but from a natural inclination that the will has toward something as its ultimate end, which it cannot not will. For example, the human will cannot not will happiness, nor can it will wretchedness. From this, it is evident that everything of which the will as such is the source can be or not be, be such and such, and then or now.

Everything that is so disposed is something created, since there is no potentiality to exist or not exist in what is uncreated. Rather, there is intrinsically necessary existing, as Avicenna proves.[7] Therefore, if one considers the Son as begotten by the divine will, it necessarily follows that he is created. For this reason, the Arians, who considered the Son a creature, said that the divine will generated him. But Catholics say that the divine nature, not the divine will, begot the Son, since nature is determined to one thing. Accordingly, because the Father by nature generates the Son, the Son cannot not be generated or be in any other way than he is. Nor can he not be consubstantial with the Father, since what proceeds by nature proceeds into the likeness of that from which it proceeds. This is what Hilary says:[8] "The will brought the substance of God to creatures, but perfect birth gave the Son his nature." And so all things are such as God willed them to be, but the Son is such as God is.

As I have said, although the will is disposed in alternate ways regarding some things, it nonetheless has a natural inclination regarding its ultimate end. Likewise, the intellect has a natural movement regarding the first principles of knowledge. But the source of divine knowledge is God himself, and he is the end of his will. And so what proceeds in God by the act of his intellect knowing himself proceeds in reality, and what proceeds by the act of his will loving himself also does. And because the Son proceeds as the Word by an act of the divine intellect inasmuch as the Father knows himself, and the Holy Spirit by an act of his will inasmuch as the Father loves the Son, it follows that both the Son and the Holy Spirit proceed by nature, and further that they are consubstantial, coequal, and coeternal with the Father and one another.

Obj. 2. You will say that the Father begot the Son by the will accompanying generation, not by the will preceding or succeeding it. On the contrary, it seems that this reasoning is insufficient. For, inasmuch as whatever is in God is eternal, nothing in God can temporally precede anything being in God. And yet we find that something in him has the nature of a source in relation to something else, such as his will for the choice whereby he chooses the just only because it proceeds from his intellect. Therefore, although the willing does not temporally precede the generation of the Son, we can, it seems, still consider it the source of the Son's generation because it proceeds from his intellect.

Reply Obj. 2. We should say that there is no antecedent will in God regarding anything, since whatever God once wills he willed from eternity. Rather, his will is concomitant with respect to all the goods, both those in himself and those in creatures, since he wills that he and a creature exist. But it is temporally preceding and antecedent only regarding the creature, which has not existed from eternity. His understanding is precedent with regard to the eternal acts that we designate as terminating in creatures, such as the arrangement of things, predestination, and the like. But the generation of the Son is not a creature, nor do we designate it as terminating in a creature. And so, regarding his generation, there is no preceding willing, whether temporally or conceptually, but only a concomitant will.

Obj. 3. The Son proceeds by an act of the intellect inasmuch as he proceeds as the Word, since there is an intellectual word only when we in thought understand something, as Augustine says.[9] But the will is the source of intellectual action inasmuch as the will commands an act of the intellect, just as it does other powers, as Anselm says,[10] since I understand because I will to do so, just as I walk because I will to do so. Therefore, God's will is the source of the procession of the Son.

Reply Obj. 3. As an act of the intellect seems to follow an act of the will, inasmuch as the will commands it, so, conversely, an act of the will seems to follow an act of the intellect, inasmuch as the intellect presents its object, which is the understood good, to the will. And so it would be to regress infinitely unless we were to establish a position, whether in an act of the intellect or in an act of the will. We cannot posit a position in the act of the will, since the will's object is presupposed for its act. And so we need to posit a position in an act of the intellect, an act naturally produced by the intellect and so not commanded by the will. And the Son proceeds as the Word by an act of the divine intellect in this way, as what I said in the body of the article makes clear.

Obj. 5. According to Aristotle,[11] what causes its own movement can be moved or not be, and by the same reasoning, what acts by itself acting can act or not act. But nature cannot act or not act, since it is determined to one thing. Therefore, it does not act by itself acting but as moved by another, as it were. But this cannot be in the Godhead. Therefore, no action in the Godhead, and so no generation, is by nature. And so generation is from the will, since we trace all active things to nature or the will, as the *Physics* makes clear.[12]

Reply Ob. 5. We should say that something else is needed to determine nature only regarding things for which its own essential sources do not suffice, not regarding things that nature can reach by its own sources. And so the actions proper to heat and cold as such did not lead philosophers to consider the work of nature a work of intelligence, since even those who held that natural things happen by a necessity of matter traced all the actions of nature to those of heat and cold. But the actions for which the power of heat, cold, and like qualities cannot suffice (e.g., bodily members integrated in an animal in such a way as to preserve it) induced them to do so. Therefore, since generation is an action of the divine nature as such, there is no need for a will to determine the nature to the action. Or we should say that something determines nature for an end. But being determined by something does not belong to the nature that is the end and not for an end.

Obj. 6. If the action of nature precedes action of the will, something improper results, namely, that the essence of willing is taken away. For, inasmuch as nature is determined to one thing, if nature should move the will, it will move the will to only one thing, and this is contrary to the essence of the will, which, as such, is free. But if the will should move nature, neither nature's essence nor the will's would be taken away, since nothing prevents what is disposed to many things from moving to one thing. Therefore, the action of the will more reasonably precedes the action of nature than the converse. But the generation of the Son is pure action or activity. Therefore it proceeds from the will.

Reply Obj. 6. We should say that, in considering different things, the action of the will precedes the action of nature. And so the action of the whole of lower nature proceeds from the will of the one governing it. But in the same thing, the action of nature necessarily precedes the action of the will, since nature conceptually precedes the will, inasmuch as we understand nature to be the source whereby a thing subsists, but the will as the ultimate thing whereby that thing is ordered to its end. Nor does it follow that the nature of the will is taken away. For, although, regarding its natural inclination, the will is determined to something that is the ultimate end intended by nature, it still remains undetermined regarding other things, as is clear in the case of a human being, who by nature and necessarily wills happiness but not other things. Therefore, the action of nature in God naturally and conceptually precedes action of the will, since the generation of the Son is the exemplar of all the things that the will produces, namely, creatures.

Article 4

Can There Be Several Sons in God?

We should say that there cannot be several Sons in the Godhead. This is made clear as follows. Only relations and none other than those of origin can distinguish the divine Persons, since the Persons, as mutually essential to one another, are one in all absolute things. For some other relations, such as equality and likeness, presuppose distinction, and some designate inequality (e.g., master and slave, and the like). But relations of origin by their nature signify like form, since what originates from something else, as such retains the likeness of the other.

Therefore, there is nothing in the Godhead to distinguish the Son from the other Persons except the relation of sonship, which is his personal property and constitutes him the Son and this existing individual or this person.

But that whereby an existing individual is this particular thing cannot be in several things, since then the existing individual thing itself could be shared, which is contrary to the nature of an existing individual thing or a person. And so in no way can there be more than the one Son in God. For one cannot say that one sonship constitutes this Son, and another sonship another, since, inasmuch as sonships do not differ conceptually, there would necessarily be matter in the Godhead, or something else distinguishing them, if matter or any existing individual were to distinguish them.

But we can assign another, special reason why the Father can beget only one Son, since nature is determined to one thing. And so, when the Father begets the Son, he can generate only one. Nor can we say that there are numerically several Sons existing in the same species, as in the case of human beings, since there is no matter in God to be the source of numerical distinction in the same species.

Obj. 6. You will say that the Father does not generate another Son because something unseemly would result, as Augustine holds, namely, that there would be an infinite number of divine generations if the Father were to generate many Sons, and the Son a grandson to the father, and so on. On the contrary, there is no power in God that is not actual, since he would then be imperfect. Therefore, if it is in the power of the Father to generate several Sons, with nothing improper preventing it, there will be several Sons in the Godhead.

Reply Obj. 6. We should say that, in an argument drawing an unsuitable conclusion, avoidance of the impropriety is not necessarily the only reason to eliminate the position from which the impropriety results, but there are also reasons that manifest the impropriety. And so there should not be several Sons in the Godhead only to avoid an infinite number of generations,

Obj. 7. It belongs to the nature of the begotten that he comes into the likeness of the begetter. But as Son is like the Father, so also is the Holy Spirit, and so the Holy Spirit is a Son, and so there are several Sons in divinity.

Reply Obj. 7. We should say that the Holy Spirit proceeds as Love. But love does not signify something shaped or specified in the form of the lover or the beloved, as a word signifies the form of the one uttering it and of what we say possesses it. And so, inasmuch as the Son proceeds as the Word, he, by the very nature of his procession, has a procession into the like form of the begetter, and so to be the Son, and we call his procession generation. But the Holy Spirit does not have this by reason of his procession but rather has it from a property of the divine nature, since there cannot be anything in God that is not God. And so the divine Love itself is God inasmuch as it is divine, not inasmuch it is Love.

Obj. 8. According to Anselm,[13] to say that the Father generates the Son is only to say that the Father expresses himself. But, as the Father can express himself, so also can the Son and the Holy Spirit. Therefore, the Father, the Son, and the Holy Spirit can generate Sons. And so there can be several Sons.

Reply Obj. 8. We should say that we may understand the word *express* in two ways: strictly and broadly. By understanding it strictly, it is the same as to utter a word, and then it is notional, belonging only to the Father, and Augustine understands *express* in this way. And so he holds in his work *Trinity* that only the Father expresses himself.[14] In the second way, we can understand it generally, as expression is the same as understanding, and so essential. And Anselm in the *Monologion* understands it in this way, when he says that the Father, Son, and Holy Spirit express themselves.[15]

Obj. 11. Goodness is the source of diffusion. But, as there is infinite goodness in the Father and the Son, so is there in the Holy Spirit. Therefore, as the Father by generating the Son communicates his nature by infinite sharing, so does the Holy Spirit by producing a divine Person, since the divine goodness is not infinitely communicated to a creature. And so it seems that there can be several Sons in the Godhead.

Reply Obj. 11. We should say that there can be only spiritual procession in the Godhead, and this is only by intellect and will. And so no other divine person can proceed from the Holy Spirit, since the Spirit proceeds by way of the will as Love. The Son proceeds by way of the intellect as the Word.

Article 5

Is the Power to Generate Included in Omnipotence?

We should say that the power to generate belongs to the omnipotence of the Father, not omnipotence absolutely. This is made clear as follows. Since we understand that power is rooted in the essence and is the source of action, we should judge about the power and the action the same as we judge about the essence. But we should consider regarding the divine essence that, because of its supreme simplicity, everything in God is the divine essence. And so also the very relations that distinguish the Persons from one another are really the divine essence. And although one and the same essence is common to the three Persons, still the relation of one Person is not common to the three Persons because of the contradiction of the relations to one another. For example, fatherhood itself is the divine essence, but fatherhood is not present in the Son because of the contradiction between fatherhood and sonship.

And so we can say that fatherhood is the divine essence as fatherhood is in the Father, not as it is in the Son, since the divine essence is not in the Father and Son in the same way, but in the Son as received from another and not in the Father in that way. Nor does it follow that, although the Son does not have the paternity that the Father has, the Father has something that the Son does not have, since the very relation as such, by reason of its nature, consists only of being in relation to something, not of being a thing. That something is real is due to the respect whereby it is in a subject, whether really the same thing, as in God, or having a cause in the subject, as in creatures. And so, since anything absolute is common to the Father and the Son, only a relation to something, not a thing, distinguishes them. And so we cannot say that the Father has anything that the Son does not have, but should say that something belongs to the Father in one respect, and to the Son in another.

Therefore, we should say likewise about action and power, since generation signifies power with a respect, and the power of generating signifies power with a respect. And so generation itself is the action of God, but as it belongs to the Father alone, and the very power of generating is likewise the omnipotence of God, but as it belongs only to the Father. Nor does it follow that the Father can do something that the Son cannot. Rather, the Son can do all the things whatsoever the Father can, although the Son cannot generate, since we predicate generating in relation to something.

Obj. 3.We attribute omnipotence to God inasmuch as it extends to all the things in themselves possible. But the generation of the Son, or Son himself, concerns necessary things, not possible things. Therefore, the power to generate is not included in omnipotence.

Reply Obj. 3. We should say that we should not understand the possible to which omnipotence extends as only the contingent, since divine power also brought necessary things into existence. And so nothing prevent us from including the generation of the Son among the things possible for divine power.

Obj. 4. What belongs commonly to many things belongs to them by something common to them. For example, having three angles belongs to equilateral and oblong triangles insofar as they are triangular. Therefore, what belongs only to something belongs to it by what is proper to it. But omnipotence is not proper to the Father. Therefore, since the power of generating in the Godhead belongs only to the Father, it does not belong to him insofar as he is omnipotent. And so generation does not belong to omnipotence.

Reply Obj. 4. We should say that, although omnipotence, absolutely considered, is not proper to the Father, it is nonetheless proper to the Father as we understand with it a determined way of existing, that is, a determined relation. For example, calling God Father is proper to the Father, although God is common to the three Persons.

Obj. 6. Things not belonging to the same consideration do not fall in the same distribution. For example, when one says *every dog*, we do not understand the distribution to apply to the animal and the constellation. But the generation of the Son and the production of other things subject to omnipotence do not belong to same consideration. Therefore, when we say that God is omnipotent, the power of generating is not included in it.

Reply Obj. 6. We should say that the generation of the Son and the production of creatures belong to the same consideration only analogously, not univocally. For Basil says that the Son has receiving in common with every creature, and so we call him "the firstborn of all creation" (Col. 1:15).[16] And for this reason, his generation can be shared in the same distribution with the production of creatures.

Article 6

Are the Power to Generate and the Power to Create the Same?

We should say, as I have said before (A. 5), that we should consider things predicated about power in the Godhead according to the divine essence. But, although one relation in the Godhead is really distinguished from another because of the contradiction between the relations, which are real in God, still the very relation is only conceptually, not really, different from the essence itself, since there is no contradiction between the relation and the essence. And so we should not allow that anything absolute in the Godhead is multiple, as some say that there are two things in the Godhead: the essential and the personal.

For every existing in the Godhead is essential, and the person exists only through the existing of the essence. But in power, besides what is the power itself, we consider a respect or order to what is subject to the power. Therefore, if we should compare the power about an essential act, such as the power to understand or create, to the power about a notional act, such as the power to generate, there is one and the same power regarding what is the power, as there is one and the same existing of the nature and the Person. But we understand with each power different aspects about the different acts to which the powers are related.

Therefore, the powers to generate and create are one and the same if we should consider what power consists of, but they differ by their different respects to different acts.

Obj. 1. Generation is an action or work of nature, as Damascene says,[17] but creation is a product of the will, as Hilary makes clear in his work *Councils*. But the will and nature are not the same source but divided as contraries, as the *Physics* makes clear.[18] Therefore, the power of generating and the power of creating are not the same.

Reply Obj. 1. We should say that, although nature and the will differ in creatures, they are really the same in the Godhead. Or we can say that the power of creating denotes God's power as commanded by his will, not his purpose or will. But the power of generating acts as nature so inclines. But this does not cause a difference in power, since nothing prevents a power from being commanded to one act by the will and being inclined to another act by nature. For example, our intellect is inclined by the will to believe and led by nature to understand first principles.

Obj. 2. Acts distinguish powers, as the *De anima* maintains.[19] But generation and creation are very different acts. Therefore, the power of generating and the power of creating are also really different.

Reply Obj. 2. We should say that the higher the power, the more things it reaches, and so different objects are less capable of distinguishing it. For example, imagination is one power with respect to all sensibly perceptible things, regarding which the proper senses differ. But divine power is the absolutely highest. And so different acts introduce no difference in the power itself, regarding what it is. Rather, God by one and the same power is able to do all things.

Obj. 4. There is no order among the same things. But the power of creating is conceptually prior to the power of generating, as the essential is to the notional. Therefore, the aforementioned powers are not the same.

Reply Obj. 4. We should say that the aforementioned powers are ordered by what is prior and what is posterior only as they are distinguished. And so we note their order only in relation to acts. And so the power of generating is clearly prior to the power of creating, as generation preceded creation. But inasmuch as they are related to the essence, they are the same, and there is no order regarding them.

Question 3

CREATION, THE FIRST EFFECT OF DIVINE POWER

Article 1

Can God Create Something Out of Nothing?

We should say and firmly hold that God can make something out of nothing and does so. To prove this, we should note that every active thing acts insofar as it is actual, and so we need to attribute action to an active thing in the way in which actual existing belongs to it. But a particular thing is particularly actual, and this in two ways. First, it is actual in a particular way in relation to itself, since, inasmuch as such-and-such a thing is composed of matter and form, its whole substance is not actuality, and so a natural thing acts by its form, by which it is actual, not by its whole self. Second, it is actual in a particular way in relation to things that are actual. For no natural thing includes the actuality as perfection of all actual things, but each has an actuality limited to a genus and a species, not the actualities and perfections of all actual things, and so each is active insofar as it is this being, determined in this or that species, not insofar as it is a being, since an active thing produces something like itself.

And so an active natural thing produces a preexistent being and one limited to this or that (e.g., the species of fire, whiteness, or the like), not a being absolutely. For this reason, an active natural thing acts by moving something, and so requires matter, which is the subject of change or movement, and so cannot make something out of nothing. But God, on the contrary, is totally actuality, both in relation to himself, since he is pure actuality without any mixture of potentiality, and in relation to actual things, since the source of all things is in him. And so he, as the one who is the source of all existing, by his action produces the totality of subsistent being, with nothing presupposed, and by his whole self. For this reason, he can make something out of nothing, and we call this action of his creation.

And so the *Liber de causis* says that a thing's existing is by creation, but that living and the like are by communicating a form.[1] For we trace the causing of a being to the first universal cause, but the causality of other things added to existing, or things by which existing is a specific kind, belongs to secondary causes, which act by communicating a form, with the effect of the universal cause presupposed, as it were. And so also a thing confers existing only inasmuch as it shares in divine power. For this reason, the *Liber de causis* also says that a noble soul has a divine activity inasmuch as it confers existing.[2]

Obj. 2. Everything that is made could have existed before it did, since, if it could not have existed, it could not have been made. But the power whereby something can exist, can be only in a subject, unless, perhaps, it is the subject, since an accident cannot exist without a subject. Therefore, everything that is made is made from matter or a subject. Therefore, something cannot be made from nothing.

Reply Obj. 2. We should say that before the world existed, it was possible for it to exist. But matter, in which power would be founded, needed to pre-exist, since the *Metaphysics* says that we say that something is at some time possible because there is nothing contradictory in the terms of the statement, as the possible is contrary to the impossible, not regarding a particular power.[3] Therefore, we say that, before the world existed, it was possible for the world to be made, since there was no contrariness between the predicate and the subject of the statement. Or we can say that it was possible because of the active power of an active thing, not because of the passive power of matter. Aristotle uses this argument regarding natural generations against the Platonists, who said that separate forms are the sources of generation.[4]

Obj. 3. One cannot bridge an infinite distance. But there is an infinite distance from absolutely nonbeing to a being, and this is clear because the less disposed a potentiality is for an actuality, the more distant it is from actuality. And so, it is impossible for something to go absolutely from nonbeing to a being.

Reply Obj. 3. We should say that there is always in some way an infinite distance between a being and absolutely nonbeing, but not in the same way. Sometimes distance is infinite from both extremities, as when we compare nonexisting to divine existing, which is infinite, as if we should compare infinite whiteness to infinite blackness. And sometimes it is finite from only one extremity, as when we compare nonexisting absolutely to created existing, which is finite, as if we should compare infinite blackness to finite whiteness. Therefore, no transition from nonexisting to divine existing is possible, but such a transition to finite existing is possible, as one extremity limits the distance from nonexisting to finite existing. On the other hand, it is not a transition in the proper sense, since transition in the proper sense consists of continuous movements, by which one phase succeeds another. In the latter way, nothing in any way infinite makes the transition.

Obj. 7. If something should be made from nothing, the preposition *from* denotes either a cause or an order, and it seems to denote only an efficient or material cause. But "nothing" cannot be either the efficient or the material cause of a being, and so, on the point at issue, *from* does not denote a cause. Nor does it denote an order, since, as Boethius says, there is no order of a being to nothing. Therefore, in no way can something be made from nothing.

Reply Obj. 7. We should say that, when we say that something is made from nothing, there are two meanings, as Anselm makes clear in his *Monologion.*[5] The negation signified in the word *nothing* can negate the preposition *from*, or be included in the preposition. And if it should negate the proposition, there can still be two meanings. One is that the negation is borne to the whole, and both the preposition and the word are negated, as if to say that something is made from nothing because it is not made, as we can say about someone silent that such a one is speaking about nothing. And we can thus say about God that he is made from nothing, since he is not made at all, although this is not the usual way of speaking. The other meaning is that the word stays positive, but the the negation is borne only to the preposition. And so the statement says that something is made from nothing because it is truly made, but nothing preexists from which it is made, as we say that someone is sad from nothing, since that one has no reason to be sad, and we say in this way that something is made from nothing. But if the preposition includes negation, then there are two meanings, one true and the other false. There is a false sense if the position should signify a causal relationship, since nonbeing can in no way cause a being. There is a true sense if the position should signify only an order, so as to say that something is made from nothing because it is made after nothing, which also is true about creation. And we should understand what Boethius says, that there is no order of nonbeing to a being, about the order of a determined proportion or the order that is a real relation, which cannot exist between a being and nonbeing, as Avicenna says.[6]

Obj. 11. Something made necessarily comes to be at some time, and something created is created at some time. Therefore, something created either at the same time comes to be and was made, or not at the same time. But we cannot say it is not at the same time, since the creature does not exist before it has been made. Therefore, if its coming to be should be before it was made, there will need to be a subject of the making, which is contrary to the nature of creation. And if it at the same time comes to be and has been made, then it at the same time comes to be and does not come to be, since something made consists of permanent things, but something coming to be does not. But this is impossible. Therefore, it is impossible that something comes to be from nothing, or is created.

Reply Obj. 11. Something made from nothing at the same time comes to be and has been made, and it is likewise in the case of all instantaneous changes, as, for example, air at the same time is illuminated and has been illuminated. For we call the very fact of such things having been made their coming to be, insofar as their coming to be consists of the first moment in which they were made. Or we can say that we mean that something made from nothing comes to be when it has been made by an effluence from an active thing into the thing made, not by the movement from one terminus to another. For we find these two things in natural generation, namely, a transition from one terminus to another and an effluence from an active thing into the thing made, only the latter of which is in the proper sense true in the case of creation.

Obj. 12. Every active thing produces something like itself. But every active thing causes insofar as it is actual. Therefore, only something actual is made. But prime matter is not an actuality. Therefore, it cannot come to be, especially by God, who is pure actuality. And so everything made is made from presupposed matter, not from nothing.

Reply Obj. 12. We should say that we do not, properly speaking, say that matter or form or an accident is made. Rather, the thing made is the subsistent thing, since, inasmuch as coming to be terminates in existing, coming to be, in the proper sense, belongs to that to which existing belongs, namely, the subsistent thing. And so we properly say that matter, form, and accidents are created along with the subsistent thing, not created separately, and the subsistent thing, whatsoever it is, is created in the proper sense. But if this has no force, we should then say prime matter has a likeness with God inasmuch as it shares in being. For as a stone is like God as a being, although it is not intellectual like God, so prime matter has a likeness with God as a being, but not as an actual being. For being is in a way common to potentiality and actuality.

Article 2

Is Creation a Change?

We should say that it is required in a change that something the same be common to both termini of the change, since, if the opposite termini of a change were not to be one in something the same, we could not call it a transition from one terminus to the other. For, in the words *change* and *transition*, we designate something the same to be differently disposed now and before. Also, the very termini of a change are compatible, which is required in order to be the termini of the change, only inasmuch as they are related to the same thing, since two contraries, if they should be related to different subjects, may exist simultaneously.

Therefore, it may be that sometimes there is one common, actually existing subject for both termini, and then there is movement in the proper sense, as happens in alteration, increase, decrease, and locomotion. For, in all these movements, one and the same actually existing subject is changed from one contrary to the other. Sometimes there is the same subject common to both termini, not actually but only potentially a being, as happens in coming to be and passing away absolutely, since the subject of a substantial form and of a privation of form is prime matter, which is not actually a being. And so we in the proper sense call coming to be and passing away changes, not movements.

Sometimes there is no common subject actually or potentially existing. Rather, there is the same continuous time, in the first part of which there is one contrary, and in the second of which there is the other, as when we say that this thing is from that thing, that is, after it. For example, noon follows morning. But we metaphorically, not properly, call this a change, as we imagine time itself as if the subject of the things taking place in time.

But there is nothing common in creation in any of the aforementioned ways. For there is in creation no common subject actually or potentially existing. Also, time is not the same thing if we are speaking of the creation of the universe, since there was no time before the world. Only the imagination finds that there is a common subject, namely, we image one common time when the world did not exist and after the world was made to exist. For, as there is no real magnitude outside the universe, we can still imagine it, so also there was no time before the beginning of the world, although we can imagine it. And in this regard, creation in the proper sense has the nature of change only regarding a certain imagination, not in reality but metaphorically, not in the proper sense.

Obj. 2. Everything made is in a way made from a nonbeing, since what exists is not being made. Therefore, as coming to be, whereby a thing is made as to part of its substance, is related to privation of form, and privation is non-existing in one respect, so creation, whereby a thing is made as to its whole substance, is related to nonexisting absolutely. But privation, properly speaking, is the terminus a quo of coming to be. Therefore, nonexisting absolutely, properly speaking, is also the terminus a quo of creation, and so creation, properly speaking, is a change.

Reply Obj. 2. We should say that, in coming to be, whereby something is made as to part of its substance, there is a subject common to privation and form, and it is not actually an existing thing. And so, as we understand in the proper sense a terminus a quo in it, so also we understand in a proper sense a transition in it, but this is not the case in creation.

Obj. 4. Something not similarly disposed now and before, is changed or moved. But something created is not similarly disposed now and before, since it was beforehand absolutely nonbeing and afterward becomes a being. Therefore, something created is moved or changed.

Reply Obj. 4. We should say that something not similarly disposed now and before is changed, presupposing the same subject; otherwise, nonbeing would be changed, since nonbeing absolutely is neither similarly nor dissimilarly disposed now and before. And in order that there be change, it is necessary that something the same be dissimilarly disposed now and before.

Article 3

Is Creation Something Really in a Creature, or If It Is, What Is It?

We should say that some said creation is something in the world in between the creator and the creature. And since a mid-point is not one of the extremes, so it followed that creation was neither the creator nor the creature. But master teachers have judged this erroneous, since every thing existing in whatever way has existing only from God and so is a creature.

And so others said that creation itself does not suppose anything as such regarding the creature. But this also seems improper, since, in all things related with respect to one another, one of which depends on the other, and not the converse, there is really a relation in the one that depends on the other, but only conceptually a relation in the other, as Aristotle says.[7] A creature by its name is related to the creator, but a creature depends on the creator, not the converse. And so the relation whereby a creature is related to the creator is necessarily real, but the relation in God is only conceptual. Lombard says this explicitly.[8]

And so we should say that we can understand creation actively and passively. If we should understand it actively, then it designates God's action, which is his essence, with a relation to a creature that is only conceptual, not real. But if we should understand it passively, since, as I have already said (A. 2), creation is not a change, properly speaking, we can say that there is something in the genus of relation, not anything in the genus of undergoing action. This is made clear as follows. In every real change and movement, there is a two fold process. One is the movement from one terminus to another, as from whiteness to blackness. The other is from the active thing to the passive thing, as from the producer to the product. But these processes are differently disposed regarding the very movement in progress and the end of the movement. For, while the movement is in progress, the thing moved departs from one terminus of the movement and comes to the other, but this is not so regarding the end of the movement. This is clear in the case of something being moved from whiteness to blackness, since, regarding the end of its movement, it does not yet become black but begins to be black. Likewise, the active thing changes the thing acted upon or produced while the latter is being moved, but the active thing does not change it further when it is at the end of the movement. But the thing produced gains a relation to the active thing, as the former has existing from the latter and is somehow similar, For example, the son born at the end of human generation acquires sonship.

But, as I have said before (A. 2), we cannot understand creation as a movement in progress, which precedes the end of movement. Rather, we understand creation as existing in the thing made. And so only the beginning of existing and a relation to the creator from which the creature receives existing, not an approach to existing or a transformation by the creator, is signified in creation itself. And so creation is nothing really different from a relation to God with the new existing.

Obj. 2. Everything in the world is either the creator or a creature. But creation is not the creator, since creation would then be from eternity, or a creature, since a creative act would create it, and so on endlessly. Therefore, creation is something in the world.

Reply Obj. 2. We should say that creation in the active sense signifies divine action with a relation understood in connection with it, and so it is uncreated. But in the passive sense, as I have said in the body of the article, creation really signifies a relation by way of change by reason of the newness or beginning signified. And this relation is a creature, with the word *creature* understood generally as anything from God. Nor do we need to regress endlessly, since the relation of creation is related to God by itself, not by another real relation. For no relation is related to another relation, as Avicenna says.[9] But if we should understand the word *creation* more strictly, as only what subsists, which is made or created in the proper sense, since it has existing in the proper sense, then the aforementioned relation is not created but accompanies creation. Just so, it is not a being in the proper sense but inheres in a being, and the like is true about all accidents.

Obj. 3. Everything that exists is either a substance or an accident. But creation is not a substance, since it is neither matter nor form nor a composite, as can easily be made clear. Nor is it an accident, since an accident is posterior to its subject. But creation is by nature prior to the created thing, since it presupposes no subject. Therefore, creation is nothing in the world.

Reply Obj. 3. We should say that the relation is an accident, and considered as to its existing, as it inheres in a subject, is posterior to the created thing, as an accident is conceptually and naturally posterior to a subject, although not an accident such as one that the sources of the subject cause. But if one should consider it by its nature, as the aforementioned relation springs from the action of the active thing, it is then in a way prior to the subject, since divine action itself is its proximate cause.

Obj. 6. If creation should signify the relation of a created thing to God, from whom it has existing, something would be continuously created, since the relation always remains in the creature, both when it begins to exist and as long as it does. But this seems impossible. Therefore, creation is not a relation, and so creation is nothing in the world.

Reply Obj. 6. We should say that creation signifies the aforementioned relation with the newness of existing. And so it is not necessary that a thing is being created whenever it exists, although it is always related to God. Nonetheless, it would not be improper to say that, as the sun illumines the air as long as the air sheds light, so also God is making a creature as long as it has existing, as Augustine also says in his *Literal Commentary on Genesis*.[10] But there is in this only a verbal distinction, as one can understand the word *creation* with or without the newness of existing.

Article 4

Is the Power to Create or the Act of Creation Communicable to a Creature?

We should say that some philosophers held that God created lower creatures by means of higher creatures, as the *Liber de causis*,[11] Avicenna,[12] and Algazel make clear, and they were moved to think this because they believed that only one thing could come directly from a simple thing, and many things proceeded from the first thing by means of the second thing. They said this as if God were to act by a necessity of nature, whereby one simple thing produces only one thing.

But we hold that things come from God by way of knowledge and understanding, in which way nothing prevents many things coming directly from one first and simple God, insofar as his wisdom contains all things. And so we hold in accord with the Catholic faith that God directly created all spiritual substances and the matter of material substances, deeming it heresy to say that an angel or any creature created anything. And so Damascene says:[13] "Let anyone who will say that an angel creates anything be anathema."

Some Catholic writers, however, have said that, although no creature can create anything, it could nonetheless be communicated to a creature that God create something by the creature's service. Lombard holds this position.[14] On the other hand, other Catholic writers say that it could in no way be communicated to a creature to create anything, and this is the more common opinion.

To prove these things, we should note that creation designates an active power whereby things are brought into existing and so presupposes no preexisting matter or any prior active thing, since only such causes are presupposed for action. For the form of the thing coming to be is the terminus of the action causing the thing to come to be, and this is also the end of the coming to be that results from, and does not precede, the action as to the form's existing.

The very meaning of the word makes clear that creation does not presuppose matter, since we say that something made out of nothing is created. Also, what Augustine says in his work *Trinity* makes clear that creation does not presuppose any prior efficient cause.[15] He proves there that angels are not creators because they act by the seeds of nature implanted in them, that is, the active powers in nature.

Therefore, if we so understand creation strictly, it evidently can belong only to the first active thing, since a second cause acts only by the influence of the first cause, and so every action of a second cause exists by presupposing the first efficient cause.

Nor did philosophers themselves hold that angels or intelligences create anything except by the divine power existing in them, as we understand that a second cause can have two kinds of action: one by its own nature and the other by the power of a prior cause. But a second cause by its own cannot be the source of existing as such, since this is proper to the first cause, inasmuch as the order of effects is according to the order of their causes.

The first effect is existence itself, which is presupposed in all other effects, and it does not presuppose any other effect. And so conferring existing as such is necessarily the effect of the first cause alone by its own power. And whatever other cause confers existing does so inasmuch as the power and activity of the first cause is in it, not by its own power, just as a tool effects instrumental action by the power of the cause moving it, not by the power of its own nature. For example, natural heat by the soul's power generates living flesh, but it only heats and dissolves by the power of its own nature.

In this way, some philosophers held that the first intelligences create second intelligences, inasmuch as the former, by the power of the first cause in them, confer existing on the latter. For existing is by creation, but goods, life, and the like by communication of form, as the *Liber de causis* holds.[16] This was the origin of idolatry, when people manifested the cult of worship to created substances as if they were creative of other substances. But Lombard holds that the power to create is communicable to a creature instrumentally, as if a tool, not by its own power, as if on its authority.[17]

But this is evidently impossible for one who considers it carefully, since the action of anything, even if it belongs to the thing as an instrument, needs to come from it by its power. And since every creature's power is finite, no creature can act in order to create, even as if an instrument. For creation requires infinite power in the power from which it comes, and five arguments make this clear.

The first is from the fact that the power of making something is proportionate to the distance between what is made and the opposite thing from which it is made. For example, the colder something is, and so the more remote from heat, the greater the power of heat needed to make something cold hot. But not existing absolutely is infinitely remote from existing, and this is made clear by the fact that not existing is more distant from any limited being than any other being is from it, however remote one being is from another. And so it can belong only to infinite power to make something completely out of nothing.

The second argument is that a thing is made in the way its maker acts, and an active thing acts insofar as it is actual. And so only what is entirely actual acts by its whole self, and this belongs only to the infinite actuality, that is, the first actuality. And so also producing a thing regarding its entire substance belongs only to infinite power.

The third argument is that, since an accident needs to be in a subject, and the subject of an action receives the action, only the thing whose action is its very substance, not an accident, requires no receptive matter when making something, and this belongs to God alone. And so it belongs to him alone to create.

The fourth argument is that, since all second efficient causes have from the first efficient cause the very fact that they act, as the *Liber de causis* proves,[18] the first imposes the mode and order on all the second causes, and nothing imposes the mode or order on the first. And since the mode of an action depends on the matter receiving the action of an efficient cause, it will belong only to the first efficient cause to act without any matter presupposed from another efficient cause, and to provide matter for all second efficient causes.

The fifth argument leads to something impossible, since, regarding the distance of potentiality from actuality, there is a proportion between powers bringing something from potentiality to actuality. For the more remote the potentiality from the actuality, the greater the power needed. Therefore, if there should be a finite power that produces something from no presupposed potentiality, there needs to be a proportion between it and an active power that brings something from potentiality to actuality, and so a proportion between no potentiality and some potentiality, which is impossible. For there is no proportion between nonbeing and a being, as Aristotle holds.[19]

Therefore, we conclude that no power of a creature can create anything, neither by its own power nor as the instrument of another.

Obj. 2. The power of the creator, which can establish even new genera of creatures, can communicate to a creature anything that does not draw a creature beyond its limits. But the ability to create, if it were to be communicated to a creature, would not exceed the creature's limits. Therefore, the ability to create can be communicated to a creature. The minor premise is proved as follows. We say that anything contrary to a creature's nature exceeds the creature's limits. But the ability to create is contrary to a creature's nature only because of the infinite power that seems to be required for creation. But infinite power is not required, it seems, since each thing is remote from one contrary insofar as it shares in the nature of the other. For example, something is white insofar as it is remote from black. But a created being shares in the nature of a being finitely. Therefore, it is finitely remote from nonexisting absolutely. But bringing something into existence from a finite distance does not demonstrate infinite power. And so we conclude that the act of creating can belong to finite power. And so the ability to create is not contrary to a creature's nature, nor does it exceed the creature's limits.

Reply Obj. 2. We should say that nothing prevents us from imagining a distance infinite on one side and finite on the other. We imagine an infinite distance on both sides when we consider both of two contraries infinite, for instance, if heat and cold should be infinite. But we imagine a distance finite on one or the other side when one or the other is finite, as, for instance if the heat should be infinite, and the cold finite. Therefore, the distance of an infinite being from nonexisting absolutely is infinite on both sides. But the distance of a finite being from nonexisting absolutely is infinite on only one side and yet requires an infinite active power.

Obj. 5. Nothing and something are more distant than something and existing, since nothing and something have nothing in common, and something is part of being. But God causes by creating, so that what was nothing becomes something, and so that no power becomes a power. Therefore, much more can he cause that a limited power, such as a creature's power, be omnipotent, to which creating belongs. And so the power to create can be communicated to a creature.

Reply Obj. 5. We should say that something cannot cause something, not only because of the distance between the extremes, but also because something cannot be done at all, as if we should say a material substance cannot cause God because God cannot be caused at all. Therefore, we should say that no particular power can cause omnipotence, both because of the distance between a particular power and omnipotence and because omnipotence cannot be caused at all. For nothing caused can be pure actuality, since, by reason of having existing from another, we comprehend potentiality in it. And so there cannot be infinite power in it.

Obj. 7. Inasmuch as substantial forms do not come to be, since only a composite does, as Aristotle proves,[20] only creation can bring them into existence. But created nature disposes matter for form. Therefore, something acts to assist in creation, and so it can be communicated to a creature to have an assisting role in creation.

Reply Obj. 7. We should say that we can consider form in two ways. We can consider it in one way insofar as it is potential, and then God creates matter along with a form, with no intervening action of nature disposing matter. We can consider form in a second way insofar as it is actual, and then it is not created. Rather, an active natural thing educes it from the potentiality of matter. And so nature does not need actively to dispose matter in order for something to be created. But because there is a natural form that creation brings into existence, namely, the rational soul, whose matter nature disposes, we should note that, since an act of creation does not elevate matter, we say in two ways that something is created. For some things (e.g., angels and heavenly bodies) are created with no matter presupposed, neither from which nor in which they are created, and nature can do nothing to dispose matter for their creation. But other things (e.g., human souls) are created with the matter in which they exist, but no matter from which they come, presupposed. Therefore, nature can actively dispose that they have the matter in which they exist, but not that the action of nature extend to the very substance of the created thing.

Obj. 16. The greater the resistance, of the thing acted upon to the active thing, the greater the difficulty in acting. But a contrary resists more than nonbeing does, since nonbeing cannot act, as a contrary does. Therefore, since a creature can make something from its contrary, it seems that it can much more make something out of nothing, that is, create. Therefore, a creature can create.

Reply Obj. 16. We should say that we can note difficulty in action in two ways. We can note it in one way in that the thing acted upon resists the efficient cause, and this is common, not to all things, but to things that mutually act on, and are acted upon, by one another, in which the active thing is acted upon by the reaction of the thing acted upon. And thus heavenly bodies, which have nothing contrary to their action, undergo no difficulty in acting from the reaction of the thing acted upon, and far less does God. We can note difficulty in a second way, which is general, insofar as the thing acted upon is distant from the action. For the more distant potentiality is from actuality, the greater the difficulty in the active thing's action. And so, since absolute nonbeing is more remote from actuality than matter subject to any contrary, howsoever intense, is, it evidently belongs to greater power to produce something from nothing than to make one contrary from the other.

Article 5

Can There Be Anything That God Did Not Create?

We should say the ancients proceeded in considering the world according to the order of human reason. And so, since human knowledge comes to understanding, beginning from the senses, the first philosophers were preoccupied about sensibly perceptible things and little by little arrived at intelligible things. And because accidental forms as such are sensibly perceptible and not substantial, the first philosophers said that all forms are accidental, and that only matter is a substance. And because substance suffices to cause the accidents that the substantial elements cause, the first philosophers held that matter is the only cause, and they said that it causes all the things that we observe in sensibly perceptible things. And so they were compelled to hold that matter has no cause and to completely deny an efficient cause.

Later philosophers began to consider substantial forms to some extent but did not arrive at knowledge of universal things. Rather, their whole attention was engaged about particular forms. And so some posited certain efficient causes that change matter to this or that form, not efficient causes that universally bring existing to things. For example, there were sensation, attraction, and repulsion, whose action they posited in processes of separation and cohesion. And so also, according to them, not all beings resulted from an efficient cause, and they presupposed matter for the action of an efficient cause.

But later philosophers, such as Plato, Aristotle, and their followers, came to consider universal existing itself, and so only they considered a universal cause of things, from which all other things come into existing, as Augustine makes clear in the *City of God*.[21]

The Catholic faith agrees with this opinion, and three arguments can prove it. The first is that, if there is any one thing common to many things, a single cause necessarily causes it in them. For the thing common to many cannot belong to each from itself, since each by itself differs from the others, and different causes produce different effects. Therefore, since existing is common to all things, which differ from one another by what they are, we necessarily need to attribute existing from a single cause, not from the things themselves. This seems to be the argument of Plato, who wanted that both numerical and real unity be prior to every multiplicity.

The second argument is that, when many things share in something in different ways, we need to ascribe it to all the things in which it is imperfectly by the thing in which it is perfectly. For things that we positively predicate by more or less have more or less by approaching closer to, or being more remote from, one thing, since, if the thing were to belong to each of them by itself, there would be no reason that it would be more perfectly in one than the other. For example, we see that fire, which consists of extreme heat, is the source of heat in all hot things. This is to posit one being, the most perfect and the most real being, and the fact that there is a cause of motion that is altogether unmoved and most perfect proves it, as philosophers have demonstrated. Therefore, all other, less perfect things necessarily receive existing from that cause, and this is the argument of Aristotle.[22]

The third argument is that we trace what exists by another as to its cause to what exists intrinsically. And so, if one heat were to exist intrinsically, it would necessarily cause all hot things, which have heat by sharing in it. But this to posit a being that is its very existing, and this is so because there needs to be a first being that is pure actuality, in which there is no composition. And so all other things, the ones that are not their existing but have it by participation, are from that one being. This is the argument of Avicenna.[23]

Therefore, reason demonstrates and faith holds that God created all things.

Obj. 2. We say that all the things made by God are his creatures. But creation terminates in existing, since the first created thing is existence, as the *Liber de causis* maintains.[24] Therefore, since a thing's essence is in addition to its existing, it seems that the thing's essence is not from God.

Reply Obj. 2. We should say that, because existing is ascribed to an essence, we say that both existing and the very essence are created. For, before it has existing, it is nothing, except, perhaps, in the creator's intellect, where it is the creative essence, not a creature.

Obj. 3. Every action terminates in an actuality, just as it proceeds from an actuality, since every active thing acts inasmuch as it is actual, and every active thing produces something like itself in nature. But prime matter is pure potentiality. Therefore, the creator's action cannot terminate in it, and so God has not created all things.

Reply Obj. 3. We should say that the argument proves that prime matter as such is not created but it does not follow from this that prime matter is not created under a form, since it then has actual existing.

Article 6

Is There Only One Source of Creation?

We should say, as I have said (A. 5), that ancient philosophers, considering only particular natural sources, proceeded from considering matter into the error of believing that not all things were created. As a result, they proceeded from considering contraries, which they held to be sources in nature along with matter, to establish two first sources of things, and this was due to three defects in their consideration of contraries.

The first defect was that they considered contraries only insofar as they differ in specific nature, not insofar as they have something common in generic nature, although contraries belong to the same genus. And so they ascribed to them a cause by that in which they differ, not regarding what is common to them. Accordingly, they traced all contraries to two first contraries as two first causes, as the *Physics* holds.[25] But among them, Empedocles also posited the first contraries, namely, attraction and repulsion, as the first efficient causes, and he first posited good and evil as sources, as the *Metaphysics* maintains.[26]

The second defect was that they equated both contraries, although one contrary is necessarily always deprived of the other, and so one is perfect and the other imperfect, one better and one worse, as the *Physics* maintains.[27] In consequence, they held both good and evil, which seemed to be more general contraries, to be different natures, as it were. And so Pythagoras posited two genera of things, namely, good and evil. He posited all perfect things, such as light, male, rest, and the like, in the genus of good, and all imperfect things, such as darkness, female, and the like, in the genus of evil.

The third defect was that they judged things only insofar as one considers them in themselves or according to the order of one thing to another particular thing, not in relation to the whole order of the universe. And so, if they found a particular thing harmful to another thing or imperfect in relation to other, perfect things, they judged the thing absolutely evil by its nature and not indicating its origin from the cause of good. For this reason, Pythagoras posited female, which is something imperfect, in the genus of evil.

It came from this root that the Manicheans did not hold that corruptible things, visible things, and the Old Testament, which are imperfect in relation to incorruptible things, invisible things, and the New Testament, are from the good God but from a contrary source. And they held the latter especially because they saw that some harm comes to a good creature, such as a human being, from visible and corruptible creatures.

This error is completely impossible. Rather, we need to trace all good things to one first source, which is good. For the moment, three arguments prove this. The first is that, in whatever things we find one common thing, we need to trace the things to one cause regarding what is common to them, since either one thing causes the other, or there is a common cause of both. For it is impossible that the one common thing belong to both by what particularly belongs to each of them, as I held in the body of A. 5. But all contrary and different things in the world share in one thing, whether specific or generic nature, or at least in the aspect of existing. And so there is necessarily one source of all of them that causes their existing. But existing as such is good. This is evident from the fact that each thing seeks to exist, of which the nature of good, namely, that a thing is desirable, consists. And so it is evident that we need to posit a single cause superior to any of the different causes, as even philosophers of nature posit above the contrary active things in nature one first active thing, namely, the heavenly bodies, which cause the movements in the things here below. But because the heavenly bodies occupy different locations, to which, as the cause, we trace the contrariety of material substances here below, we need to trace the heavenly movements to the first cause of motion, which is not intrinsically or incidentally moved.

The second argument is that every active thing is such inasmuch as it is actual, and so insofar as it is perfect in some way. But insofar as something is evil, it is not actual, since we call each thing evil because its potentiality is deprived of its proper and due actuality. But each thing is good insofar as it is actual, since it has perfection and entity in this respect, of which the nature of good consists. Therefore, nothing acts insofar as it is evil, but each active thing is such inasmuch as it is good. Therefore, it is impossible to posit an active source of things other than something good. And since every active thing produces something like itself, something is also produced only insofar as it is actual, and so insofar as it is good. Therefore, the position holding that there is an evil source of creation's evils is impossible on both counts. And the words of Dionysius,[28] who says that evil acts only by the power of good, and that evil is outside the striving and production of things, is in accord with this argument.

The third argument is that, if different beings were not totally from contrary sources not traceable to one source, they could only incidentally coalesce into one order. For only someone who orders many things produces their coordination, unless the things coalesce into the same thing by chance. We see that corruptible and incorruptible things, spiritual and material things, perfect and imperfect things coalesce into one order. For spiritual things move material things, which is evident in the case of human beings. Also, incorruptible material substances arrange corruptible things, as is evident in the alterations of elements by heavenly bodies. Nor can we say that these things happen by chance, since such would happen only in rather few cases, not always or for the most part. Therefore, we need to trace all the different things to a single first source that orders them into a unity. And so Aristotle in the *Metaphysics* concludes that there is one governing principle.[29]

Obj. 5. What happens by accident happens in rather few cases, as the *Physics* maintains.[30] But evil happens for the most part, as the *Topics* maintains.[31] Therefore, evil is not by accident.

Reply Obj. 5. We should say that evil is found only in rather few cases if effects are related to their proper causes, and this is evident in natural things. For fault or evil happens in the action of nature only because of an intervening impediment to the efficient cause, and this happens in only rather few cases, as there are monsters and the like in nature. In voluntary things, evil seems to happen rather more frequently regarding deeds than skills, inasmuch as skill, since it imitates nature, fails in only rather few cases. On the other hand, in deeds, with which virtue and vice are concerned, there are two kinds of appetite causing action, namely, the rational and the sensory. And what is good regarding one appetite is evil regarding the other, as, for example, pursuit of pleasurable things is good regarding the sensory appetite, and we call this sensuality, but it is evil regarding the rational appetite. And because more follow their senses than their reason, there are more evil human beings than good ones. But one following the rational appetite is rightly disposed in more things and evilly disposed in only rather few things.

Obj. 10. What does not exist cannot be a genus or a species. For Aristotle says in the *Categories* that good and evil do not belong to a genus but are the genera of other things.[32] Therefore, evil is a being and so needs something to create it. And so, since good does not create it, it seems that we need to posit an evil source of creation.

Reply Obj. 10. We should say that we should understand the words of Aristotle as regards the opinion of Pythagoras, who held that good and evil are genera, as I have said in the body of the article. But his opinion has some truth, since, inasmuch as we speak of good positively and of evil privatively, as I have said, as every form has the nature of good, so every privation has the nature of evil, and so good and evil are somehow convertible with being and the privation of being. And in any contraries, as the *Metaphysics* proved,[33] privation and possession are included, and so we trace the contrary that is more perfect to a good, and the other that is more imperfect, to an evil. And so Aristotle says in the *Physics* that one or the other side of the contrariety relates to an evil, and as such we call good and evil genera of contraries.[34]

Obj. 12. Constitutive specific differences signify a nature, and so a nature in one way gives each thing a specifically different form, as Boethius says.[35] But evil is a constitutive specific difference, since good and evil are specifically different habits. Therefore, evil is a nature, and so evil is a source of creation.

Reply Obj. 12. We should say that we do not consider evil, as only a privation, a constitutive specific difference of an evil habit. Rather, we consider evil the difference insofar as evil accompanies the intention of an improper end, in which there is the nature of evil from the intended end only inasmuch as the proper end is incompatible with such an end, as, for example, the good of reason is incompatible with the end of carnal pleasure. And so we particularly say that we consider good and evil in dispositions of the soul, since the end, which is the form, as it were, of the will, the proper source of evil acts, specifies moral acts and so moral habits, and we call them good and evil in relation to their end.

Obj. 15. Mt. 7:18 says: "A good tree cannot bear bad fruit." But we find some evil in the world. Therefore, it cannot be the fruit, that is, the effect, of a good cause, which the good tree signifies. And so a first evil must be the cause of all evils.

Reply Obj. 15. We should say that the Lord understands by the good tree the cause of good, not the first cause but the cause closest to an individual effect, and the like about the bad tree. And so he wishes us to understand by the bad tree heretics, whose works make them known, as a tree is by its fruits. And the analogy also makes this clear to one who attends to it, for the root, not the tree, is the first cause of the fruit. But if we should generally understand by the tree every cause, then we should reply that good does not intrinsically cause evil, as I said in reply to the first objection.

Obj. 16. Gen. 1:2 says that there was at the beginning of the world "darkness over the face of the abyss." But good, which has the nature of light, cannot create darkness. Therefore, the creation described there is from an evil, not a good, source.

Reply Obj. 16. We should say that the darkness mentioned in connection with the beginning of creation was only the lack of light, not a creature, but not evil, since only the lack of what can and ought to be present introduces the aspect of good and evil. For example, it is not evil for a stone not to have senses, or for a newborn child not to walk. But it was not due to an imperfection of the active cause that he created air without light. Rather, it comes from his wisdom, whose order requires that something be brought from the imperfect to the perfect.

Article 7

Is God Active in the Actions of Nature?

We should say that we should absolutely grant that God acts in nature and willing its actions. But some did not understand this and fell into error, attributing the whole activity of nature in such a way that the entirely natural thing did nothing by its own power, and different arguments moved them to hold this position.

Some, speaking about the law of the Moors, as Rabbi Moses relates,[36] said that all such natural forms are accidents. But since an accident cannot pass into another subject, they considered it impossible for a natural thing by its form somehow to introduce a like form into another subject. And so they said that God creates heat in something heated, not that fire heats the thing.

But one might argue against them that heating always results from applying fire to something to be heated unless an obstacle were to hinder the fire, and that this shows that fire intrinsically causes the heat. To one who so objected, they replied that God established the course to be observed in things in such a way that he would never cause heat except when fire is present, not that fire when present would contribute anything to the heating process.

But this position is evidently contrary to the senses. For, inasmuch the senses perceive only because a sensible object acts upon them, it follows that a human being would not perceive the heat of fire if the active fire should not produce a likeness of the fire's heat in the sense organ (Although there is doubt in the case of sight because of those who say this happens by sight projecting out to the object, it is evident in the case of touch and the other senses). For, if another active thing were to cause the form of heat in an organ, touch would perceive the heat but would not perceive fire's heat, or that the fire is hot, contrary to the sense's judgment, which does not err about its proper object.

It is also contrary to reason, which demonstrates that nothing regarding natural things is in vain. But unless natural things were to produce something, the natural forms and powers would be allotted to them in vain. For example, if a knife were not to cut, it would have sharpness in vain. Also, in vain would application of fire to wood be required if God were to burn wood without the fire.

It is also contrary to divine goodness, which communicates itself, and by that communication caused things to be made like him in both existing and acting. The argument that the proponents of the aforementioned position introduce in their favor is altogether frivolous. For when one says that an accident does not pass from one subject to another, one understands this about the numerically same accident, not that the power of the accident in a natural subject could not introduce a specifically like accident into another subject. This necessarily happens in every natural action. Also, they falsely suppose that all forms are accidental, since there would be no substantial existing in natural things, and its source can only be a substantial, not an accidental, form. Also, coming-to-be and passing away would be eliminated, and many other unfitting things would result.

Also, Avicebron says in his book *Fountain of Life* that no material substance acts. Rather, a spiritual force penetrating through all material substances acts in them, and the purer and subtler, and so the more penetrable by a spiritual force, something is, the more active it is. He introduces three arguments for this. The first is that every active thing after God requires a material subject on which to act, and no matter is subject to a material substance, and so it seems that it cannot act. The second argument is that quantity hinders action and movement, and he considers as evidence of this the fact that a large quantity slows movement and adds weight to a material substance, and so a material substance, which is bound to quantity, cannot act. The third argument is that a material substance is the furthest removed from the first active thing, which is only active and not being acted upon, and substances in between are active and passive. And so a material substance, the last substance, is necessarily only acted upon, not active.

But there is clear deception in this, since he understands all material substances as if numerically one and the same, and as if they would differ only in accidental, not substantial, existing. For if we should understand different material substances to be substantially different, then not every material substance will be the last substantial being and the furthest removed from the first active thing. Rather, one will be superior to another and closer to the first active thing, and so it will be able to act on another.

Likewise, in the aforementioned things, he considers a material substance by its matter, not its form, although it is composed of both. For it belongs to a material substance by reason of its matter, not its form, to be the last being and not to have a lower subject, since, by reason of its form, every substance in whose matter the form actually in the designated thing is potential, is a lower subject.

And so there is mutual action in material substances, since the form of one is potentially in the matter of another, and vice versa. And if the very form is insufficient for action, then neither is the force of a spiritual substance, which a spiritual substance needs to receive in its own way.

Nor does quantity take away movement and action, since only something quantified is moved, as the *Physics* proves.[37] Nor is it true that quantity causes weight, as the *De coelo* proves.[38] And so also quantity adds to the speed of natural motion, since the greater a heavy material substance is, the swifter its downward motion, and a light material substance is borne upward in like fashion. Also, although quantity as such is not the source of action, we cannot assign a reason that it hinders action. For it is rather the instrument of an active quality, except insofar as the active forms received in matter subject to quantity receive an existing limited and individuated to that matter, so that it by the forms' action does not extend to other matter. But although they obtain individuated existing in matter, they do not lose their specific nature, whereby they can produce something specifically like themselves, even if they themselves cannot be in another subject.

Therefore, we should understand that, in every natural thing, God is active in the nature or will that acts, not that he is active as if the natural things did nothing, and we need to show how we can understand this.

For we should note that we can in many ways call another thing the cause of a thing's action. One way is that the former gives to the latter the power of acting, as the *Physics* says that the producer moves heavy and light things, inasmuch as it gives them the power by which such movement results.[39] God produces all natural actions in this way, since he gave natural things the powers by which they can act, not only as the producer endowed heavy and light things with their power without further preserving it, but also as keeping the power in existence. For he causes the power bestowed, both as to being made a power to produce and as to existing, so that we can call God the cause of the action inasmuch as he causes and preserves the natural power in existence.

For we say in a second way that something preserving a power causes action, as we say that medicines preserving sight cause seeing. But nothing moves or acts by itself unless it should be the unmoved cause of motion.

We say in a third way that one thing causes another's action insofar as it moves the other to act, regarding which we understand application of a power to action, not the bestowal or preservation of the active power. For example, a human being causes a knife to cut because one applies the knife's sharpness to cutting by moving it. And an active lower nature acts only when moved to do so, since such lower material substances cause change and are themselves changed. But a heavenly body causes change without undergoing change, although it does not cause motion unless it is moved, and this process does not end until we arrive at God. Therefore, it necessarily follows that God causes the action of any natural thing, as the one moving and applying the power to act.

We further find that there is an order of effects according to the order of causes, and this is necessarily because of the likeness between effects and causes. Nor is a second cause by its own power able to produce an effect by the first cause, although it is the instrument of the first cause regarding that cause's effect. For an instrument does not by its own form and power cause the effect of the first cause. Rather, it somehow causes that effect inasmuch as it shares in the power of the first cause by being moved by the first cause. For example, an axe causes the product of a craftsman by the craftsman's power that moves it, and somehow shares in that power, not by its own form and power.

And so, in a fourth way, one thing causes the action of another, as the chief active thing causes the action of an instrument, and we also need to say in this way that God causes every action of a natural thing. For the higher a cause is, the more universal and efficacious it is, and the more efficacious it is, the deeper it penetrates into its effect, and the more remote the potentiality from which it brings the effect into actuality.

And in any natural thing, we find that it is a being, that it is a natural thing, and that it is such-and-such a nature. The first is common to all beings, the second to all natural things, the third in a single species, and a fourth, if we should add accidents, is proper to a particular individual. Therefore, an individual thing cannot by acting constitute something in a like species except as it is an instrument of the cause that regards the whole species, and, further, unless the whole belongs to a lower nature. And so nothing acts to produce a species in the lower things except by the power of a heavenly body, nor acts to produce existing except by the power of God. For existing is itself the most universal first effect and more internal than all other effects, and so such an effect belongs only to God by his own power. And so also, as the *Liber de causis* says,[40] an intelligence bestows existing only as it has power from God to do so.

Therefore, God causes all action, as any active thing is the instrument of divine power acting. Therefore, if we consider the active existing individual things, any particular active thing is directly related to its effect. But if we should consider the power that causes the action, then the power of the higher cause will be more directly related to the effect than the power of the lower cause, since the lower power is joined to the effect only by the power of the higher cause, as the *Liber de causis* says that the power of the first cause acts first in producing the effect and penetrates more forcibly into it.[41]

Therefore, divine power needs to be present in each active thing, as the power of a heavenly body needs to be present in each active physical element. But there is a difference in that the divine essence is wherever there is divine power, but the essence of a heavenly body is not wherever its power is. And again, God is his power, but the heavenly body is not.

And so we can say that God acts in any thing inasmuch as each thing needs his power in order to act, but we cannot in the proper sense say that a heavenly body always acts in an elementary material substance, although the elementary material substance acts by the heavenly body's power. Therefore, God causes each action inasmuch as he bestows the power to act, preserves it, and applies it to action, and inasmuch as every other power acts by his power. And when we have added to these things that God is his power, and that he is within each thing as what holds the thing in existence, not as part of the thing's essence, we will conclude that he acts directly in each active thing, without excluding action by the will and nature.

Obj. 3. If God should act in every activity of nature, God and nature act either by one and the same act or by different acts. But they do not by one and the same act, since the unity of action attests to the unity of nature. And so, since there are two natures in Christ, there are also in him two kinds of activity. But God and a creature evidently have different natures. Likewise, it is impossible that the actions are different, since different actions do not seem to terminate in the same product, inasmuch as termini distinguish movements and actions. Therefore, it is in no way possible that God acts in nature.

Reply Obj. 3. We should say that nature does not act in the action whereby God acts by moving nature, as the action of an instrument is by the power of the chief active thing. Nor are nature and God prevented from acting to produce the same thing, because of the order between God and nature.

Obj. 7. If God is acting in nature acting, he by his action necessarily contributes something to the natural thing, since an active thing by acting causes something actual. Therefore, either this suffices for nature to be able to act on its own, or it does not. If it suffices, then, since God gave nature even its natural power, we can by the same reasoning say that natural power was also enough for nature to act, nor will it be necessary for God, after he conferred the power of nature, to do anything further for its action. But if the contribution does not suffice, he again needs to do something else in nature, and if that does not suffice, he again needs to do something else, and so on endlessly. But this is impossible, since an effect cannot depend on an infinite number of actions. For, inasmuch as one cannot pass through an infinite number of things, it would never be completed. Therefore, we should rest in the first alternative and say that natural virtue suffices for natural action, without God acting further in it.

Reply Obj. 7. We should say that the natural power conferred on natural things at their institution is in them as a form having fixed and constant existing in nature. But what God does in a natural thing, whereby it actually acts, is only as an extension, having an incomplete existing, as colors are in air, and the power of a craft in the tool of the craftsman. An artisan's skill could give sharpness to an axe, so that the sharpness would be a permanent form in it, but his skill could not give the axe the power to cut wood as a permanent form, so to speak, unless the axe were to have an intellect. Just so, therefore, a natural thing's proper power, whereby it acts to produce, could be conferred as a permanent form in it, but not the power as an instrument of the first cause unless it were given to it to be the universal source of existing. Nor also could it be conferred on a natural thing to move itself or to preserve itself in existing. And so, as no power to act apart from a craftsman's skill needed to be conferred on a craftsman's tool, so no power to act apart from divine power could be conferred on a natural thing.

Obj. 9. Things altogether disparate can be separated from one another. But God's action and nature's action are altogether disparate, since God acts by his will, and nature by necessity. Therefore, God's action can be separated from nature's, and so God does not need to act in nature acting.

Reply Obj. 9. We should say that, although nature and will are disparate as to existing, they have an order in acting. For, as nature's action precedes the action of our will, by reason of which things by the will in the practice of a craft need the action of nature, so God's will, which is the source of all natural movement, precedes the action of nature. And so also his action is necessary in every action of nature.

Obj. 12. Sir. 15:14 says: "God made human beings and left them in the hands of their own deliberation." But God would not have so left them if he were always to act in human beings' will. Therefore, he does not act in their will.

Reply Obj. 12. We should not say that God left human beings in the hands of their own deliberation without acting in their will. Rather, he did so because he gave human beings' will mastery over their acts, so that they would not be bound to the one or the other contradictory alternative. He did not give this mastery to nature, since nature's form determines it to one thing.

Article 8

Does God Act in Nature by Creating, That Is, Is Creation Involved in Nature's Action?

We should say that there were different opinions about this question. The root of all of them seems to have had one and the same principle, namely, that nature cannot make anything out of nothing.

From this principle, some believed that nothing was made otherwise than by being extracted from another thing in which it was hidden, as Aristotle relates in the *Physics* about Anaxagoras,[42] who seems to have been deceived because he did not distinguish between potentiality and actuality. For he held it to be necessary that the things produced actually preexisted. But the thing produced needs to exist potentially, not actually, since, if it were not to exist potentially, it would be made out of nothing, and if it were to exist actually, it would not be produced, as what exists is not produced.

But because the thing produced is potential by matter and actual by its form, others held that a thing was produced regarding its form with preexisting matter. And because the action of nature cannot be out of nothing, and so presupposes something that exists, nature, according to them, acts only regarding matter, by disposing it to receive its form. But the form, which needs to come to be and not be presupposed, is necessarily from an active thing that presupposes nothing and can make something out of nothing. This is the supernatural active thing that Plato considered the giver of forms, and Avicenna said that it was the last intelligence of the separate forms.

Some contemporaries, following in their steps, say that this is God. But this seems inappropriate. Each thing has been constituted to produce something like itself. (For each thing produces insofar as it is actual, namely, produces what is potentially the thing to be produced.) Therefore, there would be no need for a likeness according to the substantial form in the natural active thing unless the substantial form of the product were to proceed from the action of the active thing. This is the reason that we find what is to be acquired in the product actual in the natural producer, and everything acts insofar as it is actual. It seems inappropriate to look for another external producer, when this one has been ignored.

And so we should note that these opinions seem to have arisen because they did not know the nature of form, just as the first arose because they did not know the nature of matter. We do not univocally say that the natural form exists in the thing produced. For we say that the natural thing produced exists intrinsically and properly, having existing, as it were, and subsisting in its existing, but we do not say that the form exists in this way, since it does not subsist, nor does it have existing intrinsically. Rather, we say that a form exists, or that it is a being, because it is something, just as we say that accidents are beings because they qualify or quantify a substance, not that a substance exists by them, as a substance does by a substantial form. And so we more properly say that accidents belong to a being than that they are beings, as the *Metaphysics* makes clear.[43]

And we say that each thing made comes to be in the way in which it exists, since existing is the terminus of production. And so, in the proper sense, the thing intrinsically produced is the composite. But the form is that by which a thing is produced, that is, a thing is made by its acquisition, not produced in the proper sense. Therefore, the fact that nature produces nothing out of nothing does not at all prevent us from saying that natural action causes substantial forms to exist. For what is produced is the composite, not the form, and the composite is produced out of matter, not out of nothing. And the composite is produced out of matter, inasmuch as matter is potentially the composite because it has the form potentiality. And so we do not properly say that form is produced in matter, but rather that it is brought out of the potentiality of matter.

And because the composite is produced, Aristotle in the *Metaphysics* shows that forms result from natural active things.[44] For, since the thing produced needs to be like its producer, and the thing produced by the producer is composite, the producer needs to be composite and not an intrinsically existing form, as Plato said. Thus, as the thing produced is the composite, and that by which it is produced is the form in matter brought into actuality, so the producer is a composite, not only a form, but the producer's form is that by which it produces. That form, I say, exists in this particular matter (e.g., this flesh, these bones, and such like).

Obj. 3. Augustine says:[45] "As only God can inform the soul with righteousness in our present life, and even human beings can preach the Gospel externally, so God internally acts to create visible things and adds to the world in which he creates all things the external actions of good or evil angels or human beings, or any animals (e.g., husbandry to the soil)." But God informs our soul with righteousness by creation in the proper sense, since we say that grace exists by creation. Therefore, God creates natural forms by creation in the proper sense.

Reply Obj. 3. We should say that, since grace is not a subsistent form, neither existing nor becoming intrinsically belong to it in the proper sense, and so it is not created in the proper sense, as intrinsically subsistent substances are. But the infusion of grace approaches the nature of creation inasmuch as grace does not have a cause regarding its subject, neither an efficient cause nor a material cause in which it is potential in such a way that a natural active thing can bring it into actuality, as is true in the case of other, natural forms.

Obj. 7. One might say that, although natural forms do not have matter as a constitutive part of them, they have the matter in which they exist, and so they are not created. On the contrary, like natural forms, so also the rational soul is a form in matter. But we hold that the rational soul is created. Therefore, we should hold likewise about other natural forms.

Reply Obj. 7. We should say that, although the rational soul has the matter in which it exists, it is not educed from the potentiality of matter, since its nature is superior to every material order, and its intellectual activity evidences this. Again, this form is an intrinsically existing thing, since it abides when the body has been destroyed.

Obj. 8. You will say that the rational soul, unlike other natural forms, is not educed from matter. On the contrary, nothing is educed from something that is not in the subject. But before the end of its production, the form that is the terminus of the production was not in matter; otherwise, there would be contrary forms in matter at the same time. Therefore, natural forms are not educed from matter.

Reply Obj. 8. We should say that the form that is the terminus of a production preexists potentially in the matter before complete production, not actually, and it is not unfitting that one contrary is actual, and the other potential.

Obj. 14. Something imperfect cannot cause something perfect. But the power of an animal is only imperfectly in the semen of an irrational animal. Therefore, the natural action of seminal power does not produce the soul of an irrational animal, and so it, and, by like reasoning, all other natural forms, need to exist by creation.

Reply Obj. 14. We should say that, even in semen, heat acts as an instrument of the soul's power in the semen. Although that power is imperfect, an imprint of the perfect soul still remains, since the power is in the semen from the soul of the generating animal, and semen's heat also acts under the power of a heavenly body, of which it is an instrument, so to speak. And so we say that the animal's soul and the sun, not the animal's semen, begets offspring.

Article 9

Does Creation Bring the Rational Soul into Existence, or Does the Transmission of Semen?

We should say that different peoples in ancient times said various things about this question. Some said that the soul of an offspring is propagated from the soul of its parent, just as the offspring's body is propagated from its parent's body. Others said that all souls are created separately but held that they were created together from the beginning without bodies, and the souls were later united to humanly conceived bodies, either by the will's own motion, according to some, or at God's command and action, according to others. Still others said that souls are infused at the same time as they are created.

Although these opinions were held at one time, and it was doubtful which of them were closer to the truth, as Augustine makes clear in his *Literal Commentary on Genesis*[46] and *Origin of the Soul*,[47] the judgment of the church later condemned the first two and approved the third. And so *Church Dogmas* says:[48] "We do not believe that the souls of human beings existed with other intellectual creatures from the beginning, nor that they were created together, as Origen imagined, nor does intercourse beget them with bodies, as the Luciferians, Cyril, and some rather presumptuous Latin writers affirm. Rather, we say that conjugal intercourse begets only the body, and that the soul is created and infused after the body has been formed."

To one studiously considering the matter, it is evident that the opinion that held that the rational soul is propagated along with the semen, which the present question concerns, was rightly condemned. Three arguments can suffice for the present to demonstrate this. The first is that the rational soul differs from other forms in that the existing in which other forms subsist does not belong to them, but rational souls have the existing whereby the things to which they give form subsist. The different ways of acting make this clear. For, since only what exists can act, each thing is related to producing or acting as it is related to existing. And so, since the body needs to share in the action of other forms but not that of the rational soul, which is understanding and willing, we need to ascribe existing to the rational soul itself as a subsistent thing, as it were, but not to other forms. And so, of forms, only the rational soul is separate from the body.

Therefore, it is clear that the rational soul comes into existing unlike other forms, to which being produced does not properly belong, but which we say come to be when a certain thing has been produced. But the thing produced is in the proper sense and intrinsically produced, and the thing produced is produced either out of matter or nothing. But what is produced out of matter needs to be produced out of matter subject to contrariety, since the productions are out of contraries, according to Aristotle.[49] And so, since the soul does not have matter at all, or at least no matter subject to contrariety, it cannot be produced out of anything. And so it comes into existing by creation, produced out of nothing, as it were. And to hold that the production of the body causes it is to hold that it is not subsistent, and so that it passes away with the body.

The second argument is that the action of a material power cannot be raised to the power to cause an intrinsically spiritual and immaterial power, since nothing produces something beyond its species. Indeed, the active thing needs to be more excellent than the thing acted upon, according to Augustine.[50] But the power to generate, which has a bodily organ, causes the generation of a human being. Also, the power in semen acts only by means of heat, as the *Generation of Animals* says.[51] And so, since the rational soul is intrinsically spiritual, not depending on the body or sharing with the body in its action, the generation of the body cannot at all propagate the rational soul or bring it into existing by the power in semen.

The third argument is that every form that comes into existence by generation or a natural power is educed from the potentiality of matter, as the *Metaphysics* proves.[52] But the rational soul cannot be educed from the potentiality of matter, since forms whose actions are not performed with the body cannot be educed from corporeal matter. And so we conclude that the power of the one generating does not propagate the rational soul. This is the argument of Aristotle.[53]

Obj. 3. An accident cannot be transmitted unless its subject is, since an accident does not pass from one subject into another. But the rational soul is the subject of original sin. Therefore, since original sin is transmitted from parent to offspring, it also seems that the rational soul of a child is transmitted from its parent.

Reply Obj. 3. We should say that we call original sin the sin of our entire nature, as we call actual sin personal sin. And so the relation of original sin to the whole of human nature handed down from our first parent, in whom the original sin was, and by whose will we consider original sin as if voluntary in all, is the same as the relation of personal sin to an individual person. Therefore, original sin is in the soul inasmuch as it belongs to human nature. But human nature is transmitted from parent to child by the begetting of the flesh, into which the soul is later infused, and so the soul incurs the infection because it is one nature with the flesh transmitted. For, if the soul were not united to the flesh to constitute a nature, as an angel is united to an assumed body, it would not receive the infection.

Obj. 6. According to Aristotle in the *Physics*,[54] an efficient cause in its effect is the specifically same thing. But the rational soul gives a human being its species. Therefore, it seems that what the begetter causes in the begotten is the rational soul.

Reply Obj. 6. We should say that the begetter begets something specifically like himself, inasmuch as his action produces the begotten in order to share in the begetter's species, and this is because the begotten acquires a form like the begetter's. Therefore, if that form should not be subsistent, but its existing should consist only of being united to that of which it is the form, the begetter necessarily causes the form itself, as happens in the case of all material forms. But if it should be one that has subsistence, and its existing should not completely depend on union with matter, as is the case with the rational soul, it then suffices that the begetter causes the union of such a form with matter, since it disposes the matter for the form, and he does not need to cause the form itself.

Obj. 9. The embryo, before the rational soul perfects it, has some activity of the soul, since it grows, is nourished, and has sense perception. But activity of the soul indicates life. Therefore, the embryo is alive. But the soul is the source of life in a material substance. Therefore, the embryo has life. But we cannot say that another soul comes to it, since there would be two souls in one body. Therefore, the soul that was first propagated in semen is the rational soul.

Reply Obj. 9. We should say that some thought in different ways about the life of an embryo.

For example, some likened the progression of the rational soul in human generation to the progression of the human body. They said that the human body is in semen virtually without actually having the human body's perfection, which consists of distinct organs, and comes little by little to such perfection by the power of semen. Just so, the soul is in the body at the beginning of generation, having by some power all the perfection that later appears in the complete human being. But it does not actually have the perfection, since actions of the soul are not apparent. Rather, the soul acquires perfection little by little over time, so that actions of the vegetative soul first appear in it, then actions of the sensory soul, and finally actions of the rational soul. And Gregory of Nyssa touches on this opinion in his work *Human Being.*[55]

But this opinion cannot stand, since it understands that the soul specifically exists in the semen from the beginning, without yet having perfect actions because of lack of bodily organs. Or else it understands that there is in the semen from the beginning a power or form that does not yet have the species of the soul (as semen does not have the visible form of a human body), but the action of nature little by little produces the species, so that the same soul is first vegetable, second sensory, and then rational.

First, the authority of Aristotle rebuts the first alternative, since he says in the *De anima* that the potential life in an organic material substance, whose actuality is the soul, is not jettisoning the soul, as one ejects semen and cuts off fruit,[56] and we are given to understand that semen, which lacks a soul, has the potentiality for one. Second, the semen does not yet resemble bodily members in ultimate assimilation, since its dissolution would then be its passing away, but is a superfluity of the final stage of digestion, as he says in the *Generation of Animals.*[57] Therefore, the soul did not yet perfect the semen in the body of the begetter, and so the soul cannot be in it at the beginning of its ejection. Third, given that a soul were to be ejected with it, we still cannot say this about the rational soul, which cannot be excised when a bodily part is excised, since the rational soul is not the actuality of any bodily part.

The second aforementioned alternative is also evidently false. For, since a substantial form is brought into actuality instantly, not continuously and successively (otherwise, the movement would necessarily have been in the genus of substance as movement is in the genus of quality), the power from the beginning in semen cannot successively progress to different grades of the soul. For example, the form of fire is not introduced into air so as to proceed from the imperfect to the perfect. For no substantial form receives more or less, but preceding change only alters the matter, so that it is disposed more or less for the form. But the form begins to be in the matter only in the last moment of the change.

Others say that there is in semen a vegetative soul first, and the power of the begetter, with the vegetative soul abiding, introduces a sensory soul later, and creation finally introduces a rational soul, so that they posit three essentially different souls in a human being.

But contrary to this is what the work *Church Dogmas* says:[58] "We say that there are not two souls in one human being as James and other Syrians will assent, one animating the body and intermingled with the body's blood, and the other spiritual to serve reason." Again, several substantial forms cannot belong to one and the same thing. For, inasmuch as a substantial form causes existing absolutely, not only in some respect, and constitutes this thing in the genus of substance, if a first form does this, and a second comes when the subject has already been constituted in substantial existing, the second will come to the subject accidentally. It would then follow that the sensory soul and the rational soul in a human being were united to the body accidentally. Nor can we say that the vegetative soul that is the substantial form in a plant is not the substantial form in a human being but a disposition for that form, since what belongs to the genus of substance cannot be the accident of anything, as the *Physics* says.[59]

And so others said that the vegetative soul is in potentiality regarding the sensory soul, and the sensory soul is the vegetative soul's actuality. And so the action of nature brings the vegetative soul, which is first in semen, to the perfection of the sensory soul, and, further, the rational soul is the actuality and perfection of the sensory soul. And so the act of the creator, not the action of the begetter, brings the sensory soul to its perfection, namely, the rational soul. And so they say that the rational soul in a human being is partly from within, namely, regarding its intellectual nature, and partly from without, namely, regarding its vegetative and sensory nature.

But this can in no way stand, since it means that the intellectual nature is a different soul than the vegetative and sensory natures and so returns to the same position as the second opinion, or that the substance of the soul, in which the intellectual nature will be as the formal element, is constituted from the three natures, and the sensory and vegetative natures will be as the material element. And so, since the sensory and vegetative natures, as educed from matter, can pass away, the substance of the human soul cannot be everlasting.

Also, the same impropriety introduced against the first opinion, namely, that the substantial form is successively brought into actuality, results.

Others say that the embryo has no soul until the rational soul perfects it, and the vital actions evident in it are from the mother's soul. But this cannot be. For the vital things in it differ from nonliving things, since living things move themselves by vital actions, and we cannot say this about nonliving things. And so being nourished and growing, which are the proper actions of a living thing, cannot be in the embryo from an external source, namely, the mother's soul. Besides, the mother's nutritive power would assimilate food for the mother's body, not the embryo's body, since nutritive power serves the individual as generative power serves the species. And again, there cannot be sense perception in the embryo from the mother's soul.

And so others say that there is no soul in the embryo before infusion of the rational soul, but there is a formative power that performs such vital activities in the embryo. But this cannot be, since, inasmuch as diverse vital actions are evident in the embryo before its final perfection, they cannot be from the same power. And so there needs to be in the embryo a soul that has different powers.

And so we should say otherwise, that there is in semen at the beginning of its ejection a power of the soul, and it is based on an animating source contained in the semen, which is by its nature foaming and so contains a material animating source. This power acts by disposing matter for the reception of the soul. And we should note that it is in one way in the generation of a human being or an animal and in another way in the production of air or water. For the production of air is simple, since only two substantial forms are evident in the whole production of air, one eliminated and the one introduced, and all of this happens at once in an instant. And so the form of water always remains present before the introduction of the form of air. But in the generation of an animal, different substantial forms are evident, since there is sperm first and blood later, and so on until there is the form of a human being or an animal.

And so such generation is necessarily complex and includes in it several comings to be and passings away, since one and the same substantial form cannot be gradually brought into actuality, as I have shown. Therefore, the formative power in the semen from the beginning introduces another form when the form of the sperm has been ejected, and another is again introduced when the former form has been ejected. And so the vegetative soul is introduced first. Then, when that soul has been ejected, a soul both sensory and vegetative is introduced, and when that soul has been ejected, the creator, not the aforementioned power, introduces a soul that is both rational, sensory, and vegetative. And so we should say according to this opinion that the embryo is live and has a soul before it has a rational soul, and when that soul has been ejected, the rational soul is introduced. And so it does not follow that there are two souls in the same body, or that the rational soul is transmitted with semen.

Obj. 22. According to Aristotle in the *Generation of Animals*,[60] the sources whose actions are performed with the body are produced with the body. But the action of the rational soul is not performed without the body, since understanding would then take place without the body, which is obviously false. For understanding does not take place without a sense image, as the *De anima* says,[61] and a sense image does not take place without the body. Therefore, the rational soul is transmitted with the body.

Reply Obj. 22. We should say that the intellect in the body, in order to understand, does not need anything material that is the source of intellectual activity along with the intellect, as happens in sight, since the source of vision is both the power of sight and the eye, consisting of the power and the pupil. But the intellect needs a material substance as an object, as sight needs a wall in which there is color, since a sense image is related to the intellect as colors are related to sight, as the *De anima* says.[62] And the intellect is for this reason prevented from understanding when the organ of imagination is injured, since the intellect, as long as it is in the body, needs sense images both to receive, so to speak, from sense images when it acquires knowledge and to relate intelligible forms to sense images when it employs the acquired knowledge. And examples are necessary in the sciences for the latter.

Article 10

Is the Rational Soul Created in the Body or outside It?

We should say, as I have said before (A. 9), that some held the opinion that all souls were created together outside of the body. For the present, four arguments suffice to show the falsity of this opinion. The first is that created things are from God in their natural perfection, since the perfect by nature precedes the imperfect, according to Aristotle.[63] And Boethius says that nature begins with perfect things.[64] But the soul does not have the perfection of its nature outside the body, since it is part of human nature, not by itself the complete species of a nature. Otherwise, there would necessarily be one thing of soul and body only accidentally. And so the human soul was not created outside the body.

Whoever held that souls existed outside bodies before they were united to them thought that souls are perfect natures, and that the natural perfection of the soul consists of it being united to the body only accidentally, like a human being is to one's garments. Just so, Plato said that a human being is not composed of a soul and a body but is the soul using the body. Therefore, all who held that souls are created outside the body held transmigration of souls, so that the soul drawn out of one body was united to another, as a human being, having doffed one garment, dons another.

The second argument is that of Avicenna.[65] For, inasmuch as the soul is not composed of matter and form, the *De anima* distinguishing the soul from both the matter and the composite, only a difference of form could distinguish souls from one another if they were to be differentiated by themselves. Difference of form introduces difference of species, but numerical difference in the same species comes from different matter. The latter difference can belong to a soul by the matter in which it is produced, not by the nature of which it consists.

Therefore, we can only hold that several souls of the same species are numerically different if they should be united to bodies from their beginning, so that their difference comes somehow from their union to a body as the material source, although such a differentiation is from God as the efficient source. But if human souls were to have been created outside bodies, they would necessarily be specifically different, since the material source of distinction has been eliminated, just as philosophers consider all separate substances specifically different.

The third argument is that the rational human soul does not differ substantially from the sensory and vegetative souls, as I have shown before (A. 9), and the vegetative and sensory souls originate only in the body, since they act in certain parts of the body. And so the rational soul can be created only in the body as becomes its nature, but without prejudice to God's power.

The fourth argument is that, if the rational soul was created outside the body and had in it the perfection of its natural existing, one cannot assign a suitable reason for its union with the body. For we cannot say that it joined itself to bodies by its own movement, since we see that abandoning the body is not subject to the power of the soul, which it would be if it were to be united to the body by its will. Besides, if souls are created altogether separate, one cannot say why union with the body attracted the will of the separate soul.

Nor, again, can one say that a natural desire came to it after a period of some years, and that natural activity causes such a union. For we trace things done by nature in a fixed period of time to the movement of a heavenly body as the cause, which measures periods of time. But separate souls cannot be subject to the movements of heavenly bodies.

Likewise, one cannot say that God united separate souls to bodies. For, if we should say that he did this for their perfection, there would have been no reason why they were created without bodies. But if he did this for their punishment, so that he put them in bodies as if in prison, as Origen said, because of sins they committed, the formation of natures from spiritual and material substances would consequently be by accident and not by God's original intention. This is contrary to what Gen. 1:31 says: "God saw all the things that he had made, and they were very good." In this passage, it is clearly shown that God's goodness, not the wickedness of any creature, was the reason for the good works made.

Obj. 2. Every imperfect whole thing is one that lacks a part that belongs to its perfection. But rational souls belong to the perfection of the universe more than even material substances do, since an intellectual substance is more excellent than a material substance. Therefore, if rational souls are created daily when bodies are generated and had not been created at the beginning, then the universe is imperfect because it lacks its most excellent parts. This seems to be improper. Therefore, rational souls were created at the beginning without bodies.

Reply Obj. 2. We should say that the universe at its beginning was perfect regarding species, not regarding all individual things, or it at its beginning was perfect regarding the causes of natural things, from which other things can be later propagated, not regarding the things' effects. And although rational souls are not from natural causes, the action of nature produces the bodies in which God infuses them, as connatural to them.

Obj. 5. Macrobius in the *Dream of Scipio* posited two parts in the heavens: one of the gods and the other of animals, namely, Cancer and Capricorn, through one of which souls come down into bodies.[66] But this would be only if souls were created in heaven without bodies. Therefore, souls were created without bodies.

Reply Obj. 5. We should say that the Platonists held that the nature of souls is intrinsically complete and incidentally united to bodies. And so also they posited the transition of souls from one body to another. They were especially induced to hold this because they held that human souls are immortal, and that generation is never lacking. And so, in order to eliminate an infinite number of souls, they held that there is a circle, so that souls on leaving bodies were united to new ones. And Macrobius speaks in accord with this opinion, which is false, and so we should not accept his authority in this respect.

Obj. 15. God produces all things according to justice. But different and unequal things are given according to justice only if there preexists a merited inequality in them. Therefore, since we note much inequality in the birth of human beings regarding their souls both in that some are united to bodies fit for the soul's action, and others are not, and in that some are the offspring of unbelievers, and others, who are saved through reception of the sacraments, are the offspring of believers. It seems that merited inequality preexisted in the souls, and so it seems that the souls existed before their bodies.

Reply Obj. 15. We should say that it belongs to justice to render what is due, and so it is contrary to justice if unequal things are given to equal things when one renders due things, but it is not contrary to justice when one gives things freely, which is the case in the creation of souls. Or one can say that the difference derives from the different dispositions of bodies, not the different merits of souls. And so also Plato said in *Laws* that God infuses forms according to the merits of matter.[67]

Obj. 16. It seems things that begin at the same time depend on one another regarding existence. But the soul does not depend on the body regarding the soul's existence, and the fact that the soul abides when the body has passed away evidences this. Therefore, the soul does not begin at the same time as the body.

Reply Obj. 16. We should say that, although the soul depends on the body regarding its beginning, in order to begin to be in the perfection of its nature, it does not depend on the body regarding its end, since it acquires existing in the body for itself as a subsistent thing. And so, after the body has passed away, the soul abides in its existing, although not in the fulfillment of its nature, which it has in union with the body.

Article 11

Does Semen Create or Transmit the Sensory and Vegetative Souls?

We should say that there are different opinions of philosophers on the production of substantial forms. Some said that an active natural thing only disposes the matter, but the form, the final perfection, comes from supernatural sources.

Two things show this opinion to be false. First, since the existing of natural and material forms consists only of their union with matter, it seems to belong to the same active thing to produce them as to one that alters the matter. Second, since such forms do not surpass the power, order, and capacity of the active sources in nature, there seems to be no need to trace the forms' origin to higher sources. And so Aristotle says that the form in particular flesh and bones produces flesh and bones.[68] In his opinion, an active natural thing both disposes the matter and brings the form into actuality, contrary to the foregoing opinion.

We need to exclude the rational soul from this general way of forms, since it is the very substance intrinsically subsisting, and so its existing does not consist only in being united to matter; otherwise, it could not be separate, and its activity, which belongs to the soul as such without the body sharing in the activity, also shows this to be false. Nor can it act otherwise than it exists, since what does not intrinsically exist does not intrinsically act. Again, an intellectual nature surpasses the whole order and capacity of material and corporeal sources, since the intellect by understanding can transcend all material nature, which would not be the case if the soul's nature were to be confined to the bounds of material nature.

But we can say neither of these things about the sensory and vegetative souls. The existing of such souls can consist only of union with a material substance. Their actions, which cannot exist apart from a bodily organ, show this. And so their existing does not belong absolutely to them without dependence on the body, nor, again, are they produced except insofar as the body is brought into existing. And so, as the natural generative act produces the body, so too are the aforementioned souls. And to hold that they are created separately seems to echo the opinion of those who held that such souls survived their bodies, although *Church Dogmas* condemns both of these opinions.

Such souls also do not surpass the order of natural sources, and their actions make this clear to those considering them. For the order of actions are also according to the order of natures, and we find some forms that do not reach further than what material sources can do. For example, the forms of elements and mixed material substances, which do not act beyond the action of heat and cold, do not. And so they are intrinsically immersed in matter.

On the other hand, although the vegetative soul acts only by means of the aforementioned qualities, its action attains to something in which the aforementioned qualities do not reach, namely, to produce flesh and bones, to fixing the limit to growth, and the like. And so also it is still kept within the order of material sources, although not so much as the aforementioned forms.

And the sensory soul does not necessarily act by the power of hot and cold, as is evident in the action of sight, imagination, and the like, although a fixed temperature of heat and cold is required for the constitution of the organs, apart from which the aforementioned actions do not happen. And so the sensory soul does not totally transcend the order of material sources, although it is not so low as the aforementioned forms.

But the rational soul also performs action to which the power of heat and cold does not reach, nor does it perform the action by the power of heat and cold or by a bodily organ. And so only it transcends the order of natural sources, and the sensory soul in irrational animals and the vegetative soul in plants do not.

Obj. 2. You will say that sensory and vegetative souls are in plants and irrational animals as forms and perfections but in human beings as dispositions. On the contrary, the more excellent something is, the more excellent the way in which it comes into existence. But it is more excellent that form and perfection exist than that a disposition does. Therefore, if the sensory and vegetative souls, which are in human beings as dispositions, come into existence through creation, which is the most excellent way of coming into existence, since the most excellent creatures begin in this way, it seems much more that creation has produced them in plants and irrational animals.

Reply Obj. 2. We should say that we do not speak of the sensory soul in a human being as a disposition as if it is something other than the rational soul in substance and as disposition for it. Rather, we call the sensory soul in a human being a disposition because the sensory soul is distinguished from the rational soul only as a power from a power. But the sensory soul in an irrational animal is distinguished from the rational soul of a human being as one substantial form from another. And yet, as the sensory and vegetative powers in a human being flow from the soul's essence, so also do those powers in irrational animal and plants. They differ in that only vegetative powers flow from the soul's essence in the case of plants, and so we designate the soul of a plant from those powers. In irrational animals, there are both vegetative and sensory powers, and we designate the soul of an animal from the latter powers. And in a human being, there are in addition also intellectual powers, and we designate the soul of a human being from those powers.

Obj. 5. You will say that the power in semen, although it is not actually a sensory soul, acts in the power of the sensory soul that is in the father from whom the semen is ejected. On the contrary, what acts in the power of another, acts as an instrument of the other. But an instrument moves only when moved, and the cause of movement and the thing moved need to be together, as the *Physics* proves.[69] Therefore, since the power in semen is not joined to the sensory soul of the begetter, it seems that it cannot act as the instrument of the begetter's sensory soul, nor in its power.

Reply Obj. 5. We should say that we understand that the chief active thing causes the motion of an instrument as long as the instrument retains the power imparted by the chief active thing. And so an archer moves an arrow as long as the archer's imparted force lasts. So also, in heavy and light things, their producer causes their motion as long as they retain the form given them by the producer. And so also we understand that the soul of the begetter causes the semen's action as long as the power imparted by that soul lasts in it, although it has been physically separated from the begetter. And the thing causing motion and the thing moved need to be together as to the beginning of the motion, not the whole motion, as is evident in the case of projectiles.

Obj. 7. When an effect falls short of the perfection of a cause, it cannot achieve the proper action of the cause, since different actions evidence different natures. But although the power in semen is an effect of the sensory soul of the begetter, it evidently falls short of that soul's perfection. Therefore, it has no power for the action that in the proper sense belongs to the sensory soul, namely, to produce a soul specifically like itself.

Reply Obj. 7. We should say that sensory and vegetative souls are educed from the potentiality of matter, just like other material forms for whose production a power transforming matter is required. But the power in semen, although it falls short of other activities of the soul, has that power. For, as the soul transforms matter so as to convert it into the whole body in nutritive action, so also the aforementioned power in the semen transforms matter so as to generate the thing conceived. And so nothing prevents the aforementioned power from accomplishing in this regard the action of a sensory soul in its power.

Obj. 12. Animals generated by semen as more perfect animals are more excellent than those generated by putrefaction, and they generate their like. But in things generated by putrefaction, souls exist by creation, since there is no specifically like active thing that brings them into existence. Therefore, it seems much more that the souls of animals generated by the semen of begetters exist by creation.

Reply Obj. 12. We should say that the more imperfect something is, the fewer things required for its constitution. And so, since animals generated by putrefaction are more imperfect than animals generated by semen, the power of a heavenly body, which also acts in semen, alone suffices in the former animals, although it does not suffice without the power of the soul to produce animals generated by semen. For the power of a heavenly body remains in lower material substances inasmuch it, as the first cause of their alteration, transforms them. And Aristotle for this reason says in *Animals* that all material substances in the lower world are replete with the powers of the soul. But although the heavens are specifically different from such animals generated by putrefaction, there is nonetheless a likeness regarding the fact that an effect preexists virtually in its efficient cause.

Article 12

Is a Sensory or Vegetative Soul in the Semen at the Moment of Its Emission?

We should say that some were of the opinion that such a soul was in semen from the moment of its emission. They wished that, as the matter of the semen was separated from the body of the inseminator, so the soul of the inseminator would at the same time propagate the soul of the thing begotten, so that the soul would immediately be there along with the particle of matter.

But this opinion seems false, since, as Aristotle proves in the *Generation of Animals*,[70] semen is not separated from what was actually a part of the inseminator but was a surplus after final digestion. It was not yet definitely assimilated. But the soul actually perfects a part of the body only if it should be definitely assimilated. And so the soul did not yet perfect the semen before its emission, so that the soul would be its form. But there would be in it some power, regarding which the soul's action already altered and brought it to the nearest disposition for the final assimilation. And also a power of the soul, not the soul, is in it after emission. And so also Aristotle says in the *Generation of Animals* that there is in the semen power from the soul as its source.[71]

Besides, if the soul were to be in the semen from the beginning, it would either actually have a specific soul, or not but as a certain power that would be turned into a soul. The first cannot be, since, inasmuch as the soul is the actuality of an organic body, the body cannot receive the soul before any provision of organs. And it also then follows that only disposition of the matter is all that the soul produces in the semen, and so there would be no generation, since generation precedes rather than succeeds the substantial form. But one might perchance say that another substantial form belongs to the body besides the soul, from which it follows that the soul would not be substantially united to the body, coming to it after something constituted already exists by another form.

It would further follow that the generation of a living thing would be a separation rather than a generation, as, for example, part of a log is cut off from it in order to be actually a log.

The second alternative of the aforementioned division cannot be, since it would accordingly follow that a substantial form would come to be in matter successively, not immediately. Then there would be movement in substance as there is in quantity and quality, which is contrary to Aristotle,[72] and substantial forms would receive more or less perfection, which is impossible.

And so we conclude that such a soul is not in semen, but there is a power of the soul, derived from the begetter's soul, that acts to produce the sensory or vegetative soul in the begotten.

Obj. 1. Gregory of Nyssa says in his work *Creation of Human Beings*:[73] "The assertion of either opinion is not without fault, both the opinion of those who fabricate that souls previously live in a certain state and order, and the opinion of those who think them created after our bodies." But if the soul was not at its beginning, it would necessarily be made after the body. Therefore, the soul is in the semen from the beginning.

Reply Obj. 1. Before the advent of the soul and the power to produce the soul, we should say that the material substance of a living thing, such as a lion or an olive tree, is only the seed of the substance before the soul, not by the soul, since the relation of the seed to such a power is the same as that of the body to the soul.

Obj. 5. The ejection of semen belongs to nature, and the cutting up of a wormlike animal is contrary to nature. But a soul is in part of a cut up worm-like animal, as Aristotle says. Therefore, much more is the soul in the semen ejected.

Reply Obj. 5. We should say that, since the cutting up of a wormlike animal is by force and contrary to nature, the part cut off was actually a part of the animal and perfected by its soul, and so, by cutting up the matter, the soul, which was actually one in the whole and potentially several, remains in each part. This happens because such animals are almost alike in the whole and the parts, since their souls, as more imperfect than other souls, require little diversity of bodily organs. And so a cut-off part, having as many organs as suffice for receiving such a soul, can do so, as happens in other like material substances, such as wood, stone, water, and air. And Aristotle proves by this in *Generation of Animals* that sperm was not actually a part of the begetter before its ejection, since its ejection would have not been natural but the way of a kind of destruction.[74] And so, by ejection of semen, the soul need not abide in the semen.

Obj. 11. Everything lacking a soul is inanimate. Therefore, if semen lacks a soul, it will be inanimate, and so an inanimate material substance will be transformed and become animate. Therefore, the soul is from the beginning in semen.

Reply Obj. 11. We should say that, although semen is not actually animate, it is virtually animate, and so it is not absolutely inanimate.

Article 13

Can Any Being from Another Being Be Eternal?

Since we hold that the Son of God proceeds by nature from the Father, we should say that the former is necessarily from the latter in such a way that the Son is nonetheless coeternal with the Father, and this is evident as follows. The difference between will and nature is that nature is determined to one thing regarding what the power of nature produces, and regarding whether to produce or not to produce, but the will is determined regarding neither. One can do this or that by willing to do so, as, for example, a craftsman can make a bench or a box, and also make those things and stop doing so. But fire can only heat if the subject matter of its action should be present, nor can it produce anything else in matter than an effect like itself.

And so, although we can say about creatures, which proceed from God by his will, that he could make such-and-such a creature and do so at this or that time, we cannot say this about the Son, who proceeds by nature. For the Son by nature could not be in a different way than the nature of the Father is disposed. Nor could the Son exist before or after than when the nature of the Father existed. For we cannot say that the perfection of nature was lacking at any time to the divine nature, and the Son of God was generated when this power of this nature proceeds to him, since the divine nature is simple and immutable. Nor can we say that such generation was delayed because of the absence or indisposition of matter, since this generation is altogether immutable. And so we conclude that, since the nature of the Father existed from eternity, the Father eternally generated the Son, and also that the Son is coeternal with the Father.

But the Arians, because they held that the Son did not by nature proceed from the Father, considered the Son neither coequal with the Father nor coeternal, as happens in other things that God produces by a decision of his will. And it was difficult to consider the generation of the Son as coeternal with the Father because of the usual way of acquiring human cognition in considering the perfection of natural things, in which one thing is produced from another thing by movement, and the thing brought by movement into existence begins to be at the beginning of the movement before its termination. And since the beginning of a movement necessarily precedes the end in time, which is necessary because movement is successive, and since movement cannot begin or start without a cause acting to produce it, the cause acting to produce it needs to precede in time the thing it produces.

And so what proceeds from something without movement is at the same point of time as that from which it proceeds, such as the brilliance in fire or the sun; and brightness proceeds from a bright material substance immediately, not successively, since illumination is the terminus of a movement, not the movement. We conclude, therefore, that, in the Godhead, in which movement has no place at all, the one who proceeds exists as long as the other from whom he proceeds. And so, since the Father is eternal, the Son and the Holy Spirit proceeding from him are coeternal with him.

Obj. 1. Nothing that always exists needs anything in order to exist. But everything from another, in order to exist, needs the thing from which it exists. Therefore, nothing that exists from another always exists.

Reply Obj. 1. We should say that, if need should signify deficiency or lack of what is needed, what always exists does not need anything in order to exist. But if it should signify only the order of origin to that from which it exists, then nothing prevents what always exists from needing something in order to exist, inasmuch as it is not from itself but has existing from another.

Obj. 3. What already exists is not generated or produced or in any way brought into existence, since what comes to be does not yet exist. Therefore, everything generated or produced or brought into existence would at one time not exist. But everything that exists from another is such. Therefore, everything that exists from another at one time does not exist. But what at one time does not exist does not always exist. Therefore, nothing that exists from another is eternal.

Reply Obj. 3. We should say that the argument is valid regarding production by movement, since what is being moved into existing does not yet exist. And so we say that what is being produced does not yet exist, but what has been produced does. And so, when there is no difference between something being produced and something having been produced, it is not necessary that what is produced at one time not exist.

Obj. 4. What has existing only from another, considered in itself, does not exist. But such necessarily does not exist at some time. Therefore, everything that exists from another would necessarily at one time not exist and so not be eternal.

Reply Obj. 4. We should say that what has existing from another, considered in itself, is nonbeing if it should be a different existing that it receives from the other. But if it should be the same existing, then, considered in itself, it cannot be nonbeing, since we cannot consider nonbeing as if existing. On the other hand, we can consider in a being what is other than its existing, since what exists may have something mixed in, but existing itself cannot, as Boethius says in his work *De hebdomatibus*. The first condition belongs to a creature, but the second is the condition of the Son of God.

Obj. 5. Every effect is posterior to its cause. But what exists from another is the effect of that from which it exists. Therefore, it is posterior to that from which it exists and so cannot be eternal.

Reply Obj. 5. We should say that we cannot call the Son of God an effect, since he is begotten, not made. For something is made whose existing is different from its maker, and so we, properly speaking, call the Father the source, not the cause, of the Son. Nor is it necessary that every cause precede its effect temporally but only by nature, as is evident in the case of the sun and its light.

Article 14

Can What Essentially Differs from God
Have Always Existed?

We should say that, according to Aristotle,[75] we sometimes speak of possible as an active or passive power, and sometimes as no power. We speak of possible as an active power if, for example, we should say that a builder can build, and as a passive power if, for example, we should say that wood can be burned.

And we sometimes call something possible, not regarding a power but either metaphorically, as we say in geometry that a line is potentially a rational number, or absolutely, namely, when the terms of a statement are not mutually contradictory. (I pass over the metaphorical meaning for the moment.)

Conversely, we call something impossible when the terms are mutually contradictory, as we say that one cannot at the same time affirm and deny something, not because it is impossible for an active thing or something being acted upon, but because it as such is impossible, as self-contradictory.

Therefore, if we should consider the statement, we cannot say that something substantially different from God always existing, as such, is impossible, as if self-contradictory. For existing from another is not contrary to always existing, except when something proceeds from another by movement, as I have shown before (A. 3). And this does not happen in the procession of things from God. And by adding the words *substantially different*, we are given to understand no contradiction, absolutely speaking, with having always existed.

If we should understand the statement in regard to active power, God does not lack the power to produce from eternity an essence different from his. But if we relate the statement to passive power, then, presupposing the truth of the Catholic faith, we cannot say that anything essentially different proceeding from God could always exist. For the Catholic faith supposes that everything that is outside God at some time did not exist. And as it is impossible that what we hold to have once existed never existed, so it is impossible that what we hold to have once not to have existed always existed. And so also some say that this is possible regarding God creating but not regarding an essence proceeding from God if one supposes the contrary, which faith does.

Obj. 6. If God produced a creature at a certain time or moment, and if his power has not been increased, he could also have produced a creature before that time or moment, and, by the same reasoning, before that time or moment, and so on endlessly. Therefore, he could have produced from eternity.

Reply Obj. 6. We should say that, if we should hold that a creature existed before any given date, the position of the faith, which holds that nothing but

God always existed, is preserved, but it is not if one should hold that a creature has always existed. And so there is a distinction. Also, we should note that the argument is invalid, since God can make whatever better creature but not one of infinite goodness, inasmuch as the infinite goodness of a creature, not any amount of limited goodness, is contrary to reason.

Also, we should note that, if one says that God could have made the world before he did, if one relates this priority to the power of the maker, it is undoubtedly true, since the power to make abounds in him from eternity, but his eternity precedes the time of creation. And if one should relate the statement to "the existing of the thing made," so that one understands that there existed before the moment of creation a real time in which the world could have existed, the statement is evidently altogether false. But we can imagine a time before the world, as we can imagine height and dimensions outside the heavens. And we can in this way say both that God could have positioned the heavens higher, and that he could have created sooner, since he could have made time longer and height higher.

Counterobj. 1. Augustine says in his work *Literal Commentary on Genesis*:[76] "Since the nature of the Trinity is incommunicable, it is for this reason eternal, and nothing is coeternal with it."

Reply Counterobj. 1. We should say, according to Boethius at the end of his *Consolation of Philosophy*,[77] that even if the world were to have always existed, it would not be coeternal with God, since its duration would not be all at once, and this belongs to the nature of eternity. For eternity is the "all at once and complete possession of life," as Boethius says there. But motion causes temporal succession, as Aristotle makes clear.[78] And so what is subject to change, even if it always exists, cannot be eternal, and Augustine because of this says that no creature can be coeternal with the unchangeable essence of the Trinity.[79]

Counterobj. 7. If a creature has been made, it is either from nothing or something. But it is not from something, since that would be either from the divine essence, which is impossible, or from something else. If the latter were not made, there will be something besides God not created by him, and I have disproved this before (A. 5); if something else made it, either we will regress endlessly, which is impossible, or we will come to something that has been made from nothing. But what has been made from nothing cannot have always existed. Therefore, no creature can have always existed.

Reply Counterobj. 7. We should say that the first creatures were produced from nothing, not something. But by the truth that faith presupposes, not the very nature of their production, they necessarily at first did not exist and later came into existence. For, according to Anselm,[80] one sense of the aforementioned statement, that a creature was made from nothing, may be that it was not made from something, so that the negation includes the preposition and the preposition does not include the negation. And so the negation denies an order to something, which the preposition signifies, and the preposition does not signify an order to nothing. But if an order to nothing should still be affirmed, with the preposition including the negation, it is not still necessary that a creature at one time did not exist. For one can say, as Avicenna does, that nonexisting precedes the existing of the thing by nature, not temporally, namely, that, if it were to be left to itself, it would be nothing, and it has its existing only from another, since what has been constituted to belong to something by itself belongs to it by nature prior to what has been constituted to belong to it only by something else.

Article 15

Did Things Proceed from God by a Natural Necessity or by a Decision of His Will?

We should say that we should hold without any doubt that God brought creatures into existences by a freely willed decision of his, not by any natural necessity. Four arguments can, sufficiently for the moment, demonstrate this. The first is that one needs to say that the universe has an end. Otherwise, all the things in the universe would happen by chance, unless, perhaps, one were to say that the first creatures exist by a natural necessity, not because of an end, and subsequent creatures exist for an end. Just so, Democritus held that heavenly bodies happened by chance and lower material substances by fixed causes. The *Physics* disproved this by arguing that more excellent things cannot be less ordered than less worthy things can.[81] Therefore, we need to say that, in God's production of things, there is an intended end.

We find that both the will and nature act for the sake of an end in different ways. For nature, inasmuch as it does not know either an end or the nature of an end, nor the relationship between means and an end, cannot prescribe an end for itself, nor move, order, or direct itself toward an end. This belongs to an active thing by the will, to which it belongs to understand both the end and all the aforementioned things. And so an active thing acts by the will for the sake of an end, so that it prescribes the end for itself and somehow moves itself to the end by ordering its actions to the end. But nature strives for an end as something moved and directed by an intelligent and willing thing, as is evident in the case of an arrow, which strives for a target because of the archer's aiming it. Philosophers say in this way that the action of nature is an action of intelligence. But what exists by another is always consequent to what exists by itself. And so the first thing directing things to an end needs to do this by the will, and so God produced creatures by his will, not by his nature. Nor is there a valid objection about the Son, that he by nature proceeds from the Father, and his generation precedes creation, since the Son does not proceed as ordained for an end but as the end of all things.

The second argument is that nature is determined to one thing. And since every active thing produces something like itself, nature needs to strive to produce a likeness determined in one thing. And since unity causes equality, and the multiplicity disposed in various ways causes inequality (wherefore, something is only equal to another thing in one way, and unequal in many degrees), nature always produces something equal to itself unless it fails to do so because of the deficiency of an active power or a receptive and passive power. But lack of passive power is without prejudice to God, since he himself does not require matter, and, again, his power is infinite, not deficient. And so only what is equal to him, namely, the Son, proceeds by nature from him. But the creature, being unequal to him, proceeds by his will, not by nature, since there are many degrees of inequality. Nor can we say that divine power is limited to only one thing, since it is infinite. And so, since divine power extends to different degrees of inequality in constituting creatures, it was by a decision of his will, not a natural necessity, that he constituted a creature in a particular fixed degree.

The third argument is that, since every active thing produces something like itself in some way, an effect needs to preexist in some way in its cause. But everything in something is in it in the way of that in which it is. And so, since God himself is intellect, creatures preexist in him intelligibly, because of which Jn. 1:3 says: "What he created was life in him."[82] But what is in the intellect proceeds from it only by means of the will, since the will gives effect to the intellect, and the intelligible thing moves the will. And so created things need to have proceeded from God by his will.

The fourth argument is that, according to Aristotle,[83] there are two kinds of action. The kind that stays in the active thing itself, such as understanding, willing, and the like, perfects and actualizes the active thing. The kind that goes out from the active thing into the thing acted upon, such as heating, moving, and the like, both perfects and actualizes the thing acted upon. But we cannot understand God's action in the way of the second kind of action, since, inasmuch as his action is his essence, it does not go out of him. And so we need to understand it in the way of the first kind of action, which is only in the one understanding and willing, or sensibly perceiving. (The latter does not happen in God, since sense perception, although it tends toward an external thing, is caused by the action of the external thing.) Therefore, God by this produces whatever he produces outside himself, which he understands and wills. Nor does this prejudice the generation of the Son, which is natural, since we do not understand such generation to terminate in anything outside the divine essence. Therefore, we need to say that every creature proceeded from God by his will, not by a necessity of nature.

Obj. 10. God acts inasmuch as he is good, as Augustine says.[84] But he is the necessary good. Therefore, he acts necessarily.

Reply Obj. 10. We should say that, although God acts inasmuch as he is good, and goodness necessarily belongs to him, it does not follow that he acts necessarily. For goodness acts by means of the will, inasmuch as it is the object and end of the will, and the will is not necessarily related to means to the end, although it has a necessary relation to the ultimate end.

Obj. 12. 2 Tim. 2:13 says: "God remains faithful and cannot deny himself." But, since he is his goodness, he would deny himself if he were to deny his goodness, and he would deny his goodness if he were not to pour it out by communicating it. Therefore, God cannot fail to produce a creature by communicating his goodness. Therefore, he necessarily produces a creature, since possible nonexisting and necessary existing cannot be converted, as the work *De interpretatione* makes clear.[85]

Reply Obj. 12. We should say that, if God were to deny his goodness in making something contrary to his goodness or in which his goodness was not expressed, it would follow, impossibly, that he would deny himself. But this would not follow even if he were not to communicate his goodness to anything, since nothing would be lost if it were not communicated.

Obj. 18. An effect proceeds from an efficient cause. Therefore, an active thing is related to an effect only because it is related to an action or activity. But the relation of divine activity or action to God is natural, since his action is his essence. Therefore, he is likewise related to an effect by producing it naturally.

Reply Obj. 18. We should say that an effect results from an action by way of its active source. And so, since we, in our way of understanding, consider the divine will, which does not have a necessary relationship to a creature, the source of divine action as regards a creature, a creature need not proceed from God by a necessity of nature, although the action itself is his essence or nature.

Obj. 19. Something intrinsically good makes only something good and well made. Therefore, something intrinsically necessary also makes only something necessary and necessarily made. But God is intrinsically necessary. Therefore, all things proceed from him necessarily.

Reply Obj. 19. We should say that a creature is like God regarding general conditions but not regarding its way of sharing in them. For existing, and likewise goodness, is in God in one way and in a creature in a different way.

And so, although all good things are from the first good thing, and all beings from the first being, all things from the supreme good are not supremely good, nor do all things from the necessary being exist necessarily.

Article 16

Can Multiplicity Proceed from One First Thing?

We should say that the impossibility of many things proceeding directly and properly from one source seems to derive from the determination of a cause for an effect, whereby it seems to be required and necessary that, if there is such-and-such a cause, such-and-such an effect results. And there are four kinds of causes: two, namely, the material and the efficient, precede the effect regarding internal existing; the third, the end precedes the effect regarding its purpose, not its internal existing; the fourth, the form as such precedes in neither way, since, inasmuch as the effect exists by it, it exists at the same time as the effect, but inasmuch as it is also the end, it precedes in the purpose of the active thing. And although the form is the end of an action, for which the action of an active thing is determined, still not every end is a form, since the end of one's intention is outside the end of the action. For example, in the case of a house, its form is the end determining the action of the builder, but the builder's purpose does not end there and is for a further end, that is, a dwelling. Just so, we say that the end of the builder's action is the form of a house, but the builder's purpose is to provide a dwelling.

Therefore, such-and-such an effect of existing cannot be required by reason of its form as such, since it thus accompanies the effect, but by reason of the power of the efficient cause, the matter, or the end, whether the end intended or the end of the action. But we cannot say regarding God that an effect of his necessarily exists by reason of matter. For, inasmuch as he is himself the author of all existing, his action in no way presupposes anything having existence, so that we need to say that such-and-such an effect of his exists by reason of the disposition of matter. Likewise, neither is an effect necessary by reason of his productive power, since, inasmuch as his active power is infinite, it is determined to one thing only regarding what would be equal to him, which cannot belong to any effect.

And so, if it should be necessary for him to produce an effect less than himself, his power as such is not limited to this or that degree of distance from him, so that the active power necessarily produces such-and-such an effect.

Likewise, neither is the effect necessary by reason of the end intended, since this end is the divine goodness, which gains nothing from producing effects. Again, effects cannot completely represent it, nor can it be completely communicated to them, so that we can say that such-and-such an effect is required in order to share completely in divine goodness. Rather, an effect can share in it in many ways. And so the end necessitates none of these things. Thus we understand necessity from the end when the intended end cannot be attained at all or suitably except with this or that thing existing.

We conclude, therefore, that something in divine works can be necessary only by reason of the form that is the end of the action. For, since the form is not infinite, it has fixed sources, without which it cannot exist, and a fixed way of existing. This is as if we should say that, supposing that God intends to produce a human being, it is necessary and required that he confer a rational soul and an organic body on the human being, without which a human being cannot exist. We can say the same about the universe, since what God wished the universe to contain is neither necessary not required by reason of its end, the power to produce it, or its matter, as I have shown.

But supposing that he wished to produce it, it was necessary for him to have produced such-and-such creatures, from which such a form of the universe would arise. And inasmuch as the perfection of the universe requires both multiplicity and diversity of things, since that perfection cannot not exist in one of them because of its remoteness from the fullness of the first goodness, it was necessary, supposing the intended form, for God to have produced many and diverse creatures. Some were not composite, others composite, and some destructible, others indestructible.

Certain philosophers, not considering this, departed from the truth in different ways. Some, the oldest natural philosophers, perceived only the material cause of things. They, not understanding that God is the author of the universe, held that matter did not exist from another, and that its necessity produced the diversity of things, whether by the rarity or the density of matter causing the diversity of things, or by the action of an efficient cause, which produced different effects in different matter. For example, Anaxagoras held that a divine intellect produced different things by isolating them from their combination in matter, and Empedocles considered effects differing and combined in various ways by their attraction and repulsion according to different matter.

Two things show the falsity of these philosophers. First, they did not hold that all existing flows from the first and supreme being, which I have shown (A. 5). Second, according to them, it followed that the distinction of the parts of the universe and their order were by chance, since this was necessary because of a necessity of matter.

Others, such as Avicenna[86] and his followers, posited the plurality of things and their different ways from the necessity of an efficient cause. For

Avicenna held that the first being, inasmuch as it understood itself, produces only one effect, the first intelligence, which necessarily fell short of the simplicity of the first being, since potentiality began to be mixed with actuality, and what receives existing from another is not its own existing but in a way potentiality for it. And so, inasmuch as the first intelligence understands the first being, another, lower intelligence proceeded from it, and inasmuch it understands its own potentiality, a heavenly body proceeded from it and is moved by it, and inasmuch as it understands its own actuality, the soul of the first heavenly body proceeds from it. And so intermediate things multiply different things.

But this position also cannot stand. First, it cannot because it holds that divine power is determined to only one effect, which is the first intelligence. Second, it cannot because other substances than God create other things, which I have shown to be impossible (A. 4). It also follows from this position, just as with the first positions, that the beauty of the order in the universe is by chance, since it ascribes the diversity of things to the determination of active powers regarding their effects, not to an intended end.

Others, like Plato and his followers, erred regarding the necessity of a final cause, since he held that such-and-such a universe was necessary for God's goodness as understood and loved by him, so that the best produced the best. This can be true if we should regard only things that exist, but not if we should regard things that can exist, since this universe is the best of things that exist and has the fact that it is thus the best from the supreme goodness of God. But the goodness of God is not so bound to this universe that it could not have made a different good universe that was better or worse.

Still others, not noting the necessity of a formal cause but only that of divine goodness, erred. For example, the Manicheans, who considered God most good, believed that only the best creatures, namely, spiritual and indestructible ones, are from God, and they attributed material and destructible things to another source. The error of Origen,[87] although contrary to this, also derived from a like source, since he considered that God is most good and just. And so he thought that he first established only the best and equal creatures, namely, rational creatures. He said that, when they by free decision acted for good or evil in various ways, different grades of things were as a result constituted in the universe, and that the rational creatures that turned to God were promoted to the rank of angel, and in different ranks as they merited more or less. Conversely, other rational creatures, who sinned by their free decision, were, he says, cast into things here below and bound to material substances: some, who sinned less, to the sun, the moon, and the stars, and some to human bodies, and some were turned into devils.

Both errors seem to ignore the order in the universe by considering only its individual parts. For the very plan of the universe could have shown that one source, with no distinction of merits, necessarily instituted different grades of creatures in order that the universe be perfect, with the universe representing in the many and various ways of creatures what preexists in the divine goodness without composition or distinction. Just so, the perfection of a house and the human body requires different parts, and neither would be complete if all the parts were the same, as, for example, if all the parts of the human body were an eye, the functions of other parts would be lacking. Likewise, if all the parts of a house were to be a roof, the house would not acquire its perfection and end, namely, that it would be able to protect against storms and disasters.

Therefore, we should say that the multiplicity and diversity of creatures did not proceed from one first thing because of a necessity of matter, a limitation of power, goodness, or a necessity of goodness. Rather, the multiplicity and diversity proceeded by the order of wisdom, in order that the perfection of the universe would consist of the diversity of creatures.

Obj. 3. As good and evil are privatively contrary if we should understand them in general, although they are contraries as belonging to different habits, so one and many are contrary privatively, as the *Metaphysics* says.[88] But we say that wickedness happens from a defect of secondary causes and in no way from God. Therefore, neither should we hold that God causes multiplicity.

Reply Obj. 3. We should say that wickedness consists totally of nonexisting, and being causes multiplicity, since the difference that separates beings from one another is a being. And so God does not cause tending toward nonexisting but, rather, causes all existing. He is not the source of wickedness but is the source of multiplicity. And we should note that there are two kinds of unity. One is convertible with a being and adds nothing to a being except lack of division, and this unity excludes multiplicity, inasmuch as division causes multiplicity, not the extrinsic unity that a unit constitutes as a part, but the intrinsic multiplicity that is contrary to unity. For, in saying that something is one, we deny the division of something into many things, not that nothing is outside it and constitutes a unity with it. The second kind of unity is the one that is the source of number and adds measure to the consideration of a being. Multiplicity excludes such unity, since division of something continuous constitutes number. But multiplicity does not totally exclude unity, since, when a whole thing has been divided, undivided parts still remain, although multiplicity eliminates the unity of the whole. On the other hand, wickedness as such, which neither in any way constitutes goodness nor is constituted by it, eliminates goodness.

Obj. 4. Causes and effects necessarily happen in proportion to each other, namely, that individual things cause individual things, and universal things universal things, as Aristotle makes clear.[89] But God is the most universal cause. Therefore, his effect is the most universal effect, namely, existing. But multiplicity is not because things have existing, since the cause of multiplicity is diversity or difference. But all things agree in existing. Therefore, multiplicity is from secondary causes, from which the particular conditions that differentiate things result, not from God.

Reply Obj. 4. We should say that a being is related to things included in it in a different way than animal or any other genus is related to its species. For a species adds to a genus (e.g., human being to animal) a specific difference outside the essence of the genus. Animal, for example, designates only a sensory nature, in which rational is not included. But things included in being do not add to being anything that is extraneous to its essence. And so what causes an animal as such does not necessarily cause the rational as such. But it is necessary that what causes a being as such, causes all of its differences and so the entire multiplicity of beings.

Obj. 5. It belongs to each effect to have its proper cause. But one thing cannot be proper to many things. Therefore one thing cannot cause multiplicity.

Reply Obj. 5. We should say that we note the appropriateness of a cause for an effect by the likeness of the effect to the cause. And we note the likeness of a creature to God by the fact that the creature fulfills what is in the intellect and will of God regarding it, as the products of a craft are like the craftsman inasmuch as they express the craft's forms and manifest the craftsman's intention regarding their constitution. For, as a natural thing acts by its form, so a craftsman acts by his intellect and will. Therefore, God is the proper cause of each creature, inasmuch as he understands and wills it to exist. And we should understand the statement that the same thing cannot be proper to many things when there is appropriateness by equality, but this does not touch on the point at issue.

Obj. 24. Anselm says in the *Monologion* that the creature in God is his creative essence.[90] But he has only one essence. Therefore, there is also only one creature in God. But God creates a creature in this way insofar as it preexisted in him. Therefore, only one creature is from God, and so a multiplicity does not come from God.

Reply Obj. 24. We should say that one says in two ways that a creature is in God. One says it in one way as in the cause governing and preserving the existing of a creature, and so one presupposes its separate existing from the creator, so as to say that the creature is from God. For we understand that a creature is preserved in existing only insofar as it already has existence in its own nature, as the existing of a creature is distinguished from God. And so a creature being in God in this way is not his creative essence. One says in a second way that a creature is in God as in the power of its active cause or in the one who knows it, and so the creature in God is the very divine essence, as Jn. 1:3 says: "What was made was life in him."[91] And although a creature being in God in this way is the divine essence, there are many creatures, not only one, in the essence in this way, since God's essence is the sufficient means to know different creatures and sufficient power to produce them.

Article 17

Has the World Always Existed?

We should say that we should firmly hold that the world has not always existed, as the Catholic faith teaches. Nor can any demonstration from nature effectively refute this. To show this, we should note that, as I have maintained (A. 16), we cannot understand about God's action any necessity regarding a material cause, the active power of an active thing, or the ultimate end. But we can understand a necessity regarding the form (i.e., the end of the action), by the presupposition of which it is necessary that such things as belong to the form exist.

And so we should speak of the production of a particular creature in one way and of the whole universe coming from God in another way. For, inasmuch as we are speaking about the production of an individual creature, we can assign a reason why such a creature is from another creature, or at least from the order of the universe, to which any creature is ordered, as a part to the form of the whole. But when we are speaking about the whole universe coming into existence, we cannot find further anything created by which we can understand the reason why such or such a creature exists. And so, since we cannot understand the plan of the fixed disposition of the universe, neither regarding divine power, which is infinite, nor regarding divine goodness, which things need, we necessarily understand the plan from the absolute will of the one producing it. For example, if one should ask why the size of the heavens is so big and not bigger, no explanation can be given for this except that it is by the will of the maker.

Also for this reason, as Rabbi Moses says, divine Scripture brings human beings to considering heavenly bodies, the disposition of which especially shows that all things are subject to the will and providence of the creator. For we cannot assign a reason that one star is only so far from another, or any other things that we may consider in the disposition of the heavens, except the order of God's wisdom. And so Is. 40:26 says: "Lift your eyes to the heavens and see who created them."

Nor is it an obstacle if one should say that such-and-such a size results from the nature of the heavens or heavenly bodies, just as the nature of constant things is a fixed size, since, as divine power is not limited to this size rather that one, so it is not limited to the nature to which such size is required. And so the same question about nature, that is, size, will recur, although we concede that the nature of the heavens is not indifferent to any size, nor can they have another size than the one they have.

But we cannot speak in this way about time and its duration, since time, just like place, is extrinsic to a thing. And so also in the case of the heavens, in which there is no possibility of another size or internally inhering accident, there is the possibility of another place or position, since they move in space, and of another time, since one point of time always succeeds another as there is succession in movement and place. And so we cannot say that time or place results from their nature, as we said about size. And so it clearly depends on the absolute will of God that a fixed length of time is appointed, just as a fixed size is. And so we cannot conclude anything demonstratively about the duration of the universe, so that we can thereby demonstrate that the world always existed.

But some, not considering the procession of the world from God, were forced to fall into error about its beginning. Some, like the oldest natural philosophers, omitting the efficient cause and positing only matter created by no one, necessarily had to say that matter always existed. For, inasmuch as nothing brings itself from not existing to existing, what begins to exist necessarily has another cause. And they held that the world always continually existed, since they considered only things active by nature that were determined to one thing, so that the same effect would always necessarily follow, or else that the world always existed intermittently. For example, Democritus held that the world, or rather the worlds, were often composed and dissolved by chance, because of the causal motion of atoms.

But it seemed unfitting that all the harmonious combinations and benefits existing in natural things were by chance, since we find such always or for the most part, and this operation by chance was necessarily the consequence if one were to posit only matter, especially since there are some effects that the causality of matter does not suffice to explain. Therefore, others posited an efficient cause, such as the intellect by Anaxagoras and attraction and repulsion by Empedocles. Still, they held these to be efficient causes in the way of other particular active things, by transforming matter from one thing into another, not the efficient causes of the universe. And so they needed to say that matter was eternal, as something having no cause of its existing, but that the world had a beginning, since every effect of an efficient cause by movement follows its cause in time, inasmuch as the effect exists only at the end of the movement. Before the end, there is the beginning of motion, and with it the active thing, from which the movement begins, necessarily exists simultaneously.

On the other hand, Aristotle, considering that, if one should hold that the cause constituting the world acted by movement, there would consequently be an infinite regress, since there will be movement before any movement, held that the world always existed.[92] For he proceeded from considering the position that holds that an active thing begins to act by movement, which belongs to a particular cause and is not universal, not from considering the position that understands that the world proceeds from God. And because of movement and the immobility of the first cause of motion, he takes up his arguments in order to show the eternity of the world. And so, to one studiously considering them, his arguments seem to be the arguments of a disputant against a position, as it were, And so he also in the *Physics*, on the question about the eternity of movement there considered, begins by posing the opinions of Anaxagoras and Empedocles, against whom he intends to debate.[93]

The followers of Aristotle, considering the procession of the universe from God by his will, not by movement, attempted to show the eternity of the world from the fact that the will is not slow to do what it intends except because of a novelty or change, at least one that we need to imagine in the course of time, when one wishes to do something and not before.

But these also fell into a failure like the one into which that aforementioned fell, since they considered the first active thing like an active thing that performs its action in time, even though it acts by its will. The latter presupposes time and does not cause it, but God causes even time, since even time is included in the universality of things made by God. And so, when we speak about the procession of the universe's existing from God, we should not consider that he made things at such-and-such a time and not before, since this consideration presupposes time at the making and does not subject it to the making.

But if we should consider the production of all of creatures, among which there is also time itself, we should consider why he from the beginning allotted such-and-such a duration to such-and-such a time. And the allotment of the duration of time depends on the absolute will of God, who willed that the world would begin to exist and not always exist, just as he willed that the heavens would be greater or lesser.

Obj. 3. We should say that the heavens are not absolutely indestructible, since they would fall into nothing if the power of God were not to keep them in existence. But we should not consider that a statement is possibly or contingently true because it would be false if a consequence were false, since, although it is true that a human being is necessarily an animal, it would be false if its consequence, that a human being is a substance, were false. Therefore, it does not seem that one can say that the heavens are destructible because they would not exist if we should suppose that God withdraws his support from creatures.

Reply Obj. 3. We should say that one cannot, absolutely speaking, say that the heavens are destructible because they would fall into nonexisting if God were not to sustain them. But that God keeps a creature in existence depends on God's unchangeability, not on a necessity of nature such that we can say that it is absolutely necessary, since it is necessary only on a supposition of the divine will, which unchangeably established this Therefore, we can concede the objection insofar as the heavens are destructible, namely, conditionally, if God were not to sustain them.

Obj. 6. Something remaining the same always produces the same effect unless it is prevented. But God always remains the same, as we read in Ps. 102:27: "And you yourself are the same." Therefore, since he, because of his infinite power, cannot be prevented in his activity, it seems that he always produces the same effect. And so, when he once produced the world, it seems that he also produced it from eternity.

Reply Obj. 6. We should say that, since every active thing produces something like itself, an effect necessarily results from its cause acting efficaciously, so that the effect retains a likeness of its cause. And what is from a cause acting by nature retains the cause's likeness, as the effect has a form like the form of the active thing. Just so, what is from a voluntary active thing retains the active thing's likeness, as the effect has a form like the cause, insofar as what is in the will's disposition is produced in the effect, as is clear in the case of a craft product in relation to a craftsman. But the will disposes regarding not only the form of the effect but also the place, time, and all its conditions. And so an effect of the will necessarily results when the will disposes to act, not when there is an act of the will, since the effect is like the will as to what the will disposes, not as to existing. Therefore, although the divine will is always the same, it is not necessary that the effect eternally result from it.

Obj. 12. Every active thing that newly begins to act moves from potentiality to actuality. But this cannot belong to God, since he is altogether unchangeable. Therefore, it seems that he did not begin newly to act, and he produced the world from eternity.

Reply Obj. 12. We should say that the objection is valid regarding an active thing that begins to act by new action, but God's action is eternal, since it is his substance. And we say that he begins to act by reason of a new effect, which results from his eternal action by the disposition of his will, which we understand as the source, so to speak, of his action in relation to the effect. For an effect follows from an action by the form that is the source of the action, as the heating action of fire makes something hot by the heat of the fire.

Obj. 14. Only God's goodness moves his will to act. But his will is always disposed in the same way. Therefore, his will is also always disposed to produce creatures, and so he produced them from eternity.

Reply Obj. 14. We should say that, if we should understand movement in the proper sense, the divine will is not moved, but we say metaphorically that its object moves it. And so only his goodness moves his will, as Augustine says that God moves himself apart from space and time.[94] Nor does it follow that creatures would be produced whenever his goodness existed, since creatures proceed from God by a simple act of the will, not by a duty or a necessity of his goodness, since God's goodness does not need creatures, nor does anything accrue to him from them.

Obj. 15. What always exists at its beginning and at its end never begins or ceases to exist, since each thing exists after its beginning and before its end. But a period of time always exists at its beginning and at its end, since nothing belongs to time except a moment, which is the end of the past and the beginning of the future. Therefore, a period of time never begins or ceases but always exists, and so movement and the whole world always exist, since time always accompanies movement, nor is there movement without something moveable, nor something moveable without the world.

Reply Obj. 15. We should say that, since successive motion causes the first succession of time, as the *Physics* says,[95] it is true that, as every moment is both the beginning and end of a period of time, every moved thing is the beginning and end of movement. And so, if we should suppose that a moved thing has not always existed or will not always exist, it will not be necessary to say that any moment is the beginning and end of a period of time. Rather, there will be a moment that is only the beginning and a moment that is only the end. And so the argument of the objection is clearly circular and so not a demonstration, but it is effective according to the aim of Aristotle, who introduces it to refute a position, as I have said in the body of the article. For many arguments that are not absolutely demonstrative are effective to refute a position because of the things that adversaries hold.

Obj. 23. Everything finite is communicable to a creature. But eternity is something finite; otherwise, nothing could exist beyond eternity, as Ex. 15:18

says: "The Lord will rule unto eternity and beyond." Therefore, it seems that a creature will have been capable of eternity, and so it was proper to God's goodness that he produced a creature from eternity.

Reply Obj. 23. We should say that the Greek text of Exodus says: "The Lord will reign for age upon age and beyond," and Origin, explaining the text, says in a gloss that one understands *age* as the space of one generation, the limit of which we know, and *age upon age* as the immense space of time, which has a limit but not one known to us, and God's reign will extend even *beyond.* And so eternity means a long duration of time. But Anselm in the *Proslogion* explains eternity to mean forever,[96] which is never to have an end, and yet the text says that God exists beyond that, for three reasons. First, one may understand that there are no eternal things. Second, they would not exist if God were not to sustain them. Third, they do not have all of their existing at once, since there is a successive change in them.

Article 18

Were the Angels Created before the Visible World?

We should say that all Catholic teachers agree that angels have not always existed, since God brought them into existence from nothing. But some considered that they were created before the visible world began, not at the same time as it. Different arguments convinced them to hold this.

Some thought that God did not initially intend to produce material creatures but said that he had occasion to produce them by the merit or demerit of a spiritual creature. For example, Origen held that all immaterial and rational creatures were created from the beginning at the same time, and that they were equal, as divine justice requires. For it does not seem that there can be inequality in benefits, if justice is observed, except because of different merit or demerit. And so he held that a diversity of merit and demerit preceded the diversity of creatures, so that, insofar as some spiritual creatures adhered more to God, they were promoted to the ranks of angels, and those who sinned more grievously were bound to baser and viler bodies, as the very difference of merits required that God produce different grades of bodies.

Augustine refutes this opinion in *The City of God.*[97] For it is evident that the reason for producing both spiritual and material creatures is simply the goodness of God, inasmuch as his creatures, created by his goodness, represent in their own way the uncreated goodness. And so Gen. 1:31 says about the individual works of God and then about all the works collectively: "God saw all the things that he had made, and they were good," as if to say that God established creatures in order that they would have goodness. But according to the afore-mentioned opinion, material creatures did not exist in order that it would be good that they exist, but that the spiritual wickedness of a creature would be punished. It would also follow that the order of the universe, which we observe, would exist by chance, inasmuch as different rational creatures happen to sin in various ways. For if all were to have sinned equally, there would be, according to them, no natural differences in bodies.

And so, with this position eliminated, others, by considering the nature of spiritual substances, which is more excellent than all material nature, held that spiritual substances were established before material substances were, so that, as a created spiritual nature is by the order of nature in between God and a material creature, so also it exists by an intermediate duration of time. Since this was the opinion of great teachers, namely, Basil, Gregory Nazianzen, and others, we should not condemn it as erroneous.

But if we should consider another opinion, that of Augustine and other teachers, which is now also commonly held, we find it more reasonable. For we should consider angels both absolutely and as parts of the universe, and inasmuch as the good of the universe is more important than the good of any particular creature, as the good of the whole is more important than the good of a part, we should attend more to this consideration. And insofar as we consider angels as parts of the universe, it is proper for them to be established along with the material creature, since there seems to be one production of the whole universe. But if angels were to be created separately, they would seem completely foreign to the order of a material creature, as if constituting another universe by themselves. And so we should say that angels were established along with the material creature, but without prejudice to the other opinion.

Obj. 4. Scripture at the beginning of Genesis treats of things made with the visible world but makes no mention of the angels. Therefore, it seems that they were not created with the world but before it.

Reply Obj. 4. We should say, as Basil says in the *Hexameron*,[98] Moses, the lawgiver at the beginning of Genesis, began to explain the beginning of the visible creature, omitting the spiritual creature that had been previously established and making no mention of it because he was speaking to an unedu-cated people. But, according to Augustine,[99] Moses understands by the heavens the spiritual creature and by the earth the material creature when he says: "In the beginning, God created the heavens and the earth." And we can assign the same reason as the one above, namely, the people's lack of educa-tion, for Moses to reveal the creation of angels metaphorically and not ex-pressly. Also he may have done so to avoid the idolatry to which the people were prone. An occasion for idolatry would have been given to them if many spiritual substances more excellent than the heavens were posited in addition to the one God, and especially since the pagans called such substances gods. And according to Strabo[100] and others before him, the heavens in the cited text signify the empyrean heaven that is the dwelling place of the holy angels, by metonymy, the container substituted for its content.

Obj. 6. Everything before time exists before the visible world, since time began with the visible world. But angels were created before time, since there was no time before the day. And angels were created before the day, as Augustine says.[101] Therefore, angels existed before the visible world.

Reply Obj, 6. We should say that, according to Augustine,[102] the creation of the heavens and the earth did not temporally precede the formation and production of light. And so he understands that the creation of a spiritual nature was before the first day by an order of nature, not temporally, since a spiritual nature and unformed matter, essentially considered, are not subject to the changes of time. And so also we cannot gather from this that a spiritual creature existed before a material one did, since, before the formation of day, it is a question of the creation of a material creature, which he understands by the earth. But according to others, the creation of the heavens and the earth belongs to the first day, since time was created with the heavens and the earth, although the distinction of time regarding day and night began by light. And so time is posited as one of the four things first created, which are the angelic nature, the empyreal heavens, unformed matter, and time.

Obj. 10. People call a human being a lesser world, since a human being bears the likeness of the greater world. But the more excellent part of a human being, namely, the heart, is formed before other parts, as Aristotle says.[103] Therefore, it seems that the angels, who are the more excellent part of the greater world, were established before visible creatures.

Reply Obj. 10. We should say that, although the heart is formed before other bodily members, there is one continuous generation of the whole animal body, not that the heart is formed separately by one production, and the other bodily members successively formed later by other productions, with some periods of time in between. And we cannot say regarding the creation of angels and material creatures that they were established in one production, namely, a spiritual creature before a material one, as if the universe was continuously produced, since producing successively consists of producing things from matter, in which one part is nearer to perfection than another. And so, in the first creation of things, succession has no place, although it can in the formation of things from created matter. And so also teachers who held that angels were created before the world held that the creation of angels and that of material substances were distinct, and that much time intervened between them. Besides, the heart is necessarily first formed in an animal because the power of the heart acts to form the other bodily members. But a spiritual creature does not act in creating material creatures, since it belongs only to God to create. And so also Averroes criticizes Plato for having said that God first created angels and later committed the creation of material creatures to them.[104]

Obj. 17. Sir. 1:4 says: "Of all things, wisdom was created first." But we cannot understand this about the Son of God, the wisdom of the Father, since the Son was begotten, not made. Therefore, angelic wisdom, which is a creature, was made before all other things.

Reply Obj. 17. We should say that we understand the authority of Sirach, according to Augustine,[105] to refer to the created wisdom in the angelic nature, which was in itself created prior in dignity, not prior in time. But according to Hilary in his work *Councils*, it refers to the uncreated wisdom, that is, the Son of God. And we call it at once both created and begotten, as Prov. 8:23 and various texts of Scripture make clear, in order to exclude every imperfection from the birth of the Son of God. For we note in creation imperfection regarding the thing created, inasmuch as it is brought into existence from nothing, but we note perfection regarding the creator, who, without any change, produces creatures. But it is contrariwise in birth, since birth signifies perfection regarding the begotten inasmuch as the begotten receives the nature of the begetter but imperfection regarding the begetter by way of earthly generation, inasmuch as the begetter generates with a change in himself and a separation from his substance. And so we call the Son of God both created and begotten in order that creation exclude change in the begetter, and that birth exclude imperfection in the begotten, and so both establish one perfect understanding.

Obj. 22. Dionysius likens the divine action on things to the action of fire on the material substances that fire burns. But fire acts on close material substances before it acts on material substances further away. Therefore, the divine goodness produced angelic creatures, which are close to it, before material creatures, which are more distant from it, and so angels existed before the world.

Reply Obj. 22. We should say that, in the action of fire on material substances, we should consider two orders, namely, position and time. There is an order of position in each of its actions, since each action is in a place, and fire exercises its action more fully on material substances closer to it. And so, by proceeding further, it is weakened, so that it finally fails. But we note the order of time only in an action of fire that acts by movement, not in every one of its actions. And so, since fire illumines and heats material substances, the order of position and that of time are observed in heating, but in illumination, which is the terminus of movement, not the movement, we note only the order of position. Therefore, since God's action regarding creation is without movement, we note only a likeness regarding an order of position, not one regarding an order of time. For the different grade of nature in a spiritual action is the same as the different position in material action. Therefore, we note the comparison of Dionysius regarding this, that, as fire pours out its power more fully on material substances nearer to it, so God distributes his goodness more copiously to things closer to him in grade of dignity.

Article 19
Could the Angels Have Existed before the Visible World?

We should say that, as Boethius says,[106] we ought not to be drawn into imagination about God or any material things, since, inasmuch as imagination is a product of the senses, as Aristotle makes clear,[107] it cannot reach beyond quantity, which is the subject of sensibly perceptible qualities. But some, not noting this or able to transcend imagination, could understand something only by it being situated in a place, and so some philosophers of old said that what is not in a place does not exist, as the *Physics* says.[108]

And by a like error, some modern theologians said that angels cannot exist apart from a material creature, understanding angels like things that they imaged to be situated in different places. This is prejudicial to the opinion of older theologians, who held that angels existed before the world. It is also prejudicial to the excellence of the angelic nature that, since it is prior by nature to a material creature, depends in no way on a material creature. And so we say absolutely that angels were able to exist before the world.

Obj. 1. Any things so disposed that two different ones cannot occupy the same place require different places. But two angels cannot occupy the same place, as people commonly say. Therefore, we cannot understand that there would be two different angels unless they are in two different places. But there was no place before a visible creature, since place, according to Aristotle,[109] is only the extremity of an adjacent material substance. Therefore, angels could not have existed before the visible world.

Reply Obj. 1. We should say that lack of coordination in the actions of two angels, not their difference, prevents them from being in one indivisible place. And so the objection fails.

Obj. 2. The production of a material creature took nothing away from angels regarding their natural power. Therefore, if the angels could have existed apart from a place before the world was made, they would be able to exist apart from a place even now, after the world has been made. But this seems to be false, since, if they were not in a place, they would not exist. And so they would seem not to exist.

Reply Obj. 2. We should say that even now nothing prevents angels not being in a place, were they to wish, even though they are always in a place because of the order whereby a spiritual creature presides over a material one, according to Augustine.[110]

Question 4

Article 1

Did the Creation of Unformed Matter Precede in Time the Creation of Things?

We should say, as Augustine says,[1] that there can be two ways of discussing this question: one about the objective truth; the second about the sense of the text in which Moses, inspired by God, explains to us the origin of the world.

Regarding the first, one should avoid two things: one, that one not assert anything false regarding this question, especially anything contrary to the true faith; the second, that we wish to assert that whatever one has thought to be true belongs to true faith. For, as Augustine says:[2] "If one should think that something false belongs to the beauty of pious teaching, namely, that one believes and dares pertinaciously to affirm something of which one is ignorant, such a one is an obstacle to others." He calls this an obstacle because unbelievers mock the true faith when a simple-minded Christian proposes as part of the faith something that the most certain evidence demonstrates to be false, as Augustine also says in his *Literal Commentary on Genesis*.[3]

Regarding the second way of discussion, one should avoid two things. One is that one ought not say that something patently false should be understood in the words of Scripture, which teaches the creation of things, since the divine Scriptures handed down by the Holy Spirit cannot be subject to falsehood, just as the faith taught by Scripture cannot. The second is that one not wish to force Scripture into one sense so as completely to exclude other senses that in themselves include truth and can accommodate Scripture in its context. For it belongs to the dignity of divine Scripture that it include many senses in one text, so that it is suitable for the diverse intellects of human beings, and so each marvels that each can find in divine Scripture the truth that each mentally conceived. For this reason, Scripture is also more easily defensible against unbelievers, since, if something that one wishes to understand from sacred Scripture should appear false, recourse can be had to another sense. And so it is not incredible that the Godhead has granted to Moses and the authors of Scripture to know the different things that human beings can understand, and to design them in a running text in such a way that each sense is the author's sense. And so, even if commentators should adapt to the text of sacred Scripture some true things that the author does not intend, there is no doubt that the Holy Spirit, who is the chief author of sacred Scripture, so understood. And so every truth that can be adapted to divine Scripture, without prejudice to the literal context, is the sense of Scripture.

Therefore, presupposing these things, we should note that commentators understood different senses of sacred Scripture at the beginning of Genesis, none of which is contrary to faith. And insofar as it relates to the present question, they differed in two ways, understanding in two ways the infinity of matter that the text at the beginning of Genesis indicates: "And the earth was void and empty."

Some understood that the aforementioned words signify such unformed matter insofar as we understand it without any form but having potentiality for all forms, and such matter cannot exist in a real nature without receiving a form. For whatever is in a real nature actually exists, which matter has only by reason of a form, which is matter's actuality. And so there cannot be matter without form in a real thing.

Also, since nothing can be in a genus without being determined by a specific difference, matter cannot be a being without being determined to a specific way of existing, and only a form does this. And so, if one so understands matter, it cannot have temporally preceded its receiving form, but it is prior only by the order of nature, insofar as that from which something is made is by nature prior to that thing, as God created night before day. This was the opinion of Augustine.[4]

Others did not understand unformed matter as matter lacking all form but as we call unformed something that does not yet have the final complement and elegance of its nature, and one can hold in this regard that lack of such form was also temporally prior to things receiving that form. If one should hold this, it seems congruous with the orderly wisdom of the creator, who in bringing things into existence from nothing did not immediately establish them in the final perfection of nature but first made them in an imperfect existing and later brought them to perfection. And so their existing would be shown to proceed from God against those who consider matter uncreated, and yet the author of the perfections of things would be apparent, contrary to those who ascribed the formation of lower things to other causes. And so Basil the Great, Gregory Nazianzen, and their followers so understood. Therefore, since neither sense contradicts the true faith, and the text's context allows each sense, let us reply to the arguments on each side sustaining each side.

Obj. 2. Augustine says in his *Literal Commentary on Genesis* that unformed matter precedes matter formed from it, as voice precedes singing.[5] But one might say that he is speaking about matter with respect to its formation, which is by the forms of elements in matter from the beginning. On the contrary, as water and earth are elements, so also are fire and air. But Scripture, dealing with matter's lack of form, mentions earth and water. Therefore, were matter to have had elementary forms from the beginning, Scripture would have, by like reasoning, mentioned air and fire.

Reply Obj. 2. We should say that thinkers held many opinions about this. For example, people say that Plato, in a vision of Genesis,[6] understood the number of elements and the order there signified to express land and water by their proper names. He understands water to be over the earth because Gen. 1:9 says: "Let the waters be gathered into one place, and let the dry land appear." Above these two elements, he understood air in the expression: "The Spirit of the Lord was borne over the waters," understanding air in the word *spirit*, And he understands fire by the word *heavens*, which are over all the others.

But according to the proofs of Aristotle,[7] the heavens cannot be of a fiery nature, as their circular motion demonstrates. And Rabbi Moses, following the opinion of Aristotle and agreeing with Plato on the first three elements, said that darkness signifies fire, since fire in its own sphere is not luminous, and the words *over the face of the deep* declare its position. And he understands that the word *heavens* signified a fifth essence.

But since, as Basil says in the *Hexameron*,[8] it is not the custom of sacred Scripture to understand air by the spirit of the Lord, Scripture gave us to understand intermediate things by the extreme material substances that it posited. Scripture does so especially because it is obvious to the senses that water and the earth are material substances, but air and fire are not so manifest to the simple, also for the instruction of whom Scripture was handed down.

But according to Augustine,[9] one understands formless matter, not formed elements, by the words *earth* and *water*, which Scripture mentions before the formation of light. And so these two kinds of matter rather than the other elements express formlessness, since the former, having more matter and less form, are closer to formlessness, and they, as elements better known, also show us more clearly the matter of the other elements. And so Scripture wished to signify this by two elements, not one, lest, were one to posit only one or the other, one would truly believe that one is unformed matter.

Obj. 5. If one calls matter formless insofar as the elements did not yet have their proper place, it seems to follow that we understand its formation by assigning a natural position to the elements. But this is not evident in different things, since some waters are positioned above the heavens, although the natural position of waters is beneath the air and immediately above the earth, as the *De coelo* makes clear.[10] Therefore, we do not understand the formlessness of matter because of the aforementioned confusion of the elements' position.

Reply Obj. 5. We should say that thinkers held different opinions about the waters above the heavens. For example, some said that those waters are spiritual natures, which is attributed to Origen. But this does not seem possible to understand in accord with the text, since position does not belong to spiritual natures, so that the firmament is between them and the lower material waters, as Gen. 1:6 holds.

And so others say that we understand by the word *firmament* the air near us, over which evaporation lifts up vaporous waters, which are the matter of rains, so that, the airy heavens are in between the higher waters, which float vaporously in mid-air, and the material waters that we see on the earth, and Rabbi Moses agrees with this explanation. But this does not seem to fit the context, since Gen. 1:16–17 later adds that God made two great luminaries and stars and placed them in the firmament of the heavens.

And so others say that one understands by the firmament the starry heavens, and that the waters above the heavens concern the elementary waters, and divine providence places them there to moderate the power of fire, which they say sustains the whole heavens, on which Basil touches. And to add to this, Augustine says that some introduce two arguments.[11] The first is that, if water by evaporation can rise to mid-air, where rains are generated, if it should be further divided and rarefied (since it is infinitely divisible like every continuous thing), it could by its rarefaction rise above the starry heavens and be fittingly there. The second argument is that the planet Saturn, which ought to be the hottest planet because its movement is the swiftest, inasmuch as its orbit is the greatest, is found to have a cold effect. And they say this happens from the closeness of the water cooling the aforementioned planet.

But this explanation seems to fail in that it asserts certain things through sacred Scripture that sufficiently evident arguments refute by proving their contraries. First, the very position seems to distort the natural position of material substances, since, inasmuch as the greater the form that each thing has, the higher it should be, it does not seem to befit the nature of things that water, which, of all material substances besides the earth, is the most material, is located even above the starry heavens. Again, as things belonging to a species are allotted a different natural place, what will be the case if one part of the element of water will be immediately above the earth, and another part above the heavens? Nor is it a sufficient response that the omnipotence of God sustains the waters, contrary to their nature, above the heavens, since one is presently asking how God instituted the natures of things, not how he wished to exercise miraculous powers over them, as Augustine says.[12]

Second, the argument from rarefaction or division of the waters seems altogether pointless, since, although mathematical quantities can be infinitely divided, natural material substances are divisible up to a fixed limit, inasmuch as quantity is by nature determined for each thing, just as other accidental things are. And so neither can rarefaction be infinite but is up to the fixed limit that is the rarity of fire. Besides, water could only be rarefied because it was already air or fire, not water, if it were to transcend the mode of rarity of water. Nor could water by nature go beyond the spaces of air and fire unless it, having lost the nature of water, were to surpass their rarity. Again, nor could an elementary material substance, which is destructible, have more form than the starry heavens, which are indestructible, and so be located by nature above them.

Third, the second objection seems altogether frivolous, since heavenly bodies do not receive impressions from extraneous sources, as philosophers prove. Nor could those waters cool the planet Saturn unless they were also to cool all the stars in the eighth sphere, but we find many of them to be hot by reason of their effects.

And so it seems that one should say otherwise in order to defend the truth of Scripture from every calumny, namely, that those waters do not have the same nature as the elementary waters, Rather, they have the nature of a fifth essence, having transparency in common with our waters, just as the empyrean heavens have brilliance in common with our fire. And one calls these waters the crystalline heavens because of the solidity of those heavens, just as Job 37: 18 says of all the heavens: "They are most solid, as if cast in bronze," not because they are frozen in the shape of crystal, since,as Basil says in the *Hexameron*,[13] it belongs to childish foolishness and an imbecilic mind to hold such an opinion about the heavens. And astronomers also consider these heavens the ninth sphere. And so Augustine does not assert any of the aforementioned explanations but hesitantly dismisses all of them, saying in his *Literal Commentary on Genesis*:[14] "Howsoever the waters are there, and whatever kinds they are, let us not at all doubt that they are there. The authority of the Scripture is surely greater than all the capacity of human talent."

Obj. 7. We designate the formlessness of matter regarding what Gen. 1:2 says: "The earth was void and empty." But we attribute the voidness of matter regarding the power to produce, and the emptiness of matter with regard to adornment, as the saints explain, and this consists of things that move on the earth. Therefore, we note the formlessness of matter regarding position, so that one can say that the formlessness of matter temporally preceded the formation of matter.

Reply Obj. 7. We should say that if, according to the explanation of Basil[15] and his followers, one should understand by earth the element earth, we can then consider it inasmuch as it is the source of some things, namely, the planets, of which it is like a mother, as the book *Planets* says. And so it was void with respect to them before it produced them, since we call void or vain what does not attain its proper effect or end. And we can consider it empty inasmuch as it is a home and place of animals, with regard to which we say that it was empty.

Or according to the Septuagint text, which reads "invisible and not composite," part of the earth was invisible inasmuch as it was covered by water, and also inasmuch as light, whereby it could be seen, was not yet produced. And it was not composite inasmuch as it lacked the adornment of both plants and animals, and a suitable place for their generation and preservation. And if one should understand by earth prime matter, according to the opinion of Augustine,[16] then one speaks of voidness in its relation to the composite in which it subsists, since being void is contrary to being firm and solid, and one speaks of emptiness in relation to the forms that do not fulfill the earth's potentiality. And so also Plato relates the reception to place, insofar as what is in a place is received,[17] and we properly speak of emptiness and fullness about place. We also call matter, considered in its formlessness, invisible, insofar as it lacks form, which is the source of all knowledge, and not composed inasmuch as it does not subsist apart from a composite.

Obj. 15. The works of the six days of creation formed different kinds of things from unformed matter. But among the other works of the six days, the firmament was formed on the second day. Therefore, if unformed matter was subject to elementary forms, it will follow that the heavens were made from the four elements, which Aristotle disproved.[18]

Reply Obj. 15. We should say that there are many opinions about the firmament formed on the second day. Some say that the firmament is the same as the heavens, which Scripture says were made on the first day, but they say that Scripture first mentioned collectively the things made and then explained how the things were made over the course of six days. This is the opinion of Basil in the *Hexameron*.

Others say that the firmament made on the second day was one thing, and the heavens said to be created on the first day another, and they say this in three ways. Some said that by the heavens, which we read were created on the first day, they understand a spiritual creature, whether formed or still unformed, and they understand by the firmament, which we read was made on the second day, the material heavens that we see. This is the opinion of Augustine, as he makes clear in his *Literal Commentary on Genesis*[19] and *Confessions*.[20]

Others say that they understand by the heavens the empyreal heavens that we read were created on the first day, and they understand by the firmament made on the second day the starry heavens that we see. This is the opinion of Strabo, as he makes clears in the ordinary gloss on Gen. 1.

Others say that they understand by the heavens made on the first day the starry heavens, and they understand by the firmament made on the second day the space of the air near the earth that separates waters from waters, as I have said above. Augustine touches on this explanation in his *Literal Commentary on Genesis*,[21] and Rabbi Moses holds it.

Therefore, according to the last opinion, it is easy to resolve this question, since the firmament made on the second day does not concern the nature of a fifth element. And so nothing prevents the firmament, regarding itself, from it having proceeded from formlessness to formation, whether regarding its rarefaction, when the massing of the waters into one place diminished the vapors from the waters that have risen upward, or regarding its position, since air takes the place of the receding waters.

But regarding the first three opinions, which understand by the firmament the starry heavens, it is not necessary to say that there is a process in the heavens from formlessness to formation, as if they acquired a new form, since Scripture does not compel us to hold this regarding the lower elements. But Scripture compels us to understand that a power has been conferred on the firmament to produce mixed material substances and the firmament's formation in this regard, as I have said about the production of mixed material substances (replies to objs. 4 and 13). For, as lower elements are the matter of mixed substances, so the firmament is the efficient cause of those substances.

And so we can understand the separation of the lower waters from the higher ones as a mean within two extremes distinguishes between both, since the lower waters are subject to change, inasmuch as the movement of the firmament makes them mixed matter, but the higher waters are not. But according to Augustine in his *Literal Commentary on Genesis*,[22] if one should hold that unformed matter existed beforehand, it is of no serious consequence, since one necessarily in some way posits matter in a heavenly body, in which we also find movement. And so nothing prevents us from understanding the matter before the form by the order of nature, although no formation has come to it later. Nor are we compelled because of this to say that one nature is common to a heavenly body and lower elements, although a single word, such as *earth* or *water*, signifies this, according to the opinion of Augustine, since we understand such unity proportionally, as we consider every matter as potential in relation to its form, not substantially.

Obj. 17. If there was no formation of matter at the beginning of its creation, then the massing of waters, which we read happened on the third day, never was. But this seems impossible, since, if the waters entirely covered the earth, there was no place where they could be massed. Therefore, it seems that unformed matter did not precede the formation of things. But it is evident that water entirely covered the earth because the elements were separate, as the *De coelo* proves.[23]

Reply Obj. 17. We should say that, according to the opinion of Augustine,[24] who holds that the earth and water mentioned first signified prime matter, not the elements, nothing unsuitable follows about the massing of the waters. For, as he says,[25] as the statement "Let the firmament be made" on the second day signified the formation of the heavenly bodies, so the statement "Let the waters be gathered together" on the third day signifies the formation of the lower elements, and that statement signifies that water received its form. And the statement "Let the dry land appear" signifies the same thing about the earth. And so God used these words about the formation of the elements, not the word *making*, as in the case of the heavens, in order to say: "Let water and earth be made," as he had said: "Let the firmament be made," in order to signify the imperfection of these forms and their closeness to unformed matter. For he used the words *gathering together* for water in order to signify its mobility, and the word *appearance* regarding the earth in order to signify its stability. And so Augustine says:[26] "Thus it was said about water that it is gathered together, and about the earth that it appears, since water flows in waves, and the earth remains stable."

But if, according to the opinion of Basil and other saints, one should say that Scripture signifies the same earth and the same water in both cases but disposed in different ways before and later, one responds in many ways. For some said that there was a part of the earth that was not covered by the waters, in which part the water that occupied habitable land was at God's command gathered together. But Augustine disproves this from the text, saying:[27] "If part of the earth was exposed, where the waters would be gathered together, dry land already appeared before, which is contrary to the context." And so others said that the water was vaporized, as a cloud, and later condensed and transposed to a smaller place. But this also produces no less difficulty, both because there was truly no water if it had assumed the form of vapor, and because it would have replaced air, and a similar difficulty would remain about the displaced air. And so others say that the earth had caverns in which it could receive much water by the action of God. But that one part of the earth is incidentally farther distant from the center seems to be contrary to this, and nature took its own way in the formation of things, as Augustine says in the same work.[28]

And so it seems better that we should say, as Basil says,[29] that the waters had been dispersed into many parts and were later gathered together into one, and the text, using the word *gathering together*, also seems to signify this. For, although water covered the whole earth, it would not necessarily first cover the earth everywhere in such depth as it now is in some places.

Obj. 20. Either the water entirely covering the earth occupied its natural position, or it didn't. If it had its natural position, then it could be removed from that disposition only by force, since a material substance is removed from the place in which it rests only by force. But this does not belong to the first institution of things, which establishes nature, and force is contrary to nature. And if this position of water was by force, it could by its nature return to the disposition that it did not have, since nature moves something from the place in which it rests by force. And so it was not necessary to consider among the works of formation that waters were massed in one place.

Reply Obj. 20. We should say that, if one should consider the natural position of the elements, which belongs absolutely to their natures, it is then natural for the water to surround the whole earth entirely, just as the air surrounds the water. But if one should consider the elements in relation to the production of mixed things, toward which the heavenly bodies also cause movement, then such position belongs in the way in which it was later established. And so, immediately when dry land appears in one of the earth's parts, the text explains about the production of plants. And what happens in the elements by the influences of heavenly bodies is not contrary to nature, as Averroes says in his *Commentary on the De coelo*,[30] as is evident in the ebb and flow of the sea. Although this is not the natural movement of water inasmuch as it is heavy, since it is not at the center of the earth, it is natural movement inasmuch as a heavenly body moved it instrumentally. It is far more fitting to say this about things that the divine ordinance causes in the elements, the ordinance whereby their whole nature subsists. But in the present consideration, both seem to concur in gathering the waters together, chiefly the divine ordinance of power, secondarily the power of the heavenly body. And so, immediately after the establishment of the firmament, the text unites to it the massing of the waters. But there can be an aptitude of water by reason of its nature, since, inasmuch as what contains has more form than what it contains, as Aristotle makes clear in the *Physics*,[31] water falls short of being the perfect container of the earth insofar as it is not so perfectly formed as fire and air, being closer to the density of earth than to the rareness of fire.

Counterobj. 5. Spiritual and material creatures were established together, as Q. 3, A. 18, made clear. But in the spiritual creature, formlessness preceded formation even temporally. Therefore, by like reasoning, this is also the case regarding the material creature. The minor premise is proved as follows. We understand the formation of a spiritual creature insofar as it is turned toward the Word, which is its enlightenment. But once light has been made, there is a division between light and darkness, and we understand by darkness in a spiritual creature sin. But there could not be sin in the first moment of the angels' creation, since then the devils would never have been good. Therefore, the spiritual creature was not formed in the first moment of its creation.

Reply Counterobj. 5. We should say that we can understand the creation of a spiritual creature in two ways: one by the infusion of grace; the other by the perfection of glory. According to Augustine, the first formation flows immediately to a spiritual creature at the beginning of its creation, and then we do not understand by darkness, from which light is distinguished, the sin of the evil angels. Rather we understand the formlessness of nature, which was not yet formed but was to be formed by subsequent actions, as Augustine says in his *Literal Commentary on Genesis.*[32] Or, as he also says in that work,[33] we signify by day knowledge of God, by night the knowledge of a creature, which is dark in comparison to divine knowledge. Or if we should understand by darkness the sinning angels, the division is related to future sin, which God foreknew, not present sin. And so Augustine says in a work addressed to Orosius:[34] "Because God foreknew that some of the angels out of pride will fall, he by the incommunicable order of his foreknowledge divided the good ones from the evil ones, calling the bad angels darkness and the good angels light." The second formation belongs to the completion of things, for which divine providence governs them, not the beginning of the establishment of things. According to Augustine, the last is true about all the things in which the action of nature is required, namely, what is necessary to have arrived at in this formation, since some by the movement of free decision have been turned to God so as to stand fast, others turned away from him so as to fall.

Article 2

Was the Formation of Matter All at Once or Successively?

We should say that, if one should hold that the unformed matter preceded the formation of things only by origin, not temporally (which one needs to say if one should understand unformed matter without any form), it necessarily follows that the whole formation of things was accomplished at the same time. For it cannot be the case that a part of matter is altogether unformed even for a moment. Besides, regarding the part, matter would already precede the formation of things. And so, regarding things determined in the preceding article, there is no room for this further question if we follow the opinion of Augustine. Rather, it is altogether necessary to say that all things were formed at the same time, except insofar as it remains to explain how one explains the six days of creation that Scripture relates. For, if we were to understand them as the days that now take place, there would be something contrary to the aforementioned position, since it would then be necessary to understand the formation of things over successive days.

Augustine explains these days in two ways. For he says in his *Literal Commentary on Genesis* that one understands the distinction of formed matter from unformed matter, which remains to be formed by the order of nature, not temporally, by the distinction of light from darkness.[35] He says that day and night imply the very order between being formed and between unformed, insofar as God orders them, since day and night signify the order between light and darkness. He says that we understand by evening the termination of finished activity, and by morning the future beginning of activity, but we understand future only by the order of nature, not by the temporal order, since a sign, as it were, of the future activity to be done preexists in the first activity. We ought to understand the days as different in this way, namely, there are different receptions of forms and so deprivations of forms.

But it follows from this that even the seventh day (Gen. 2) differs from the first six, and the first six differ from one another. (It seems to follow from this that either God did not make the seventh day, or that he after the seventh day did something in which he perfected his works.) Therefore, Augustine holds that the seven days are to be understood as one day, namely, the knowledge of the angels, and the number pertains to the different things they knew rather than to different days, namely, that one understands by six days the knowledge of the angels related to the six kinds of things produced by God. And one day is the knowledge of the angels related to the rest of the creator, as he rested in himself from the things established. And then one understands by evening the knowledge of a thing in its own nature, and by morning the knowledge of it in the Word.

According to other saints, these days show both a temporal order and successive production. For, according to them, one notes in the works both a natural order and an order of time and duration, inasmuch as they hold that, as, unformed matter temporally preceded receiving forms, so also one formation preceded another temporally. But, as I said in the preceding article, they do not understand unformed matter as the lack and exclusion of all form, since there were already the heavens, water, and the earth. And so they understand heavenly bodies, spiritual substances, and the four elements subsisting under their own forms. But they understand matter to be unformed insofar as it signifies only the lack and exclusion of the requisite distinction and complete beauty of each thing, since it did not have the beauty and decorum now apparent in material creatures.

And so, as we can understand from the text of Gen. 1, material nature lacked three kinds of beauty, on which account one calls it unformed. For a heavenly body and the whole of a diaphanous material substance lacked the decorum and beauty of light, and the word *darkness* indicates this. The element of water lacked proper order and distinction from the element of earth, and the word *deep* indicates this, since the word signifies an inordinate expanse of the waters, as Augustine says.[36] The earth lacked two kinds of beauty. One is the kind that it has by reason of the waters having ceased to cover it, and this lack is designated by the words: "And the earth was void," that is, invisible, since it could not be visible because of the waters covering it on all sides. The other is the kind that it has by reason of having been adorned with plants, and this lack is touched upon by the words *empty*, or *without composition*, that is, unadorned.

And so, before the works of distinguishing things, Scripture mentions that many distinctions preexisted in the world's elements themselves at the beginning of its creation. First, it touches on the distinction of the heavens and the earth insofar as one understands by the heavens the whole diaphanous material substance, in which are included fire and air, because of the diaphanous nature that they have in common with the heavens. Second, it touches on the distinguishing the elements regarding their substantial forms by naming *water* and *earth*, which are more apparent to the senses, and this lets us understand the other, less apparent elements. Third, it touches on distinguishing position, since the earth was under the waters, which make the earth invisible, and the air, which is the subject of darkness, is indicated to have been over the waters by saying that "the darkness" (i.e., the dark air) "was over the face of the abyss."

Therefore, the formation of the first material substances, the heavenly bodies, was accomplished on the first day by the production of light. This brought the property of brightness to the sun and the heavenly bodies, which by reason of their substantial forms had already existed, and brightness removed the formlessness of darkness. This formation caused the distinction of movement and time, namely, of night and day. And so the text distinguished light from darkness, since the sun's substance caused light, and the earth's opaqueness caused darkness. There was light in one hemisphere and darkness in the other, and there was light in each hemisphere in one part of time and darkness in another part. This is what the text says: "He called light day and darkness night."

On the second day, the formation of the firmament formed and distinguished the middle material substance, namely, water, taking on differences and an order, so that one understands by the word *water* all the diaphanous material substances and so the firmament. And so the firmament (i.e., the starry heavens) produced on the second day regarding an accidental perfection, not substantially, divided the waters over the firmament from those beneath it. The firmament is the whole diaphanous heavens without the stars, and we call it aqueous or crystalline, and philosophers call it the ninth sphere and the first cause of motion, which revolves the whole heavens in daily motion, so that it produces by that motion a continuous process of coming to be. Just so, the starry heavens by the movement of the zodiac produce the diversity in coming to be and passing away by approaching toward, and receding from, us through different powers of the stars. The firmament, I say, divided the crystalline heavens, which are above the firmament, from the waters, that is, from the other diaphanous, destructible material substances beneath the firmament. And so the lower material substances designated by the word *waters* received through the firmament an order and the requisite distinction.

On the third day, the final material body, namely, the earth, was formed by no longer being covered by the waters, and the distinction of the sea from dry land in the lower world. And so, as the text congruously enough expressed the earth's lack of form, saying that "the earth was invisible," or "void," so it expresses its formation by saying: "And let the dry land appear, and the waters were collected into one place" separate from dry land, "and he called the waters sea and dry land earth." And he adorned it with plants and herbs, since it was hitherto unformed and empty.

On the fourth day, there was adornment of the first part of material creation, which had been divided on the first day, namely, the heavens by production of the luminaries. These were created as to their substance at the beginning, but their substance was unformed. Now, on the fourth day, it is formed, not by a substantial form but by conferring fixed power on it, insofar as determined power to produce determined effects is ascribed to the luminaries, as we see that solar, lunar, and stellar rays have different effects. And because of this determined power, Dionysius says that the light of the sun, hitherto unformed, was formed on the fourth day.[37] But Genesis made mention of the luminaries only on the fourth day, not at the beginning, as Chrysostom says, so that Scripture would by this keep the people from idolatry, showing that the luminaries are not gods and so did not exist at the beginning.

On the fifth day, the second part of the material nature that was distinguished on the second day was adorned by the production of birds and fish, and so, on the fifth day, Scripture makes mention of waters and the firmament of the heavens, so as to show that the fifth day corresponds to the second, in which there was mention of them. Therefore, on this day, the birds and fishes were at God's word produced as actual and in their own natures out of the elementary matter previously created, for the adornment of the air and the water, in which they are by nature suitably fit to be in motion by animal movement.

On the sixth day, the third part and final material body, namely, the earth, is adorned by the production of land animals, which are by nature fit to move themselves on land. And so the text indicates three parts of material creation in the work of creation, namely, the first, which is signified by the word *heavens*; the middle one, which is signified by the word *waters*; and the lowest, which is signified by the word *earth*. The first part, namely, the heavens, is distinguished on the first day and adorned on the fourth day. The middle part, namely, water, is distinguished on the second day and adorned on the fifth day, as I have said. Just so, it was fitting that the lowest part, namely, the earth, which is distinguished on the third day, is adorned on the sixth day by the production of actual land animals according to their proper species.

And so Augustine clearly differs from other saints in explaining the works of the six days. First, he understands by the earth and water first created completely unformed prime matter, and by the production of the firmament the collection of the waters, and by the appearance of dry land the impression of substantial forms on corporeal matter. But other saints understand by the initially created earth and water the elements of the world existing under their proper forms, and by the following works a distinction in preexisting material substances by some powers and accidental properties conferred on them, as I have said.

Second, regarding the production of plants and animals, other saints hold that they were actually produced in the works of the six days, and in their own natures, but Augustine holds that they were produced only potentially.

And in that Augustine holds that all the works of the six days happened at once,[38] there does not seem to be a difference from the others regarding the production of things. First, both agree that matter was under the substantial forms of the elements in the first production of things, so that prime matter did not temporally precede the substantial forms of the elements of the world. Second, both agree that plants and animals existed only potentially, not actually, in the first establishment of things by the work of creation, so that the power of God's word could produce them out of the elements.

But there still remains a difference between them regarding a fourth point. For, according to the other saints, there was after the production of the elements of the world and the heavenly bodies with their substantial forms a time when there was no light. Likewise, there was a time when there was no formed firmament or ordered and distinct diaphanous material body. Likewise, there was a time when the earth was still covered by the waters and the heavenly luminaries not yet formed. This is a position that the explanation of Augustine, who held that all the aforementioned things were formed together and at the same moment of time, did not need to consider. And that the works of the six days, according to the other saints, were produced successively, not together, was not due to lack of power of the creator, who could have produced all things at once. Rather, it was in order that the order of divine wisdom, which, bringing things into existence from nothing, instituted them in the final perfection of nature subsequent to nothingness, would be manifested in their institution. God made them first in an imperfect state of existing and brought them later to the perfect state so that the world would come gradually from nothing to its final perfection, and that different days would be devoted to different grades of perfection. So also it would show that their existing proceeds from God, contrary to those who considered matter uncreated, and yet God would appear the author of the perfection of things against those who will ascribe the formation of things in the lower world to other causes.

Therefore, the first explanation of these things, namely, Augustine's, is more subtle and a better defense of the Scriptures against the ridicule of unbelievers, and the second, namely, that by other saints, is fuller and ostensibly more consonant with the words of the text. But since neither of the explanations contradicts the true faith, and the context admits either sense, we, upholding each opinion, should reply to the arguments on each side.

Obj. 2. Several parts of time cannot be at once, since the whole of time passes successively. But Gen. 1 mentions the formation of things done at different points of time. Therefore, it seems that the formation of things was done successively, not all at once.

Reply Obj. 2. We should say that all the things in the six days, in which we read the works of God were done, are a single day as present to the six distinctions of things, whereby each day is numbered, not that the formation of things was done successively or at different points of time. Just so, one Word, namely, the Son of God, made all things, although we repeatedly read: "God said . . ." And as those works are preserved in subsequent things, which nature's activity multiplies from the works, so also the six days remain in the whole succession of time. This is made clears as follows. The angelic nature is intellectual, and we properly call it light, and so we should call its brilliance day. And the angelic nature at the first establishment of things received knowledge of the works, and so, in a way, the light of the angel's intellect was made present to them, inasmuch as the light of the angelic mind knows them.

And so we call this knowledge of things signifying the presence of the light of the angelic mind on the things known day, and the different kinds of things known and their order distinguishes and orders the days. Thus the first day is the knowledge of the first divine work concerning the formation of the spiritual creature by its turning to the Word. The second day is the knowledge of the second work insofar as the production of the firmament formed a higher material creature. The third day is the knowledge of the third work concerning the formation of a material creature as to the lower part of the universe, namely, formation of the earth, water, and the air over them. The fourth day is the knowledge of the fourth work insofar as the production of the luminaries adorned the higher part, namely, the firmament. The fifth day is the knowledge of God's fifth work insofar as the production of birds and fishes adorned air and water. The sixth day is the knowledge of God's sixth work insofar as the production of animals adorned the earth. The seventh day is the angelic knowledge related to the rest of the creator whereby he himself rested from establishing new works.

Since the light, God, is full, and there is no darkness in him, the knowledge of God himself in himself is full light, but inasmuch as a creature has in it the darkness of potentiality and imperfections, since it is from nothing, the knowledge whereby one knows a creature is mixed with darkness. But one can know a creature in two ways. One can know it in one way in the Word insofar as it comes from divine skill, and then we call knowledge of it morning knowledge, since, as morning is the end of darkness and the beginning of light, so a creature, after it first had not existed, receives the beginning of light from the light of the Word. One also knows a creature as existing in its own nature, and we call such knowledge evening knowledge because, as evening is the end of light and the tendency toward night, so a creature subsisting in itself is the end of the action of the light of the divine Word, as made by the Word, and of itself deficient, tending toward darkness unless the Word were to sustain it.

And so we call such knowledge divided into morning and evening day, since, as it is dark in relation to the Word, so we call it light in relation to an ignorance that is only dark. And so we note a circularity between morning and evening insofar as an angel, knowing itself, related this knowledge to praise of the Word as its end, in which as source the angel received this knowledge of the forthcoming work. And as such morning is the end of the preceding day, so it is also the beginning of the following day, since day is part of time and the effect of light. We understand different days regarding spiritual light insofar as the light of an angelic mind knows diverse and different kinds of things, not by the difference in time.

Obj. 5. Ex. 20:9 says: "You will work for six days, and you will do no work on the seventh day, the sabbath of the Lord your God." And the reason is later added: "God in six days made the heavens and the earth, the sea, and all the things in them and rested on the seventh day." But the law speaks literally about material days, in six of which it allows work and on the seventh prohibits it. Therefore, we should also relate what Genesis days about the action of God to material days.

Reply Obj. 5. We should say that one understands by the six days, in which the text says that God created the heavens, the earth, the sea, and all the things in them, the angelic knowledge related to the six kinds of things God produces, not a temporal succession. On the seventh day, there is the angelic knowledge related to the rest of the maker. For, according to Augustine in his *Literal Commentary on Genesis*,[39] the text says that God rested on the seventh day, inasmuch as he revealed to the angelic mind his own rest, whereby he rests in himself from the things he established, and whereby he, not needing creatures but sufficient for himself by himself, is happy, and Augustine calls knowledge of it day. And the text says that he ceased work on the seventh day, since he afterward made nothing new that did not in some way precede, whether materially or causally or by like species or genus, in the works of the six days.

And because God in himself rested after establishing all his works, Scripture and the Law commanded that the people keep the seventh day holy, since the sanctification of anything consists most of all in it resting in God, and so we call things dedicated to God, such as the tabernacle, vases, and ministers, holy. The seventh day is dedicated to the worship of God, and so sanctified. Thus God, who established six kinds of things and revealed them to the angelic mind, abided in himself, in whom his happiness consists, apart from the things established and did not rest in the things established, as if they were his end. (For he is happy because he has sufficiency in himself and does not need the things made, not because he made the things). Just so, let us also learn not to rest in his or our works as our end, but let us rest in God himself, in whom our happiness consists, apart from the works. For this reason, it was instituted that a human being working for six days on his own works would rest on the seventh and be free to worship and quietly contemplate God, in which contemplation the sanctification of a human being consists.

The newness of the world also especially shows that God exists and does not need creatures. And so it is established in the Law that the people rest and celebrate festively on the seventh day, on which the world was consummated, so that, through the newness of the world produced at once and through the six different kinds of things, human beings would always remain conscious of God, show thanks to him regarding so useful and special a benefit, and put their peace of soul in him as their end, at present by grace and in the future by glory.

Obj. 8. Augustine says in his *Literal Commentary on Genesis* that one understands by the words "God said: 'Let it be made'" that the things to be made preexisted in the Word; by the words "It was so made" the knowledge of the thing produced in an intellectual creature; and by the words "God made" that the creature was made in its own genus.[40] Therefore, if we understand by day the knowledge of an angel, after the text mentioned a particular work, "And so it was made," in which we understand angelic knowledge, it would be superfluously added: "The evening and morning became the first or second day."

Reply Obj. 8. We should say that, according to Augustine, the three things signify three kinds of existing of things. The first is the existing of things in the Word, since things have existing in God's skill, that is, the Word, before they have it in themselves. And the text "God said: 'Let it be made'" signifies this, that is, God begot the Word, in whom the thing was in order to be made. The second is the existing of things in the angelic mind, and the text "It was made" signifies this, namely, by the influence of the Word on the angelic mind. The third is the existing of things in their own nature, and the text "He made it" signifies this. For, as the nature in which a creature is established is in the Word before it is in the creature that is established, so also knowledge of the same nature is by the order of nature in the angelic mind before the production of the creature. And so an angel has a triple knowledge about things, namely, as the things are in the Word, as they are in the angelic mind, and as they are in their own nature. We call the first knowledge morning knowledge, and the other two are included in evening knowledge.

To show this twofold way of knowing things in a spiritual creature, the text says: "Evening and morning became one day." Therefore, by the six days in which we read God made all things, Augustine understands one day, that is, the angelic knowledge present to the six kinds of things, not the customary days produced by the course of the sun, since we read that the sun was made on the fourth day. And so, as the presence of material light on the things here below causes a temporal day, so the presence of the spiritual light of the angelic intellect on created things causes a spiritual day, so that the six days are distinguished insofar as the light of the angelic intellect is applied to knowing the six kinds of things. For example, the first day is knowledge of God's first work, the second day knowledge of the second work, and so forth.

And so the natural order of the things known distinguishes the six days, as one known work is by the order of nature prior to another, not by the order of time or succession of things. And as morning in a natural and material day is the beginning of day, and evening the end and terminus, so we call knowledge of each work, regarding its primordial existing, namely, as it has existing in the Word, morning knowledge, and we call knowledge of the work regarding its final existing, as it subsists in its own nature, evening knowledge. For the source of each thing's existing is in the cause from which it flows, and the terminus is in the thing in which it is received, and in which the cause's action terminates. And so there is primitive knowledge of something insofar as we consider the thing in the cause from which it flows, and there is final knowledge of the thing insofar as we consider it in itself.

The final existing of things flows from the eternal Word, as its primordial source, and this effect terminates in the existing of things that they have in their own nature. Therefore, it follows that we call the knowledge of things in the Word, which belongs to the primitive and primordial existing of things, morning knowledge by comparison to the morning that is the beginning of day. But we should call the knowledge of a thing in its own nature, which belongs to its final and determined existing, evening knowledge, since evening is the terminus of day. And so, as the six kinds of things related to angelic knowledge distinguish days, so the unity of the thing known, which one can know by different concepts, constitutes the unity of a day and distinguishes day by evening and morning.

Obj. 10. Several actions cannot be from one and the same power, as neither can a straight line terminate at an end except in a point, since action determines power. But considering a thing in the Word and in its own nature consists of several actions, not one. Therefore morning and evening knowledge are not simultaneous, and so it still follows that there is succession in the six days.

Reply Obj. 10. We should say that two actions, one of which is related and ordered to another, can belong simultaneously to one power, and it is evident that the will simultaneously wills an end and the means to it, and that the intellect simultaneously understands first principles and conclusions by the principles, provided that it acquired knowledge scientifically. And the evening knowledge in angels is related to morning knowledge, as Augustine says,[41] as natural knowledge and love are ordered to the knowledge and love of heavenly glory.

And so nothing prevents an angel from simultaneously having morning and evening knowledge, as an angel simultaneously has natural knowledge and the knowledge of heavenly glory. For two actions proceeding from two forms of the same kind, one of which is not ordered to the other, such as all created forms inhering in the intellect, cannot simultaneously belong to one power. And so an angel cannot simultaneously produce different intellectual acts by different forms created together. But if the two actions should proceed from forms of different kinds and natures, one of which is ordered to the other, such as a subsistent uncreated form and an inhering created form, they could exist together.

And a created and inhering intelligible form causes the knowledge whereby an angel sees things in their own nature, called evening knowledge, but the essence of the Word, which does not inhere, causes the knowledge whereby an angel sees things in the Word, called morning knowledge. These ways of knowing are of different kinds and natures. And one is ordered to the other. Therefore, both kinds of knowledge could be simultaneous. For the accompanying created form inhering in the intellect is not repugnant to the union of the intellect with the essence of the Word, which actualizes the intellect only regarding understanding, not regarding existing, since it is of a different order, not of the same nature. And the inhering form and any perfection in the created intellect is a quasi-material disposition for the union and beatific vision whereby an angel sees things in the Word.

Thus, as the disposition for a form and the form can exist together in what is actually perfected, so an inhering intelligible form coexists in what is actually perfected with union to the essence of the Word. And so a twofold action proceeds from the intellect of a blessed angel: one by reason of the union to the essence of the Word, whereby it sees things in the Word, called morning knowledge; the other by reason of the form inhering in it, whereby it sees things in their own nature, called evening knowledge. Nor does attention to one way of knowledge weaken or attenuate the other. Rather, one strengthens the other, since one is the reason for the other, as the imagination of a thing seen is strengthened when it is actually visible to the external eye. The action whereby the blessed see the Word and things in the Word is the reason of any action found in them. And two actions one of which is the reason for the other, or ordered to the other, can at the same time belong to the same power.

And then the same power by different forms ordered to one another terminates in different acts in different respects, not the same respect, since a perfect act can simultaneously unite forms of different kinds and orders, that is, different natures, as is evident about the color, smell, and taste in an apple.

The divine essence, whereby the angelic intellect sees things in the Word, is uncreated and intrinsically subsistent; the essence of an angel, whereby it always sees itself and things insofar as they have existing in it, is created and intrinsically subsistent by the existing received whereby its intellect subsists; and an accompanying infused and created form, whereby it sees things in their own nature, inheres in the intellect. These three are said to belong to different orders and kinds, and different natures, so that the first is, as it were, the reason of the others, and the second, as it were, the reason of the third. Thus the angelic intellect could simultaneously have three actions by reason of the three forms, just as the soul of Christ simultaneously understands things by the form of the Word, infused forms, and acquired forms.

Obj. 14. Night is between evening and morning, and midday is between morning and evening. Therefore, as Scripture made mention of evening and morning, so should it make mention of midday.

Reply Obj. 14. We should say that Augustine calls knowledge that is in full light morning knowledge, and this includes midday knowledge, since he sometimes calls it day knowledge and sometimes morning knowledge. Or one may say that every knowledge of the angelic intellect has a mixture of darkness regarding the one knowing, and so we can call only the knowledge whereby God knows all things in himself, not any knowledge of an angelic intellect, midday knowledge. Likewise, since God is full light, and no darkness is in him, we can call the knowledge of God in himself and absolutely, since it is full light, midday knowledge. But because a creature, inasmuch as it is from nothing, has the darkness of potentiality and imperfection, the knowledge of a creature is mixed with darkness. Morning and evening signify this mixture, insofar as one can know a creature in two ways. One can know a creature in the Word, insofar as it proceeds from God's skill, and then we call knowledge of it morning knowledge, since, as morning is the end of darkness and the beginning of light, so also a creature after darkness, that is, after it existed, receives the beginning of light from the Word. One can know a creature existing in its own nature by a created form, and we call such knowledge evening knowledge, since, as evening is the end of light and tends into night, so a creature subsisting in itself is the terminus of the action of the Word, who is light, as if made by the Word, and inasmuch as it of itself tends toward the darkness of deficiency unless the Word were to support it.

Nevertheless, we call this knowledge day, since, as it is darkness in relation to the knowledge of the Word, so we call it light in relation to ignorance, which is altogether dark, just as we call the life of the just cloudy in relation to to the life of glory, and yet we call it light in relation to the life of sinners. Likewise, since morning and evening are parts of day, and day in angels is knowledge illumined by the light of grace, morning knowledge and evening knowledge reach only to the gratuitous knowledge of good angels. And so we call knowledge of God's works by an enlightened angel day, and different kinds of God's known works distinguish days, and their different rank orders the days.

An enlightened angel knows each of these works in one way in the Word, or by the form of the Word, and then we call such knowledge morning knowledge. An enlightened angel knows each work in another way in its own nature, or by a created form, and good angels do not rest in this knowledge as if considering their end in it, since they, like the evil angels, would become night. Rather, they relate it to praise of the Word and the light of God, in which as the source they know all things. Therefore, we do not call such knowledge of a creature related to praising God nocturnal, which it would be if they were to rest in it, since they would then become night, enjoying the creature, so to speak.

Therefore, morning knowledge and evening knowledge distinguish day, that is, the knowledge that good angels enlightened about the created works have. But the knowledge of a creature by the good angels, whether by an uncreated or a created means, always has a mixture of obscurity. Therefore, we do not call it midday knowledge, like God's knowledge regarding himself is. Nor do we call it nocturnal, as the knowledge of a creature unrelated to the divine light is. Rather, we call it only morning and evening knowledge, since evening as such terminates in morning. And so we can call only the knowledge of things in their own nature related to the praise of God, not any knowledge of things, evening knowledge. And so we cannot properly call the knowledge that devils have about things morning or evening knowledge, since we understand morning and evening in angelic knowledge by a likeness regarding the nature of its origin and end, not every likeness.

Obj. 15. All sensibly perceptible days have both evening and morning. But we do not find this in the seven days, since the first day does not have morning, and the seventh day does not have evening. Therefore, we do not suitably speak of ordinary days as like those days.

Reply Obj. 15. We should say that an angel, although created in grace, was not at the beginning of its creation blessed or beheld the Word essentially. And so it did not have morning knowledge of itself, which expresses knowledge of a thing by the form of the Word. Rather, it first had evening knowledge of itself, insofar as it by nature knew itself in itself, since natural knowledge in each thing precedes supernatural knowledge, as the foundation of the latter, and an angel's knowledge by nature results from the angel's existing in its own nature. Thus it at the beginning of its creation had evening knowledge of itself, not morning knowledge. And it related this knowledge to praise of the Word and thereby merited arrival at morning knowledge. And so we significantly say that the first day had only evening and not morning, and that evening became morning, since the spiritual light, which we read was made on the first day, knew itself as soon as it was made. This belonged to evening knowledge, and an angel related this knowledge to praise of the Word, whereby it deserved to receive morning knowledge of the following work. For we can call only knowledge of things in their own nature related to praise of the creator, not whatever knowledge, evening knowledge, as evening recedes and terminates in morning.

And so the knowledge that devils have from themselves about things is neither morning nor evening knowledge; only the gratuitous knowledge in good angels is such. And so the knowledge of things in their own nature that is related to praise of the Word is always evening knowledge, nor does such a relation cause it to be morning knowledge. Rather, the relation causes it to terminate in morning knowledge, and an angel by such a relation deserves to obtain morning knowledge. And as the first day, which signifies the formation and knowledge of a spiritual nature regarding its own nature, has only evening, so also the seventh day, which signifies contemplation of God, has only morning. No defect encompasses this contemplation, and it corresponds to the angelic knowledge related to the rest of God in himself, in which the enlightenment and sanctification of anything consists. For, since God ceased establishing new creatures, we say that he consummated his work and rested in himself from his works. And as God rests in himself alone and is happy by enjoying himself, so also we by enjoying him alone become happy, and so also he makes us rest in himself from his and our works.

Therefore, the first day, which corresponds to the knowledge that a spiritual nature enlightened by the light of grace had about itself has only evening, but the seventh day, which corresponds to the angelic knowledge related to the rest and enjoyment of God in himself, has only morning, since there is no darkness in God. For the text says that God rested on the seventh day, inasmuch as he displayed to the angelic nature his own rest, whereby he rests in himself from the things established, and Augustine calls this knowledge day.[42] And since the rest of a creature, insofar as it stands firm in God, has no end, just as the rest of God whereby he rests in himself from the things established, not by needing them, has no end, since he will never need them. Thus the seventh day corresponding to such rest has only morning and not evening. But the other days, which correspond to the angelic knowledge related to other things have morning and evening, as I have already said.

Obj. 22. Augustine raises the question whether Adam's soul was made with the angels without a body or made in a body.[43] But this question would be pointless if all things had been formed at once, since even the human body would have been formed at the same time as the angels were. Therefore, it seems that not all things were formed at once, even according to opinion of Augustine.

Reply Obj. 22. We should say that Augustine wants certain things, such as the four elements, which were produced out of nothing, heavenly bodies, and spiritual substances, to have been produced by their different forms at the beginning of creation.[44] Such production presupposes neither the matter out of which nor the matter in which they were produced. But he says that other things were produced in seminal forms only in animals, plants, and human beings, and all of these were later produced in their own natures in the work whereby God, after the six days, assists the nature previously established. Jn. 5:1 says about this work: "My Father works up to now." And he wants us to note the order of nature, not the order of time, in the production and distinction of things. For all the works of the six days were accomplished at once at the same moment of time, whether actually or potentially in their causal forms, namely, that either the Word or the active powers implanted at the creation of a creature could later make them out of preexisting matter.

And so he does not hold that the soul of the first human being, which he says by way of inquiry, not assertion, was actually created along with the angels, was made before the sixth day, but he holds that the soul of the first human being was actually made on the sixth day, and the first human being's body by causal forms. For God implanted a passive power of the earth, so that the active power of the creator could form the human being's body out of it. And so the soul actually and the body in passive power in relation to the active power of God were made simultaneously.

Or supposing in truth that the soul does not have a complete species by itself but is united to a body as its form, and it is by nature part of human nature, as Aristotle holds, one needs to say that the soul of the first human being was not actually produced before the formation of the body. Rather, the soul was created simultaneously with the formation of the body and infused in it, as Augustine expressly holds about other human souls.[46] For God established the first things in the perfect condition of their nature, insofar as the species of each thing required. And the rational soul, since it is part of human nature, has natural perfection only insofar as it has been united to a body. And to exist outside a body is for it contrary to nature. Thus it would have been improper that the soul be created without a body.

Therefore, in upholding the opinion of Augustine about the works of the six days, one can say that, as the body of the first human being was created and produced in those days only potentially in causal forms, not actually, so also the first human being's soul was not then produced actually and in itself but in its generic likeness. And so the soul preceded the body in the six days in generic likeness, as the soul has an intellectual nature in common with the angels, not actually and in itself. Later, in the work whereby God assists the creature first established, the soul was actually produced together with a formed body.

Obj. 25. Morning knowledge, whereby an angel knows things in the Word, needs to have been by a form, since all such knowledge is. But it could not be by a form proceeding from the Word, since the form would be a creature, and so the knowledge would be evening knowledge rather than morning knowledge, since knowledge caused by a creature belongs to evening knowledge. Nor can we say that the aforementioned knowledge was by a form that is the Word itself, since it would then be necessary that an angel saw the Word itself, which was not so before an angel was beatified, inasmuch as the vision of the Word beatifies. But angels were not beatified at the first moment of their creation, just as, contrariwise, devils did not sin at the first moment. Therefore, if we should understand by morning knowledge of things that angels had in the Word, we need to say that not all things were made at once.

Reply Obj. 25. We should say that, according to Augustine,[47] the angels at the beginning saw in the Word the creatures to be made, since the things that we read were made in the works of the six days were made at the same time. And so, immediately at the beginning of the creation of things, there were the six days, and consequently a good angel at the beginning necessarily knew the Word and things created in the Word. For created things have three kinds of existing, as I have said before. They have the first kind of existing in the divine skill, which is the Word, and the text "God said: 'Let it be made'" signifies this, that is, the Word, in whom it was to make such a work, begot it. They have the second kind of existing in angelic intelligence, and the text "It was made" signifies this, namely, by the influence of the Word. They have the third kind of existing in the very things and their own nature.

So also an angel has three kinds of knowledge about things, namely, as they are in the Word, in his mind, and in their own nature. An angel also has two kinds of knowledge of the Word. One is natural, whereby an angel knows the Word by its likeness reflected in the angel's own nature, in which its natural happiness consists, at which it can arrive by the power of its nature. The second kind is supernatural knowledge of the Word and heavenly glory, whereby an angel knows the Word essentially, in which its supernatural blessedness, which exceeds the power of nature, consists. And a good angel by each kind of knowledge knows things or creatures in the Word. By natural knowledge, it imperfectly knows things in the Word, and by the knowledge of heavenly glory, it knows the things in the Word more fully and more perfectly. The first knowledge of things in the Word flows to an angel at the beginning of its creation, and so *Church Dogmas* says:[48] "The angels who persevered in the blessedness in which they were created possess by grace, not nature, the good that they have." Likewise, Augustine in his *Letter to Peter, on Faith* says:[49] "Angelic spirits received from God the gift of eternity and blessedness in the creation of their spiritual nature." But they were not thereby blessed absolutely, since they were capable of greater perfection, but in a qualified sense, namely, regarding that time, as Aristotle says that some are happy in this life as human beings, not absolutely.[50]

The second kind of knowledge, namely, of heavenly glory, does not come to an angel at the beginning of its state, since the angels were not created with perfect blessedness. Rather, the second kind of knowledge comes to angels at the moment when they become blessed by turning perfectly to the good. Therefore, all the six kinds of things were created together with the angel, and it knew all the things in the Word by a natural knowledge that it later knew in the Word more fully by supernatural knowledge, which angels received immediately after they related natural knowledge of self to praise of the Word. And this natural knowledge, since eternity measures it, always coexists with the supernatural knowledge of the Word and the knowledge whereby an angel knows creatures in their own nature by forms implanted in it. And so these three kinds of knowledge coexist, and one does not come after the other, since we call knowledge of things in the Word, whether things already made or things to be made, morning knowledge, and we call knowledge of things by a created medium, whether a present thing or a future thing, evening knowledge.

Obj. 27. People also say that prophets saw future things in the mirror of eternity, insofar as they saw the divine mirror, as it is the plan of things to be made. Therefore, there would be no difference in this respect between the morning knowledge of an angel and the knowledge of a prophet.

Reply Obj. 27. We should say that there were some who, wishing to distinguish prophetic knowledge from the knowledge of the blessed, said that the prophets saw the divine essence, which they call the mirror of eternity, not insofar as the divine essence is the object of the blessed and the end of blessedness but as it is the plan of things to be done, insofar as there are in it the plans of future events, as the objection says.

But this is altogether impossible, since God is the object of blessedness and the end of the blessed, according to the saying of Augustine:[51] "Blessed is one who knows you even if one does not know those things," namely, creatures. But one cannot see the natures of creatures in the divine essence without seeing it. For the divine essence is the plan of all the things that come to be, inasmuch as the ideal form, the form of the thing to be made, adds to the divine essence only the relation to a creature, and knowing something in itself, which is knowing God as the object of blessedness, precedes knowing it in relation to something else, which is knowing God by the forms of things in him. And so the prophets cannot see God by the forms of creatures and not as the object of blessedness.

And they do not see the divine essence as the object of blessedness, inasmuch as vision removes prophecy, as 1 Cor. 13:8 says, and the vision signifies the divine essence as close by, not far away, since they see it face to face. Therefore, it follows that prophets do not know the divine essence as the plan of things to be made or things in the Word, as the angels know them by morning knowledge. For the vision of a prophet is not the vision of the divine essence itself, nor do they see in the divine essence the things they see, as the angels do. Rather, they see what they see in certain likenesses by the illumination of the divine light, as Dionysius says,[52] and such likenesses illumined by the divine light have the nature of vision in a mirror rather than a vision of the divine essence. For a mirror is where forms result from other things, and we cannot say this about God, but we can call such illumination of a prophet's mind a mirror, inasmuch as a vision of God's true foreknowledge results in the prophet's mind. And so we call a prophet's mind the mirror of eternity, as if representing by those forms the foreknowledge of God, who in his eternity sees all things as present. And so a prophet's knowledge is more akin to an angel's evening knowledge than its morning knowledge, since an uncreated medium causes morning knowledge, but a created medium, namely, implanted forms, that is, forms illumined by the divine light, as I have said, causes a prophet's knowledge.

Obj. 29. As Ps. 104:24 says, God made all things in his wisdom. But it belongs to a wise person to direct, as the beginning of the *Metaphysics* says.[53] Therefore, it seems that God made all things successively in a temporal order, not all at once.

Reply Obj. 29. We should say that it belongs to the wisdom of a craftsman such as God, all of whose works are perfect, that he does not produce the whole apart from the chief part or parts separately from the whole, since neither the whole apart from the chief part nor parts separate from the whole have perfect existing. The angels by their forms, the heavenly bodies, and the four elements are the chief parts constituting one universe, since they have an order to one another and serve one another. Therefore, it belongs to the wisdom of God that he produced the whole universe with all its parts at once and not successively, since there ought to be a single production of a whole and all of its parts, and one thing is not produced before another except because of a deficiency of the active thing. And God is infinite power and has no deficiency, and his chief effect is the whole universe. Therefore, God created the whole universe with all of its chief parts at once with a single production.

Although no temporal order was observed in producing the universe, an order of origin and nature was, since, according to Augustine, the work of creation preceded the work of distinguishing things by the order of nature, not time, just as the work of distinguishing preceded the work of adornment by the order of nature. And the creation of the heavens and that of the earth belong to the work of creation. By the heavens, he understands the production of the unformed spiritual nature, and by the earth, he understands the unformed matter of material substances. And these two things, since they are outside time, considered essentially, are not subject to temporal changes, as Augustine says.[54] Thus he posits the creation of both before the first day, not that this lack of form preceded formation in time, but only by the order of origin and nature, as sound precedes singing.

And, according to Augustine, one formation preceded another only by the order of nature, not temporally. By this order of nature, we would need to posit a first formation of the highest spiritual nature, as we read that God made light on the first day, since a spiritual nature is more excellent and more eminent than a material nature. Therefore, a spiritual nature was to be formed first, and it is formed because it is enlightened to adhere to the Word of God. But as spiritual light is more excellent than even the divine natural order, so also higher material substances are more eminent than lower material substances. And so the text touches on higher material substances in the second day, saying: "Let the firmament be made." One understands by this the imprint of a heavenly form on unformed matter as first only in origin, not first in time.

In the third place, there is an imprint of elementary forms on unformed matter, which precedes in origin and the order of nature, not temporally. And so we understand by the words "Let the waters be gathered together, and the dry land appear" that the substantial form of water was imposed on corporeal matter, by which such-and-such motion belongs to it, and the substantial form of the earth was imposed, by which it belongs to it then to be visible. For water flows in waves, and earth is firmly fixed, as Augustine says.[55] Under the word *water*, he also understands the other higher formed elements.

In the following three days, the text posits the adornment of material nature, since it was necessary that parts of the world be first formed and distinguished by the order of nature, and that individual parts be later adorned by being replete with their occupants, so to speak. On the first day, as I have said, the spiritual nature is formed and distinguished. In the second day, the heavenly bodies are formed and distinguished, and they are adorned on the fourth day. But on the third day, lower material substances, namely, air, water, and earth, are formed and distinguished, of which air and water, being more excellent, are adorned on the fifth day, but earth, which is the lowest material substance, is adorned on the sixth day. And so the perfection of God's works corresponds to the number six, which arises from its many parts at once united, and they are one, two, and three. One day is assigned to the formation and distinction of the spiritual creature, two days to the formation and distinction of the material creature, and three days to their adornment. For one plus two plus three makes six, one times six makes six, two times three makes six, and three times two makes six. Therefore, since six is the first perfect number, it designates the perfection of things and God's works. Therefore, the order of nature, not time, is preserved in the production of God's works.

Counterobjs. Gregory and others hold that there was a temporal succession in those days, and that the production of the things was done successively, so that, when the heavens and the earth were created, there was not yet light, nor was the firmament formed, nor was the earth uncovered from the waters, nor were the heavenly luminaries formed. If one wishes to uphold this opinion, one can reply to objections as follows.

Counterobj. 4. There is a greater distance between the material creature and the spiritual creature than there is between material creatures in relation to one another. But the spiritual creature and the material creature were created at the same time, as was maintained before in Q. 3, A. 18. Therefore, much more were all spiritual creatures created at the same time.

Reply Counterobj. 4. One should say that, although the Greek teachers held that the spiritual creature was created before the material creature, the Latin teachers hold that the angels were produced at the same time as material nature, so that they guarantee that the universe as to its chief parts was produced at the same time. For, inasmuch as material creatures are one thing in created matter, and the matter of the material creature was created at the same time as the angels, we can somehow call all the things created actual or potential. But the angels do not belong in matter with the material creature. Thus, when the angels were created, there would in no way be material created nature, and so also not the universe itself. And so it is reasonable that they were produced along with material nature. And so all material things were created at the same time regarding matter somehow unformed, not actually. Later, the distinction and adornment of the already actually preexisting creature successively produced all things.

Counterobj. 5. Because of the immensity of God's power, he acts immediately. Therefore, the work of each day was done immediately and instantly. Therefore, one would foolishly hold that God waited to perform the next work until another day and so was inactive for a whole day.

Reply Counterobj. 5. One should say that, as a creature does not have existing from itself, so it also has perfection from God, not from itself. Thus, as he, in order to show that a creature has existing from God, willed that it did not first exist and later did, so also, in order to show that a creature did not have its perfection from itself, he willed that it was first imperfect and later successively perfected by the work of distinction and adornment. Or one should say that, in the creation of things, both the might of his power and the order of divine wisdom ought to be manifested, so that the things that are first in nature would also be established first. And so it is not from the impotence of God, as if he needs time in order to produce, that all things were not produced and distinct and adorned at the same time, but that the order of wisdom would be observed in establishing things. And so it was necessary that different days be devoted to different conditions of the world. For, after a work of creation, the next work added a new condition of perfection to the world. Thus, in order to show the perfection and newness of the condition, God willed one day to correspond to each distinction and adornment of things, not from a lack of power or the active thing's weariness.

Counterobj. 6. If the days mentioned in the formation of things were material days, it seems that one could not completely distinguish night from day and light from darkness. For, if the light that we read was made on the first day enveloped the earth everywhere, there never was darkness, which is from the shadow of the earth blocking the light that causes day. And if the light by its movement enveloped the earth, so as to cause day and night, then there was always day on one side and night on the other. And so night was not completely distinct from day, and this is contrary to Genesis.

Reply Counterrobj. 6. One should say that, according to Gregory and Dionysius, the day that we read was made on the first day is the light of the sun. The light, along with the substance of the luminaries, that is, the light's substance, was produced on the first day regarding the general nature of light. But determined power for determined effects was assigned to the luminaries on the fourth day, as it is evident that the rays of the sun have certain effects, and the rays of the moon other effects, and so forth. And so Dionysius says that this light was that of the still unformed sun regarding what was already the sun's substance and had the power to illuminate in a general way. But it was formed later, on the fourth day, regarding certain accidental conditions by conferring a determined power, insofar as a particular and determined power for determined effects was later given to it, not indeed by the substantial form that it already had on the first day.

And so, in the production of this light, light was distinguished from darkness regarding three things. First, light was distinguished from darkness regarding their cause, insofar as the cause of light was in the substance of the sun, but the cause of darkness was in the opaqueness of the earth. Second, light was distinguished from darkness regarding place, since, there was light in one hemisphere and darkness in the other. Third, light is distinguished from darkness regarding time, since, in the same hemisphere, there was light in one part of time and darkness in the other. And this is what Gen. 1:5 says: "He called light day and darkness night." Thus the light did not envelop the earth everywhere, since there was light in one hemisphere and darkness in the other. Nor was there always light on one side and night on the other. Rather, there was in the same hemisphere day in one part of time and night in the other.

Counterobj. 7. We distinguish day and night by the sun and other heavenly luminaries. And so Genesis 1:14 says about the work of the fourth day: "Let the luminaries in the firmament of the heavens be made," and adds: "Let them be for signs and times and days." Therefore, since an effect does not precede its cause, these three days cannot be of the same nature as the days that the sun now produces. And so one does not on account of those days need to say that all the things were made successively.

Reply Counterobj. 7. One should say there are two kinds of movement in the heavens. One is common to the whole heavens, which we call diurnal, and it causes day and night. This movement seems to have been established on the first day, in which the unformed substance of the sun and the other luminaries was produced, as I have said before (in the body of the article and the reply to counterobj. 6). The other is particular, which various heavenly bodies differentiate, the movements of which cause the different days in relation, to one another, and the different months and years. On the first day, diurnal movement, that is, the general movement of the whole heavens, caused the distinction of time in general into day and night, and we can understand this to have begun on the first day. And so there is mention in the first day only of the distinction of day and night that the diurnal movement common to all the heavens causes. On the fourth day, there was made the distinction regarding the special distinctions of days and times, as one day is hotter than another, and one period of time hotter than another, and one year hotter than another. The special and particular movements of the stars, which we can understand to have begun on the fourth day, cause this. And so there is mention in the fourth day of the different days and times and years when Gen. 1:14 says: "And let there be times and days and years," and particular movements cause this diversity. And so the first three days that preceded the formation of the luminaries were of the same nature as the days that the sun produces regarding the general distinction of time into day and night, which the diurnal movement common to the whole heavens causes, not regarding the special distinction of days that particular movements cause.

Counterobj. 8. If there was another light that by its movement then made day and night, there needed to be something that, moved in circular motion, bears the other light, so that it illumined the earth everywhere. But this is to bear the firmament, which we read was made on the second day. Therefore, at least the first day could not be of the same nature as the days that are now produced.

Reply Counterobj. 8. One should say that some say that the light that we read was made on the first day was a luminous cloud that, when the sun was made, was later brought into surrounding matter. But this is not fitting, since Scripture at the beginning of Genesis recounts the establishment of nature, which remains constant, and so we ought not to say that something that was then made ceased to exist after a little while. And others say that the luminous cloud still remains and was joined to the sun, so that it cannot be distinguished from it. But the cloud in this respect would remain superfluous, and nothing is in vain or superfluous in the works of God. And so still others say that the material substance of the sun was formed out of the cloud. But one also cannot say this if one should hold that the material substance of the sun does not naturally consist of the four elements but is naturally indestructible, since then its matter cannot exist under another form.

And so one should say, as Dionysius says,[56] that that light was the light of the sun not yet formed, in that the sun's substance already existed and had the power of illumination in general. But later, on the fourth day, the substance of the sun was given a special and determined power for its own particular effects. And so the circular motion whereby the light acceded or receded caused day and night. Nor is it unsuitable that the substances of the spheres, which by their general and diurnal movement caused the light to revolve, existed from the beginning of creation, to which some powers were later added in the works of distinction and adornment.

Question 5

THE PRESERVATION OF THINGS IN EXISTENCE BY GOD

Article 1

Does God Preserve Things in Existence, or Do They Remain in Existence Intrinsically, with All God's Action Circumscribed?

We should say that we should without any doubt grant that God preserves all things in existence, and that they would instantly return to nothing were God to abandon them. We can understand the reason as follows. An effect necessarily depends on its cause, since this belongs to the nature of an effect and a cause. This is manifest in formal and material causes, since a thing immediately ceases to exist when any material or formal source has been removed, inasmuch as such sources enter into the thing's essence.

We should judge the same about efficient causes as about material and formal causes, since an efficient cause causes a thing insofar as it induces a form or disposes matter. And so the thing has the same dependence on its efficient cause as on its matter and its form, since, by one of them [the efficient cause], it depends on the others. And we should judge the same about final causes as about an efficient cause, since the end causes only insofar as it moves an efficient cause to act. It is the first thing only in striving, not in existing. And so also there is no final cause where there is no action, as the *Metaphysics* makes clear.[1]

Accordingly, therefore, the existing of the thing made depends on the efficient cause insofar as the existing depends on the form of the thing made. But there is an efficient cause on which the form of the thing made depends only incidentally, not intrinsically and by reason of the form. For example, the form of the fire produced does not intrinsically and by reason of its species depend on the fire producing it, since it has the same grade in the order of things, and the form of fire is the same in the thing produced and in the thing producing. Rather, the form of fire in the thing produced differs from the one in the thing producing only by reason of different matter, namely, as the form of fire is in different matter. And so, since the form of fire belongs to the fire produced from a cause, the form itself needs to depend on a higher source, which causes the form intrinsically and according to the form's own specific nature.

And since the existing of a form in matter, absolutely speaking, signifies no movement or change except, perhaps, incidentally, and every material substance acts only when moved, as Aristotle proves, the source on which the form depends needs to be an immaterial source. For the effect by the action of a source depends on the active cause. And if a material source is in some way the cause of a form, it has this power insofar as it acts by the power of the immaterial source, as if its instrument, and this is necessary in order that the form begin to exist, inasmuch as the form begins to exist only in matter. For matter being disposed in whatever way can be subject to a form, since the particular thing produced needs to exist in its proper matter.

Therefore, when matter is disposed in such a way that it is unsuitable for a particular form, it cannot immediately obtain the form from the immaterial source on which the form intrinsically depends. And so something needs to alter the matter, and this is an active material thing, to which acting belongs by causing movement. And this thing acts in the power of the immaterial source, and its action is determined to this form insofar as such a form is in it actually, as in univocal active things, or virtually, as in nonunivocal active things.

Therefore, such material active things of the lower world are the sources in things made only as far as the causality of change can extend, since they act only by causing change, as I have said (Q. 3, AA. 7 and 8), and this is inasmuch as they dispose matter and educe form from the potentiality of matter. Therefore, regarding forms being educed from the potentiality of matter but not regarding absolute existing, the forms of the things produced depend by nature on the things producing them.

And so also, when the action of the producing thing has been removed, educing the form from the potentiality of matter into actuality, that is, the coming to be of the things produced, ceases. But the forms themselves, by which the things produced have existing, do not cease. And so, when the action of the producing thing ceases, the existing of the things produced remains but not their coming to be. But if the forms do not exist in matter, such as intellectual substances, or exist in matter in no way indisposed to their forms, such as the heavenly bodies, in which there are no contrary dispositions, the source of the forms can be only an immaterial active thing, which does not act by movement. Nor do the latter depend on something in their coming to be from which they do not depend in their existing.

Therefore, as, when the action of the efficient cause that acts by movement ceases, the coming to be of the things produced ceases at that very moment, so, when the action of the immaterial active thing ceases, the very existing of the things created by it ceases. But this immaterial active thing, which creates all things, both material and immaterial, is God, as I have shown in a previous question (Q. 3, AA. 5, 6, and 8), from whom both the forms of things and their matter exist. And regarding the question at issue, it makes no difference whether he made them all immediately or in an order, as some philosophers held. And so the consequence is that, if the divine action should cease, all things would fall into nothingness at the same moment, as the authorities cited in the counterarguments proved.[2]

Obj. 2. Someone said that the works of God are perfect in their nature, not absolutely. To the contrary, something perfect in its nature has that of which its nature is capable. But whatever has the whole of which its nature is capable can abide in existing, with all external preservation by God ceasing. Therefore, if any creatures are perfect by their nature, they can abide in existing without preservation by God. Proof of the minor: God, in preserving things, does something, and Jn. 5:17 says on that account: "My Father is active even now, and I am active," as Augustine says.[3] But when an active thing produces something, an effect receives something. Therefore, as long as God preserves things, the things preserved by God always receive something from him. Therefore, as long as a thing needs preservation, it does not yet have the whole of which it is capable.

Reply Obj. 2. We should say that God does not by one action bring things into existing and by another preserve them in existing, since the very existing of permanent things is divisible only incidentally, as it is subject to movement, and it is as such instantaneous. And so God's action intrinsically causing a thing to exist does not differ insofar as it causes the beginning and the continuation of existing.

Obj. 4. God causes things as an efficient cause. But when the action of an efficient cause ceases, the effect remains. For example, when the action of a builder ceases, the house abides, and when the action of fire producing fire ceases, the fire produced still abides. Therefore, also when all action by God ceases, creatures can still remain in existence.

Reply Obj. 4. We should say that such lower active things cause things regarding their coming to be, not their existing, properly speaking. But God by himself causes existing, and so there is no comparison. And so Augustine says:[4] "Unlike when one has built a structure and departs, and the work remains when the builder ceases to be active and departs, the world could not abide even for the blinking of an eye were God to have withdrawn his governance from it."

Obj. 5. Someone said that lower active things cause coming to be, not existing, and so the existing of effects abides when the action of the causes of coming to be has been removed. But God causes both things' coming to be and their existing. And so the existing of things cannot abide when divine action ceases. On the contrary, everything produced has existing by its form. Therefore, if lower productive causes do not cause existing, they will not cause forms. And so the forms in matter are not from forms in matter, contrary to the opinion of Aristotle, who says in the *Metaphysics* that a form in particular flesh and bones is from a form in particular flesh and bones.[5] And so, following the opinion of Plato, the forms in matter are from forms without matter, or, following the opinion of Avicenna,[6] from the giver of forms.

Reply Obj. 5. We should say that, since material active things act only in causing change, and nothing is changed except by reason of matter, the causality of material active things can only extend to things that are somehow in matter. And because Platonists and Avicenna did not hold that forms are educed from the potentiality of matter, they were thus forced to say that natural active things only disposed the matter, and the introduction of a form was from a separate source. But if we, following the opinion of Aristotle, should hold that substantial forms are educed from the potentiality of matter, natural active things cause both the dispositions of matter and substantial forms, exactly as they are brought into actuality from the potentiality of matter, as I have said (Q. 3, AA. 9 and 11). And so natural active things are the sources of existing regarding the beginning to exist but not regarding existing absolutely.

Obj. 6. Things whose existing is in the state of coming to be cannot abide when the action of the active thing ceases, as is evident in the case of motion, a physical contest, and the like, but things whose existing is in the state of actual existing can abide even when the active things have been removed. And so Augustine says:[7] "The presence of light is making the air lucid, but it has not finished doing so, since, if light were to have finished making the air lucid, it would not still be making the air lucid. Rather, the air would remain lucid if light were absent." But there are many creatures whose existing consists of actual existing, not of coming to exist, as is evident regarding angels and all material substances. Therefore, when the action of God producing ceases, creatures can remain in existence.

Reply Obj. 6. We should say that some of the forms that begin actually to exist in matter by the action of a material active thing are produced according to a perfect specific nature and perfect existing in matter just like the form of the thing producing them. For no contrary sources remain in the matter, and such forms abide after the action of the thing producing them up to the time of their dissolution.

Some forms are produced according to a perfect specific nature but not perfect existing in matter. For example, the heat in hot water has the perfect form of heat but not perfect existing, which is by application of form to matter, since a form contrary to such a quality remains in the matter. And such forms can remain for a while after the action of the active thing, but the contrary source in the matter prevents them from long enduring.

And some forms are produced in matter imperfect in both form and existing, such as light in air from a luminous material substance, since light is in air by way of extension, not as a perfect natural form. And so, as the likeness of a human being remains in a mirror only as long as the mirror is in front of the human being, so the light in air remains only with the presence of a luminous material substance, since such extensions depend intrinsically, not incidentally, on the natural forms of material substances. And so the existing of these things does not abide when the action of active things ceases. Therefore, we say that such things, because of the imperfection of their existing, are in a state of coming to be, but that perfect creatures are not in a state of coming to be because of the imperfection of their existing, although God's action in causing them abides unfailingly.

Obj. 8. If anything ceases to exist, this is either because of matter or because of the fact that it exists out of nothing. But matter causes dissolution only insofar as it is subject to contrariety, and matter is not subject to contrariety in all creatures. Therefore, things in which there is no matter subject to contrariety (e.g., heavenly bodies and angels) cannot cease because of matter, nor because they exist out of nothing. For nothing results from nothing, and nothing produces nothing, and so nothingness does not cause dissolution. Therefore, when every divine action ceases, such things would not cease to exist.

Reply Obj. 8. We should say that a creature would cease to exist if divine action were to cease, because a creature exists out of nothing, not because of something contrary in its matter, since the contrary would cease along with the matter. This is because nothingness would do nothing to preserve a creature, not because nothingness would do anything to destroy it.

Obj. 12. Sir. 33:15 says: "Look on all the works of the most high. They come in pairs, one thing contrary to the other thing." But of the works of the most high, there is something that needs preservation by God. Therefore, there is also among the works of God its contrary, namely, something that does not need preservation by God.

Reply Obj. 12. We should say of the works of God that, if there is one contradictory, it is not necessary that there be the other, since, inasmuch as there is something created, there then would be something uncreated, although the argument is true about other contraries. But the things about which the objection is concerned are contradictories. And so the argument does not follow.

Article 2

Can God Communicate to a Creature to Be Intrinsically Preserved in Existing without God?

We should say that it does not belong to the omnipotence of God to be able to make two contradictory things true simultaneously. But in saying that God makes something that does not need preservation by him signifies a contradiction, since I have shown that every effect depends on its cause insofar as the cause causes the effect. Therefore, in saying that God makes the thing, we hold that it is created.

Therefore, as it would signify a contradiction to say that he makes something that he did not create, so would it be if one were to say that God makes something that did not need preservation by him. And so, by like reasoning, God cannot do either.

Obj. 1. Creating is greater than intrinsically preserving in existence. But creating could have been communicated to a creature, as Lombard says in the *Sentences.*[8] Therefore, so could intrinsically preserving a creature in existence have been.

Reply Obj. 1. We should say that, since creating consists of causing something, and not needing preservation by another belongs only to what has no cause, not needing to be preserved by another is obviously greater than creating, as not having a cause is greater than being a cause. But it is also not at all true that creating is communicable to a creature, as creating is the act of the first active thing, as I have said (Q. 3, A. 4).

Obj. 2. There is more in the power of things and God than in the power of our intellect. But our intellect can understand a creature apart from God. Therefore, God can far more powerfully give to a creature to be intrinsically preserved in existence.

Reply Obj. 2. We should say that, although our intellect can understand a creature without understanding God, it cannot understand that God does not preserve the creature, since this signifies a contradiction, just as one cannot understand that God did not create the creature, as I have said (Q. 3, A. 5).

Article 3
Can God Annihilate a Creature?

We should say that one says that something is possible in two ways regarding things made by God. Something is possible in one way only by the power of an active thing, as, for example, it was possible before the world was made that the world will exist, by the power of God, who was able to bring the world into existence, not by the power of a creature, which did not exist. Something is possible in a second way by the power in the things made, as, for example, it is possible that a composite material substance pass away.

Therefore, if we should be speaking about the possibility not to exist regarding things made, some had opinions about this in two ways. For example, Avicenna held that anything besides God had in itself the possibility to exist or not to exist.[9] Since existing is in addition to the essence of any created thing, the very nature of a created thing, considered in itself, can exist, but it has a necessity to exist only from another, whose nature is its existing, and so its existence is intrinsically necessary. This other is God.

But Averroes holds the contrary, namely, that there are some created things in whose nature there is no possibility not to exist, since what has in its nature the possibility not to exist cannot acquire everlasting existing from something external, namely, to be by its nature everlasting.[10] This position seems more reasonable, since the potentiality to exist or not exist belongs to something only by reason of matter, which is pure potentiality. Matter also, since it cannot exist without form, cannot have potentiality for not existing except insofar as it, being under one form, has potentiality for another form.

Therefore, it can happen in two ways that there is in the nature of a thing no possibility not to exist. It happens in one way because the thing is only a form subsisting in its own existing, as in the case of immaterial substances, which are completely immaterial. For, if a form by being in matter is the source of existing in material things, and a material thing can cease to exist only by separation of the form, its form, when subsisting in its own existing, could in no way cease to exist, as neither can existing be separated from itself. It happens in a second way because there is in matter no potentiality for another form, and the whole possibility of its matter is limited to one form, as in the case of heavenly bodies, in which there is no contrariety of forms.

Therefore, only those things in which there is matter subject to contrariety have in their nature the possibility not to exist. But the necessity of existing belongs to other things by their nature, with the possibility of not existing removed by their nature. Nonetheless, this does not eliminate the necessity of their existence being from God, since one necessary thing can cause another, as the *Metaphysics* says.[11] For God causes the created nature to which everlasting existence belongs. Also, in the things in which there is the possibility not to exist, the matter abides, but, as forms are brought into actuality out of the potentiality of matter, so they in passing out of actuality are reduced to being potential. And so we conclude that there is not in the whole of created nature any potentiality whereby something can incline to nothingness.

But if we have recourse to the power of God, the creator of things, then we should consider that we say in two ways that something is impossible for God. We say in one way that it is as such impossible, in that it is by nature not subject to any power, as are those things that signify a contradiction. We say something is impossible in a second way because of a necessity for the contrary. And this happens in an active thing in two ways. It happens in one way regarding the natural active power, which is limited to only one thing, such as the power of something hot to heat. In this way, God the Father begets the Son and cannot fail to do so. We say in a second way regarding the final end, for which everything necessarily inclines, just as, for example, a human being necessarily wills happiness and cannot will wretchedness. Likewise, God necessarily wills his goodness and cannot will things with which goodness is incompatible, as we say that God cannot lie or will to lie.

But it is not in itself impossible that creatures not exist, absolutely speaking, as if signifying a contradiction; otherwise, they would have always existed. That they not exist is possible because they are not their existing. Thus, if one says that a creature does not exist at all, the contrary of the predicate is included in the definition of the subject, as if one should say that a human being is not a rational animal, for such things signify a contradiction and are as such impossible. Likewise, God does not produce creatures by a necessity of nature, so that his power is determined to the existing of a creature, as I have proved in another question (Q. 3, A. 15). Nor does God depend on creatures, so that he could not exist without creatures, since creatures add nothing to his goodness.

Therefore, we conclude that it is not impossible that God annihilate things, since it is not necessary that he give existing to things, except on the supposition of his decree and foreknowledge, in that he so ordained and foreknew that he would keep things in existence forever.

Obj. 2. Destructible creatures, which have a weaker existing than that of other creatures, cease to exist only through the action of an efficient cause, as fire is destroyed by something contrary acting on it. Therefore, far less can other creatures cease to exist except through an action. Therefore, if God were to annihilate a creature, only an action would cause this. But an action cannot do this, since, as every action is from an actual being, so it terminates in an actual being, inasmuch as a product is necessarily like its producer. But an action that constitutes an actual being in no way annihilates. Therefore, God cannot annihilate anything.

Reply Obj. 2. We should say that destructible things cease to exist because their matter receives another form, with which the prior form cannot exist. And so the action of an active thing, which educes a new form from potentiality to actuality, is required for their destruction. But if God were to reduce a thing to nothing, no action would be necessary. It would only be required that God cease from the action whereby he bestows existing on things, as the absence of the sun's illumination causes privation of light in the air.

Obj. 6. Some said that God will not be the actual cause if creatures will be annihilated. On the contrary, God's action is his existing. And so also Augustine says that we exist because God exists.[12] But his existing never comes to him. Therefore, he never ceases to exist in his action, and so he will always actually cause.

Reply Obj. 6. We should say that we should consider two things regarding God's action in producing things, namely, the substance of the action and its order to an effect. The substance of his action, since it is the divine essence, is eternal, and the substance necessarily exists. But its order to an effect depends on the divine will, since an effect in any action of one producing results only according to the necessity of the action's source, as, for example, fire heats according to mode of heat. And so, since the source of things made by God is his will, there is accordingly in divine action an order to an effect as the will determines. And so, although God's action cannot cease substantially, the order to an effect could cease, if God were so to wish.

Obj. 8. Averroes says in his *Commentary on the Metaphysics* that what in itself can exist or not cannot acquire the necessity of existing from another.[13] Therefore, whatever creatures have a necessity to exist, have no possibility to exist and not to exist. All such things (e.g., immaterial substances and heavenly bodies) are indestructible. Therefore, for all of these things, there is no possibility not to exist. Therefore, if they should be left to themselves, with the divine action removed, they will not fall into nonexisting, and so God does not seem able to annihilate them.

Reply Obj. 8. We should say that something in whose nature there is the possibility not to exist does not receive the necessity of existing from another, so that necessary existence belongs to it by nature, since this would signify a contradiction, namely, that the nature could not exist, and that it would have the necessity of existing. But having indestructibility from grace and glory is not prevented. Just so, the body of Adam was somehow indestructible through the grace of innocence, and the bodies of the risen will be indestructible by glory, by the power of the soul inhering in its source. On the other hand, a nature in which there is no possibility not to exist may have the necessity of existing from another, since whatever perfection it has, it has from another. And so, when the action of its cause ceases, it would cease to exist because of the power in God not to give existing, not because of a potentiality not to exist.

Obj. 13. As God is the supreme good, so he is the most perfect being. But inasmuch as he is the supreme good, it is proper to him to be incapable of causing the evil of sin. Therefore, inasmuch as he is the most perfect being, it does not belong to him to be capable of causing the annihilation of things.

Reply Obj. 13. We should say that God, although he can reduce creatures to nothing, cannot fail to cause them as long as they remain. And he is their cause both as efficient cause and final cause. Therefore, as God cannot cause that a creature abiding in existence not be from him, so he cannot cause that a creature not be ordered to his goodness. And so, since the evil of sin takes away the order toward himself as the end, inasmuch as sin is turning away from the incommunicable good, God cannot cause the evil of sin, although he can cause annihilation by altogether ceasing to preserve a creature.

Article 4

Should a Creature Be Annihilated, or Is Any?

We should say that the created universe will not be annihilated. Although creatures capable of passing away have not always existed, they will endure forever substantially. But some have held that all creatures capable of passing away will cease to exist at the final consummation of things, and this is ascribed to Origen, who nonetheless seems to say so only by citing the opinion of others.

We can understand the reason from two things. First, we can understand why from the divine will, on which the existing of creatures depends. Although the will of God, absolutely considered, is disposed to contrary things regarding creatures, since he is not bound more to one thing or another, it has a necessity when one makes a supposition. For, regarding creatures, we understand that something disposed to contrary things is necessary if one makes an assumption, as Socrates can sit or not sit, but he necessarily sits while he sits. Just so, the divine will, which, as concerning itself, can will something or its contrary, as, for example, to save or not save Peter, cannot will not to save Peter if he wills to save Peter. And because his will is immutable, if we suppose that he at some time wills something, it is by supposition necessary that he always wills it, although it is not necessary that he wills what he wills to exist at one time to exist always.

And whoever wills something for its own sake wills that it always exist, since he wills it for itself. For what one wills to exist at some time and later not to exist, one wills to exist in order to perfect something else, and when the other thing has been perfected, one does not need the thing that one willed to perfect the other. But God wills the created universe for its own sake, although he also wills that it exist for his sake, since these two things are not contradictory. For God wills that creatures exist for the sake of his goodness, namely, that they imitate and represent it in their own way, and they do this inasmuch as they have existing from it and subsist in their own natures. And so to say that God made all things for his own sake, as *Proverbs* 16:4 does ("The Lord produced all things for his own sake"), is the same as to say that he made creatures for the sake of their existence, as *Wisdom* 1:14 says ("He created all things in order that they exist"). And so, since God established creatures, he evidently willed that they always endure, and the contrary will never happen because he is unchangeable.

Second, we can understand the reason from the very nature of things, since God so established each nature as not to take away its own property. And so a gloss on Rom. 11:24 ("You were grafted contrary to nature") says that God, who is the founder of nature, does not act contrary to nature. (He sometimes, however, does something above nature in created things as evidence for faith.) And the natural property of immaterial things, which lack contrariety, is that they endure forever, since there is no potentiality in them not to exist, as I have shown before (A. 3). And so, as he does not take away from fire the natural inclination whereby it tends to rise, so he does not take away from the aforementioned things their perpetuity so as to annihilate them.

Obj. 1. As a finite power cannot cause motion in infinite time, so nothing can exist in infinite time by a finite power. But every power of a material substance is finite, as the *Physics* says.[14] Therefore, there is in no material substance a power capable of enduring in infinite time. But some material substances, such as the heavenly bodies, cannot be destroyed, since they have no contrary. Therefore, they are at some time necessarily annihilated.

Reply Obj. 1. We should say that, according to Averroes,[15] although all the power in a material substance is limited, not every material substance needs to have a finite potentiality to exist, since there is in naturally destructible material substances only a potentiality to be changed, not a potentiality to exist, whether finite or infinite. But this analysis does not seem valid, since the potentiality to exist is received both by way of passive power, which regards matter, and by way of active power, which regards form, which in indestructible things cannot fail. For the more form each thing has, the more power of existing it has. And so Aristotle says in the *De coelo* that some things have the power and potentiality to exist always.[16]

And so we should say otherwise, that one can infer from the infinite time of something that it has infinity only if it is measured by time, whether intrinsically, like movement, or incidentally, like the existing of things subject to movement, and these things last for a period of time, beyond which they cannot. But time and movement in no way affect the existing of a heavenly body, since the latter is altogether unchangeable. And so the heavens' existing has no infinity from the fact that they are in infinite time, as they exist altogether outside the continuity of time. For this reason, theologians say that eternity measures the heavens. And so the heavens do not require infinite power in order to exist forever.

Obj. 6. Justice requires that one who is ungrateful be deprived of a benefit received or acquired. But a human being by mortal sin is ungrateful. Therefore, justice demands that such a one be deprived of all the benefits received from God, among which is existence itself. And God's judgment on sinners will be just, as Paul says in Rom. 2:2. Therefore, sinners will be annihilated.

Reply Obj. 6. We should say that, although God could justly withdraw existing from a creature sinning against him, it is more suitable justice that he preserve the creature in existence for punishment. This is for two reasons. First, that justice would not have any mixture of mercy, since nothing would remain for which God could show mercy, as Ps. 25:10 says: "All the ways of the Lord are mercy and truth." Second, the more congruent justice corresponds to sin in two things. It corresponds in one way because the will in sinning acts against God, but the nature that observes the order implanted by God does not. And so the punishment ought to be such that it afflicts the will by harming the nature that the will abuses. But if a creature were to be altogether annihilated, there would be only harm to the nature and not affliction of the will. It corresponds in a second way because, inasmuch as there are two things in sin, namely, turning away from the incommunicable good and turning to a transient good, the turning to a transient good involves turning away from God. For a sinner does not intend to be turned away from God but seeks to enjoy a temporal good with which one cannot simultaneously enjoy God. And so, since the pain of loss corresponds to the turning away of sin, and the pain of sense for actual sin corresponds to the turning to a transient good, it is fitting that the pain of sense accompany the pain of loss. But if a creature were to be annihilated, there would be the eternal pain of loss, but there would not remain the pain of sense.

Article 5

Does Heavenly Motion at Some Time Cease?

We should say that we, following the example of the saints, hold that heavenly motion will at some time cease, although one holds this by faith rather than one can demonstrate it by reason. And in order that one can clearly manifest on what the difficulty of this question depends, we should note that heavenly motion is not natural to a heavenly body in the same way that the movement of an elementary material substance is natural to it. The latter motion has its source in the movable thing, a source not only material and passive but also formal and active, since such motion results from the form of the elementary material substance, just as other natural properties result from essential sources. And so we say that their efficient cause causes their motion inasmuch as it gives them the form from which movement results.

But we cannot say the same about a heavenly body, since, inasmuch as nature, not being disposed for many things, always inclines to one thing in a fixed way, no nature inclines to movement as such. For there is a lack of uniformity in any movement, inasmuch as the thing moved is disposed differently before and after the movement, and uniformity of the movable thing is contrary to the nature of movement.

And so nature never inclines to movement for its own sake but for the sake of something determined that results from movement, as, for example, a heavy nature inclines to rest in the center of the earth and consequently inclines to downward movement, so as to arrive by such movement in such a place. But a heavenly body by its movement does not arrive at a place toward which it inclines by its nature, since any place is the starting point and end of its motion. And so its natural movement cannot result from an inclination of a natural power inhering in it, as the natural movement of fire is to be borne upward.

But we say that circular motion is natural to the heavens inasmuch as they have in their nature a disposition for such movement and so have in themselves the passive source of such movement, but the active source of such movement is a separate substance. Such a separate substance is God, an intelligence, or a soul, as some hold. As to the present question, it does not matter which one is the source.

Therefore, we cannot understand the reason of the permanent motion from the particular nature of a heavenly body whereby there is only the disposition for movement. Rather, we need to understand it from the separate active source. And because every active thing acts for the sake of an end, we need to consider what is the end of heavenly motion. For, if it should be compatible with its end that the movement at some time terminates, the heavens will be stationary, but if being at rest should not be compatible with its end, the movement will be everlasting. For the movement cannot fail by reason of a change in its efficient cause, since God's will is immutable just like nature, and if there are any intermediate causes of the motion, they obtain immutability by his will.

In considering this, we ought to avoid three things. The first is that we do not say that the heavens are moved for the sake of their movement, as we said that the heavens exist for the sake of their existing, in which they are like God. For movement, by its very nature, is contrary to being able to be considered an end, since movement is tending toward something. And so it does not have the nature of an end but rather of the means to an end, and to confirm this, it is also said to be an imperfect act, as the *De anima* and the *Physics* say.[17] But the end is the ultimate perfection.

The second thing to avoid is considering heavenly motion for the sake of anything less excellent, since, inasmuch as the end is that by which we understand its essence, the end needs to be more excellent than the means to the end. But it can happen that a less excellent effect results from the action of a more excellent thing, although this is not the end striven for. For example, the safety of a peasant is an end that results from the action of the king's governance, but the king's governance is directed to something better than that peasant's safety as its end, namely, the common good. And so one cannot say that the production of the things in the lower world is the end of heavenly motion, although it was an effect or terminus, since a heavenly body is also superior to the things in the lower world, and its movement to the movements and changes of those things.

The third thing to avoid is considering the end of heavenly motion something infinite, since, as the *Metaphysics* says,[18] one who posits something infinite in a final cause destroys the end and nature of the good, since it is impossible to attain what is infinite, and nothing is moved to what is impossible to obtain, as the *De coelo* says.[19] And so one cannot say that the end of heavenly motion is to obtain actually what is potential, although Avicenna seems to say this. For this is impossible to obtain, since it is infinite, because, when it is actually in one place, it will be potential for another place, in which it previously actually existed.

Therefore, we need to consider the end of heavenly motion something that the heavens can obtain by their movement, something other than the movement and more excellent than it. We can consider this in two ways. In one way, we consider the end of heavenly motion something in the heavens themselves that exists along with the movement, and so some philosophers hold that likeness to God in causing is the end of heavenly motion, and this happens while the movement continues. And so it is unfitting in this respect that heavenly motion cease, since, when the movement ceases, the end proceeding from the movement would cease. In a second way, we can consider the end of heavenly motion something outside the heavens, at which the heavens arrive by their motion, and which can abide when the motion ceases. This is our position.

For we hold that heavenly motion is for the sake of filling up the number of the elect. The rational soul is more excellent than any material substance, even the heavens. And so there is nothing unfitting if we should consider the end of heavenly motion the multiplicity of rational souls, but not to an infinite number, since this could not result from heavenly motion, and so the heavens would be moved to achieve something that they cannot obtain. And so we conclude that the fixed multiplicity of rational souls is the end of heavenly motion. And so, when this is had, the heavenly motion will cease.

And although each of the aforementioned positions can be reasonably sustained, the second, which belongs to faith, seems to be more probable, for three reasons. First, there is no difference between saying that a thing's end is likeness to God in some respect, or saying that the end is the thing insofar as we note the likeness. As I have said above, we can call the end of things either the likeness to God's goodness or the things' existing as likened to God. Therefore, it is the same thing to say that the end of heavenly motion is to be likened to God in causing, or to say that the end consists of causing. But causing cannot be an end, since it is an action having an effect and tending toward something, since effects are of more importance than the actions producing them, as the beginning of the *Ethics* says.[20] And so such productive acts cannot be the ends of active things, since they perfect the things produced, not the things producing the effects. And so also the very things made are more the ends, as the *Metaphysics* and the *Ethics* make clear.[21] But the effects themselves are not the ends, since they are less excellent than the heavens, as I have said above. And so we conclude that it is unfitting to say that the end of heavenly motion is being likened to God in causing.

Second, since the heavens have in them only an aptitude for movement and an external active source moves them, they are moved and act as an instrument. For such is the way in which an instrument is disposed, as is evident in the works of a craft (e.g., an axe has only an aptitude for its proper movement, but the source of its movement belongs to a craftsman). And so also, according to philosophers, what moves when moved moves as an instrument. And in action by an instrument, there cannot be an end in the instrument itself except incidentally, inasmuch as we understand the instrument as a product, not as an instrument. And so it is probable that the end of heavenly motion is something outside itself, not a perfection of itself.

Third, if likeness to God in causing is the end of heavenly motion, we especially note this likeness by the causality of what God causes immediately, namely, the rational soul, in the causality of which a heavenly body also acts at the same time by disposing the matter. And so it is more probable that the end of heavenly motion is the number of the elect than being likened to God in the causality of coming to be and passing away, as philosophers held. And so we concede that heavenly motion ends when the number of elect is complete.

Obj. 3. Things that have necessity from something antecedently necessary are absolutely necessary, as Aristotle makes clear in the *Physics.*[22] For example, the death of an animal is necessary because of a necessity of matter. But the actions of indestructible things, among which one needs to posit heavenly motion, are because of the substances of the things to which the actions belong. And so the actions seem to have necessity from something antecedent, although the converse is true in the case of destructible things, whose substances are such because of their actions. And so those destructible substances have necessity from something subsequent, as Averroes, commenting on the cited text of Aristotle, says. Therefore heavenly motion is absolutely necessary and so will never cease.

Reply Obj. 3. We should say that the prepositional phrase *because of* denotes a cause, and so it sometimes signifies a final cause, which is subsequent in existence, and sometimes a material or efficient cause, which is antecedent. But when one says about indestructible things that acts are because of the active things, the phrase *because of* denotes the efficient cause because of which there is necessity in the acts, not the final cause. Therefore, if we should relate heavenly motion to the moveable thing, the motion does not have necessity from the moveable thing as its efficient cause, as I have shown, but has this necessity from the thing causing motion. This cause, which acts voluntarily, brings necessity in the motion insofar as the order of divine wisdom has determined, and not to be in motion forever.

Obj. 7. Everything potential is imperfect unless it is brought into actuality. But in the consummation of the world, God will not leave anything imperfect. Therefore, since only movement brings the potentiality in the heavens for a place into actuality, it seems that heavenly motion even in the consummation of the world will not cease.

Reply Obj. 7. We should say that we do not call a thing imperfect if every potentiality in it has not been brought into actuality. Rather, this is true when a thing obtains its completion by a potentiality brought into actuality. For example, someone with a potentiality to be in India will not be imperfect if that one were not there, But we call someone imperfect if a one lacks knowledge or virtue, which nature designs to perfect a human being. But position does not perfect the heavens, unlike lower material substances, which are preserved in their proper place. And so, although the potentiality whereby the heavens can be in a fixed position is never brought into actuality, it does not follow that the heavens are imperfect. For, if we should consider the heavens as such, there is no greater perfection for them to be in one position than in another, and they are indifferently disposed for all positions, since nature moves them to any position. This indifference leads to a state of rest rather than perpetual motion unless one should consider the will of the one who causes the motion and intends its end. Just so also, some philosophers assigned the cause of the earth's rest in the center because of the center's equidistance from any part of the circumference of the heavens.

Obj. 9. God will never take away eternity from something that receives eternity, as is evident in the case of angels, rational souls, and the heavenly substance. But heavenly motion receives eternity, since only circular motion may be eternal, as the *Physics* proves.[23] Therefore, heavenly motion will last forever, just like other things that nature intends to be eternal.

Reply Obj. 9. We should say that the heavens are by their nature capable in one way of eternal motion and in another way of eternal existing. For their existing depends on the sources of their nature, from which the necessity of existing results, since it is impossible for them not to exist, as I have shown before. But their motion in its nature has only an aptitude for perpetuity, and it has necessity from the cause of its motion. And so also, according to Averroes,[24] the eternity of existing in the heavens is from the sources of their nature, but the eternity of motion from an external source. And so also, according to those who say that the motion never ceases, the cause of the duration of the heavens' motion and its eternity is the divine will. But the immutability of his will does not necessarily have the power to prove the eternity of heavenly motion, as they wish, since his will is not altered if he should will that different things succeed one another insofar as the end that he immutably wills demands. And so we should rather seek the reason of the eternity of motion from the end rather than from the immutability of the cause of the motion.

Obj. 13. There needs to be an order and proportion of things that succeed one another. But there is no proportion of the finite to the infinite. Therefore, one improperly says that the heavens are moved in finite time and later rest in infinite time. And yet one is forced to say this if heavenly motion began and will end, never to begin again.

Reply Obj. 13. We should say that if heavenly motion were not to be because of something else, it would then be necessary to note its proportion to subsequent rest if we were to hold it not to be eternal. But because it is ordered to another end, we note its proportion in relation to the end, not in relation to the subsequent rest. Thus we understand that God, bringing all creatures into existence out of nothing, by himself established the first perfection of the universe, which consists of the essential parts of the universe and different species. But for the final perfection of the universe, which will consist of fulfilling the order of the blessed, he ordained different movements and actions of creatures. Some are natural, such as heavenly motion and the actions of the elements, which prepare matter for receiving a rational soul, and some are voluntary, such as the ministries of the angels, who are sent for the sake of those who receive the inheritance of salvation. And so, when this consummation has been accomplished and remains forever without change, things ordained for it will cease forever.

Article 6

Can a Human Being Know When the Heavenly Motion Ends?

We should say that the exact time of the world's end is completely unknown, except by God and the incarnate Christ. The reason for this is that there are two ways in which we can foreknow future things, namely, by natural knowledge or by revelation. We foreknow some future things by natural knowledge through causes that we see present and thereby await their future effects. We foreknow future things through the certitude of scientific knowledge, if there should be causes from which effects necessarily follow. Or we foreknow through conjecture, if there should be causes from which effects for the most part result, as an astronomer foreknows a future eclipse, or a doctor an impending death. One cannot precisely foreknow the time of the world's end, since the cause of heavenly motion and its cessation is only the divine will, as I have shown (Q. 5, A. 5), and we cannot by nature know that cause. But we can by natural knowledge foreknow other things that heavenly motion or any other sensibly perceptible cause causes (e.g., the particular destruction of some part of the earth hitherto inhabitable and later not).

Although it can be known through revelation were God to will to reveal it, it would be fittingly revealed only to the incarnate Christ, for three reasons. First, the world will end only when the number of elect is complete, and its completion is an execution, as it were, of all of divine predestination. And so it is fitting that there be revelation about the world's end only to the one to whom there is revelation about all of divine predestination, namely, the incarnate Christ, who in a way fulfills all of the divine predestination of the human race. And so Jn. 5:20 says: "The Father loves the Son and reveals to him all the things that he does." Second, since we do not know how long this condition of the world ought to endure, whether for a short or long time, we consider things of this world as if about to pass away immediately. And so 1 Cor. 7:31 says: "Let those who enjoy this world be as if they do not enjoy it, since the form of this world is passing away." Third, human beings are ever ready to await God's judgment when the precise time is altogether unknown. And so Mt. 24:42 says: "Be watchful, since you do not know at what hour the Lord will come." And so Augustine says that one who says that he does not know when the Lord will come, whether in a short or a long time, is in accord with the view of the Gospel.[25] But of two who say they know, the statement of the one who says that Christ will come shortly, or that the end of the world is imminent, is more dangerous, since this can be an occasion to lose all hope that it will come if it will not occur at the time when it is predicted to happen.

Obj. 5. A sign is ordered to knowing something. But the Gospels posit some signs of the coming of the Lord, which will be at the end of the world, as Mt. 24:24 and Lk. 21:9 make clear. Paul in 1 Tim. 4:1, 2 Tim. 3:2, and 2 Thess. 2:3 also makes this clear. Therefore, it seems that we can know the time of the coming of the Lord and the end of the world.

Reply Obj. 5. We should say that the signs were given in order to manifest that the world will end at some time, not to manifest the fixed time when it will end. For some of the signs have occurred almost from the beginning of the world (e.g., nation will rise against nation, and there will be earthquakes in many places), but these things will happen more frequently when the end of the world is impending. But it cannot be manifest to us what is the measure of these signs about the end of the world.

Obj. 7. In the second coming, Christ will come more openly than in the first coming, since then all the people and those who pierced him (Rev. 1:7) will see him. But Scripture foretold the first coming even as to the exact time, as Dan. 9:24–27 makes clear. Therefore, it seems that Scripture ought to foretell the second coming regarding the exact time.

Reply Obj. 7. We should say that the first coming of Christ prepared the way for us to merit by faith and other virtues, and so knowledge of the first coming was required on our part, so that, by believing in him who had come, we can merit by his grace. In the second coming, rewards are rendered for merits, and what we do or what we know will not be required on our part. Rather, it will be a question of what we receive. And so we do not need to know exactly the time of his coming. But we call this coming manifest because he will be manifest when he will be present, not because it is manifestly foreknown.

Obj. 9. We predicate large and small, long and short, relatively, of one thing in relation to another. But we say that the time from the coming of Christ until the end of the world is short, as 1 Cor. 7:29 ("The time is short"), 1 Cor. 10:11 ("We upon whom the ends of the ages will come"), and 1 Jn. 2:18 ("It is the last hour") make clear. Therefore, we can at least know that it is a much shorter time from Christ's coming until the end of the world than from the beginning of the world until Christ.

Reply Obj. 9. We should say that the words in Scripture that seem to pertain to shortness of time, or even to the closeness of the end, are to be related not only to the quantity of time but also to the disposition of the world's condition. For no other condition succeeds the evangelical law, which brought things to perfection, as that law succeeded the Old Law, and the Old Law the natural law.

Article 7

Do the Elements Remain When Heavenly Motion Ceases?

We should say that all universally agree that the elements in some way remain and will in some way pass away, but there are different opinions regarding the way of remaining and passing away.

Some say that all the elements remain regarding their matter, but some, namely, water and fire, will receive a more excellent form, namely, a heavenly form, so that we can call three elements the heavens, namely, air, which Scripture sometimes calls the heavens because of its nature, and water and fire, which assume a heavenly form. And so one understands to be verified what Rev. 21:1 says: "I saw a new heaven and a new earth," with the three, namely, fire, air, and water, included under the word *heaven.*

But this position is impossible. For the elements have no potentiality for a heavenly form, since a heavenly form does not have a contrary, and all the matter with potentiality for such a form is under it. If not, the heavens would come to be and pass away, which Aristotle shows to be false.[26] And the argument supporting the position is frivolous, since, as Basil says in the *Hexameron.*

Scripture understands intermediate things by the extremes, as when Gen. 1:1 says: "In the beginning, God created the heavens and the earth." For the text also understands by the creation of the heavens and the earth the middle elements. And sometimes things of the lower world are included under the word *earth*, as Ps. 148:7 makes clear: "Praise the Lord from the earth," and then "fire, hail," and so on. And so nothing prevents us from saying that Scripture also understood by the beginning of the heavens and the earth the beginning of the intermediate elements, or that it includes all the elements under the word *earth*.

And so others say that all the elements remain substantially both as to their matter and as to their substantial forms. For, as, according to the opinion of Avicenna, the substantial forms of the elements remain in a mixed material substance, with their active and passive qualities reduced to a mean, not in their excellences, so the elements can remain in the final condition of the world without the aforementioned qualities. This seems consonant with what Augustine says:[27] "In that conflagration of the world, the qualities of destructible elements that were compatible with our bodies, will completely perish by fire, and the substance will have those qualities that are suitable for immortal bodies by a wondrous alteration."

But this does not seem a reasonable assertion. First, it is unreasonable because, inasmuch as active and passive qualities are intrinsically accidents of the elements, essential sources of the elements necessarily cause them. And so the qualities cannot be lacking while the essential sources remain in the elements, except by force, which cannot be of long duration. And so neither does the opinion of Avicenna seem to be probable, that the forms of the elements actually remain in a mixed material substance, although they remain only virtually, as Aristotle says. For it would be necessary that the forms of different elements be preserved in different parts of matter, and this would be so only if they were in different places. And so there would be only a mixture according to the senses, not a real one, and the qualities of one element in a mixed material substance nevertheless counteract the qualities of another. We cannot say this about the consummation of the world where force will altogether cease.

Second, because active and passive qualities belong to the integrity of the nature of elements, it would follow that imperfect elements remain. And so the adduced authority of Augustine is speaking about the dispositions of things that come to be, pass away, and are changed, not active and passive qualities.

And so it seems that we should say that the elements remain substantially and also in their natural qualities, but the mutual comings to be, passings away, and alterations will cease, since such things order the elements to completing the number of the elect, just as the movements of the heavens order the heavens to that purpose. But the substances of the elements will remain, just as the substance of the heavens will, since, inasmuch as the universe remains forever, as I have shown above, it is necessary that things belonging to the perfection of the universe first and intrinsically remain.

This belongs to the elements, since they are essential parts of the universe, as Aristotle proves.[28] For, if the universe is spherical, it must have a center, and this is the earth. And given the earth, which is heavy, absolutely speaking, and its centrality, we need to suppose its contrary, namely, fire, which is light, absolutely speaking, since if one contrary exists in a nature, the other also does. But given the extremes, we need to suppose intermediate things. And so we need to suppose air and water, which are light in relation to fire and heavy in relation to the earth, one of which is closer to the earth than the other is.

And so this configuration of the universe makes clear that the elements are essential parts of it. This is made evident when we consider the order of causes to effects, since, as the heavens are the universal active cause of things that come to be, the elements are the universal matter of the same. And so it is required for the perfection of the universe that the elements remain substantially and also have for that their natural aptitude. And passing away happens in one way in mixed material substances and in another way in the elements. For there is an active source of passing away in mixed material substances because they are composed of contrary things, but there is in the elements which have an external contrary and are not composed of contrary things, a passive, not an active, source of passing away, inasmuch as they have matter in which there is an aptitude for another form that they lack. And from this source, coming to be and passing away in the elements are natural movements or changes, not because of an active source as Averroes says.[29]

Therefore, since a heavenly body has the source of its motion external to it, its motion can cease without the use of force, as I have said, and it can remain. Just so, the passing away of the elements can cease when the external cause of passing away ceases, while their substances remain, and we need to trace this cause of passing away to heavenly movement as the first source of coming to be and passing away.

Obj. 4. Someone said that divine power will cause the elements to remain without active and passive qualities, although this is naturally impossible. On the contrary, as nature was instituted at the beginning of the world, so nature will be consummated at the end of the world. But at the beginning of the world, as Augustine says,[30] it does not suffice to ask what God can do, but we should ask what the nature of things possesses. Therefore, we should note this also at the end of the world.

Reply Obj. 4. We should say that the nature of material substances was instituted at the beginning of the world insofar as their nature is ordered to coming to be and passing away, which completes the number of the elect. But the substance of the elements will remain at the consummation of the world insofar as their substance is ordered to the perfection of the universe. And so not all the things that the elements needed to have at the beginning of the world need to present in them in their final state.

Obj. 7. Augustine says that water and earth exhibit the capacity to be acted upon, and air and fire the capacity to act.[31] Therefore, if one says that some elements are appropriate because of their active power, it seems that we should understand this about fire and air rather than earth and water.

Reply Obj. 7. We should say that, if one should consider action and being acted upon in the elements regarding their substantial sources, then Augustine's statement is true, that water and earth show an aptitude to be acted upon, and fire and air an aptitude for action, since fire and air have more form, which is the source of action, and earth and water more matter, which is the source of being acted upon. But if one should consider action and being acted upon regarding active and passive powers, which are the immediate sources of action, then fire and water are more active, and air and earth more passive.

Obj. 16. Someone said that the elements are indestructible as a whole, although they are destructible as to parts. On the contrary, this belongs to the elements because of heavenly motion, inasmuch as one part of an element is destroyed, and another part produced. Thus the totality of the element is preserved. Therefore, when heavenly motion ceases, one could not assign a cause of the indestructibility in the whole element.

Reply Obj. 16. We should say that the elements are indestructible as a whole, with parts produced and destroyed as long as heavenly motion lasts, but when heavenly motion ceases, there will be another cause of their indestructibility, namely, in that only something external can destroy them, and a destructive external thing will cease when heavenly motion is lacking.

Article 8

Do Action and Being Acted Upon Remain
When Heavenly Motion Ceases?

We should say that, as the *Liber de causis* maintains, when the first cause withdraws its action from an effect, the second cause also necessarily withdraws its action from it, since the second cause has the fact that it acts from the action of the first cause, in whose power it acts. And since every active thing acts insofar as it is actual, it is necessary to understand the order of active causes according to their rank in actuality.

Lower material substances have less actuality than heavenly bodies have. For actuality does not fulfill the whole potentiality in lower material substances, as the matter underlying one form remains potential for another form, but this is not so in heavenly bodies, since the matter of a heavenly body has no potentiality for another form, and so the form that it has exhausts all of its potentiality.

But separate substances are more perfect than even heavenly bodies, since they are particular subsistent forms and not composed of matter and form. Nonetheless, they fall short of the actuality of God, who is his existing, which is not the case with other subsistent forms. Just as we see that elements also surpass one another according to the grade of their actuality, since water has greater form than earth, air greater form than water, and fire greater form than air, so also is this the case regarding heavenly bodies and separate substances.

Therefore, elements act in the power of heavenly bodies, and heavenly bodies act in the power of separate substances. And so, when the action of separate substances ceases, the action of a heavenly body necessarily ceases, and when the latter ceases, the action of elementary material substance necessarily ceases.

But we should note that a material substance has two kinds of action. One is by a property of the substance, namely, that it acts by movement, since this is proper to a material substance, so that it, being moved, causes movement and acts. The other has action insofar as it attains the order of separate substances and shares part of their way. For example, lower natures were accustomed to share in the property of a higher nature, as is evident in certain animals that share in a likeness of practical reason, which is proper to human beings. But this is the action of a material substance that is not related to the transformation of matter. Rather, it is related to communicating a likeness of its form to a medium by analogy to the immaterial representation received in the senses and the intellect about a thing. And the sun in this way illumines air, and color multiplies its form in a medium.

And heavenly bodies cause each way of action in the lower things. For fire also by the power of a heavenly body transforms matter by its heat, and perceptible material substances by the power of light, whose source is in a heavenly body, multiply their forms in the medium. And so also, if both actions of a heavenly body were to cease, no action would remain in lower things. But when heavenly motion ceases, the first action, but not the second, will cease.

And so, when heavenly motion ceases, there will be in lower things the action of sensibly perceptible things illuminating and affecting the medium, but there will be no action whereby matter is changed, from which coming to be and passing away result.

Obj. 4. What belongs to the perfection of an element is not taken away from it. But it belongs to the perfection of each being to produce something like itself, since the communication of existing itself comes from the first good into all beings. Therefore, it seems that the elements in the consummation of the world will produce their like, and so they will have action and being acted upon.

Reply Obj. 4. We should say that lower things never attain the grade of perfection of higher things. But it belongs to the nature of the supreme active thing that its perfection suffices for him to act when another active thing has been removed. And so one cannot attribute this to lower active things.

Obj. 5. As it is a property of fire to be hot, so also it is a property of fire to heat, since, as heat comes from the essential sources of fire, so heating comes from heat. Therefore, if fire and its heat will remain at the consummation of the world, it seems that heating will also remain.

Reply Obj. 5. We should say that it is a property of fire to heat, supposing that it has any action, but its action depends on another thing, as I have said.

Article 9

Do Plants, Irrational Animals, and Minerals Remain after the World's End?

We should say that no mixed material substance besides the human body will remain in the renovation of the world. And to understand the reason for this, we should proceed by the order that Aristotle teaches,[32] namely, that we consider first the final cause and then the material, formal, and efficient causes, and we can in two ways consider the end of minerals, plants, and animals. The first end is the fulfillment of the universe, to which all the parts of the universe are ordered as their end. But the aforementioned mixed material substances are not ordered to that end, as if they intrinsically and essentially belong to the perfection of the universe, since nothing exists in them that is not in the chief parts of the world (i.e., the heavenly bodies and the elements) as active and material sources. And so the aforementioned things are certain effects of universal causes, which are essential parts of the universe, and so they belong to the perfection of the universe only insofar as they proceed from their causes, which movement does. And so they belong to the perfection of the universe being subject to movement, not to the perfection of the universe absolutely. And so, when the changeability of the universe ceases, the aforementioned things necessarily cease to exist.

The second end is the human being, since, as Aristotle says in the *Politics*,[33] imperfect things in nature are ordered to perfect things as their end. And so, as he says in the same place, animals have imperfect life in relation to human life, which is perfect, absolutely speaking, and plants imperfect life in relation to animals. Plants are for the sake of animals, by nature provided as food for them, and animals are for the sake of human beings, necessary for them in providing food and other helpful things. But this need, as long as the life of the animal human being endures, is taken away in the renovation of things, since a spiritual, not an animal, body rises at the resurrection, as 1 Cor. 15:44 says. And so animals and plants will then also cease to exist.

And the matter and form of the aforementioned things have an aptitude for the same thing, since, inasmuch as they are composed of contrary things, they have in themselves the active source of passing away. And so, if only an external source prevents them from passing away, this would be by force and unsuitable for perpetual existence, since things that exist by force cannot always exist, as Aristotle makes clear in the *De coelo*.[34] And they do not have an internal source that can prevent them from passing away, since their forms, as not intrinsically subsisting but having their existing dependent on matter, are by nature capable of passing away. And so they cannot remain forever numerically or specifically the same when coming to be and passing away cease.

The same conclusion follows from considering their efficient cause, since the existing of plants and animals is a living existing, one that does not exist in material things without movement. And so animals cease to exist when the heart stops beating, and plants when nourishment ceases. And there is in these things no source of motion that does not depend on the first mobile thing, since the souls of animals and plants are completely subject to the influences of the heavenly bodies. And so, when heavenly motion ceases, neither movement nor life will be able to remain in them. And so, in the renovation of the world, the aforementioned things will evidently be unable to remain.

Obj. 9. As the elements have assisted human beings in the condition of this life, so also have plants and animals. But the elements will remain. Therefore, animals and plants also will, and so it does not seem that they will cease to exist.

Reply Obj. 9. We should say that the elements are rewarded inasmuch as human beings will be rewarded in them, namely, as their brilliance will proceed to the glory of the elect, not as such, since they as such do not merit anything. But human beings will not need animals and plants, as they will need the elements, which will be the place of their glory, as it were. And so there is no comparison.

Obj. 15. The final purification of the world will be by the action of fire. But some minerals are of so strong a composition that they are not consumed by fire, as is evident in the case of gold. Therefore, it seems that at least those minerals remain after that fire.

Reply Obj. 15. We should say that, although there are some things that fire does not consume at once, there is nothing that fire does not finally consume, if the fire should remain for a long time, as Galen says. But the fire of the conflagration of the world will be much stronger than the fire we use. Again, the cessation of heavenly motion and not only the action of fire will destroy mixed material substances in the fire.

Obj. 16. The universal is eternal. But the universal exists only in singular things. Therefore, it seems that singulars of any universal will always exist. Therefore, irrational animals, plants, and mineral substances will always exist.

Reply Obj. 16. We should say that one can consider a universal in three ways, and it is true in some way that the universal is eternal in whatever way one considers the universal. One can in one way consider the universal nature insofar as it abstracts from any existing. And then it is true that a universal is eternal, by removal of the cause determining it to a particular time rather than by positing the cause of its perpetuity, since it does not belong to a universal nature that it be more at this time than that. (Also in this way, we say that prime matter is one.) In the second way, one can consider the universal according to the existing that it has in singulars. And then it is true that it is eternal, since it exists whenever its singular exists, just as we say it is every-where, since it exists wherever its singular exists, although there are many places where its singulars do not exist, and so there is no universal there. One can consider the universal in a third way according to the existing that it has in the intellect, and then it is also true that the universal is eternal, especially in the divine intellect.

Article 10

Do Human Bodies Remain When Heavenly Motion Ceases?

We should say that, as Augustine says,[35] Porphyry held that human souls should avoid every material substance in order to be perfectly happy, and so, according to him, the soul in perfect happiness cannot be united to a body.

Origen touches on this in his *Peri archon*. He says that some were of the opinion that the saints will at some time lay aside the bodies resumed at the resurrection, so that they live in perfect happiness in likeness to God.

But this position, besides being contrary to faith, as the cited authorities and many others make clear, is also contrary to reason, since there will be no perfect happiness where the perfection of nature is lacking. And since there is a natural substantial, not accidental, union of the soul and the body, the nature of the soul can be perfect only if it is united to the body. Therefore, Augustine also says at the end of his *Literal Commentary on Genesis* that the souls of the saints do not so perfectly enjoy the vision of God before the resurrection as they do after it.[36] And so it will be necessary in the final state of perfect happiness that human bodies be united to the souls.

The first position proceeds according to the opinion of those who say that the soul is accidentally united to the body, like a sailor to his ship or a human being to his clothes. And so also Plato said that the human being is a soul clothed in a body, as Gregory of Nyssa relates.[37]

But this cannot be so, since a human being would then be one being accidentally, not intrinsically, it would belong to the genus of accident, not the genus of substance, like what I call clothed or shod. It is also clear that the arguments about mixed material substances introduced in the previous article have no force regarding the human being. For a human being is ordered to the perfection of the universe as an essential part of it, since there is in a human being something that is not virtually contained in the elements or the heavenly bodies, namely, the rational soul. And the body of a human being is ordered to the human being for the perfection of the human being's nature and not only regarding the human being's animal life. And although the body of a human being is composed of contrary things, there will be in it an indestructible source that, without force, will be able to preserve it from passing away, since that source is intrinsic to the human being. And this source can suffice as the source of movement when heavenly motion ceases, since it does not depend on heavenly motion.

Obj. 6. Perfect action of the intellect is required for the perfect blessedness of a human being. And the activity of the intellectual soul is more perfect when separated from the body than when united to the body, since, as the *Liber de causis* says, every united power is more infinite than a multiple power. But separate forms are united in themselves, while forms united to matter are in some way diffused to many things. Therefore, souls in perfect blessedness will not be united to a body.

Reply Obj. 6. We should say that a soul united to a body remains in itself simple and one, not multiple in the way of material forms, which are divisible by division of the subject. And so the union with the body does not hinder the soul's activity when the body will be completely subject to the soul. But union with the body in this life does, since the soul is not perfectly in control over the body.

Obj. 7. The elements in a mixed material substance naturally seek their proper places. But a natural appetite cannot be in vain. And so what is contrary to nature cannot be forever. Therefore, the elements in a mixed material substance necessarily at some time tend toward their proper places, and then the mixed material substance is dissolved. Therefore, after the condition of dissolution, human bodies, which are mixed material substances, will not remain.

Reply Obj. 7. We should say that the mastery of the soul over the body will hold back the natural appetite of elements to tend toward their proper places, lest the elements be dissolved. For the elements will have more perfect existing in the body of a human being than they would have in their proper places.

Question 6

MIRACLES

Article 1

Can God Do Anything in Created Things Outside Natural Causes, Whether Contrary to Nature or Contrary to the Course of Nature?

We should say that God can undoubtedly act in created things outside created causes, just as he acts in all created causes, as I have shown elsewhere (Q. 3, A. 7), and by acting outside created causes, he can produce the same effects that he does by means of them and in the same order, or other things and another order. And so he can do something contrary to the general and usual course of nature. The reason for this being true will be manifested if we should consider things that seem contrary to this truth. There are three such things.

The first is the opinion of some ancient philosophers, who held that material things do not have a higher cause than the one causing them to exist, and so some of them, such as Anaxagoras, considered an intellect the cause of a movement in them, such as retraction. According to this position, no supernatural cause can change natural forms, which are the sources of natural actions, or hinder their actions, and so nothing can be done contrary to the course of nature, which the necessity of these material causes ordains. But this position is false, since what is the source in beings causes the existing of all other things, as, for example, the hottest thing causes the heat in all other things, as the *Metaphysics* says.[1] I have treated about this elsewhere (ST I, Q. 44, A. 1), where I showed that nothing can exist except by God.

The second thing is that what can prevent the aforementioned truth is the opinion of other philosophers who said that God causes all beings by his intellect. But they say that he has a universal knowledge of all things inasmuch as he knows himself, and that he is the source of existing for all things but does not have proper knowledge about each. And particular effects result from general and universal knowledge only by means of particular conceptions. For example, if I should know that I should avoid any fornication, I would avoid a particular act only if I should accept that that act is one of fornication. And some accordingly say that particular effects proceed from God only by means of other causes in order, the higher of which are more universal, and the lower more particular. And so God could not do anything contrary to the course of nature. But this position is false, since, inasmuch as God perfectly knows himself, he necessarily knows whatever is in him in whatever way. But there is in him the likeness of any effect, since there can be nothing that does not imitate him. And so he necessarily has proper knowledge about all things, as I have shown elsewhere (ST I, Q. 14).

The third thing that could prevent the aforementioned truth is the position of some philosophers, who said that God does things by a necessity of nature, and so his action is limited to the course of nature that nature has ordained, and so he could not act contrary to it. But this is also patently false, since, above everything that acts by a necessity of nature, there is necessarily something that determines nature to one thing, as I have shown elsewhere (ST I, Q. 19, A. 4). And so God, who is the first active thing, cannot act by a necessity of nature, as I have shown in many other places (ST I, Q. 19, A. 3, and Q. 3, A. 15).

Therefore, with these things considered, namely, that God causes the existing in natural things, that he has proper knowledge and providence about each, and that he does not act from a necessity of nature, then he can do something in particular effects outside the course of nature. Or he can do something regarding existing, inasmuch as he introduces a new form in natural things that nature cannot, such as the form of glory, or into particular matter, such as sight in a blind man. Or he can do something regarding action, inasmuch as he restrains the actions of natural things from doing what they are by nature inclined to do, such as fire from burning, as Dan. 3:24 makes clear, or water from flowing, as Jos. 3:16 makes clear about the water of the Jordan.

Obj. 1. A gloss on Rom. 11:24 ("You have been grafted," etc.) says: "God, who establishes all natures, does nothing contrary to nature."

Reply Obj. 1. We should say that both God and natural things act contrary to a particular nature. For example, it is contrary to the particular nature of this fire that it be extinguished. And so Aristotle says that the passing away of the elderly and every deficiency is contrary to nature.[2] But no natural thing is contrary to nature in general, since we call nature particular by the order of a particular cause to a particular effect, but nature in general by the order of the first active thing in nature, that is, the heavens in relation to all lower active things. Therefore, since all lower material substances act only by the power of a heavenly body, a natural material substance cannot act against nature in general. But the very thing that something does against a particular nature is in accord with nature in general.

And as the heavens are the universal cause with respect to all lower material substances, so God is the universal cause with respect to all beings, regarding which even the heavens themselves are particular causes. For nothing prevents one and the same cause being universal with respect to lower things and particular in relation to higher things, just as happens in the predicables (e.g., animal, which is universal with respect to human being, is particular with respect to substance). Therefore, as the power of the heavens can do something contrary to a particular nature, and this is not absolutely contrary to nature, since this is according to nature in general, so the power of God can do something contrary to nature in general, which is from the power of the heavens. But this will not be absolutely contrary to nature, since it will be according to the most universal nature, which we consider by the order of God to all creatures. And by this understanding, Augustine says in the quoted gloss that God does nothing contrary to nature. And so he adds that what God does is proper to each nature.

Obj. 4. Whenever God acts in creatures by natural causes, nothing is done contrary to the course of nature. But God cannot suitably act in nature contrary to innate natural causes. Therefore, God cannot suitably work contrary to the course of nature. Proof of the minor: Augustine says that the ministry of angels revealed apparitions to the fathers, since God governs material substances by the spirits.[3] But higher material substances likewise govern lower ones, as he says in the same work,[4] and one can likewise say that he governs whatever effects by their causes. Therefore, since the plans of nature are implanted in natural causes, it seems that God can suitably act in natural effects only by natural causes. And so he will do nothing contrary to the course of nature.

Reply Obj. 4. We should say that, as God can cause effects contrary to natural causes in material things, so he can act contrary to the ministries of angels, but there is a different way of acting contrary to each. For he acts contrary to natural causes so that a human being is compelled to trace the effect to a higher cause, which one cannot attribute to visible causes, so that a visible miracle manifests divine power. But the actions of angels are not visible. And so the angels' miracles do not prevent a human being from being brought to consider divine power. And so Augustine does not say that God cannot act contrary to the ministry of angels, but that he does not.

Obj. 5, God cannot make an affirmation and a negation to be simultaneously true, since, inasmuch as this is contrary to the nature of a being as such, it is also contrary to the nature of a creature. First, existing belongs to created things, as the *Liber de causis* says.[5] But since the aforementioned principle is the first principle of all, in which all other principles are resolved, as the *Metaphysics* proves,[6] it is necessarily included in any necessary proposition, and its contrary is included in anything impossible. Therefore, since things contrary to the course of nature are impossible in nature, as, for example, a blind person becoming enabled to see, and a dead person restored to life, the contrary of the said principle will be included in such things. Therefore, God cannot do things contrary to the course of nature.

Reply Obj. 5. We should say that, as God cannot make an affirmation and a negation to be simultaneously true, so he cannot do things impossible in nature inasmuch as they include the aforementioned impossibility. For example, that a dead person returns to life includes a contradiction if one should suppose that an intrinsic source naturally restores a dead human being to life, since it belongs to the nature of a dead human being that the person is deprived of the source of life. And so God cannot do this, but he causes a dead human being to acquire life from an external source, and this does not include a contradiction. And there is the same argument about other things impossible by nature that he can do.

Obj. 16. What is intrinsically impossible is more impossible than what is incidentally impossible, since what is intrinsically such-and-such is more such-and-such. But that what existed did not exist is incidentally impossible, which God cannot do, as Jerome and Aristotle say.[7] Therefore, God cannot do intrinsically impossible things contrary to the course of nature, such as that a blind person see.

Reply Obj. 16. We should say that we trace everything incidental to something intrinsic. And so nothing prevents something incidentally impossible from being more impossible when traced to what is intrinsically impossible. For example, snow by its whiteness dazzles sight more than the whiteness of a wall, since the whiteness of the snow is greater than that of the wall. Likewise, it is impossible to deny Socrates' previous running because we can trace the running to what is intrinsically impossible, that the past did not exist, and this implies a contradiction. And so nothing prevents this being more impossible than what is impossible for something, although it is not impossible incidentally.

Obj. 18. Since every genus is divided into potentiality and actuality, as the *Physics* makes clear,[8] and passive power belongs to potentiality, and active power to actuality, there is only passive power in nature for which there is active power, since they belong to the same genus. Averroes says the same in his *Commentary on the Metaphysics*.[9] But there is no natural active power for things contrary to the course of nature. Therefore, there is also no passive power. But we say that things with respect to which there is no passive power in a creature cannot be done, although God by his omnipotence can do all things. Therefore, things contrary to the course of nature cannot be done because of the deficiency of a creature, not because of a lack of divine power.

Reply Obj. 18. We should say that the higher an active power, the more it can bring the same thing to a higher effect. And so nature can make gold out of the earth with other elements intermingled, which skill cannot do. And so something is in potentiality for different things by relationship to different active things. And so nothing prevents a created nature from being in potentiality for some things to be done by divine power that a lower pwer cannot do, and we call this obediential power, insofar as every creature obeys its creator.

Article 2

Can We Call All the Things God Does without Natural Causes or Contrary to the Course of Nature Miracles?

We should say that we understand the word *miracle* from wonderment, and two things combine to occasion wonderment, as we can understand from the words of Aristotle in the beginning of the *Metaphysics*.[10] One thing is that the cause of what we wonder about is hidden. The second is that we perceive in the thing we wonder about something that makes that thing seem contrary to what it ought to be, as, for example, one could wonder if one were to see iron rising toward a magnet but not know the power of a magnet, since it seems that iron by its natural movement ought to tend downward.

This happens in two ways: in one way, in itself; in the other way, as regards us. It is in our regard when the cause of the effect we marvel at is hidden to this or that individual, not absolutely. Nor is there really in the thing we marvel at a disposition contrary to the effect we marvel at but only in the opinion of the one wondering. And so it happens that what is wonderful or astonishing to one is not to another, as, for example, one who knows the power of a magnet by learning or experience does not wonder about the aforementioned effect, but one ignorant of a magnet's power does.

As such, however, something is wonderful or astonishing whose cause is absolutely hidden, and when the disposition in the thing is contrary regarding the nature of an effect that is evident, and we can call these things not only actually or potentially wonderful but also miraculous, as things having in themselves the cause of astonishment. And the cause most hidden and most remote from our senses is the divine cause, which acts most secretly in natural things. And so we can properly say that the things that only divine power causes in things that have a natural order for the contrary effect, or the contrary way of causing, are miracles. But we can only call things caused by nature but hidden to all or even one of us, or things that God causes but are of such a nature as to be produced only by God, wonderful or marvelous, not that they are miracles.

And so Augustine posits in the definition of miracle[11] something that surpasses the order of nature in the words *above the capacity of nature*, corresponding to which is the word *difficult*. And he also posits something that surpasses our knowledge in the words *apparently beyond the expectation of the one wondering*, corresponding to which is the word *unusual*. For something comes more familiarly into our knowledge through usual occurrence.

Obj. 2. We cannot call what happens frequently unusual. But such divine actions outside natural causes were often accomplished in the time of the apostles. And so Acts 5:15 says that the sick were placed in the streets, etc. Therefore, such things were not unusual and so not miracles.

Reply Obj. 2. We should say that we call a miracle unusual because it is contrary to the usual course of nature, even if it were to be repeated daily, as the transubstantiation of bread into the body of Christ is repeated daily and does not cease to be a miracle. For one ought to call what happens generally in the whole order of the universe usual rather than what happens in only one thing.

Obj. 3. What nature can do is not above the capacity of nature. But sometimes God does outside natural causes things that nature could do, as is evident when the Lord cured Peter's mother-in-law of the fever that she suffered, as Lk. 4:38–39 says. Therefore, this was not above the capacity of nature and so not a miracle.

Reply Obj. 3. We should say that one usually makes a distinction about the things that God does miraculously. We say that some deeds are above nature, some contrary to nature, and some outside nature. They are above nature inasmuch as nature in no way has power for the effect that God causes. This happens in two ways. It happens in one way because nature altogether lacks the power to induce the form that God does, such as the form of glory, which God induces in the bodies of the elect, and the incarnation of the Word. Or it happens because, although nature can induce such a form into some matter, it cannot into this matter, as, for example, nature is able to cause life but not in this dead person.

We say that deeds are contrary to nature when a contrary disposition for the effect that God causes remains in nature, as when he preserved the children in the furnace without harm, with the power to burn remaining in the fire, and when the water of the Jordan stood still, with the force of gravity remaining in it, and when a virgin gave birth. We say that God does something outside nature when he produces an effect that nature can, but not in the way nature can. Or because the means whereby nature acts are lacking, as when Christ changed water into wine (Jn. 2:3–11), but which nature in a way can do when the water a vine takes in for nourishment is in season converted into the juice of a grape by a process of absorption. Or because there is a greater quantity in God's production than nature usually produces, as is evident about the frogs that were produced in Egypt, or regarding the time, as when one whom nature could cure over time and at a different time is cured immediately at the invocation of a saint. And thus it happens in the cited miracle about Peter's mother-in-law. And so all such things, if we should understand both their mode and effect, exceed the capacity of nature.

Obj. 9. God works miracles to confirm faith. But the incarnation of the Word is an object of faith, not to confirm faith as a proof. Therefore, it is not a miracle, and yet only God does this, with no other cause active. Therefore, not all the things that God does outside natural causes are miracles.

Reply Obj. 9. We should say that the incarnation of the Word is the miracle of miracles, as the saints say, since it is greater than all miracles, and all the other miracles are ordered to it. And so it leads to believing other things, and other miracles lead to believing it, since nothing prevents one miracle leading to belief in another, as the resurrection of Lazarus leads to believing in the future resurrection.

Article 3

Can Spiritual Creatures by Their Natural Power Cause Miracles?

We should say that, after Augustine in *Trinity* had diligently treated of this question, he concludes:[12] "It is altogether useful for me to remember my powers and admonish my brothers to remember theirs, lest human weakness go further than it is safe to go, since how the angels do this, or rather, how God does this by his angels, I am unable to penetrate with sharp eyes or to unravel with trust in reason or to understand by mature mind. And so I do not speak with great certainty to all the things that can be inquired about these things, as if I were an angel or prophet or apostle." And so also, using this moderation, we should proceed without apodictic assertion or prejudice to a better opinion, as much as reason and authority would be able to help.

Therefore, we should note that philosophers have disagreed about this question. For example, Avicenna held that the spiritual substance that moves the heavens causes effects in lower material substances both by means of heavenly motion and without any action of a material substance. He wants the material substance to obey the plan and the command of a spiritual substance far more than the contrary active things in nature or any active material substance. And he says that this cause produces changes in the air currents and the curing of the sick, which we call miracles. And he gives the example of the soul moving the body, as the soul's imagination without any other material active thing causes the body to become hot or cold, and sometimes feverish or leprous.

This position is sufficiently fitting for the principles supposed by it, since active natural things only dispose matter, but substantial forms are from a spiritual substance, which he calls the giver of forms. And so the matter from the natural order obeys the spiritual substance in order to receive the form from it, and so it is not strange if, even outside the order of material active things, the spiritual substance should imprint some forms in the matter. For, if matter obeys the separate substance in order to receive a substantial form, it will not be unfitting if matter should also obey it to receive dispositions for the form, since this evidently consists of less power.

But according to Aristotle and his followers, this cannot be sustained. He gives two arguments to prove that forms are not imprinted in matter by a separate substance, and that the action of a form existing in matter brings forms into actuality from the potentiality of matter. He proposes the first argument in the *Metaphysics*, which is that, as he proves there, what is in the proper sense produced is the composite, not the form or matter, since the composite has existing in the proper sense.[13] But every active thing produces something like itself. And so it is necessary that what causes natural things actually to exist by coming to be is a composite, not form without matter, that is, a separate substance.

The second proof is in the *Physics*.[14] Inasmuch as the same thing is by nature always disposed to produce the same thing, and what comes to be, passes away, or is changed, whether by increase or decrease, is not always disposed in the same way, what causes coming to be or movement regarding such movement is necessarily disposed in different ways, not always in the same way. But this cannot be a separate substance, since every such substance is unchangeable, as the *Physics* proves.[15] And so the immediate cause bringing form into actuality from potentiality by causing a coming to be or a change is a material substance disposed in different ways insofar as it accedes and recedes by locomotion.

And so a separate substance by its command directly causes locomotion in a material substance, and by means of it causes other movements whereby the moveable thing acquires a form. This happens reasonably, since locomotion is the first and most perfect movement, inasmuch as it changes a thing only regarding its external position, not its internal makeup. And so, by a material substance's first, namely, local, motion, a spiritual nature moves it. Therefore, a material creature accordingly obeys the command of a spiritual creature by the latter's natural relation to locomotion, not to the reception of any form, and we should understand this about a created spiritual nature, whose power and essence are limited by being a limited kind of thing, not about the uncreated spiritual substance, whose power is infinite, not limited to one kind of thing by the rule governing that kind of thing.

And faith agrees with this opinion in one respect, and so Augustine says that corporeal matter does not obey angels at their whim.[16] But the judgment of faith differs from the position of the philosophers in another respect, since the aforementioned philosophers held that separate substances move heavenly bodies at their command by locomotion, but a separate substance does not directly cause locomotion in lower things. Rather, other causes do so by nature, their will, or force.

And so also the commentator Alexander of Aphrodisias ascribed all the effects that we ascribe to angels or devils in lower things to the action of heavenly bodies. But this seems inadequately expressed, since such effects do not come to be in a fixed course, as those that come to be by the action of higher and lower material substances. Besides, there are some effects for which heavenly bodies in no way have power, as, for example, that rods are instantly changed into serpents, and such like.

But the judgment of faith is that both heavenly bodies by their command and other material substances cause locomotion, with God ordaining and permitting it. Therefore, they by their command cause the locomotion of material substances in which there is an active natural force to produce an effect, which forces Augustine calls seeds of nature.[17] And so their actions will be skillful, not miraculous, since a supernatural cause produces effects miraculously without natural actions. But it belongs to skill by means of the action of natural sources to produce an effect that nature either cannot produce or cannot produce so suitably. And so Aristotle says in the *Physics* that skill imitates nature and perfects certain things that nature cannot make, in some of which it also assists nature.[18] For example, a doctor helps nature in healing, by adding things that have a natural power to heal by processes of change and separation.

In producing such effects, the skill of a good or evil angel is more efficacious and causes better effects than human skill, and this for two reasons.

First, inasmuch as material effects in lower things especially depend on heavenly bodies, skill can chiefly obtain its effect when the power of a heavenly body cooperates with it. And so, in agricultural and medical activities, it avails to consider the movement and position of the sun, moon, and stars, whose powers, movements, and positions angels by their natural knowledge know with far greater certainty than human beings do. And so they can select better the time when the power of a heavenly body cooperates more to produce intended effects. This seems to be the reason that magicians in their invocations observe the positions of the stars.

Second, angels know the active and passive power in lower material substances better than human beings do, and angels, who by their command can cause the locomotion of material substances, can more easily and more quickly apply those powers to produce an effect. And so also doctors produce better effects in healing, since they know more about the powers of natural things.

There may be a third reason in that an instrument acts both in its own power and that of the cause of its movement. (And so also a heavenly body produces an effect by the power of the spiritual substance causing its movement. For example, it evidently causes life in the case of animals generated by putrefaction, and natural heat, as the instrument of the vegetative soul, acts to form flesh). Therefore, it is not unfitting to suppose that the natural material substances obtain a greater effect inasmuch as a spiritual substance moves them, and the words of Gen. 6:4 show this: "There were giants on the earth in those days, since, after the sons of God had intercourse with the daughters of human beings, and the women begot offspring, these are the mighty men of old, famous men." A gloss on the same text says that it is credible that some devils who had intercourse with women procreated such men, namely, giants.

Therefore, it is clear that good or evil angels cannot by their natural power work miracles, but they can produce certain marvelous effects, in which skill produces their action.

Obj. 2. The more actual something is, the more it is active, since each thing acts inasmuch as it is actual. But forms that are rational creatures are more actual than the forms in material creatures, inasmuch as the former are more immaterial. Therefore, the former are more active. But the forms in a material nature produce forms in nature like themselves. Therefore, far more can the forms in the mind of a spiritual creature. And so a rational creature could cause natural effects outside natural causes, and this is a miracle.

Reply Obj. 2. We should say that the forms of natural things existing in the angelic mind are more actual than the forms in matter. And so they are the immediate source of more perfect action, that is, understanding, but they are not the immediate source of the action that transforms matter. Rather, they are the source of such action by means of the will, and the will by means of the motive power, and that power immediately causes locomotion. And by means of that motion, it causes other movements and the introduction of a form in matter.

Obj. 4. You will say that the active forms in the intellect of an angel are applied to effects by means of a material active thing, as the forms of the human intellect are. On the contrary, every power that can go into action only by a material instrument is in vain given to something unless a bodily organ is given to it, since a power to cause movement would be given in vain to an animal unless means of movement were given to it. But a body is not by nature united to an angel. Therefore, its power does not require an active material thing to execute its work.

Reply Obj. 4. We should say that the power for which an organ corresponding to it can be used regarding every action ought to have a conjoined organ, as the power of sight has the eye. But no material substance equal to an angel's power could correspond in this way to the angel, and so an angel did not have a bodily organ conjoined to it by nature. And so also philosophers who held that separate substances have effect in the lower things only by means of the heavens held that a spiritual substance, which they called the soul of the heavens, is united to the heavens as its instrument. But they said that there is another intelligence not united to the heavens, which moves the soul of the heavens, as the object of desire moves one who desires.

Obj. 7. According to Augustine,[19] God governs all material substances by the rational spirit of life. And Gregory the Great says the same thing.[20] And so it seems that the motion of the heavens and all nature is by the angels, as the movement of a human body is by the soul. But the soul implants forms into the body outside the active natural powers of the body, since imagination alone heats and cools someone, and one sometimes incurs fever or even leprosy, as doctors say. Therefore, far more can some effects result in the lower things only by the conception of an angel moving the heavens without the action of natural causes. And so an angel can work a miracle.

Reply Obj. 7. We should say that the soul by the natural order moves the body locally at the soul's command, since the will commands movement, and the body obeys at the will's command, This is by the motive powers that are affixed to organs and flow from the soul into the body, to which the soul gives form. But other changes, such as heating, chilling, and the like, result from the soul by means of locomotion. It is also evident that there also results from the imagination the emotion that in some way changes the heartbeat and spirits, and these things, whether drawn to the heart or diffused in the members, effect an alteration in the body. And this can also cause sickness, especially if the matter is so disposed.

Obj. 13. A form in the imagination or the senses, insofar as it is more immaterial, is more excellent than a form in corporeal matter. But a spiritual creature can impress a form into a sense image or the senses, so that a thing seems otherwise than it is. And so Augustine says:[21] "Devils certainly do not create natures, but they change in appearance things that God truly created," and he later adds that they do this by altering the sense image. Therefore, much more can an angel impress a form into corporeal matter, and so angels can work miracles.

Reply Obj. 13. We should say that separate spiritual creatures can change a sense image by natural power, by stirring up the spirits and humors, not by inducing forms in the organ of imagination by command. For it is evident that, with a change in those things, fantasies appear, as in the case of the insane and those asleep. And we say that even some natural things have efficacy for this change in imagination, which magicians are said to use for deceptive visions.

Article 4

Can Good Angels and Human Beings Work Miracles by a Gift of Grace?

We should say that angels, above the natural power that they have, can do something by a gift of grace, inasmuch as they are ministers of divine power. And we can say that angels in working miracles can act in three ways. They can in one way by accomplishing it through prayers, and this way can be common to angels and human beings. The second way is insofar as angels dispose matter by their natural power to do something that becomes miraculous, as people say that they will in the resurrection collect the dust of the dead, whom divine power will bring back to life. But this proper way belongs to the angels, since human spirits, inasmuch as they are united to bodies, can act on external things only by means of the body, to which they are somehow by nature bound.

The third way is that they also do something in conjunction with God being the chief cause. Augustine leaves this way in doubt, saying this:[22] "Whether God in a wondrous way does this by himself, or through his ministers, or by the spirits of the martyrs, or by human beings still in the flesh, or all these things by angels whom he invisibly commands, or in other ways that human beings can in no way understand, these miracles attest to the faith that proclaims the resurrection of the flesh to eternity. The martyrs accomplish by their prayers, not by their works the things they are reputed to do."

But Gregory seems to decide this question, saying that holy human beings even living in the flesh work miracles both by their efficacious prayers and by their power, and so by their accompanying activity.[23] He proves this both by reason and by examples. First, by reason: if God has given to human beings the power to become his sons, it is not wondrous that they can by his power do wondrous things. And he gives examples. Peter caused the lying Ananias and Sapphira to die by his words of condemnation, as Acts 5:1–11 holds. Also, when blessed Benedict cast his eyes on the arms of a peasant in bonds, he closed his eyes to dissolve the thongs bound to the arms faster than any swift action by human beings could. And so Gregory concludes that the saints sometimes work miracles by prayer, and sometimes by their power.

We should consider how this can be. It is evident that God works miracles only at his bidding. And we see that the divine command extends to lower rational, namely, human, spirits by means of higher ones, namely, angels, as is evident in the promulgation of the Old Law. The divine command can by angelic and human spirits in this way extend to material creatures, so that the latter somehow present the divine command to nature, and human and angelic spirits somehow act as an instrument of divine power in order to work a miracle. This is not as if they can work a miracle by a power habitually in them, whether a gratuitous or natural power, since they could then work miracles whenever they wished. But Gregory asserts that this is not true and proves it by the example of Paul, who sought and did not obtain that a torment be removed from him (2 Cor. 12:9), and by the example of Benedict, whom the rain gained by his sister's prayers detained against his will.[24] Rather, we can understand the power in saints to cooperate with God in working miracles as like the imperfect forms called extensions, when the active source is present, as, for example, light in air, and movement in an instrument.

And we can understand such a power as the gift of a grace freely given, which is the grace of miraculous powers or healings. And so the grace given to produce things supernaturally is like the grace of prophecy given to know things supernaturally, whereby a prophet can prophesy only when the prophetic spirit touches his mind, not whenever he wishes to do so, as Gregory proves.[25] Nor is it strange if God in this way uses a spiritual creature as an instrument to cause miraculous effects in material nature, since he uses even a material creature for the sanctification of spirits, as is evident in the sacraments.

This makes clear the reply to objections that angels and human beings can work miracles. For it is true that only God works miracles by his authority. It is also true that he communicates the power to work miracles to a creature according to the capacity of the creature and the ordinance of his wisdom. Thus a creature works miracles ministerially by grace.

Article 5
Do Devils Also Act to Work Miracles?

We should say that, as good angels can by grace do something beyond their natural power, so evil angels can, by divine power restraining them, do less than they could by their natural power. For, as Augustine says,[26] as there are certain things that evil angels could do if they were permitted to do so, so they cannot do certain things because they are not permitted to do so. (And so we say that they are restrained in that they are prevented from doing things that their natural power could reach, and free when divine judgment allows them to do things that they can by their nature do.) But there are certain things that they cannot do even if they should be permitted to do so, as Augustine says in the same place, since the kind of nature bestowed on them by God does not permit it.

And God gives them no power to do such things above the capacity of their nature. For, inasmuch as miraculous activity is a divine witness indicative of divine power and truth, if a power to work miracles were to be given to devils, whose whole will is for evil, God would be a witness to their falsehood, which does not become his goodness. And so, when God allows them, they sometimes do only works that seem miraculous to human beings, and that their natural power reaches.

Just as what I said before (A. 4) makes clear, they can by their natural power produce by skill only those effects for which there are particular natural powers in material substances, which obey them regarding locomotion, so that they can quickly apply those substances for an effect. And such powers can cause real change of material substances, as we see according to the natural course of things that one thing produces another. But after causing a material change, they can cause some things that are not in the real world to appear in the imagination by disturbing the power of imagination regarding different spirits and humors. And some external substances also have the effect that, when they are employed in some way, something seems to be of a different form than the one it has, as is evident in the case of delirium and insanity.

Therefore, devils can act marvelously in us in two ways: in one way by the real change in a material substance; in the second way by a delusion of the senses from a change in imagination. But neither action is miraculous. Rather, it is by skill, as we have said before (A. 4). And so we say absolutely that devils cannot work miracles.

Obj. 2. Suddenly healing a sick person is a miracle, as we say that it was a miracle when Christ cured Peter's mother-in-law, as Lk. 4:38–40 relates. But devils can do this, since medicines administered to the sick facilitate health, and devils can by the agility of their nature use efficacious medicines, which they know well, to heal, and so, it seems, they can quickly heal. Therefore, they can work miracles suddenly.

Reply Obj. 2. We should say that nothing prevents the skill of devils being able to heal someone more quickly than nature can, if the healing should be left to it, since we see that the skill of a human being also accomplishes this. But it does not seem that they can suddenly heal, although they can work some effects as if suddenly, since medicines used on a human body work for health as a means, so to speak, and nature acts as the chief active thing. And so one ought to use things that nature can act on, and if too many were to be used, they would hinder rather than contribute to health. And so also the activity of devils cannot heal those sicknesses for the healing of which the power of nature in no way can. But it is otherwise in the case of those effects that depend on an external active thing as the chief cause. We should note that, even if devils were to effect health suddenly, it would not be a miracle, since they would do it by means of natural power, if they were to do it.

Obj. 5. We read in the stories that Augustine relates that a vestal virgin carried water from the Tiber in a leaky jar as proof of her chastity, and yet the water did not pour out.[27] This could happen only because no natural power kept the water from flowing out, and there was evidently a miracle when the Jordan was parted, and its waters stood still. Therefore, devils can work miracles.

Reply Obj. 5. We should say that, to commend her chastity, the true God probably worked such a miracle of retaining the water through good angels, since, if they did certain good things in the case of the pagans, the deeds were done by God. But if devils did it, this is not contrary to the foregoing. For being at rest and being moved locally are by genus from the same source, since the nature that moves something to a place brings it to rest in a place. And so, as devils can move material substances locally, so they can also keep them from moving. But this is not a miracle, as when God does it, since it happens by the natural power of a devil for such a determined effect.

Obj. 8. It was a miracle that Moses changed his rod into a serpent. But the Pharaoh's magicians likewise did this by the power of devils, as Ex. 7:8–13 relates. Therefore, it seems that devils can work miracles.

Reply Obj. 8. We should say a gloss touches on two opinions about the actions of the Pharaoh's magicians. One is that there was not a real turning of rods into serpents. Rather, only a conjuring illusion made this seem so. But Augustine in the same gloss says that there was a real turning of rods into serpents, and he gives a likely proof of this in that Scripture uses the same word *rod* for the rods of the magicians and the rod of Moses, which was evidently turned into a serpent. But that the actions of the devils turned rods into serpents was not a miracle, since the devils did this by means of collected snake semen that had the power to decompose the rods and turn them into serpents. On the other hand, what Moses did was a miracle, since he did this by divine power without the action of any natural power.

Counterobj. At the time of the Antichrist, the devil will have the greatest power to act, since, as Rev. 20:3 says, it will be necessary that he be free for a little time, and we understand this as that of the Antichrist. But true miracles will not be performed, and this is evident because 2 Thess. 2:9 says that the coming of the Antichrist will be "in every power and signs and deceitful prodigies." Therefore, devils cannot work true miracles.

Reply Counterobj. We should say to the contrary that, in the time of the Antichrist, the power of the devil is loosed inasmuch as many things are permitted to him that are not now permitted. And so also he will do many things to seduce those who by not acquiescing to the truth deserved to be seduced. And he will do some things by trickery, in which things there will be neither a real effect nor a miracle. He will also so some things by a real transformation of material substances but not a real miracle, since natural causes will accomplish them. And we call them lies regarding the intention of the perpetrator, who by such wondrous works induces human beings to believe lies.

Article 6

Do Angels and Devils Have Bodies by Nature United to Them?

We should say that the ancients proceeded in different ways regarding consideration of immaterial substances.

Some ancient philosophers said that there is no immaterial substance, and that all substances are material, and Augustine confesses that he was once in that error.[28] But philosophers have refuted this position, and Aristotle refuted it as follows.[29] There needs to be an infinite power causing motion; otherwise, it could not cause perpetual motion. Also, he shows that every quantified power is limited. And so he concludes that there needs to be a completely immaterial power that causes continual motion.

And he proved this in another way,[30] since actuality is prior to potentiality, both naturally and temporally, absolutely speaking, although, in a particular thing that goes from potentiality to actuality, potentiality temporally precedes actuality. But because an actual being needs to bring it into actuality, actuality is necessarily absolutely prior to potentiality even temporally. And so, since every material substance is potential, which its changeability shows, there needs to be an everlasting unchangeable substance prior to all material substances.

We can understand a third argument regarding this from the opinions of the Platonists, that something unshared needs to exist before finite and shared existing, as, for example, if the nature of fire is in a particular way in iron, the nature of fire needs to be first in what is fire essentially. And so, since existing and other forms and perfections are in material substances in a particular way, as it were, inasmuch as the forms and perfections have been received in matter, an immaterial substance, which has in itself perfect existing in complete fullness, not in a particular way, necessarily preexists. But they were misled in holding that only material things are substances, since they, unable intellectually to transcend their imagination, which deals only with material substances, could not attain knowledge of immaterial substances, which only the intellect can grasp.

Others considered an immaterial substance, but they said that it was joined to a body, and that there is no immaterial substance that is not the form of a body. And so they held that God himself is the soul of the world, as Augustine in *City of God* says about Varro that God is the soul governing the world by movement and reason.[31] And so Varro said that the whole world is God because of its soul, not its body, just as we call a human being wise because of the human being's soul, not because of the human being's body. And the pagans for this reason worshipped the whole world and all of its parts.

But philosophers themselves refuted this position in many ways. First, a power united to a body as its form has limited action because it is united to such a body. And so, since there needs to be a universal active thing exercising causality on all material substances, inasmuch as the first cause of motion cannot be a material substance, as I have shown, we conclude that there needs to be an immaterial thing that is not united to any body. And so Anaxagoras posited a pure intellect to command, as the *Physics* says,[32] since command belongs to something surpassing the things that it commands and not subject or tied to them.

Second, if any immaterial substance is united to a body as its form, it is necessarily the first thing that is moved, moving itself in the way of an animal, as if composed of a material and spiritual substance. But moving itself, it does so by the will, inasmuch as it seeks something, since the will is a moved cause of motion, and the will's object an unmoved cause of motion. Therefore, there needs to be above an immaterial substance joined to a body something that moves it, as a desirable object moves an appetite, and this needs to be an intellectual good, since this is desirable because it is absolutely good, while a sensible object of desire is sought because it is a particular good here and now.

An intellectual good is necessarily immaterial, since it would not be an object of understanding unless it were to exist without matter, and for that reason it itself understands, since any substance understands because it is free of matter. Therefore, above the substance joined to a body, there needs to be another, higher immaterial or intellectual substance not united to a body. And Aristotle in the *Metaphysics* proves this as follows.[33] One cannot say that something moving itself desires nothing outside of itself, since it would then never be moved. For movement is in order to acquire something in some way.

Third, inasmuch as something moving itself can be moved or not be moved, as the *Physics* says,[34] if something moved by itself is continually moved, an altogether immobile external thing needs to establish it in its movement. But we see the heavens, whose soul they call God, in continual motion. And so the substance that is the soul of the world, if there is any, needs to be another, higher substance not joined to any body but subsisting by itself.

Those who held that every substance is united to matter seem to have been deceived by their belief that matter causes subsistence and individuation in all beings, as it does in material things. And so they believed that immaterial substances cannot subsist except in a body, just as the *Commentary on the Liber de causis* touches on this by way of objection.

With these opinions rejected, Plato and Aristotle held that some substances are immaterial, and some of these are joined to a body, but some not joined to any body. For Plato held that there were two separate substances, namely, God, the father of the whole universe in the highest rank, and then God's mind, which Plato called the paternal intelligence, in which were the exemplars or ideas of all things, as Macrobius relates.[35] And he posited many immaterial substances united to bodies, some to heavenly bodies, which substances the Platonists called gods, and some joined to airy bodies, which substances they called demons. And so Augustine in *City of God* introduced this definition of demons given by Apuleius:[36] "Demons are animals rational in mind, passive in spirit, airy in body, and eternal in time." And the pagan Platonists said that one should religiously reverence all the aforementioned immaterial substances on account of their perpetual existence. They also further held that immaterial substances were united to grosser earthly bodies, namely, those on the earth and those in the seas, and these immaterial substances are the souls of human beings and other animals.

Aristotle agrees with Plato regarding two things and disagrees with him regarding two things. He agrees in positing a supreme substance neither material nor united to a body and in positing that heavenly bodies are animate. But he differs in positing several immaterial substances not united to a body, namely, those corresponding to the number of heavenly motions, and in denying that any airy animals exist, which he very plausibly denied.

The latter is evident from three things. First, a mixed material substance is more excellent than an elementary material substance and especially regarding form, since elements are the matter of mixed material substances. And so it is necessary that immaterial substances, which are the most excellent forms, be united to mixed bodies, not to pure elements. And there can be no mixed body in which earth and water do not more abound quantitatively. For even higher elements have more active power, since they have more form, and if these were to exceed quantitatively, a due proportion in the mixture would not be observed, since the higher elements would subdue the lower. And so immaterial substances cannot be united to airy bodies as their forms but are united to mixed bodies, in which earth and water are more abundant.

Second, a homogeneous and uniform body needs to have the same form in the whole and the parts. But we see that the entire mass of air belongs to one and the same nature. And so particular spiritual substances, if they have been united to particular airy parts, are also necessarily united to the whole air, and so the whole air will be an animal, which seems absurd to say. But some ancients, saying that the whole air is replete with gods, held even this, as the *De anima* says.[37]

Third, if a spiritual substance does not have in itself another power than the intellect and the will, it is united to a body in vain, since those activities are fulfilled apart from a body. For every form of a body causes some action with the body. But if spiritual substances have other powers, which the Platonists seem to have perceived about demons, saying that they are spiritually passive, and since emotion is only in the sensory part of the soul, as the *Physics*[38] proves, such substances need to be united to organic bodies, so that determined organs perform the actions of such powers. But an airy body cannot be such, since it is incapable of shape. And so spiritual substances evidently cannot be united by nature to airy bodies.

Augustine leaves in doubt whether some immaterial substances have been united to heavenly bodies,[39] although Jerome[40] and Origen[41] seem to assert it. Several modern authorities, however, seem to reject it because, inasmuch as the number of the blessed according to divine Scripture is constituted only from human beings and angels, those spiritual substances cannot be numbered with the souls of human beings, or with the angels, who are immaterial.

On the other hand, Augustine also leaves this in doubt, saying:[42] "It is not certain whether the sun, moon, and all the stars belong to the same group, namely, the angels, although they seem to some to be brilliant bodies without senses or intelligence. But the teaching of faith differs most certainly from the teaching of both Plato and Aristotle in that we posit many more substances completely apart from bodies than either of them does."

The negative position would seem more reasonable, for three reasons. First, as the bodies above are more worthy than the bodies here below, so also immaterial substances are more worthy than material substances. And the upper bodies surpass the lower bodies insofar as we relate the earth to the heavens like a point to a sphere, as the astronomers prove. And so also, as Dionysius says,[43] immaterial substances transcend the whole collectivity of material species, which Dan. 7:10 signifies by saying: "Thousands of thousands ministered to him, and 10,000 by 100,000 assisted him." This accords with the abundance of divine goodness, namely, that it more copiously produces more excellent things into existence. And since higher things do not depend on lower things, and the higher things' powers are not limited to the lower things, we need not posit in the higher things only things that lower effects manifest.

Second, there are in the order of natural things many ranks in between natures remote from one another (e.g., imperfect animals, which share with plants in having fixed places and share with animals in having sense perception, in between animals and plants). Therefore, since the supreme substance (i.e., God) is the most remote from the nature of material substances, it seems probable that there are many grades of natures in between, and not only the substances that are the sources of movements.

Third, God has both universal providence about material things and a providence reaching individual things, in which he sometimes acts outside the order of universal causes, as I have said (A. 1). Therefore, we need to posit immaterial substances serving God both in the universal causes of nature, which are the heavenly movements, and in other things that God does particularly in individual things, especially regarding human beings, whose minds are not subject to heavenly movements. Therefore, by following the true faith, we say that angels and devils do not have bodies united to them by nature but are completely immaterial, as Dionysius says.

Obj. 4. Angels are either composed of matter and form, or they are not. If they are, they need to be material substances. For, inasmuch as matter as such is one, since only forms differentiate it, we need to understand different forms of all the different things having matter, forms received in different parts of matter, since matter cannot receive different forms by the same thing. But we cannot understand different parts in matter without its division, since a substance without quantity is indivisible, as the *Physics* says.[44] Therefore, all things having matter necessarily have dimension and so matter. But if angels are not composed of matter and form, either the forms are intrinsically subsistent, or the forms are united to bodies. If the forms are intrinsically subsistent, they necessarily do not have existing caused by another. For, inasmuch as a form as such is the source of existing, what is only a form causes existing for other things and does not have caused existing. But if the forms have been united to bodies, they necessarily have bodies united to them by nature, since the union of form and matter is natural. Therefore, we conclude that we need to posit one of the following three things, namely, that angels are material substances, or that they are uncreated substances, or that they have bodies naturally united to them. But the first two are impossible. Therefore, we should hold the third.

Reply Obj. 4. We should say that, if one should consider angels composed of matter and form, they by the aforementioned argument are necessarily on that account corporeal only if one supposes that the matter of angels and that of material substances are the same. One could say that the relation to forms of different kinds of things, not dimensional division, would divide the different matter of material substances, since potentiality is proportioned to actuality. Rather, we believe that angels are only intrinsically subsistent forms, not composed of matter and form. Nor is it necessary that angels are on this account not created, since form is the source of existing, as that by which something exists, although both the existing of form and that of matter in a composite is from an active thing. Therefore, if there should be a created substance that is only a form, it can have an efficient, not a formal, cause of existing.

Obj. 8. What is alive and vivifies has life more excellently than what only lives, as light is more perfectly in what shines and illumines than in what only shines. But the human soul lives and vivifies the body united to it by nature. Therefore, an angel lives no less excellently than the soul.

Reply Obj. 8. We should say that a soul united to a body vivifies the body both effectively and formally. And so vivifying the body is less than only intrinsically being alive, absolutely speaking. For a soul can thus vivify the body, inasmuch as it has the lowest existing, one that can be common to the soul and the body in a composite of both. But since the existing of an angel is higher, it cannot be communicated to a body in this way. And so an angel only lives and does not formally vivify.

Obj. 9. Every movement of a material substance moved in different ways is the movement of something that moves itself, since something moved in only one way does not seem to be moving itself, as the *Physics* says.[45] But a heavenly body is moved in different ways. And so astronomers say that planets sometimes go forward, sometime backward, and sometimes are stationary. Therefore, the movement of higher material substances belongs to mobile things moving themselves, and so these substances are composed of material and spiritual substance. But that spiritual substance is neither a human soul nor God. Therefore, it is an angel. Therefore, an angel has a body united to it by nature.

Reply Obj. 9. We should say that the going forward and backward and the standing still seen in the planets does not come from the irregularity of the motion of one and the same mobile thing. Rather, it comes from the different movements of mobile things, whether by positing eccentrics and epicycles according to Ptolemy or by positing different movements by the poles, as others hold. And yet, even if the heavenly bodies were to be moved irregularly, this would not show that a conjoined rather than a separate voluntary cause moved them.

Obj. 13. A heavenly body is more excellent than a human body, as something everlasting to something destructible. But the human body is by nature united to a spiritual substance. Therefore, much more is a heavenly body, since there is a more excellent form of a more excellent material substance. And so a heavenly body is by nature united to an angel.

Reply Obj. 13. We should say that the human body as to its matter is less excellent than a heavenly body, but the human body has a more excellent form if the heavenly bodies are inanimate. But I call the form more excellent as such, not insofar as it gives form to the body. For the form of the heavens perfects matter, to which it gives indestructible existing, in a more perfectible way than the rational soul perfects the body. This is so because the spiritual substance that moves the heavens has a higher dignity than being united to a body.

Article 7

Can Angels or Devils Assume Bodies?

We should say that some of those who believe in sacred Scripture, in which one reads of the apparitions of angels, said that angels never assume bodies, as is clear about Rabbi Moses, who holds this opinion. And so he says that all the things that we read in sacred Scripture about apparitions of angels happen in the vision of prophecy, namely, in imaginary vision, sometimes when awake and sometimes when asleep,

This position does not preserve the truth of Scripture, since the very way that Scripture uses gives us to understand that one thing is signified as a fact and another thing as in the way of prophetic vision. For, when we ought to understand an apparition in the way of prophetic vision, Scripture proposes particular words belonging to the vision. For example, Ez. 8:3 says: "The spirit raised me in between heaven and earth and brought me to Jerusalem in the visions of the Lord." And so we clearly ought to understand absolutely as fact things said absolutely to happen, and we so read about many apparitions in the Old Testament.

And so we should absolutely admit that angels sometimes assume a body by forming a sensibly perceptible body or one subject to corporeal vision, just as they sometimes appear in imaginary vision by forming particular images. This is fitting for three reasons. First and chiefly, all these apparitions of the Old Testament are ordered to the apparition in which the Son of God appeared visible to the world, as Augustine says.[46] And so, since the Son of God assumed a real body, not an imaginary one, as the Manicheans said, it was fitting that angels by also assuming real bodies appeared to human beings.

We can take the second reason from the word of Dionysius in a letter that he wrote to Titus. He says that divine things in divine Scripture are transmitted to us under sensibly perceptible things, among other reasons, in order that sharing in divine things perfects the whole human being, as much as possible, both by the intellect grasping the intelligible truth and in sensibly perceptible nature through sensibly perceptible forms that are as if particular images of divine things. And so, likewise, since the angels appear to human beings in order to perfect them, it is fitting that they both enlighten the intellect by intellectual vision and provide for the imagination and the external senses by imaginary vision, namely, of the bodies assumed. And so also Augustine attributes this triple vision to the apparitions.[47]

There can be a third reason in that, although the angels are superior to us, we by grace obtain equality and association with them, as Mt. 22:30 says: "They will be like the angels in heaven." And so, in order to show their friendship and kinship with us, they are conformed to us in their own way by assuming bodies, so that they, by assuming what is proper to us, cause our intellect to rise to what is proper to them, just as the Son of God, when he descends to us, raises us to things that are proper to him. But devils, when they transfigure themselves into angels of light, endeavor to do for deception what good angels do for our profit.

Obj. 3. God in the Old Testament appeared to the patriarchs, just as we read that angels appeared, as Augustine shows.[48] But we should say that God assumed a body only by the mystery of the incarnation. Therefore, angels do not assume a body when they appear.

Reply Obj. 3. We should say, as Augustine says,[49] that the ministry of the angels, who form certain appearances, whether imaginary or material, that lead the mind of the beholder to God, made all the apparitions of God that we read about in the Old Testament. Just so, sensibly perceptible shapes can lead a human being to God. Therefore, angels assumed apparent bodies in the aforementioned apparitions, but we say that God appeared in them because he himself was the end for which the angels, by representing such bodies, strove to raise the mind of a human being. And so Scripture in these apparitions sometimes calls to mind that God has appeared, and sometimes that an angel has.

Obj. 4. As it is proper for a soul to be united by nature to a body, so it is improper for an angel to be by nature united to one. But the soul cannot be separated from the body when it wishes. Therefore, neither can an angel assume a body.

Reply Obj. 4. We should say that no thing has power over its own existing, since every power of a thing flows from its essence or presupposes its essence. And because the soul by its existing is united to the body as the body's form, it is not in its power to free itself from union to the body. Likewise, it is not in the power of an angel to unite itself to a body by being a body's form, but an angel can assume a body in the aforementioned way, to which the angel is united as cause of the body's motion, and as something configured to a shape.

Obj. 9. If angels assume a body, the bodies assumed by them either have or do not have the real forms that we see. If they have real forms, then, since they are sometimes seen in the form of a human being, the body assumed by them will be a real human body, which is impossible unless one says that an angel assumes a human being, which seems improper. And if there are no real forms, this also seems improper, since a fiction is not fitting for messengers of truth. Therefore, an angel in no way assumes a body.

Reply Obj. 9. We should say that the bodies that angels assume have real forms that the senses can perceive, forms that are intrinsically sensibly perceptible, such as color and shape, but not regarding the specific nature, which is incidentally sensibly perceptible. Nor is it thereby necessary that there be any fiction in it, since angels do not present themselves to human eyes in order that they be believed to be human beings, but in order that angelic virtues be recognized through human properties. Just so, metaphorical expressions, in which the likenesses of some things signify other things, are not false.

Obj. 14. A gloss on Ps. 11:4 ("The Lord in his holy temple") says that, although devils preside externally over idols, they cannot be in them, nor, by like argument, in other material substances. But if devils assume bodies, they are necessarily in the bodies assumed. Therefore, we should not say that they assume bodies.

Reply Obj. 14. We should say that we can understand being in a body in two ways. We can understand it in one way as within its quantitative dimensions, and then nothing prevents a devil from being in a body. We can understand it in another way as within the essence of a thing as giving the existing of the thing and acting in it. The latter is proper only to God, although God is not part of the essence of anything. But we can also understand in the gloss that a devil cannot be in an idol in the way in which idolaters think, namely, that the idol and the inhabiting spirit constitute one thing.

Article 8

Can an Angel or Devil with an Assumed Body Perform the Actions of a Living Body?

We should say that an action seems to receive its specific nature from two things, namely, its efficient cause and its terminus. For example, heating differs from cooling in that the former proceeds from heat and to heat, and the latter from cold and to cold. But, properly speaking, action, just like motion, has its species from its terminus and has its beginning, properly speaking, from what is natural, since we call motion and actions from an internal source natural.

Therefore, we should consider that, in actions of the soul, some both proceed from the soul as their source and terminate in the soul and the animated body. We cannot attribute such actions to angels in assumed bodies, neither by reason of specific likeness nor by reason of the naturalness of an action such as sensing, growing, nourishing, and the like. For the senses proceed by movement from things to the soul. Similarly, nourishment and growth proceed by something being produced and added to a living body.

And some actions belong to the soul that proceed from the soul as their source but terminate in an external effect, and if only bodily division or locomotion should be able to produce such an effect, we attribute such an action to an angel by means of an assumed body as to a specific likeness in the effect, but, although it will be like natural action, it will not really be such. For example, this is evident in speech, which movements of the vocal organs and air form, and in eating, which division of food and its transmission into internal parts perform.

And so the speech attributed to angels in assumed bodies is not real speech but a certain resemblance by the likeness of effect, and we should say likewise about eating. And so also the angel says in Tob. 12:18: "When I was with you, I seemed to eat and drink with you, but I ate invisible food and drank invisible drink." But if such an effect requires a change of form, an angel could not do this, except, perhaps, by means of a natural act, as is evident regarding generation.

Obj. 5. The ultimate action of the vegetative soul in one and the same individual is reproduction, since an animal is nourished and grows before it generates. But one cannot say that an angel or the body assumed by it is nourished or is moved by growth. Therefore, an assumed body cannot generate.

Reply Obj. 5. We should say that we never attribute generation to good angels, but there are two opinions about devils. Some say that devils in assumed bodies also can in no way generate, for the reasons cited in the objection. But it seems to some that they can generate, not by semen emitted by an assumed body or by the power of its nature, but by the semen of a human being used to generate, since one and the same devil is a female form to a man and pours the semen received from him into a woman with whom he lies. And this can be reasonably supported, since devils cause other natural things by using the particular semen, as Augustine says.[50]

Obj. 7. Accordingly, such semen would generate a human being only by the power of human semen. Therefore, those said to be generated by devils would not be taller or stronger than others that human semen generally generates, although Gen. 6:4 says that "when the sons of God had sexual intercourse with the daughters of human beings, and the daughters generated, giants, the mighty of old and the famous, were born."

Reply Obj. 7. We should say that the power of human semen undoubtedly causes the generation accomplished in the aforementioned way. And so the human being thus begotten would not be the son of a devil but of the man to whom the semen belonged. But it is possible that stronger and taller human beings would be generated in this way, since devils, wishing to appear wonderful in their effects, can by observing the fixed positions of the stars and the disposition of a man and a woman act to produce this. And they can especially do this if the semen that they use as means should acquire an increase of power by such use.

Obj. 8. Eating is ordered to nourishment. Therefore, if angels in assumed bodies are not nourished, it seems that neither do they eat.

Reply Obj. 8. We should say that one ascribes eating to angels in assumed bodies absolutely, regarding the act of eating, not regarding its purpose (i.e., nutrition). Likewise, one ascribes eating to Christ after the resurrection, to whose body nothing was then added. But there is a difference in that Christ's eating was truly natural, like his existing that had a vegetative soul, and so there could really be natural growth. But in neither case, was the food converted into flesh and blood. Rather it was dissolved into adjacent matter.

Article 9

Should We Attribute Miraculous Activity to Faith?

We should say that, according to Gregory in his *Dialogues*,[51] holy human beings cause miracles in two ways, namely, obtaining them by praying that God cause them and by the saints' power. Faith renders a human being suitable to work miracles in both ways, since faith appropriately merits that one's petition with respect to working miracles be heard.

Reason can show this, since we see in natural things that all particular causes get their efficacy in acting from a universal cause, but we attribute a determined and particular effect to a particular cause, as is evident regarding the active powers of lower material substances in relation to the power of a heavenly body and regarding the lower orders. (Although the latter follow the movement of the first sphere, each has its own movements.) Just so, this is the case regarding the virtues whereby we merit, since all of them have their efficacy in meriting from charity, which unites us to God, from whom we merit, and perfects the will whereby we merit, but individual virtues merit particular individual rewards corresponding proportionately to them. For example, humility merits elevation, and poverty the kingdom.

And so sometimes, when charity ceases, by reason of acts of other virtues, a divine generosity grants some congruous rewards for such acts, at least in this world, although one does not merit anything condignly. And so theologians say that some sometimes congruously merit an increase of temporal goods by things as such good done without the presence of charity.

Faith merits miraculous actions in this way, although the foundation of meriting is from charity. We can attribute three reasons for this. First, miracles are proofs of faith, since deeds surpassing nature prove the truth of things that transcend natural reason. And so Mk. 16:20 says: "They went forth and preached everywhere, with God working with them and confirming their words with the signs that followed." The second reason is that faith relies most on divine power, which serves as the reason and means for assenting to things that seem to be above reason, and so the divine power in miraculous actions is especially helpful for faith. The third reason is that miracles happen outside natural causes, and faith takes proof from divine things, not from natural and sensibly perceptible things.

And so, as poverty of temporal things merits spiritual riches, and humility merits heavenly dignity, so faith, as if contemning things that happen naturally, in some way merits miraculous actions, which happen outside natural power.

Likewise, faith especially disposes a human being to work miracles by power, and three reasons make this evident. First, as I have said before (A. 4), saints are reported to work miracles by power as instruments of God, not as if the chief authors of the miracles, manifesting in a way God's command, which nature obeys in miracles, to natural thiugs themselves. And it is by faith, which is a sharing of divine truth in us, that God's words dwell in us. And so faith disposes a human being to work miracles.

Second, the saints, who by their power work miracles, act in virtue of God acting in nature, since God's action is related to the whole of nature as the soul's action is to the body. And the soul alters the body besides the order of natural sources especially by a fixed imagination, whereby concupiscence or anger heats the body, or even becomes feverish or leprous. Therefore, the fact that one gives to one's apprehension a fixed point and firmness makes a human being disposed to work miracles. This is evident because Mt. 26:21 says: "If you have faith and do not hesitate, you will not only do this about a fig tree, but even if you say to this mountain, 'Take off and cast yourself in the sea,' it will be done." And Jas. 1:8 says: "Ask in faith, never hesitating."

Third, since one works miracles by power by way of a command, what renders one fit to command makes one fit to work miracles by power. This is by a separation and withdrawal from the things to which one ought to give commands. And so also Anaxagoras says that the intellect was unmixed with the body in order to command it. And faith draws the spirit away from natural and sensibly perceptible things and founds it on intelligible things. And so faith renders a human being fit to work miracles by power.

And so also the virtues that draw the spirit of a human being away from the most material things (e.g., continence and abstinence, which draw one away from choices that immerse one in sensibly perceptible things) especially assist in working miracles. But other virtues, which direct human beings in arranging temporal things, do not dispose them to work miracles.

Obj. 3. Charity is the source and root of meriting, without which unformed faith cannot merit. Therefore, if we attribute the action of miracles to faith because of merit, we should rather attribute the action to charity.

Reply Obj. 3. We should say that charity, since it is a greater virtue than faith, bestows the efficacy of meriting on faith itself. But faith is better suited particularly to merit miraculous works. For faith is a perfection of the intellect, whose activity consists of understood things being in some way in it, but charity is a perfection of the will, whose activity consists of the will tending toward the thing itself. And so charity puts a human being in God and makes one united with him, but faith puts divine things themselves in us. And so Hebr. 11:1 says that faith is "the substance of things to be hoped for." Besides, miracles are worked to confirm faith, not charity.

Obj. 5. Jn. 9:31 says: "We know that God does not hear sinners." But only charity takes away sins, since, as Prov. 10:12 says, "Charity covers all sins." Therefore, we ought to attribute the action of miracles to charity.

Reply Obj. 5. We should say that, as a gloss on the gospel says,[52] the words are those of a blind man, whom wisdom has not fully enlightened. And so it contains a false opinion, since God sometimes hears sinners out of his generosity, although not because of their merits. And so their petition succeeds by entreaty, although it is not meritorious. Just so, the petition of a just person is sometimes meritorious but does not obtain the request, since obtaining a request relates to the object requested and depends only on a favor, but merit relates to the faith whereby one merits and depends on justice.

Obj. 8. The intellect is the source of action only by means of the will. But faith is in the intellect, and charity in the will. Therefore, faith acts only through charity, as Gal. 5:5 says: "The faith that acts through love." Therefore, as we ascribe the activity of virtuous acts to charity rather than faith, so also we ascribe miraculous works to charity.

Reply Obj. 8. We should say that the objection proves that faith merits through charity, and we have conceded this before (Reply Obj. 3). Moreover, the objection holds regarding those things that one does by one's own power, things in which the intellect directs the will, which commands the power of execution. But regarding things in which God is the power of execution, only faith, which relies on divine power, suffices for action.

Obj. 10. It was miraculous that Sarah, old and barren, conceived a miraculous son. This was ascribed to hope, as Rom. 4:18 says: "Who believed against hope in hope." Therefore, we should ascribe the working of miracles to hope, not faith.

Reply Obj. 10. We should say that we do not properly ascribe the working of miracles to hope, since hope is ordered to obtaining something, and so concerns only eternal things. But faith concerns eternal and temporal things, and so can reach to things to be done. And for this reason, the authority cited, "who believed in hope," chiefly mentions hope rather than faith.

Article 10

Do Certain Sensibly Perceptible and Material Things, Deeds, or Words Force Devils to Work the Miracles that Magical Skills Seem to Cause?

We should say that there were many opinions about the effects of magical skills. Some, like Alexander of Aphrodisias, said that some powers and forces in lower things produced by the powers of lower material substances in conjunction with observance of heavenly movements cause the effect of magical skills. And so Augustine says that it seems to Porphyry that human beings, by plants, stones, and living things, by certain definite sounds and voices, by certain shapes and contrivances, and by things observed in the movements in the revolving heavens, fabricate on earth powers suitable for causing various effects of the stars.[53]

But this position seems inadequate, since, although the powers of higher and lower material substances can suffice for some things seemingly caused by magical skills (e.g., some changes in material substances), magical skills do other things to which material power cannot extend. It is evident that speech is only from an intellect, and magical skills cause some responses to be heard. And so it is also necessary that an intellect do this, especially since such responses teach a human being about certain occult things.

Nor can one say that only a change in imagination by magic does this, since then not all of those standing by would hear the voices, nor could those awake and having alert senses hear the voices.

And so we conclude that either the power of the soul of a human being using magical skills, or something external having an intellect does this.

It cannot be the former, and this is evident from two things. First, the soul of a human being by its own power can come to knowledge of unknown things only by some things known to it, and so the will of a human being cannot cause revelation of the occult things that magical skills cause, since the principles of reason do not suffice to cause occult things. Second, if the soul of a magician were by its own power to cause such effects, it would need to use invocations or some such external things.

It is evident that some external spirits, but not upright and good ones, cause such effects of magical skills, and this for two reasons. First, good spirits do not exhibit association with wicked human beings, such as most of those performing magical skills do. Second, they do not assist human beings in doing unlawful things, which is usually the result of magical skills. Therefore, we conclude that the evil spirits whom we call devils do this.

We can understand that devils are compelled in two ways: in one way, by a higher power, which induces the necessity for them to act; in the second way, by enticement, as we say that human beings are enticed to something to which desire entices them. In neither way can material things compel devils, properly speaking, unless one supposes them to have airy bodies by nature united to them and so sense desires like other animals, just as Apuleius held that demons are animals with an airy body and a passive soul.[54] For then they can be compelled in both ways, by bodily power and the power of heavenly bodies, by the imprints of which they would be induced to particular emotions, and also by lower material substances in which they would take pleasure. Just so, Apuleius says:[55] "they take pleasure in the smoke of sacrifices and such like." But I have shown the falsehood of this opinion in the preceding articles.

We conclude, therefore, that devils, whose magical skills produce effects, are both compelled and enticed. Something higher, sometimes God himself and sometimes saints, angels, and human beings by his power, compels them. For theologians say that it belongs to the angelic order of Powers to restrain devils, and as holy human beings share in the gift of powers insomuch as they work miracles, so they share in the gift of the Powers insomuch as they cast out devils. Higher devils themselves sometimes compel them, which compulsion alone magical skills can cause.

They are also compelled as if enticed by magical skills, not by material things because of themselves, but because of something else. First, they know by such material things how to be able to cause the effect for which they are invoked, and they desire this, namely, that people consider their power marvelous. And so, when invoked under a definite constellation, they arrive more at the desired effect.

Second, such material things are signs of some spiritual things in which they take pleasure. And so Augustine says that these things entice devils as spirits by signs, so to speak, not like animals by food.[56] For, inasmuch as human beings offer sacrifice and prostrate themselves as a sign of subjection to God, they rejoice that such signs of reverence are shown to them. And different signs entice different devils insofar as the signs befit their diverse vices.

Third, these material things entice them inasmuch as the things lead human beings into sin, and so lies and things that can induce human beings to error and sin entice them.

Obj. 2. Whoever does something contrary to one's will is in some way compelled. But devils, invoked by magicians, sometimes do something contrary to their will. For a devil's will is always to lead human beings into sin, but a human being incited to base love by magical art is freed from the violence of the incitement by the same art. Therefore, magicians compel devils.

Reply Obj. 2. We should say that it is satisfactory to a devil if he, by preventing some evil and promoting some good, more easily draws human beings into familiar converse with him and admiration. For they even transform themselves into angels of light, as 2 Cor. 11:14 says.

Obj. 3. We read about Solomon that he performed some exorcisms that compelled devils to leave possessed bodies. Therefore, solemn oaths can compel devils.

Reply Obj. 3. We should say that, if Solomon performed his exorcisms when he was in the state of grace, there could be in these exorcisms the power to compel devils by divine power. But if he performed them at a time when he worshiped idols, so that we understand that he performed them by magical arts, they had power only to compel devils in the aforementioned way.

Obj. 5. Devils endeavor to turn human beings from God. But when invoked by things that reflect reverence of God (e.g., invocation of the divine majesty), the devils become present. Therefore, they do this by compulsion, not their own will.

Reply Obj. 5. We should say that, even in the fact that they come at the invocation of divine power, they wish human beings to understand that they are not altogether excluded from divine justice. For they do not so seek divine status as to wish to be equal to almighty God, but under him rejoice that human beings show divine worship for him.

Question 7

THE SIMPLICITY OF THE DIVINE ESSENCE

Article 1

Is God Simple?

We should say that we should hold that God is simple in every way, and, for the moment, three arguments can prove this. The first is as follows. I have shown in another discussion (Q. 3, A. 5) that all beings proceed from a first being, and that we call the first being God. And although in one and the same thing that is sometimes actual and sometimes potential, the potentiality is temporally prior, but by nature subsequent, to the actuality, the latter, absolutely speaking, necessarily precedes the former both by nature and temporally, since an actual being brings all potential beings into actuality. Therefore, the being that made all beings actually exist, and itself proceeds from nothing else, is necessarily the first actual thing without any admixture of potentiality, since, if it were in any way potential, another being that made it actual would have to be prior to it. And in every composite thing, by whatever composition, there needs to be potentiality admixed with actuality, since one thing from which there is a composition in composite things is potential in relation to another, such as matter to form, a subject to its accidents, or genus to specific difference. Or at least all the parts are potential in relation to the whole, since we trace parts to matter, and the whole to form, as the *Physics* makes clear.[1] And so no composite thing can be the first actuality. But the first being (i.e., God) is necessarily pure actuality, as I have shown (Q. 1, A.1). Therefore, God cannot be anything composite, and so he is altogether simple.

The second argument is that, since there can be composition only by different things, the different things need an active thing in order to be united, since different things, as such, are not united. But every composite has existing insofar as the things of which it is composed are united. Therefore, every composite necessarily depends on a prior active thing. Therefore, the first being (i.e., God), from whom all things exist, cannot be composite.

The third argument is that the first being (i.e., God) is necessarily the most perfect and so the best, since the sources of things are not imperfect, as Pythagoras and Leucippus thought. And the best thing is one in which there is nothing lacking goodness, as the most white thing is one in which no blackness is admixed. But this is impossible in any composite, since the good resulting from a composition of parts, whereby the whole is good, is not present in any of the parts. And so the parts are not good by reason of the goodness that belongs to the whole. Therefore, the best thing is necessarily the most simple and lacks every composition. And Aristotle[2] and Hilary propose this argument, Hilary saying:[3] "God, since he is light, is not confined by obscure things, and since he is virtue, he is not confined by weak things."

Obj. 1. One simple thing by nature produces only one kind of thing, since, according to Aristotle,[4] the same thing always produces the same kind of thing. But many kinds of things proceed from God. Therefore, he is not simple.

Reply Obj. 1. We should say that Aristotle does not mean that many kinds of things cannot proceed from one thing, since, inasmuch as an active thing produces something like itself, and an effect falls short of representing its cause, what is united in a cause is necessarily multiple in its effects. For example, all the forms of producible material substances are one thing, so to speak, in the power of the sun but distinguished in the sun's effects. And so it happens that a thing by its one power can produce different effects, as fire by its heat liquefies and solidifies, softens and hardens, and burns and blackens. And a human being by the power of reason acquires different sciences and produces works of different skills. And so and far more God can by his one simple power create many kinds of things. But Aristotle means that something remaining the same does not cause different things at different times if it should be active by a necessity of nature, unless, perhaps, this should result accidentally from different matter or another accidental thing. But this is not relevant to the present question.

Obj. 7. Substance, power, and action are in every thing, as Dionysius says,[5] and it thereby seems that action results from power and substance. But there is plurality in God's actions. Therefore, there are multiplicity and composition in his substance.

Reply Obj. 7. We should say that we can consider God's action either regarding him producing or his product. If we should consider God's action regarding him producing, then there is in him only one action (i.e., his essence), since he does not produce things by an action in between himself and the thing made, although made by his understanding and his willing, which belong to his existing. But if we should consider God's action regarding the thing produced, then there are different actions and different effects of divine action. But this introduces no composition in him.

Obj. 8. There needs to be composition wherever there are many forms. But there are many forms in God, since, as Averroes says,[6] all forms are actual in the first cause of movement, as they are all potential in prime matter. Therefore, there is composition in God.

Reply Obj. 8. We should say that the form of an effect is in a natural active thing in one way and in a thing active by skill in another way. For the form of an effect is in a natural thing by nature insofar as the active thing in its nature assimilates the effect to itself, since every active thing produces something like itself. This happens in two ways. When the effect is perfectly likened to the active thing, as equal to the active thing's power, the form of an effect is in the active thing by the same measure, as is evident in the case of univocal active things, as when fire produces fire. But when an effect is not perfectly likened to an active thing, as unequal to the active thing's power, then the form of an effect is in the active thing in a higher way, not in the same measure, as is evident in the case of nonunivocal active things, as when the sun produces fire.

In things active by skill, the forms of effects preexist in the same measure but not in the same way of existing, since they have material existing in the effects but intelligible existing in the mind of the artisan. And since we say that something exists in the intellect as the thing understood and the form whereby one understands the thing, the forms of a skill are in the mind of an artisan as that whereby the artisan understands the thing. The artisan produces the form of the product in matter because the artisan conceives its form.

The forms of things are in God in both ways. When he produces things by means of his intellect, it is not without the action of nature. In inferior things produced by skills, a skill produces them by the power of an external nature, which it uses as an instrument, as a potter uses fire to bake bricks. But God's skill does not use an external nature in order to produce an effect, but he produces his effect by the power of his own nature. Therefore, the forms of things are in the divine nature as in the active power producing them, not in the same measure, since no effect is equal to that power. And so all the forms that are multiple in effects are in it as one thing. And so no composition thereby results. Likewise, there are many understood things in his intellect by one and the same thing, that is, his essence. But that one understands many things by one thing does not introduce composition in the one understanding. And so neither does composition in God result in this respect.

Obj. 9. Anything that comes to something after it completely exists is in it accidentally. But we say some things about God temporally, such as that he is creator and Lord. Therefore, those things are in God accidentally. But there is a composition of an accident and its subject. Therefore, there is composition in God.

Reply Obj. 9. We should say that the relations we predicate of God temporally are only conceptually, not really, in him, since there is a real relation where something really depends on something else, whether absolutely or in a respect. And so there is a real relation of knowledge to the knowable object but not the converse, where there is only a conceptual relation, as Aristotle makes clear.[7] And so, since God depends on nothing else, but, conversely, all things depend on him, there are in other things real relations to God, but there is in him only a conceptual relation to things, as our intellect cannot understand the relation of this thing to that thing without, conversely, understanding a relation of that thing to this thing.

Obj. 10. There is composition wherever there are many things. But there are three Persons in God, and the persons are three things, as Augustine says.[8] Therefore, there is composition in God.

Reply Obj. 10. We should say that plurality of Persons introduces no composition in God, since we can consider the Persons in two ways, We can consider them in one way insofar as they are related to the divine essence, with which they are really the same, and so it is evident that there is no composition. We can consider the Persons in a second way insofar as they are related to one another, and then they are related as distinct Persons, not as combined. And so neither can there be composition in this respect, since every composition is a union.

Article 2

Is the Essence or Substance in God the Same as His Existing?

We should say that there is no difference between existing and substance in God. To prove this, we should consider that when some causes producing different effects share in one and the same effect besides the different effects, they necessarily produce the common effect by the power of higher cause to which the common effect belongs. This is so because, inasmuch as a cause produces its proper effect by its own nature or form, different causes having different natures or forms necessarily have different proper effects.

And so, if different causes result in one and the same effect, the effect is proper to something higher, in whose power they act, not to any one of them.

Just so, different things like pepper and ginger, and the like, when combined, evidently result in causing heat, although each of them has its own effect, which differs from that of another. And so we need to trace the common effect to a prior cause to which the effect belongs, namely, fire. Likewise, in heavenly movements, individual planetary spheres have their own movements, and they have with this a common effect that needs to belong to a higher sphere revolving all of them in their daily movement.

All created causes share in one and the same effect, that is, existing, although individual causes have their own effects, regarding which we distinguish them. For example, heat causes something to be hot, and a builder causes a home to exist. Therefore, they have in common that they cause existing but differ in that fire causes fire, and the builder a house. Therefore, there needs to be a higher cause than all the others by whose power they cause existing, and that existing is a proper effect of the higher cause. And this cause is God.

But the particular effect of a cause proceeds from it by a likeness to its nature. Therefore, what constitutes existing in God is necessarily his substance or nature. And so the *Liber de causis* says that only a divine intelligence gives existing, that the first effect is existing, and that nothing was created before it.[9]

Obj. 1. Damascene in his work *Orthodox Faith* says:[10] "It is manifest to us that God exists, but what he is in substance and nature is altogether incomprehensible and unknown." But the same thing cannot be known and unknown. Therefore, God's existence and his substance, or essence, are not the same thing.

Reply Obj. 1. We should say that we speak of being and existing in two senses, as the *Metaphysics* makes clear.[11] Sometimes it signifies the essence of a thing or the act of existing, and sometimes one signifies the truth of a proposition, even regarding things that have no existing, as we say that there is blindness because a human being is truly blind. Therefore, when Damascene says that God's existence is manifest to us, he understands God's existing in the second way, not the first. For, in the first way, God's existing and his substance are the same, and as his substance is unknown, and so also is his existing. But in the second way, we know that God exists, since we conceive this proposition in our intellect from his effects.

Obj. 5. There are different things only if they have different existing. But the existing of this thing is different from the existing of that thing insofar as something is in this or that nature, not insofar as something exists. Therefore, if some existing should not be in a nature that differs from existing itself, it will not differ from another existing. And so it follows that, if God's substance is his existing, he is the common existing for each thing.

Reply Obj. 5. We should say that, as the *Liber de causis* says,[12] God's very existing is distinguished and individuated from any other existing, since he is intrinsically subsistent existing, and not coming to a nature other than his existing. But every other, nonsubsistent existing needs to be individuated by a nature and substance that subsists in such-and-such existing. And regarding them, the existing of this particular thing is truly different from the existing of that particular thing because it belongs to a nature.

Obj. 6. The being to which nothing is added is the being common to all things. But if God should be his very existing, there will be a being to which nothing is added. Therefore, it will be common to all things and so predicated of each, and God will be combined with all things. But this is heretical and contrary to Aristotle, who says in the *Liber de causis* that the first cause governs all things without being combined with them.[13]

Reply Obj. 6. We should say being in general is that to which nothing is added, although it does not belong to its nature that nothing can be added to it. But divine existing is that to which nothing is added, and it belongs to its nature that none can be. Just so, no specific difference is added to animal in general conceptually, but it does not belong to its nature that something cannot be added to it, since such belongs to the nature of irrational animal, which is a species of animal.

Obj. 7. Nothing expressed in conjunction is proper for what is altogether simple. But existing is so expressed, since it so seems that existing is related to essence as a white thing is to whiteness. Therefore, one inappropriately says that God's substance is his existing.

Reply Obj. 7. We should say that the way of signifying in words that we impose on things results from our way of understanding, since words signify concepts of the intellect, as Aristotle says at the beginning of *De interpretatione*.[14] But our intellect understands existing in the way in which it finds existing in the inferior things from which it gets its knowledge, in which things existing inheres but is not subsistent. And reason discovers that there is a subsistent existing. And so, although we signify by way of conjunction the fact that the names express his existing, our intellect in attributing existing to God transcends that way of signifying, attributing to God what is signified but not the way of signifying.

Obj. 9. We should not attribute to God, who is most perfect, what is most imperfect. But existing, like prime matter, is most imperfect, since, as all the forms determine prime matter, so all the particular categories can determine existing, since it is most imperfect. Therefore, as there is no prime matter in God, so also we should not attribute existing to the divine substance.

Reply Obj. 9. We should say that what I am calling existing is the most perfect of all things. And this is evident in that actuality is always more perfect than potentiality. But we actually understand any designated form only because we consider existing. For example, we can consider humanity or the nature of fire as existing potentially in matter, or the power of an active cause or the intellect, but what has existing is actually such. And so what I am calling existing is evidently the actuality of all actualities, and for that reason the perfection of all perfections. Nor should we understand that there is added to what I am calling existing anything more formal than it, determining it as actuality determines potentiality. For this existing is essentially different from that to which a further determination is added. And nothing extrinsic to existing can be added to it, since only nonexisting, which cannot be a form or matter, is outside it. And so nothing else determines it as actuality determines potentiality. Rather, something else determines it as potentiality determines actuality. For, in defining forms, we posit proper matter rather than specific differences, as when we say that the soul is the actuality of the physical organic body. And we distinguish this existing and that existing in this way, inasmuch as it belongs to this or that nature. And so Dionysius says that, although living things are more excellent than existing things, existing is more excellent than living, since living things have not only life but existing along with life.[15]

Obj. 10. What one signifies by way of effect does not belong to the first substance, which has no cause. But existing is such, since every being has existing by the sources of its essence. Therefore, one inappropriately says that God's substance is his very existing.

Reply Obj. 10. We should say that the order of ends is according to the order of active things, so that the ultimate end corresponds to the first active thing, and other ends to other active things proportionally in order. For, if we were to consider the governor of a city, the commander of an army, and an individual soldier, the governor of the city is evidently the first in the order of active cause, at whose command the head of the army goes to war, and under him is the soldier, who wages hand-to-hand combat at the order of the army commander. The end of the soldier is to overwhelm the enemy, and this is further ordered to the army's victory, which is the end of the commander, and this is further ordered to the well-being of the city or kingdom, which is the end of the governor or king. Therefore, what is the particular effect and end in the action of the first active cause needs to have the place of the ultimate end. And although that end is first in intention, it is last in action and the effect of the other causes. And so created existing itself, which is the particular effect corresponding to the first active cause, is caused by other sources, although the first thing causing existing is the first cause.

Article 3

Is God in a Genus?

We should say that God is not in a genus, and three arguments, for the moment, can show this. First, we posit something in a genus only by reason of its essence, not its existing. This is clear because the existing of each thing is proper to it and different from the existing of any other thing. But the nature of a substance can be common, and so also Aristotle says in the *Metaphysics* that being is not a genus.[16] But God is his very existing. And so he cannot be in a genus.

The second argument is that, although matter is not a genus, nor form a specific difference, we take the nature of a genus from the matter, and the nature of a specific difference from the form. For example, the sensibly perceptible nature in a human being from which we take the nature of animal is material in relation to reason, from which we take the specific difference of rational. For an animal is what has a sensibly perceptible nature, and rational is what has reason. And so, in everything in a genus, there needs to be a composition of matter and form, or actuality and potentiality, but this cannot be in God, who is pure actuality, as I have shown (A. 1). And so we conclude that he cannot be in a genus.

The third argument is that, since God is absolutely perfect, he includes in himself the perfection of all genera, since this is the nature of the absolutely perfect, as the *Metaphysics* says.[17] But what is in a genus is limited to things that belong to that genus. And so God cannot be in a genus, since he would not then be of infinite essence or absolute perfection. Rather, his essence and perfection would be limited under the nature of a fixed genus.

This makes further evident that God is not a species or the individual of a species and does not have a specific difference or definition, since very definition is by genus and specific difference. And so also we cannot demonstrate anything about him except by reason of his effects, since the means of demonstrating why something is so is a definition.

Obj. 1. Dionysius says:[18] "Substance in divinity signifies the common species of the specifically like Persons, and hypostasis indicates an individual, namely, the Father, the Son, and the Holy Spirit, Peter and Paul." Therefore, God is related to the Father and the Son and the Holy Spirit as a species to individuals. But wherever there is species and individual, there is a genus, since species is constituted of genus and specific difference. Therefore, it seems that God is in a genus.

Reply Obj. 1. We should say that Damascene is speaking metaphorically, not literally, since the name of God (i.e., God) has likeness to a species in that we predicate it substantially of many numerically different things. But we cannot properly call God a species, since species is only conceptually, not really, one thing common to numerically many things. But the numerically one divine substance is common to the three Persons. And so the Father and the Son and the Holy Spirit are one God, but Peter, Paul, and Mark are not one human being.

Obj. 2. Whatever things exist and differ in no way are completely the same. But God is not the same as other things. Therefore, he differs from them in some way. But everything that differs from something else differs from it by a difference. Therefore, there is a difference in God whereby he differs from other things. But the difference is not accidental, since there is no accident in God, as Boethius says in *Trinity*. But every substantial difference divides a genus. Therefore, God is in a genus.

Reply Obj. 2. We should say that difference and diversity are not the same, as Aristotle says,[19] since we call what is not the same diverse absolutely, but we say that difference is in relation to something, inasmuch as every difference differs by something. Therefore, if we should understand the word *difference* in the proper sense, then the proposition, *whatever things exist and differ in no way are the same*, is false. But if we understand the word *difference* broadly, then the proposition is true, and so we should concede the inference that God differs from other things. But it does not follow that he differs by a difference. Rather, it follows that he differs from other things by reason of his substance, since we need to say this about first and simple things. For example, a human being differs from an ass by the specific difference of reason, but rationality is not further distinguished from an ass by a difference (since the process would then go on endlessly) but is distinguished by reason of itself.

Obj. 4. Anything to which the nature of the genus of substance is proper is in a genus. But the nature of substance is to exist intrinsically, which most of all belongs to God. Therefore, God is in the genus of substance.

Reply Obj. 4. We should say that subsistent being is not the definition of substance, as Avicenna says,[20] since being cannot be the genus of anything, as Aristotle proves,[21] inasmuch as nothing can be added to being that does not share in it, and a difference should not share in a genus. But if substance could have a definition, notwithstanding that it is the most general genus, its definition will be this: a substance is a thing for whose essence existing in another is not competent. And so the definition of substance is not appropriate for God, who does not have his essence in addition to his existing. And so God is not in the genus of substance but is above every substance.

Obj. 6. Everything predicated of something else regarding what it is, and more, is either related to it as its species or its genus. But we predicate all the things predicated of God regarding what he is, since all the categories, when they have come into divine predication, are convertible with substance, as Boethius says.[22] It is also evident that the predicates belong to other things and not only to God and so are in other things. Therefore, they are related to God either as species to individual or as genus to species, and, either way, God is necessarily in a genus.

Reply Obj. 6. We should say that the nature of genus requires what is predicated univocally, and we can predicate nothing univocally about God and creatures, as A. 7 will make clear. And so, although we predicate the things we say about God substantially, we nonetheless do not predicate them about him generically.

Article 4

Do We Predicate *Good*, *Wise*, *Just* of God as Accidents?

We should say without any hesitation that one should hold that there is no accident in God, and three arguments, for the moment, can show this. The first argument is that nothing external is added to any nature, essence, or form, although what has a nature, form, or essence can have something external in it. For example, humanity receives into itself only what belongs to the nature of humanity. This is evident because, in definitions that signify the essence of things, anything added or subtracted changes the species, just as in the case of numbers, as Aristotle says.[23]

The human being who has humanity can have something else that does not belong to humanity, such as whiteness and the like, which belong to the human being but are not present in humanity. And in any creature, there is a difference between the creature that has something and the something that the creature has. For there is a twofold difference in composite creatures, since the individual existing thing, or individual thing, has a specific nature (e.g., a human being has humanity) and existing besides. For example, a human being is not humanity or the human being's existence. And so an accident can be in a human being but not in humanity itself or the human being's existence.

But in simple substances, there is only one difference, namely, between essence and existing. Any individual existing angel is its nature, since the essence of a simple thing is itself simple, as Avicenna says.[24] And so there can be an intelligible accident in such substances but not a material one.

And in God, there is no difference between him having something and the something had, or between him sharing and something shared. He is his nature and his existing, and so nothing foreign or accidental can be present in him. Boethius seems to touch on this argument, saying:[25] "What exists can have something besides itself existing, but existing itself has nothing besides itself added."

The second argument is that, since an accident is external to the essence of the subject, and a cause unites different things, a cause needs to do this if an accident should be added to God. But an external cause cannot do this, since then the external cause would act on God, and it would be prior to him, as the thing causing motion to the thing moved, and the productive thing to the thing made. For an external thing causes an accident in a subject inasmuch as it acts externally on the subject in which the accident is an effect.

Likewise, an accident cannot be from an internal cause, as is intrinsically the case regarding accidents that have their cause in a subject. For a subject cannot cause an accident by the same thing by which it receives the accident, since no potentiality moves itself to actuality. And so it is necessary that something receives an accident from one thing and causes the accident from something else, and so it is composite, as in the case of those things that receive an accident by the nature of their matter and cause the accident by the nature of their form. But I have shown before (A. 1) that God is not composite. And so there cannot be an accident in him.

The third argument is that an accident is related to a subject as actuality is to potentiality, since an accident is a form of the subject. And so, since God is pure actuality without any admixture of potentiality, he cannot be the subject of an accident. Therefore, the foregoing makes clear that there is in God no composition of matter and form or of any substantial parts or of genus and specific difference or of subject and accident. It is also clear that the cited terms (*good, wise, just*) do not predicate accidents of God.

Obj. 1. What one predicates about something, signifying what results from its nature, not its substance, predicates an accident. But Damascene says that the words *good* and *just* and *holy* predicated about God result from his nature but do not signify his substance.[26] Therefore, they predicate about him as an accident.

Reply Obj. 1. We should say that Damascene is speaking about those words regarding the thing from which they take their name, not regarding what they predicate of God, since we impose them to signify from certain accidental forms found in creatures. For he wishes to prove from this that the words expressed about God do not signify his substance for us.

Obj. 2. But someone said that Damascene is speaking about the way of signifying. On the contrary, the way of signifying that results from the nature of a genus needs to be related to a thing, since a generic predicate signifies the substance of a subject, inasmuch as it is predicated about what something is.

But it belongs to the aforementioned predicates to signify by way of resulting from a nature by reason of its genus, since they are in the genus of quality, which has a relation to a subject by reason of its own nature, inasmuch as quality is why we call them such-and-such. Therefore, this way of signifying is necessarily related to a thing, namely, that the things that the aforementioned predicates signify are consequences of the nature of that about which we predicate them, and so accidents.

Reply Obj. 2. We should say that, although quality is the genus of human goodness and wisdom and justice, it is not the genus of those things insofar as we predicate them of God, since we call quality as such a being because it inheres in some way in a subject. But we denote wisdom and justice, not by this but rather by a perfection or actuality. And so such things come into predication about God by reason of their difference, not their genus. And Augustine on this account says:[27] "Let us understand, as far as we can, good without quality, great without quantity." Therefore, it is not necessary that there is in God the way that results from a nature.

Obj. 8. We predicate as an accident that without which we can understand something, since Porphyry thereby proves that certain separable things are accidents because we can conceive a white crow and a shining white Ethiopian.[28] But we can conceive of God without good, as Boethius makes clear.[29] Therefore, good signifies an accident in God, and so do other things for the same reason.

Reply Obj. 8. We should say that everything without which one can understand an understood thing substantially has the nature of an accident, since, given that one understands a thing substantially, it cannot be the case that one does not understand what belongs to its substance, as, for example, that one should understand what a human being is and not what an animal is. But we in this life consider God from his effects and do not see him essentially. And so nothing prevents us from considering him from his effect of existence and not considering him from his effect of goodness, since Boethius speaks in this way. But we should note that, although we in some way understand God without understanding his goodness, we cannot understand God by understanding him not to be good (as we also cannot understand a human being by understanding the human being not to be an animal). To do so would take away God's substance, which is goodness. But the saints in heaven, who see God essentially, in seeing him see his goodness.

Obj. 9. We should consider two things regarding the meaning of a word, namely, the thing from which it is taken and the thing on which it is imposed. Regarding both, the word *wisdom* seems to signify an accident, since it is taken from what consists of making one wise, which seems to be the activity of a wise person, and that from which it is taken is a quality. Therefore, this word and others like it in every way signify an accident in that of which it is predicated, and so there is an accident in God.

Reply Obj. 9. We should say that the word *wisdom* is true about God regarding that from which it is taken, but it is taken from what consists of possessing wisdom intellectually, not from what consists of making one wise. For knowledge as such is related to a knowable object, but knowledge as an accident or form is related to the knower. Having wisdom is accidental to a human being but not to God.

Article 5

Do the Aforementioned Terms Signify the Divine Substance?

We should say that some held that these aforementioned terms do not signify the divine substance, and Rabbi Moses especially says this expressly. He says that we should understand these terms in two ways. We should understand them in one way by the likeness of an effect, that one calls God wise because he acts in his effects like a wise human being, namely, by ordering each thing to its requisite end, not because wisdom is anything in him, and we similarly call God living inasmuch as he acts like a living human being, acting on his own, as it were. The second way is one of negation, that, by calling God living, we remove from God the way of existing whereby nonliving things exist, but do not signify that life is anything in him. Similarly, when we call God intelligent, we remove from God the way of existing whereby irrational animals exist but do not understand that the intellect is anything in him.

Both ways seem to be inadequate and unsuitable, the first for two reasons. The first reason is that there would be, according to the explanation, no difference between saying that God is wise, angry, or fire. For example, we call God angry because he acts like an angry human being when he punishes, since angry human beings are accustomed to do this. Also, we call God fire because he acts like fire when he purifies, which fire does in its way. But this is contrary to the position of the saints and prophets speaking about God, who affirm some things about God and deny other things of him, since they assert that God is living and not a material substance or subject to emotions. According to the aforementioned opinion, we can affirm or deny all things about God, not mattering whether these things or those.

The second reason is that, inasmuch as we hold by faith that no creature has always existed, which he allows, we could not then say that he was wise or good before creatures existed. For, before creatures existed, God produced nothing regarding effects, neither like a good human being, nor like a wise one. But this is altogether contrary to sound faith, unless, perhaps, one should wish to say that one could call God wise before creatures existed because he could act like a wise human being, not because he did so. And then it would follow that this signified something existing in God and so be his substance, since everything in God is his substance.

By the same reasoning, the second way seems unsuitable, since there is no specific term that does not remove a way that does not belong to God. For any specific term includes signifying the difference that excludes the other species contradistinguished from it. For example, the term *lion* includes the difference of four-footed, which distinguishes a lion from a bird. Therefore, if the predications about God were to be introduced only to remove things from him, as we say that God is living because he does not have existing like nonliving things, as Rabbi Moses says, so we could say that God is a lion because he does not have existing like a bird. Besides, the understanding of negation is always based on an affirmation. And this is clear because an affirmative proposition proves every negative proposition, and so, unless the human intellect were to know something affirmatively about God, it could not deny anything about God. But it would not know anything if nothing said about God were to be affirmatively verified about him.

And so, according to the opinion of Dionysius,[30] we should say that such terms signify the divine substance, although defectively and imperfectly, which is made clear as follows. Since every active thing acts insofar as it is actual, and so produces something in some way its like, the form of a thing made necessarily exists in the active thing but in a different way. When the effect is equal to the power of its cause, the form in the cause and the form in the effect need to regard the same nature, since then the cause and the effect are specifically the same, which happens regarding all univocal things. For example, a human being begets a human being, and fire produces fire. But when the effect is not equal to the power of the cause, the form in the cause and the form in the effect do not regard the same nature, and the form is more eminently in the cause, since, insofar as the form is in the cause, the latter has the power to produce the effect. And so, if the whole power of the cause is not expressed in the effect, we conclude that the way whereby the form is in the cause exceeds the way whereby it is in the effect. And we see this in the case of all nonunivocal active things, as when the sun produces fire.

And evidently no effect is equal to the power of the first cause, that is, God. Otherwise, only one effect would proceed from one and the same power. But since we find that many and different effects proceed from one and the same power, this shows us that any effect of his falls short of the power of the cause. Therefore, no form of any divine effect is of the same nature in the effect as in God. Nevertheless, it needs to be in him in a higher way. And so all the forms that are different and separate from one another in different effects are united in him as one and the same universal power. Just so, the power of the sun produced all the forms in the lower things by its unique power, to which the action of the sun assimilates all the things produced in their own forms.

Likewise, the perfections of created things are likened to God regarding his unique and simple essence, and the likenesses of the perfections found in creatures, such as wisdom, virtue, goodness, and the like, give our intellect its form, since our intellect gets its knowledge from created things. And so, as created things by their perfections are in some way likened to God, although deficiently, so also the forms of these perfections give our intellect its form.

And whenever the intellect by its intelligible form is likened to something, the thing it conceives and asserts by that intelligible form is true about the thing to which the intelligible form likens the intellect, since knowledge is the assimilation of the intellect to the thing known. And so it is necessary that the things that the intellect, formed by the forms of these perfections, knows and asserts about God exist in God, who corresponds to each of the aforementioned forms as the thing to which all the forms are likened. And if such an intelligible form of our intellect were to be equal to the divine essence in likeness to him, it would comprehend that essence, and the very conception of our intellect would be the perfect definition of God, as two-footed, walking animal is the perfect definition of human being.

But the aforementioned form is not perfectly likened to the divine essence, as I have said. And so, although such terms, which the intellect by such conceptions attributes to God, signify what is the divine substance insofar as we understand it, not perfectly as it exists.

Therefore, we should say that any of those terms signify the divine essence imperfectly, not as if comprehending it. And so *He Who Is* is the most fitting name for God, since it does not affix any form to God but signifies existing without limit. This is what Damascene says,[31] that the name *He Who Is* signifies the infinite ocean of substance.

The words of Dionysius confirm this analysis. He says in *Divine Names*:[32] "Since the Godhead comprises all existing things in himself simply and unlimitedly, we fittingly praise and designate him by different things." He says *simply* because we attribute to God by his simple essence the perfections that are in creatures by different forms. He says *unlimitedly* to show that no perfection found in creatures comprehends the divine essence, so that the intellect under the definition of that perfection would define God in himself. Also, what the *Metaphysics* holds,[33] that the absolutely perfect is what has in itself the perfections of all the genera, confirms this. Averroes, commenting on this, explains it as referring to God.[34]

Obj. 2. We cannot truly deny of a thing a predicate that signifies its substance, since Dionysius says that negative judgments about God are true, but affirmative judgments are imprecise.[35] Therefore, affirmative predicates do not signify the divine essence.

Reply Obj. 2. We should say that Dionysius says that negations of those predicates are true about God in such a way as not to assert that affirmations are false and imprecise. For regarding the things signified, we truly attribute to God the things that are in him in any way, as I have already shown, but one can deny them in the way that they signify about him, since the way of these predicates signifies a definite form, and so we do not attribute it to God, as I have said. And so, absolutely speaking, one can deny the predicates about God, since they are not proper to him in the way that they signify him, since the way signified is insofar as they are in our intellect, as I have said, but they belong to him in a more eminent way. And so we call the affirmation imprecise, not altogether suitably affirmed, as it were, because of the different way the predicates are in God and us.

And so, according to the teaching of Dionysius,[36] we predicate these things of God in three ways. First, we predicate them affirmatively, so as to say: "God is wise." We need to say this about him because of the likeness of wisdom proceeding from him. But, since the wisdom in God is not of the same kind as we understand and designate, we can truly deny it, so as to say: "God is not wise." Also, since we do not deny wisdom of God because he lacks it but because it is in him more eminently than we predicate or understand it, we need to say that he is super-wise. And so, in this three-fold way of calling God wise, Dionysius gives us perfectly to understand how we attribute these predicates to God.

Obj. 4. Origen says that we call God wise because wisdom fulfills us. But this signifies God's effect, not the divine substance. Therefore, the aforementioned predicates do not signify the divine substance.

Reply Obj. 4. We should say that we should not understand the saying of Origen that, when we say that God is wise, we intend to say that God causes wisdom, but rather that the wisdom he causes leads out intellect to attribute wisdom to him more eminently, as I have said.

Obj. 8. We can know God only by the likeness of a creature, since, as Paul says in Rom. 1:20, "We perceive the invisible things of God, when understood by means of the things that he has made from the creation of the world." But we denote him insofar as we know him. Therefore, we denote him only by the likeness of something else. But when the likeness of something else denotes something, we predicate the word of him metaphorically, not substantially. This is evident because we predicate it of him secondarily, and first of the thing from which we take the likeness, although one predicates what signifies the substance of a thing first about the thing.

Reply Obj. 8. We should say that there is in an effect something whereby the effect is assimilated to its cause and something whereby the effect differs from its cause, something that belongs to the effect from its matter or some such thing. For example, this is evident in the case of a brick hardened by fire, since the brick is like fire in that fire heats it and differs from fire in that it, when heated, is condensed and hardened, and the brick has this from the condition of matter. Therefore, if we shall predicate of fire that regarding which the brick is like fire, we predicate this properly about fire, both more eminently and first, since fire is hotter than the brick and also more eminent, inasmuch as the brick is hot as heated, so to speak, but fire is hot by nature. But if we should predicate of fire that regarding which the brick differs from fire, it will be false, and we could only metaphorically predicate a term having such a condition in our intellect. It is false to call fire, which is the finest of material substances, dense. But we can call fire hard because of its violent action and the difficulty of overcoming it.

Likewise, we should consider in creatures certain perfections by which they are like God, perfections that, regarding the thing signified, signify no imperfection, such as existing, living, understanding, and the like, and we properly predicate these of God, indeed first about him and more eminently than about creatures. But there are other things by which a creature differs from God, things resulting in it as it proceeds from nothing, such as potentiality, privation, movement, and the like. And we can only metaphorically predicate of God whatever terms include such conditions in their concept, such as lion, stone, and the like, since they have matter in their definition. And we predicate such things of God metaphorically because of the likeness in the effect.

Obj. 14. Dionysius says that a human being is best united to God in knowing that his knowledge about God knows nothing.[37] But this would not be so if the things a human conceives and signifies were the divine substance. Therefore, the aforementioned predicates do not signify the divine substance.

Reply Obj. 14. We should say that, because our intellect is not equal to the divine substance, what God's substance is remains beyond our intellect, and so we do not know it. And so the ultimate human knowledge about God is that one knows that one does not know God, inasmuch as one knows that what God is exceeds everything we know about him.

Article 6
Are These Terms Synonymous?

We should say that all those understanding the question say that these terms are not synonymous. Those who said that the terms signify certain mental representations added to the divine essence, or ways of acting regarding effects, or negations of perfections as they are in creatures, not the divine essence, easily agreed with this.

But assuming that these terms signify the divine substance, as I have shown before (A. 5), the question seems to contain greater difficulty, since we find one and the same thing, that is, the divine substance signified by all these terms.

We should note that the meaning of a term is related to a thing by means of the intellect, not directly, since words are the symbols of imprints in the soul, and the very concepts of the intellect are likenesses of things, as Aristotle makes clear in the beginning of *De interpretatione*.[38]

Therefore, either the things signified or the aspects understood by the terms, which are imposed to signify the aspects, can prevent some terms from being synonymous. Therefore, the diversity of the things signified, according to what has been said, cannot prevent the terms predicated of God from being synonymous. Only the aspects of the terms that result from mental concepts can.

And so Averroes says in his *Commentary on the Metaphysics* that the multiplicity in God consists only of differentiation in the intellect, not in existing.[39] We call this something really one but conceptually many. But these different aspects in our intellect cannot be such as to have nothing really corresponding to them, since our intellect attributes to God the things those aspects concern. And so, if nothing were to be in God, whether regarding himself or his effect, corresponding to these aspects, the intellect attributing them to God, and all propositions signifying such attributions, would be false. But this is unsuitable.

But there are some aspects to which nothing corresponds in the thing understood. Rather, the intellect attributes those things of which there are such aspects only to things as it understands them, not as they are in themselves, as is evident in the consideration of genus and species, and intellectual representations. For there is in things existing outside the soul nothing whose likeness is the aspect of genus and species. The intellect, however, is not false, since we attribute things of which there are these aspects, namely, genus and species, to things only insofar as they are in the intellect, not insofar as they exist outside the soul. For, as the intellect understands things existing outside the soul, so it by reflecting on itself understands that it understands them. And so, as there is a mental concept or aspect to which the very thing outside the soul corresponds, so there is a concept or aspect to which the understood thing as such corresponds, as a thing outside the soul corresponds to the consideration or concept of human being, but only the understood thing corresponds to the concept of genus and species.

But such cannot be the aspects of the terms we predicate of God, since the intellect would then attribute them to God insofar as we understand him, not insofar as he is in himself. This is patently false, since, when we say that God is good, the sense would be that we so understand God, not that he is such.

And so some say that the connoted different things, which are the different divine effects, correspond to these different aspects, since they want the statement that God is good to signify his essence with an effect of his connoted, so that the sense is that God causes goodness, as different effects cause different aspects.

But this does not seem suitable, since, inasmuch as an effect proceeds from a cause by likeness, we need to understand a cause prior to such effects. Therefore, we do not call God wise because he causes wisdom, but he causes wisdom because he is wise. And so Augustine says in *Christian Doctrine* that we exist because God is good, and we are good inasmuch as we exist.[40]

Besides, in this view, it would follow that we predicated such terms of a creature before we predicated them of the creator, as we predicate health of a healthy person before we predicate it of the cause of health, since we call something healthy because it causes health. Likewise, if we understand the statement, God is good, to say nothing more than that God exists and causes goodness, it would follow by the same reasoning that we could predicate all the names of divine effects of him, as if one were to say that God is the heavens, since he causes them.

And if one should say this about his actual causality, it is clearly false, since, in this view, we cannot say that God was eternally good, wise, or any such thing, inasmuch as he was not actually a cause from eternity.

But if we should understand about causality according to the truth, that we call God good because he exists and has the power to pour out goodness, then we shall need to say that the word *good* signifies that power. But that power is a supremely eminent likeness of its effect, just like any power of a nonunivocal active thing. And so it would follow that the intellect conceiving goodness would be likened to what is in God, and what God is. And so something that is in God and is God corresponds to the aspect or concept of goodness.

And so we should say that all these many and different aspects have something corresponding in God himself, of which all these concepts of the intellect are likenesses. For, evidently, only one specific likeness can belong to one form, which likeness is equivalent to the form, but there can be different imperfect likenesses, any one of which falls short of perfectly representing the form. Therefore, since, as things previously said make clear, concepts of the perfections found in creatures are imperfect likenesses and not equivalent to the divine essence, nothing prevents one and the same essence from corresponding to all the aforementioned concepts, as thereby imperfectly representing it, as it were. And so all the aspects are in our intellect as their subject, but they are in God as fundamentally verifying the concepts, since there would be true mental concepts about a thing only if that thing were to correspond to the concepts by way of likeness.

Therefore, our intellect causes the diversity and multiplicity of the terms, since it cannot attain seeing the essence of God as it exists but sees it by many deficient likenesses of it in creatures, as if reflections in a mirror. And so, if one were to see the divine essence, one would not need many terms or many concepts. And for this reason, there is only one Word of God, which is the perfect conception of him. On this account, Zech. 14:9 says: "On that day, there will be one Lord and one name for him," when we shall see the very essence of God and not get knowledge of him from creatures.

Obj. 1. We call words that signify the same thing synonyms. But all the words predicated of God signify the same thing, since they signify the divine substance, which is altogether simple and one, as I have shown (A. 1). Therefore, all the predicates are synonyms.

Reply Obj. 1. We should say that, although these words signify one and the same thing, they signify by many aspects, as I have said, and so are not synonyms.

Obj. 2. Damascene says all things in the Godhead are one thing except being without generation, generation, and procession.[41] But words signifying one thing are synonyms. Therefore, all the predicates about God, except those that signify the properties of the Persons, are synonyms.

Reply Obj. 2. We should say that Damascene understands that all the things in the Godhead are really one thing except the properties of the Persons, which constitute real distinction of the Persons, but he does not exclude that the things we predicate about God differ conceptually.

Obj. 4. One might say that those predicates signify one thing in reality but different aspects of it, and so they are not synonyms. On the contrary, an aspect to which nothing really corresponds is false and empty. But if the aspects of these predicates should be many, it seems that they are empty and false.

Reply Obj. 4. We should say that the foregoing already makes clear that, although God is altogether one, the many concepts and aspects are not false, since one and the same thing represented by the concepts and aspects imperfectly corresponds to all of them. But they would be false if nothing were to correspond to them.

Obj. 5. One might say that those aspects are not empty, since something in God corresponds to them. On the contrary, things are like God insofar as they proceed from him by an exemplary likeness. But we note plurality of exemplars or aspects of exemplars in relation to creatures, since God himself by his one essence is the general exemplar. Therefore, the aspects of the words that we predicate of God from the likeness of creatures have nothing regarding the divine substance corresponding.

Reply Obj. 5. We should say that, in every way, there is unity regarding God and multiplicity regarding creatures. Therefore, as many creatures in him understanding are necessarily one intelligible form by his essence, and the relations to different creatures many, so, in our intellect ascending to God from the multiplicity of creatures, there are necessarily many forms having relations to the one God.

Article 7

Do We Predicate Such Terms of God and Creatures Univocally or Equivocally?

We should say that we can predicate nothing about creatures and God univocally, and this is made clear as follows. For every effect of a univocal active thing is equal to the power of the active thing. But no creature, since it is finite, can be equal to the power of the first active thing, since it is infinite. And so no likeness of God can be received univocally in a creature.

Likewise, it is evident that, although there is one nature of the form existing in the active thing, a different way of existing prevents univocal predication. For, although the nature of the house in matter and the house in the mind of the builder is the same, since one thing is the nature of the other, we do not predicate house univocally of both because the form of the house in matter has material existing, but the house in the mind of the builder is immaterial.

Therefore, given the impossibility that goodness in God and goodness in a creature are of the same nature, we would not predicate good of God univocally. For what is in God immaterially and simply is in the creature materially and in many ways. Besides, we do not predicate being univocally of substance and accidents, since a substance is a being as intrinsically having existence, but an accident is a being as something whose existing is to be in something else. From this, it is evident that the different disposition to existing prevents univocal predication of a being. But God is disposed to existing in a different way than any creature, since he is his existing, which is not true of any creature. And so we cannot in any way univocally predicate a creature of God, and so nothing of the other predicables, among which the first is being, since, if there is diversity in the first predicable, there needs to be diversity in the others. And so we predicate nothing of substance and accidents univocally.

But others said otherwise, that we predicate something of God and a creature purely equivocally, not analogically. Rabbi Moses is of this opinion, as what he has said makes clear.

This opinion cannot be true, since, in purely equivocal things, which Aristotle calls equivocal by chance, we do not predicate anything of one thing in relation to another. But we predicate all the things we predicate of God and creatures of God in relation to creatures, or vice versa, as all the opinions held about explaining the divine names attest. And so purely equivocal predication is impossible.

Likewise, since we take all our knowledge about God from creatures, if the commonness will be purely nominal, we would know nothing about God except purely empty words, behind which there would be nothing real.

It would also follow that all the demonstrations given by philosophers about God would be sophistical. For example, if one should say that an actual being brings everything potential into actuality and were to conclude from this that God was an actual being, since he brings all things into existing, it will be the fallacy of equivocation, and so about all the other demonstrations. Besides, an effect is necessarily in some way like its cause, and so we necessarily predicate nothing purely equivocally of an effect and its cause, as, for example, *healthy* about medicine and an animal.

And so we should say otherwise, that we predicate nothing univocally about God and a creature, but we predicate analogously, not purely equivocally, things predicated of both. There are two ways of such predication. One is by predicating something of two things by their relation to a third thing, as we predicate being of quality and quantity by their relation to substance. The second way is by predicating something of two things by the relation of one thing to another, as we predicate being of substance and a quantity.

In the first way, there needs to be something prior to the two things, to which both of the two have a relation, such as substance to quantity and quality. In the second way, there does not, but it is necessary that one be prior to the other. And so, since there is nothing prior to God, and he is prior to a creature, the second, not the first, way of analogy is proper in predication about God.

Obj. 2. Like things share in a form. But a creature can be like God, as Gen. 1:26 makes clear: "Let us make a human being in our image and likeness." Therefore, a creature shares in a form with God. But we can predicate something univocally of all things sharing in a form. Therefore, we can univocally predicate something about God and a creature.

Reply Obj. 2. We should say that the likeness of a creature to God falls short of the likeness of univocal things in two respects. First, the former likeness does not consist of sharing the same form, as two hot things share the same heat. For what we predicate of God and creatures, we predicate of God essentially, and we predicate of creatures by participation, so that we understand such likeness of a creature to God as a hot thing to heat, not as a hot thing to a hotter thing. Second, the shared form in a creature falls short of the nature that God is, as the heat of fire falls short of the nature of sun's power, whereby fire produces heat.

Obj. 3. More and less do not differentiate species. But, since we call a creature good and God good, it seems in this regard that God is better than every creature. Therefore, the goodness of God and that of a creature are not specifically different, and so we can univocally predicate good of God and a creature.

Reply Obj. 3. We should say that we can consider, and so predicate, more and less in three ways. We can consider more and less in one way only by the amount of the thing shared, as we say that snow is whiter than a wall, since whiteness is more perfect in snow than in a wall but belongs to the same nature. And so such difference by more and less does not distinguish their species. We can consider more and less in a second way insofar as one thing is shared, and another thing expressed essentially, as we might say that goodness is better than good. We consider more and less in a third way insofar as something the same belongs to one in a more eminent way than to another, as heat belongs to the sun in a more eminent way than to fire, and these two ways prevent the unity of a species and univocal predication. And we accordingly predicate something more and less of God and a creature, as what I have said before makes clear.

Obj. 6. The house in the mind of the builder and the house in matter belong to the same kind of thing. But all creatures proceed from God as buildings do from a builder. Therefore, the goodness of God belongs to the same nature as the goodness in a creature, and so we conclude as before.

Reply Obj. 6. We should say that there is a two-fold likeness between a creature and God. One is the likeness of a creature to the divine intellect, and then the form understood by God belongs to the same nature as the thing understood, although it does not have the same way of existing, since the form understood exists only in the intellect, but the form of a creature also exists in the thing. The second is the likeness insofar as the divine essence itself is the more than eminent likeness of all things but not of the same nature. And we may in this way of likeness predicate good and the like of God and creatures, but not in the first way, since it is not the essence of God if we say that God is good because he understands the goodness of a creature. For what we have said makes clear that we do not predicate house univocally of a house in the mind and a house in matter.

Counterobj. 2. Since a genus is the first part of a definition, the nature signified by a word is taken away when a genus is taken away. And so, if a word is imposed in order to signify what is in something else, it will be an equivocal word. But wisdom predicated of a creature is in the genus of quality. Therefore, since wisdom predicated of God is not a quality, as I have shown before, it seems that we predicate the word *wisdom* of God and creatures equivocally.

Reply Counterobj. 2. We should say that, although difference of genus takes away univocal predication, it does not take away analogy. This is evident as follows. Healthy, insofar as we predicate it of urine, is in the genus of sign, but insofar as we predicate it of medicine, is in the genus of cause.

Counterobj. 3. We can only equivocally predicate something commonly where there is no likeness. But there is no likeness between a creature and God, since Is. 11:18 says: "Therefore, to whom have you likened God?" Therefore, it seems that we can predicate nothing of God and a creature univocally.

Reply Counterobj. 3. We should say that we in no way say that God is like a creature, but rather the converse, since, as Dionysius says,[42] we perceive reciprocal likeness only in coordinate things, not in a cause and its effects. For example, we do not say that a human being is like the human being's image, but we say the converse, since the form by which we note likeness is first in the human being before it is in the image. And so we say that creatures are like God but not the contrary.

Counterobj. 5. Nothing regarding an accident can be like a substance. But wisdom is an accident in a creature but a substance in God. Therefore, a human being by his wisdom cannot be like God.

Reply Counterobj. 5. We should say that nothing regarding an accident can be like a substance by the likeness that we note regarding the form of a nature, but nothing prevents something regarding an accident being like a substance by the likeness between effect and cause. For the first substance necessarily causes all accidents.

Article 8

Is There a Relation between God and a Creature?

We should say that a relation differs from quantity and quality in that they are certain accidents abiding in a subject, and relation, as Boethius says,[43] signifies something in transit to something else, not something abiding in a subject. And so the followers of de la Porrée said that relations support rather than inhere, which is true in a way, as I shall show later.

What we attribute to something as proceeding from it into something else does not produce a composition of the other with it, just as action does not produce a composition with an active thing. And so also Aristotle in the *Physics* proves that there cannot be movement in a relation, since, without any movement of what is related to something else, a relation can cease only by the movement of the other.[44] Just so, it is evident about action that there is movement regarding action only metaphorically and improperly, as we say that one going from inactivity to activity is changed. This would not be the case if relation or action were to signify something abiding in a subject.

And so it is apparent that many relations between something and other things is not contrary to the aspect of the thing's simplicity. Indeed, the simpler something is, the more unlimited is its power. And so the *Liber de causis* says that unified power is less limited than multiple powers.

But we need to understand a relation between a source and things from the source, both the relation of origin, insofar as the things originate from the source, and a relation of diversity, since we need to distinguish an effect from its cause, since nothing causes itself.

And so the unlimited number of dispositions or relations between creatures and God results from his supreme simplicity, insofar as he produces creatures different from himself but in some way like him.

Obj. 1. Relative things are simultaneous, according to Aristotle.[45] But a creature cannot be simultaneous with God, since God is in every respect prior to a creature. Therefore, there can be no relation between a creature and God.

Reply Obj. 1. We should say that relative things mutually related by the same aspect, such as father to son, master to slave, and double to half, are naturally simultaneous. But relative things in which there is not the same aspect regarding each are not naturally simultaneous, but one or the other is naturally prior, as Aristotle also says about the senses and a sensibly perceptible thing, knowledge and an object of knowledge.[46] And so it is clear that it is not necessary that God and a creature be naturally simultaneous, since there is not the same aspect of relation regarding each. Nevertheless, it is not necessary, even in relative things that are naturally simultaneous, that the subjects of the relations be naturally simultaneous, but only that the relations be such.

Obj. 2. Between whatever things a relation exists, there is also a comparison to each other. But there is no comparison between God and creatures, since things that do not belong to one and the same genus cannot be compared, such as a number and a line. Therefore, there is no relation between God and a creature.

Reply Obj. 2. We should say that there is not a comparison of all the things of which there is a relation to each other, but only of those of which there is relation by a quality or quantity, so that we can thereby call one greater or better than the other, whether whiter or the like. But we can relate different relations, even those that belong to different genera, to each other, since things that belong to different genera differ from each other. Nevertheless, although God is not in the same genus with a creature as something contained in a genus, he is in all genera as the source of genus, and so there can be a relation between a creature and God as between effects and their cause.

Obj. 4. A creature cannot be contrary to its creator, since one contrary does not cause the other. But relative things are contrary to each other. Therefore, there cannot be a relation between a creature and God.

Reply Obj. 4. We should say relational opposition differs from other kinds of opposition in two things. The first is that, in other kinds of opposition, we say that one thing is contrary to another inasmuch as one excludes the other and is contrary to it in this way, and the opposition of privation, habit, and contrariety include contradictory opposition, as the *Metaphysics* says.[47] This is not the case in relative things, since a son is contrary to a father because of the nature of the son's relationship to the father, not by excluding the father. And this causes a second difference, since, in other contraries, one or the other is always imperfect, and this happens by reason of the negation included in privation or one of the contraries. This is not necessary in relative things; indeed, one can consider both relative things perfect, as is especially evident in equivalent things and those about origin, such as equal things, like things, father and son. And so we can ascribe a relation to God rather than other kinds of opposition. By reason of the first difference, we can note a relational opposition between a creature and God but no other opposition, since the positing of creatures, not their exclusion, proceeds from God, and yet there is a relationship of creatures to God. By reason of the second difference, there is in the divine Persons, in whom there can be nothing imperfect, a relational opposition and no other, as we will show later (Q. 8).

Obj. 5. Of whatever we newly begin to predicate something, we can in a sense say that it has become. Therefore, it follows that, if we predicate something of God in relation to a creature, God has in a sense come to be such, which is impossible, since he is immutable.

Reply Obj. 5. We should say that, since becoming is to be changed in the proper sense, it concerns a relation only incidentally, namely, when a thing has been changed, from which a relation results, and so neither does becoming concern a newly expressed relation except incidentally. For example, a material substance changed in size becomes equal to something else, not that the change intrinsically regards equality, but that the change is incidentally related to equality. And yet it is not necessary, regarding a relation being newly expressed about something, that there be a change in it. Rather, it suffices that there be a change in one of the termini, since the cause of a relationship between the two termini is something inhering in both And so, regarding whichever terminus there is a change of what caused the relationship, the relationship between both is removed Accordingly, because there is a change in a creature, a relation about God begins to be expressed. And so we cannot say that he has become anything except metaphorically, since he is related in the likeness of the thing that has come to be inasmuch as one says something new about God. And so we say (Ps. 90:1): "Lord, you have become our refuge."

Obj. 6. Whatever we predicate about something, we predicate about it either substantially or accidentally. But we do not substantially predicate of God things that signify a relation to a creature, since we necessarily and always predicate substantial predicates, nor do we predicate relative things as accidents. Therefore, we can in no way predicate any such relative things about God.

Reply Obj. 6. We should say that, since we begin to predicate such relations with God because of a change made in a creature, it is clear that the reason we predicate them of God regards the creature, and we predicate them accidentally of God. This is not as an accident in him, as Augustine says, but regards something existing outside him that is incidentally related to him, since God's existing does not depend on a creature, just as a builder's does not depend on a house. And so, as it is accidental to a builder that a house exists, so it is accidental to God that a creature does, since we say that anything without which a thing can exist is accidentally related to it.

Article 9

Do Such Relations between Creatures and God Really Exist in Creatures Themselves?

We should say that the relation to God is a thing in a creature. To prove this, we should note that, as Averroes says in his *Commentary on the Metaphysics*,[48] since a relation has the weakest existence of all the categories, some thought that it is one of the second things understood.[49] For the first things understood are things outside the soul, to the understanding of which the intellect is first borne. But we call the second understood things mental representations resulting from our way of understanding, since the intellect understands this by a second act as it reflects on itself, understanding that it understands and the way in which it understands.

Therefore, in this view, it would follow that a relation exists only in the intellect, not in things outside the soul, like the mental representation of genus and species, and secondary substances.

But this cannot be, since we put in a category only something existing outside the soul. For we contradistinguish a conceptual being from a real being, which is subdivided by the ten categories, as the *Metaphysics* makes clear.[50] And if a relation were not to exist in things existing outside the soul, we would not consider a relation one of the categories. Besides, we note the perfection and goodness in things outside the soul both by what absolutely inheres in them and by the order of one thing to another. Just so, the good of an army consists in the ordering of its parts, to which Aristotle compares the order of the universe.[51]

Therefore, there needs to be an order in things themselves, and this order is a relation. And so there need to be some relations in things themselves by which one thing is related to another. But one thing is ordered to another thing by quantity or by an active or passive power, since we note something in one thing in relation to something extrinsic only by these two things. For we measure something by both its external and its internal quantity. Also, each thing acts upon another by its active power, and another acts upon it by reason of its passive power. But substance orders something only to itself, not to something else, except incidentally, namely, insofar as a quality, a substantial form, or the matter has the aspect of an active or passive power, and insofar as we consider an aspect of quantity in it. For example, one substantial thing causes substantially the same thing, and one qualitative thing causes a like quality, and number or multitude causes dissimilarity and diversity in the same things insofar as we consider something more or less such-and-such than another, as, for example, we call one thing whiter than another. And so Aristotle in the *Metaphysics*, assigning the species of relations, considers some caused by quantity and others by acting and being acted upon.[52]

Therefore, things having an order to something are necessarily related to it, and something in them is a relation. But all creatures are ordered to God both as their source and as their end, since the order of the parts of the universe to one another is by the order of the whole universe to God. Just so, the order among the parts of an army is for the sake of the order of the army to its commander, as the *Metaphysics* makes clear.[53] And so creatures are necessarily really related to God, and the relation is something in creatures.

Obj. 3. Something is related only to one definite thing, as the *Metaphysics* says.[54] and so double is related to half, not anything, and father to son, and so forth. Therefore, regarding the difference between related things, there need to be differences between the objects of a relation. But God is one being absolutely. Therefore, there cannot be a relation of all creatures to him by a real relation.

Reply Obj. 3. We should say that Aristotle there concludes that, if all things should be related to the best thing, a specifically infinite thing is necessarily the best thing. And so nothing prevents an infinite number of things being related to what is specifically infinite. The latter is God, since the perfection of his substance is not limited to any genus, as I have maintained (A. 3). And so nothing prevents an unlimited number of creatures being related to him.

Obj. 5. A relation is something in between the termini of the relation. But nothing can be in between God and a creature that he immediately creates. Therefore, a relation cannot be something in a creature.

Reply Obj. 5. We should say that, when one says that a creature proceeds immediately from God, one excludes an intermediate creating cause but not an intermediate real relationship, which naturally results from the production of a creature. As equality results from producing quantity indefinitely, so a real relationship naturally results from the production of a created substance.

Obj. 6. Aristotle says that, if all apparent things were true, things would result from our opinion and senses.[55] But it is evident that all creatures result from the thought, or knowledge, of their creator. Therefore, all creatures are substantially related to God and not by an inherent relation.

Reply Obj. 6. We should say that creatures result from God's knowledge as an effect from its cause, not as its own reason of existing, so that a creature's existing consists of nothing else than being known by God. But those who say that all apparent things are true, and a thing results from one's opinion and sense perception, held this position, namely, that being perceived and thought by another would be existing for a thing.

Obj. 7. There seems to be less relation between things that are more distant from one another. But there is a greater distance of a creature from God than of one creature from another. But the relation of a creature to a creature is not a thing, as it seems, since, inasmuch as it is not a substance, it needs to be an accident. And so, without a change in the subject, it cannot be present in, nor excluded from, the subject. But we have previously stated the contrary about relation. Therefore, the relation of a creature to God is not a thing.

Reply Obj. 7. We should say that the relation that is only the order of one creature to another has one thing insofar as it is an accident, and another thing insofar as it is a relation or order. For insofar as it is an accident, it has existing in a subject, but insofar as it is a relation or order, it has only existing in relation to something else as if passing into the other and somehow supporting the related thing. And so the relation is something inherent, although not because it is a relation. (Just so, we consider action, because it is such, to issue from an active thing, but insofar as it is an accident, we consider it as in the active subject.) And so nothing prevents such an accident from ceasing to

exist without a change in its subject, since its essence is not perfected as it
exists in its subject but is perfected as it passes into something else. When the
other is removed, the essence of the accident is taken away regarding the actuality but abides regarding the cause, just as heating is taken away when
material is removed, although the cause of heating remains.

Article 10

Is God Really Related to a Creature, So That
the Relation Is Something in God?

We should say that the relations predicated about God in relation to a creature
are not really in him. To prove this, we should note that, since a real relation
consists of the order of one thing to another, as I have said (A. 9), a mutual
real relation only exists in things in which there is the same aspect of order on
the part of both. This is true about all the relations resulting from quantity,
since, inasmuch as the notion of quantity is abstracted from every sensibly
perceptible thing, the quantity in all natural material substances belongs to
the same notion. And by the same reason why one quantified thing is related
to another, the other thing is also related to it.

And one quantity, absolutely speaking, has an order to another by the
aspect of measure and measured, the name of whole and part, and the like,
which result from quantity. But in relations that result from acting and being
acted upon or from active and passive power, there is not always the same
order of movement on the part of both. For, inasmuch as effects are always
perfected by their cause and depend on it, what always has the nature of undergoing action and being moved, or caused, necessarily has an order to the
active thing or cause of motion. And so an effect is ordered to its cause as what
perfects it.

And active things, whether movers or causers, sometimes have an order to
the things acted upon, whether the latter have been moved or caused, namely,
inasmuch as we note the good and perfection of the cause or active thing in
the effect, whether by being acted upon or by things brought about by movement. For example, this is most evident in univocal active things, which by
their action bring about their specific likeness and so their perpetual existing
as far as this is possible.

This same thing is evident in all other things that, when moved, move,
produce, or cause something, since they by their movement are ordered to
producing effects, and likewise in all things in which any good comes to a
cause from its effect. But there are some things to which other things are

ordered, but not vice versa, since they are altogether external to the genus of actions or powers from which such an order results. For example, it is evident that knowledge is related to a knowable thing, since a knower by an intelligible act has an order to a known thing existing outside the soul. But such an act does not touch the thing outside the soul, since the act of the intellect does not go on to change external matter. And so also the very thing outside the soul is altogether outside the genus of intelligible things. And so the relation that results from an act of the intellect cannot be in that thing.

And the argument is similar about the senses and sensibly perceptible things. For, although a sensibly perceptible thing in its action alters a sense organ and has a relation to the organ for that reason, just like other natural active things do to things they act upon, the act of a sense power, not the alteration of an organ, perfects actual sense perception, and the sensibly perceptible thing outside the soul does not at all share in the act. Likewise, a human being to the right of a column is so related to it, by reason of the locomotive power in the human being to be able to be to the right or left, before or behind, above or below. And so such relations in a human being or an animal are real but not in a thing that lacks such a power. Likewise, money is outside the genus of the action whereby prices are set, which is the agreement between buyers and sellers. And a human being is outside the genus of the artistic actions that constitute an image of the human being.

And so a human being has no real relation to the human being's image, nor does money to prices. Rather, the converse is true. But God does not produce by means of action understood as proceeding from God and terminating in a creature. Rather, his action is his substance, and whatever is in it is altogether outside the genus of created existing, whereby a creature is related to God. Nor, again, does any good accrue to the creator from producing a creature, and so his action is most generous, as Avicenna says.[56] It is also evident that he is not moved to act. Rather, he causes mutable things without any change in himself.

And so we conclude that there is in him no real relation to a creature, although there is a relation of a creature to him, as an effect to its cause.

Rabbi Moses errs in this regard in many ways. He sought to prove that there is no relation between God and a creature because, inasmuch as God is not a material substance, he has no relation to time or place. For he considered only a relation that results from quantity, not one that results from acting and being acted upon.

Obj. 1. The thing causing movement is really related to the thing moved, and so Aristotle considers the relation between the thing causing movement and the thing moved as a species of the category of relation.[57] But God is

related to a creature as the cause of movement to the thing moved. Therefore, he is really related to a creature.

Reply Obj. 1. We should say that the natural cause of movement and an active thing moves and acts by an action or intermediate movement that is
between the thing causing movement and the thing moved, the active thing
and the thing being acted upon. And so, at least in this intermediary, the active
thing and the thing being acted upon, the cause of movement and the thing
moved, are necessarily united. And so the active thing as such is not extrinsic
to the genus of the thing undergoing action, as it is such. And so a real relation
of one to the other belongs to each, especially since the intermediate action is
a particular perfection of the active thing. And so the thing at which an action
terminates is a good of the active thing. But this does not happen regarding
God, as I have said, and so there is no comparison.

Obj. 4. Things that we properly, not metaphorically, predicate of God posit
the thing signified in God. But Dionysius posits among these predicates the
name *Lord.*[58] Therefore, the thing signified by the word *Lord* is really in God.
But this is a relation to a creature. Therefore, God is really related to a creature.

Reply Obj. 4. We should say that the word *Lord* includes three things in its
concept, namely, the power to coerce subjects, the relation to subjects that
results from such power, and the determination of the subjects' relation to the
lord, since in one relative thing is understanding of the other. Therefore, we
preserve the meaning of this word regarding God as to the first and the third
but not as to the second. And so Ambrose says that the word *Lord* is the name
of power,[59] and Boethius says dominion is the power to coerce a slave.

Obj. 5. Knowledge is really related to a knowable thing, as the *Metaphysics*
makes clear.[60] But God is related to created things as knower to the thing
known. Therefore, there is a relation to a creature in God.

Reply Obj. 5. We should say that God's knowledge is related to things in a
different way than our knowledge is, since his knowledge is related to a being
as its cause and measure. For things accord with truth as much as God by his
knowledge has ordained them, but those things are the cause and measure of
our knowledge. And so, just as our knowledge is really related to things, and
not the converse, so things are really related to God's knowledge, and not the
converse. Or we should say that God understands other things by understanding himself, and so the relation of God's knowledge is to the divine
essence itself, not to the things directly.

Obj. 11. The relative things we predicate temporally of God regard either
existence or expression. If they regard expression, they posit nothing in
either terminus. But according to what has been said before, this is false,
since they really exist in a creature related to God. Therefore, we conclude

that they regard existence, and so it seems that they really posit something in both termini.

Reply Obj. 11. We should say that the distinction between things relative regarding existence and things relative regarding expression does not cause a real relation regarding the former. For some relative things regarding existence are not real, such as right and left in a column, and some relative things regarding expression signify real relations, such as is evident about knowledge and the sense perception. We call things relative regarding existence when we impose words to signify the very relations, but we call things relative regarding expression when we impose words chiefly to signify qualities or some such thing from which relations result. Nor. regarding this issue, does it matter whether they are real or merely conceptual relations.

Article 11

Are These Temporal Relations in God Conceptually?

We should say that, as a real relation consists of the order of a thing to a thing, so a conceptual relation consists of the order of things understood. The latter can happen in two ways. It happens in one way insofar as the intellect arrives at an order, and the order is attributed to what we say relatively. Such are the relations that the intellect attributes to understood things as such, such as the relation of genus and species, since reason comes to these relations by considering the order of what is in the intellect to things outside it or by considering the order of understood things to one another.

It happens in the second way insofar as such relations result from a way of understanding, namely, that the intellect understands something in relation to something else, although the intellect does not discover that relation, but rather the relation necessarily results from the way of understanding. And we attribute such relations of the intellect to what is in the thing, not to what is in the intellect.

This happens insofar as we understand a relation in some things that do not have the relation as such, although the intellect does not understand that the things have the relation, since it would then be false. And in order that some things have a relation, each needs to be a distinct being (since there is no relation of the same thing to itself) and able to be related to something else.

The intellect sometimes considers two things as beings, only one or neither of which is such, as when the intellect considers two future things, or one present and the other future, and understands one with a relation to the other, asserting that one is prior to the other. And so these relations are only conceptual, as resulting from the way of understanding.

Sometimes, the intellect considers one thing as two things and understands those things with a relation, as when one says that something is the same as itself, and so such a relation is only conceptual.

Sometimes, the intellect considers two things as capable of a relation to each another, between which there is no relation, and one of them is itself essentially a relation, as when one says that a relation happens to its subject. And so such a relation of a relation to anything else is only conceptual.

But sometimes, the intellect considers something with a relation to something else inasmuch as it is the terminus of the relation of the other thing to it, although it is not itself related to the other thing. For example, by considering a knowable thing as the terminus of the relation of knowledge to it and so with a relation to knowledge of it, the word *knowable* signifies relatively, and the relation is purely conceptual. Likewise, our intellect attributes some relative terms to God, inasmuch as it considers God as the terminus of the relations of creatures to him. And so such relations are purely conceptual.

Obj. 1. A concept to which no thing corresponds is useless and vain, as Boethius says.[61] But these relations are not really in God, as what I have said before (A. 10) makes clear. Therefore, a concept would be useless and vain if such relations belonged to God conceptually.

Reply Obj. 1. We should say that, in such relations, something regarding a thing, namely, the relation of a creature to God, corresponds. For, as we speak of a knowable thing relatively, not because the knowable thing is related to knowledge, but because knowledge is related to the knowable thing, as the *Metaphysics* holds,[62] so we speak of God relatively because creatures are related to him.

Obj. 3. The word *Lord* signifies a relation, since it is relative categorically. But God is Lord not only conceptually. Therefore, such relations are not in God only conceptually.

Reply Obj. 3. We should say that, as one is really identical with oneself and not only conceptually (although the relation is only conceptual), since the cause of the relation is real, namely, the substantial unity that the intellect understands relationally, so the power to coerce subjects is really in God. The intellect understands this power in relation to subjects because of the relation of subjects to God. And so we call him Lord really, although the relation is only conceptual. In the same way, he evidently would be Lord were no human intellect to exist.

Question 8

THE THINGS THAT WE PREDICATE OF GOD ETERNALLY

Article 1

Are the Relations Predicated of God Eternally, Which the Terms *Father* and *Son* Signify, Real or Purely Conceptual Relations?

We should say that those who follow the opinion of the Catholic faith need to say that the relations in the Godhead are real, since the Catholic faith posits in God three Persons of one essence. But every number results from a distinction. And so there is necessarily a distinction in God both regarding creatures, which differ essentially from him, and regarding one subsisting in the divine essence.

But this distinction cannot be by anything absolute, since any absolute thing we predicate in the Godhead signifies the essence of God. And so it would follow that the divine Persons were essentially different, which is heresy. Therefore, we conclude that one notes a distinction in the divine persons only by relative things.

This distinction cannot be purely conceptual, since nothing prevents things that differ only conceptually from being predicated of one another, as we say that the beginning of a line is its end, since one and the same point is really the beginning and the end of the line, although conceptually different. And so it would follow that the Father is the Son, and the Son is the Father, since, inasmuch as we give names in order to signify the notions of the names, it would follow that we distinguish the Persons in the Godhead only nominally, which is the heresy of Sabellius.

Therefore, we conclude that one needs to say that the relations in God are real things, and we need to investigate how this is by following what the saints say, although we cannot fully arrive at the reason for this. Therefore, we need to note that, since we can understand a real relation only if it results from quantity, or from acting or being acted upon, we necessarily posit a relation in God in one of those ways.

But there cannot be quantity, whether continuous or discrete, in God, nor anything having similarity to it except the multiplicity that a relation causes (for which we need first to understand the relation) and the oneness that belongs to the essence, to which the resulting relation of identity is only conceptual, not real, like the relation that the word *same* signifies, as I have said before (Q. 7, A. 11).

Therefore, we conclude that we need to posit in him a relation resulting from action. I do not speak of the action that goes into something acted upon, since nothing can be acted upon in God, inasmuch as there is no matter in him, and there is no real relation to what is outside God, as I have said (Q. 7, A. 10).

Therefore, we conclude that the real relation in God results from an action abiding in the active thing, and actions in God consist of understanding and willing. For sense perception, inasmuch as a bodily organ completes it, cannot belong to God, who is altogether immaterial. And so Dionysius says that there is perfect fatherhood in God, that is, intelligibly, not corporally or materially.[1] And intelligence in the one understanding can have an order to four things, namely, to the thing understood, to the intelligible form that causes the intellect actually to understand, to the actual understanding, and to the intellect's concept.

The concept differs from the other three aforementioned things. It differs from the thing understood in that the thing understood is sometimes outside the intellect, but the intellect's concept is only in the intellect. Also, the intellect's concept is ordered to the thing understood as its end, since the intellect forms within itself the concept of a thing in order to know the thing known. The concept differs from the intelligible form, since we consider the intelligible form that makes the intellect actual as the source of the intellect's action, inasmuch as every active thing acts insofar as it is actual, and a form, which needs to be the source of action, makes the active thing actual. And the concept differs from the intellect's action in that we consider the aforementioned concept as the terminus of an action and as if something constituted by it, since the intellect by its action forms the definition of a thing or an affirmative or negative proposition. We properly call this intellectual concept in us a word, since it is what an external word signifies, inasmuch as an external word signifies the intellect's concept, by means of which an external word is related to a thing, and does not signify the very thing understood, the intelligible form, or the act of the intellect.

Therefore, such a concept, or word, whereby our intellect understands something different from itself, arises from, and represents, something else. It arises from the intellect by the intellect's act and is a likeness of the thing understood. But when the intellect understands itself, the aforementioned word, or concept, is an offspring and likeness of the same thing, namely, of the intellect understanding itself. This so happens because the effect is like the cause by its form, and the form of the intellect is the thing understood. And so the word that arises from the intellect is a likeness of the thing understood, whether it is the same as the intellect, or something else.

And such a word of our intellect is external to the existing of the intellect itself, since it consists of the intellect being acted upon, not part of the intellect's essence, but not external to the understanding of the intellect, since the very understanding could not be accomplished without the aforementioned word.

Therefore, if an intellect should be one whose understanding is its existing, it will be necessary that the word not be external to the intellect's existing, nor to its understanding. Such is the divine intellect, since existing and understanding are the same thing in God. Therefore, his Word is necessarily co-essential with him, not outside his essence.

Therefore, there can be in God the origin of one thing from another, namely, the Word and the one producing the Word, without prejudice to the unity of the divine essence. For whenever there is an origin of one thing from another, we need to posit in it a real relation, either only regarding what originates, when it does not receive the same nature that its source has, as is evident in the origin of a creature from God, or regarding both, namely, when the thing originating attains the nature of its source. The latter is evident in the generation of human beings, in which there is a real relation in both the father and the son. But the Word in the Godhead is co-essential with its source, as I have shown. Therefore, we conclude that there is a real relation regarding both the Word and the one producing the Word.

Obj. 3. There is in God no real relation to a creature, since he produces creatures without change in himself, as Augustine says.[2] But far more does the Father produce the Son, and the Son proceed from the Father, without change. Therefore, there is no real relation of the Father to the Son in the Godhead, or vice versa.

Reply Obj. 3. We should say that, as God is not changed in the production of his creature, so he is not changed in the production of his Word. But a creature does not attain the divine essence and nature. And so the divine nature is not communicated to a creature. And so there is a relation of God to a creature by reason of what happens regarding the creature, not because of anything happening in God. But the Word is produced as consubstantial with

God himself. And so God is related to his Word by what is in God and not only by what regards the Word. For there is a real relation regarding one and not the other when the relation results from what one and not the other causes, as is evident in the case of a knowable thing and a knower, since the act of the knower, not something knowable causes such relations.

Obj. 9. Since God is the supreme source and ultimate end of things, things that need to be traced to other, prior things cannot be in God, but only things to which other things are traceable, as we trace what is moveable to what is unmovable, and the accidental to the intrinsic. And so God is not moved, nor is there anything accidental in him. But we trace everything that we say in relation to something else to something absolute in relation to itself. Therefore, there is nothing in God in relation to something else but only something predicated in relation to himself.

Reply Obj. 9. We should say that we trace the moveable and the accidental to something prior as the imperfect to the perfect, since an accident is imperfect, and, likewise, movement is the activity of something imperfect. But a relation sometimes results from the perfection of a thing, as is evident in the case of the intellect, since a relation results from its operation, which is its perfection. And so the divine perfection does not prevent us from positing a relation in God as it prevents us from positing movement and an accident in him.

Obj. 11. Every real relation, as was held in Q. 7, A. 9, results from a quantity or from acting or being acted upon. But there is no quantity in God, since we call God great without quantity, as Augustine says in *Trinity*.[3] There is also no number in him from which a relation could result, as Boethius says,[4] although we consider a number that relations cause. Therefore, if there is a real relation in God, it necessarily belongs to him by an action of his. But it cannot be by the action whereby he produces creatures, since it was held in Q. 7, A. 10, that there is in God no real relation to a creature. Nor also can it be by a personal action that we posit in the Godhead, such as generating. For, inasmuch as generating in the Godhead belongs only to a distinct existing individual, and only relation causes distinction in the Godhead, we need to understand beforehand a relation to such action, and so a relation cannot result from such action. Therefore, we conclude that, if a relation really existing in God should result from an action of his, it results from the eternal and essential action of his that consists of understanding and willing. But this also cannot be, since a relation of one who understands to the thing understood results from such action, and such relations are not real in God. Otherwise, it would be necessary that the one understanding and the thing understood be really different in the Godhead, which is evidently false, since we predicate both of the individual Persons. For the Father is one who understands, as are the Son and the Holy

Spirit, and each of them is likewise in what is understood. Therefore, there can be no real relation in God, as it seems.

Reply Obj. 11. We should say that a real relation results from the action of the intellect, so that we understand a real relation of the one who understands to the Word, not to the thing understood, since a word, not the thing understood, proceeds from one who understands.

Obj. 12. Natural human reason can arrive at knowledge of the divine intellect, since philosophers have proved conclusively that God is intelligence. Therefore, if real relations, which we express to distinguish the Persons in the Godhead, should result from action of the intellect, it seems that human reason could discover the Trinity of Persons, and so it would not be an article of faith. For Hebr. 11:1 says: "Faith is the substance of things to be hoped for, the proof of things not apparent."

Reply Obj. 12. We should say that, although natural reason can arrive at showing that God is intellect but cannot adequately discover his way of understanding, since, as we can know about God that he exists but not what he is, so we can know about God that he understands but not how he understands. But having a conception of the Word in his understanding belongs to the way of his understanding. And so reason cannot adequately prove these things but can conjecture in a way by likeness from what is in us.

Article 2

Is Relation in God His Substance?

We should say that, assuming that relations exist in the Godhead, it is necessary to say that they are the divine essence. Otherwise, it would be necessary to posit composition in God, and that the relations are accidents in the Godhead, since everything inhering in something besides its substance is an accident. It would also be necessary that something that will not be the divine substance be eternal. All of these things are heretical.

Therefore, to prove this, we should note that the nature of an accident signifies some of the nine kinds of accident, since the nature of an accident is to be present in something. And so I say that the way of an accident signifies the things signified as inhering in something else, such as quantity and quality do, since we signify quantity as belonging to something in which it exists, and likewise quality. But we do not signify a relation by the nature of an accident, since we signify it as a relation to something external, not as part of the thing in which it rests. This is also why Aristotle says that knowledge as a relation is of the thing known, not the knower.[5]

And so some, noting the way of signifying in relative things, said that those things do not inhere in substances, namely, as if supporting the substance, since we signify them as to something in between the substance that is related and that to which the substance is related. And so it followed that relations are not accidents in created things, since the existing of an accident is to be in something.

And so also some theologians, namely, the followers of Gilbert de la Porrée extended this position to the divine relations, saying that those relations are not in the Persons but support them, as it were. And because the divine essence consists of the Persons, it followed that the relations were not the divine essence, and because every accident inheres in a subject, it followed that the relations were not accidents. And they accordingly analyzed the cited words of Augustine,[6] namely, that we do not predicate relations of God substantially or accidentally. But it follows from this opinion that the relation is purely conceptual, not a thing, since a thing is either a substance or an accident.

And so also some ancients held that relations concern second things understood, as Averroes says in his *Commentary on the Metaphysics*.[7] And so the followers of de la Porrée need to say that the divine relations are purely conceptual. And so it will follow that the distinction of the Persons will not be real, which is heretical.

And so we should say that nothing prevents something from being inherent and yet not being signified as such, just as we signify action as being by an active thing, not in it, and yet action is evidently in the active thing. Likewise, although we do not signify a relation as inhering, it is still necessary that it be inhering. This is true when the relation is real, but not when the relation is purely conceptual. And as a relation is necessarily an accident in created things, so it is a substance in God, since whatever is in God is his substance. Therefore, real relations in God are the divine substance but have a way of predicating different from things predicated substantially in God.

Obj. 4. Nothing absolute distinguishes the divine Persons, since it would follow that they differ essentially, inasmuch as things predicated of God absolutely, such as goodness, wisdom, and then like, signify his essence. Therefore, if the relations are the same as the divine substance, it will be necessary either that relations do not distinguish the Persons, or that the Persons are distinguished essentially.

Reply Obj. 4. We should say that essential attributes both signify what is the divine essence and signify it in a certain way, since they signify something existing in God. And so a difference regarding absolute things would lead to essential diversity. But divine relations, although they signify what is the divine essence, do not by way of the essence, since they signify by way of being related to something else, not by way of existing in something. And so the distinction that we note regarding relations in the divine essence do not signify difference in the essence but signify only that there is a relation to something else by way of origin, as I have just explained.

Obj. 6. Whatever we predicate of a predicate, we predicate of its subject. But if a relation is the divine essence itself, the following predications will be true: the divine essence is paternity, and sonship is the divine essence. Therefore, it will follow that sonship is paternity.

Reply Obj. 6. We should say that the objection holds regarding intrinsically predicable things, and we intrinsically predicate something of something when we predicate it according to its own nature. But we indeed do not intrinsically predicate what we do not predicate according to its own nature but rather in order to identify a thing. Therefore, when one says: *the divine essence is paternity*, one predicates paternity of the divine essence because of real, not conceptual, identity, and likewise if one predicates the divine essence of paternity, as I have already said, since divine essence and relation are different aspects. And so the logical fallacy of accident occurs in aforementioned objection. For, although there is no accident in God, there is the likeness of an accident inasmuch as things that are predicated of one another as accidents and differ conceptually are one and the same in the subject.

Obj. 7. Any things the same are so disposed that we may predicate of one whatever we predicate of the other, since, according to Aristotle,[8] "howsoever slight the difference we assign, we will be showing that they are not the same." But we predicate of the divine essence that it is wise, that it creates the world, and the like, which do not seem able to be predicated of paternity and sonship. Therefore, relation in the Godhead is not the divine essence.

Reply Obj. 7. We should say, as Aristotle says in the *Physics*,[9] that it is not necessary to predicate all the same predicates about things in any way the same but only about things by definition the same. But the divine essence and paternity, although they are really the same, are not conceptually the same. And so it is not necessary that we predicate of one whatever we predicate of the other. But we should note that there are some things that result from the particular definitions of essence and relation, such as that common existing is a consequence of essence, and difference a consequence of relation. And so one of these excludes the other, since essence does not distinguish, and relation is not common. But some things regarding the way of signifying, not the chief thing signified, have a difference from the definition of essence or relation, and we predicate them of essence or relation, although not in the proper sense. Such are adjectives and participial verbs, such as good, wise, understanding, and willing, since, regarding the thing signified, they signify the essence itself, but they signify it by way of the existing individual, not in the abstract. And so we most properly predicate good, wise, creating, and such like of the Persons and of such concrete essential titles as God, Father. But one improperly predicates them of the essence signified in the abstract and not by way of the existing individual. Still less properly does one predicate them of relations, since such belong to the existing individual by the essence, not by the relation. God is good or creating because he has the divine essence, not because he has a relation.

Obj. 11. Relation and essence in the Godhead differ art least conceptually. But where there is a different aspect, or definition, there is the existing of different things, since a definition is language indicating what something is. Therefore, one thing will be the existing of the relation in the Godhead, and the other thing will be the existing of the substance. Therefore, relation and substance differ regarding existing, and so really.

Reply Obj. 11. We should say that in no way is there existence in the Godhead except that of the essence, as there is no understanding except that of the intellect. And so, as there is in God only one act of understanding, so also there is only one existing. And so we should in no way concede that one thing is the existing of relation in the Godhead, and another is that of the divine essence. But a definition signifies being some kind of thing, that is, what something is, not its existing. And so two definitions of one and the same thing do not demonstrate two existences. Rather, they demonstrate that we can in two ways predicate of that thing what it is, as we can predicate of a point what it is as the beginning and end of a line because of the different definition of beginning and end.

Article 3

Do the Relations Constitute and Distinguish the Persons or Hypostases?

We should say that there are two opinions about this. The first is that the relations in the Godhead do not constitute or distinguish the hypostases but show them as distinct and constituted. To prove this, one should note that the word *hypostasis* signifies an individual substance, that is, one that cannot be predicated of several things. And so we cannot call genera and species in the category of substance, such as human being and animal, hypostases, since we predicate them of many things, but we call Socrates and Plato a hypostasis, since we predicate each of them of only one thing. Therefore, if we were not to assume the Trinity of Persons in the Godhead, as Jews and pagans hold, there is no need to look for anything in the Godhead other than the divine essence as constitutive and distinctive of a hypostasis, since God is by his essence something undivided in himself and distinct from all the things that are not God.

But because the Catholic faith holds one essence in three Persons, one cannot understand the divine essence as distinctive and constitutive of a hypostasis in the Godhead. For we understand that the divinity constitutes God as what is common to the three Persons and so signifies as predicated of several things, not as an incommunicable hypostasis. By the same reasoning, we can understand nothing predicated absolutely of God as distinctive and constitutive of a hypostasis in the Persons, since the way of the essence signifies things predicated absolutely of God.

Therefore, we need to consider what we first find not to be predicated of several things but to belong to only one thing as distinctive and constitutive of a hypostasis in the Godhead. But there are two such things: relation and origin, both generation and fatherhood, or being generated and sonship, which couplets, although really the same thing in God, differ conceptually and in their way of signifying. The first of these things conceptually is origin, since relation seems to result from origin.

And so this opinion holds that origin constitutes and distinguishes the hypostases in the Godhead, as, when we say that one thing is from another, and that the other is from that one, we signify that the relations of fatherhood and sonship conceptually result from the constitution and distinction of the Persons and manifest their constitution and distinction. For, by calling one the Father, we manifest that another is from him, and by calling one the Son, we manifest that he is from another. But, according to this opinion, we do not need to say that any absolute things distinguish the divine hypostases if the relations do not distinguish them, since the very origins signify a relation. For, as we speak of a father in relation to a son, so do we speak of the one begetting in relation to the one begotten.

But this opinion does not seem to be fittingly viable, since we can in two ways understand the thing distinctive and constitutive of a hypostasis. We can in one way understand it to distinguish and constitute a hypostasis by its form, such as a human being by humanity, and Socrates by being Socrates. We can in a second way understand it to distinguish and constitute a hypostasis by the process leading to differentiating and constituting a hypostasis, as it were, as if we were to say that Socrates is a human being by generation, which is the process leading to the human form, which formally constitutes it. Therefore, we evidently can understand the origin of something as constitutive and distinctive of it only because of what formally constitutes and distinguishes it. For generation, if it were not to produce humanity, would never constitute a human being. Therefore, we cannot say that being generated constitutes the Son's hypostasis except inasmuch as we understand that his being generated terminates in what formally constitutes the hypostasis. And the very relation in which being generated terminates is sonship.

Therefore, sonship necessarily and formally constitutes and distinguishes the hypostasis of the Son, not origin or the relation understood in origin, since the relation understood in origin, just like origin itself, signifies something tending toward a nature, not anything hitherto subsisting in nature. And because the same consideration of constitution and distinction belongs to all hypostases of the same nature, so it is necessary to understand regarding the Father that paternity, not active generation or the included relation, constitutes and distinguishes the hypostasis of the Father.

And the second opinion is this, that the relations constitute the Persons and hypostases, and we can understand this as follows. Paternity is the very divine essence, as I have proved (A. 2), and by the same reasoning, the Father is the same as God. Therefore, paternity, by constituting the Father, constitutes God. But as paternity, although the divine essence, is not common to the Persons, like the essence, so the Father, although the same as God, is something proper, not common, like God. Therefore, God the Father as God is something common having the divine nature, and as Father is something proper distinct from the other Persons. And so he is a hypostases, which signifies subsisting in a nature, distinct from the other hypostasis. And paternity in this way, by constituting the Father, constitutes the hypostasis.

Obj. 4. You might say that, when the relation has been excluded, the Father is the divine essence. On the contrary, what is in something relative besides the relation is related to something else by that relation, as is evident in the examples posited by Augustine.[10] For example, the relation of lordship relates a human being to a slave. But the essence in the Godhead is not related, since it neither generates nor is generated. Therefore, we cannot understand this about the divine essence but can about the relation of the existing individuals to whom generating and being generated belong.

Reply Obj. 4. We should say that, although we do not predicate a relation of the divine essence by way of a form, we do predicate it of the divine essence by way of identity. For, if we should not say that the divine essence is generating or related, we nevertheless say that it is a generation and relation. But we even formally predicate relative things of essential terms concretely signified. For we say that God generates God, and that God is related to God because we understand the same existing individual of both the relation and the essence, as I have shown (A. 2), although the essential terms are not distinguished.

And so, with the relative terms excluded, we understand the essential terms as concrete, not as distinct, which the relations express relatively.

Obj. 5. We consider each thing in itself before we relate it to something else. But what is subsequent to it in our understanding constitutes nothing. Therefore, the relation that relates the Father to something else does not constitute his hypostasis.

Reply Obj. 5. We should say that there is in any divine hypostasis what we predicate absolutely, which belongs to the divine essence, and this in our way of understanding is prior to what we predicate relatively in the Godhead. But what we predicate absolutely, since it is common, does not pertain to distinguishing the hypostasis. And so it does not follow that understanding a distinct hypostasis precedes understanding its relation.

Obj. 7. Understanding the hypostasis generating precedes understanding the generation itself, since we understand the one generating as the source of the generation, and understanding generation precedes understanding paternity. For relations are consequences of actions and being acted upon, as the *Metaphysics* says.[11] Therefore, understanding the hypostasis of the Father precedes understanding paternity. Therefore, paternity does not constitute the hypostasis of the Father, nor by the same reasoning does sonship constitute the hypostasis of the Son.

Reply Obj. 7. We should say that two things are necessary regarding the nature of a hypostasis. The first is that it be intrinsically subsistent and in itself undivided. The second is that it be distinct from other hypostases of the same nature. But if it should happen that there are no other hypostases of the same nature, there will still be a hypostasis, as in the case of Adam before Eve, when there were no other hypostases in human nature. Therefore it is always necessary to understand the hypostasis generating before generation, insofar as the hypostasis intrinsically subsists and is individual but not insofar as it is distinct from other hypostases of the same nature if other hypostases of the same nature should originate only by such generation. For example, Adam was not distinct from other hypostases of the same nature before Eve was formed from his rib, and before he generated children.

But only the procession of other Persons from one Person multiplies hypostases in the Godhead. Therefore understanding the hypostasis of the Father, insofar as it is subsistent, precedes understanding generation, but not insofar as it is distinct from other hypostases of the same nature, which proceed only with this generation presupposed. But the relations in the Godhead, although they constitute hypostases and make them subsistent, they do this inasmuch as they are the divine essence. For a relation as such does not have the power to subsist or cause subsistence, as this belongs only to a substance. But the relations as such distinguish, since they have opposition in this way. Therefore, we conclude that we understand the relation of paternity, insofar as it constitutes the hypostasis of the Father, which it has insofar as it is the same as the divine substance, before generation, but insofar as the relation of paternity distinguishes the Father, we then understand generation before paternity. But no difficulty remains regarding the Son, since birth conceptually precedes the hypostasis of the one born, since we understand birth as the way to the hypostasis, since generation is the process to a substance.

Obj. 11. One should not ask how two things differ unless they agree in something that something additional differentiates in each. For example, animal is common to a human being and a horse, but added specific differences distinguish a rational animal from an irrational animal. And so we can ask how a human being is different from a horse. And things that agree in nothing so as to be distinguishable in the aforementioned way are distinguished by themselves and not by something distinguishing them. But two hypostases in the Godhead are one only in essence, which a relation in no way distinguishes. Therefore, we should say that the hypostases distinguish themselves, not that the relations do.

Reply Obj. 11. We should say that, although there are really common things in the Godhead only in the unity of the essence, we conceptually note common things in the divine Persons in what is to be substituted for the essence. We signify this commonality in all the concrete essential terms, which signify being the existing individual Person in general, such as God is one who has divinity. Therefore, the very thing that it is to be an existing individual of the divine nature is common to the three Persons by a conceptual commonality, although the three Persons are three existing individuals, not one. Just so, Socrates and Plato are two human beings, although being a human being is conceptually common. But we seek a difference both in things in which there is something really common and in things in which there is something conceptually common.

Article 4

Does a Hypostasis Remain When We Exclude a Relation Conceptually?

We should say that, as I said before (A. 3), some held that only origin, not the relations, constitutes and distinguishes the hypostases. And they said that the relations result from the very origin of the Persons, as the termini of their origin, which designate its completion, and so belong to a dignity. And so, since *person* denotes an excellence, they said that such relations understood as added to hypostases constitute the Persons, and so they said that such relations constitute the Persons but not the hypostases.

And so some call such relations excellences, and so, as with us, when things belonging to an excellence, which make a human being a person, have been excluded from the human being, the human being's hypostasis abides, so in the Godhead, when the intellect has excluded such personal relations from the Persons, they say that the hypostases but not the Persons remained.

But because I have already shown before (A. 3) that the aforementioned relations both constitute and distinguish the hypostases, so others should say that, when the intellect has removed such relations, as the Persons do not abide, so neither do the hypostases. For, when one has removed what constitutes something, what it constitutes cannot abide.

Obj. 2. The Father does not have from the same thing that he is someone, and that he is the Father, since the Son is also someone and not the Father. Therefore, if we exclude from the Father that he is the Father, it remains that he is someone. But he is someone inasmuch as he is a hypostasis. Therefore, if the intellect excludes his paternity, the hypostasis of the Father still remains.

Reply Obj. 2. We should say that the Father has from the same thing that he is someone, and that he is the Father. I say *from the same thing* really, not conceptually, but differing conceptually, whether as the general differs from the specific, or the common from the particular. For example, it is clear that a human being has from the same substantial form that the human being is an animal, and that the human being is a human being, since there are not several really distinct substantial forms of one and the same thing. But a human being has from the soul as sensibly perceptive only that the human being is an animal, but has from the soul as sensibly perceptive and rational that the human being is a human being. And so also a horse is an animal and not a human being, since a horse does not have the numerically same sensibly perceptive soul that a human being has, and so also a horse is not the numerically same animal as a human being.

I say likewise about the proposed question, that the Father has from a relation that he is someone, and that he is the Father, but he has the former from the relation generally understood, and he has the latter from the relation that is paternity. And because of this, the Son also, in whom there is a relation, but not the relation of paternity, is someone but not the one who is the Father.

Obj. 3. Since we understand something by its definition, we can understand a thing when we exclude what we do not posit in its definition. But we do not posit relation in the definition of a hypostasis. Therefore, if relation has been excluded, we still understand the hypostasis.

Reply Obj. 3. We should say that we can in two ways consider something in a relation of something, namely, explicitly, that is, actually, and implicitly, that is, potentially. For we do not explicitly and actually posit the rational soul in the definition of animal, since then every animal would have a rational soul, but we do so implicitly and potentially, since an animal is an animated sensory substance. And as rational soul is included potentially in soul, so rational is included potentially in animated. And so, when the definition of animal is actually attributed to a human being, rational is necessarily explicitly part of the definition of animal, insofar as animal is identical with human being.

And it is likewise in the proposed question, since hypostasis, as generally understood, is a distinct substance. And so, since there can be a distinction in the Godhead only by relation, it is necessary that when I speak of a divine hypostasis, I understand a distinct relation. And so, although relation does not fall within the definition of the hypostasis that is a human being, it does within the definition of a divine hypostasis.

Obj. 5. Everything having an addition remains as it was before the addition when the addition is excluded. For example, a human being adds rational to animal, and so the human being remains an animal when we exclude rationality. But person adds a property to hypostasis, since a person is a hypostasis distinguished by a property pertaining to excellence. Therefore, when the property has been conceptually excluded from the person, the hypostasis remains.

Reply Obj. 5. We should say that there is one way to define accidents, and another to define substance, since we do not define substances by anything outside their essence. And so what we first posit in the definition of a substance is its genus, which we predicate regarding what is the essence of the thing defined. But we define accident by something outside the thing's essence, namely, the subject, on which the accident depends regarding its existing. And so what we posit in its definition, in place of genus in the definition of a substance, is the subject, as, for example, when we say: "Something pug-nosed is flat-nosed." Therefore, as the genus remains in the definition of substances after we have excluded specific differences, so, the subject remains in the definition of accidents after we have excluded the accident posited in place of a specific difference, but in different ways. For after a specific difference has been excluded, the remaining genus is not numerically the same. For example, the numerically same animal (i.e., the rational animal) does not remain after we have excluded rational. But the numerically same subject remains after we have excluded what we posited in place of the specific difference in definitions of accidents. For example, after we have excluded pug or flat, the numerically same nose remains. This is because an accident does not complete the essence of the subject as the specific difference completes the essence of a genus.

Therefore, when one says: "a person is a hypostasis with a distinct property pertaining to excellence," one posits hypostasis in the definition of person as a genus, not as subject. And so, after one excludes the property pertaining to excellence, the hypostasis does not remain the same numerically or specifically but only generically the same, as also applied to irrational substances.

Obj. 7. When we conceptually exclude paternity and sonship, there still remains in the Godhead the one who proceeds from another and the one from whom the other comes. But these denote the hypostases. Therefore, when we exclude the relations, the hypostases in the Godhead still remain.

Reply Obj. 7. We should say that when we speak of the one who proceeds from another and the one from whom another comes, they differ from paternity and sonship only as the common from the particular, since the Son signifies the one who is from another by generation, and the Father signifies the one from whom another comes by generation, unless we perhaps should say that the one from whom another comes and the one who proceeds from another signify origin, and Father and Son the consequent relations. But what I have already said before makes clear that relations, not origins, constitute the hypostases.

Question 9

THE DIVINE PERSONS

Article 1

How Is Person Related to Essence, Subsistence, and Hypostasis?

We should say that Aristotle holds that we speak of substance in two ways.[1] We say in one way that a substance is the ultimate subject, which we do not predicate of anything else, and this is a particular thing in the genus of substance, and we say in the second way that a substance is the form or nature of a subject. The reason for this distinction is because many subjects belong to one and the same nature (e.g., many human beings in one human nature). And so we need to distinguish what is one and what is multiple, since a definition signifies a common nature, indicating what a thing is. And so we call a common nature the essence or substance.

Therefore, whatever is in something belonging to a common nature is contained in the meaning of an essence, but not everything in a particular substance is such. For, if everything in a particular substance were to belong to a common nature, there could be no difference between particular substances of the same nature. But what is in a particular substance besides a common nature is the individual matter that is the source of individuality, and so individual accidents that determine the aforementioned matter.

Therefore, essence is related to a particular substance as its formal part, such as humanity to Socrates. And so, in things composed of matter and form, the essence is not altogether the same thing as the subject, and so it is not predicated of a subject, since we do not say that Socrates is humanity.

But in simple substances, there is no difference between essence and subject, since they do not have individual matter individuating a common nature.

And Aristotle[2] and Avicenna, who says in his *Metaphysics* that the essence of a simple thing is the simple thing itself, make this clear.

And the substance that is a subject has two proper things. The first is that it does not need an external foundation on which to be sustained but is sustained in itself. And so we say that it, existing in itself, as it were, and not in another, subsists. The second is that it is the foundation for accidents, supporting them, and so we say that it underlies them.

Therefore, we call the substance that is a subject, inasmuch as it subsists, a *ousiosis* or subsistence, but inasmuch as it lies under, the Greeks call it a hypostasis, and the Latins a first substance. Therefore, it is clear that hypostasis and substance differ conceptually but are really the same thing.

But the essence in material substances is not really the same thing as they, or completely different from them, since it is disposed as a formal part, and the essence in immaterial things is altogether really the same thing but conceptually different. And person adds a definite nature to hypostasis, since a person is simply the hypostasis of a rational nature.

Obj. 1. Augustine says in *Trinity* that the Greeks, when they profess three hypostases in God, and the Latins, when they profess three Persons, understand the same thing.[3] Therefore, hypostasis and person signify the same thing.

Reply Obj. 1. We should say that, inasmuch as person adds only a rational nature to a hypostasis, a hypostasis and a person in a rational nature are completely the same, as a rational animal is necessarily a human being, since human being adds rational to animal. And so it is true, as Augustine says,[4] that the Greeks, when they profess three hypostases in God, and the Latins, when they profess three Persons, signify the same thing.

Obj. 3. We impose words from concepts of the things they signify. But the same character of individuation is present in things belonging to the same rational nature, and in other substances. Therefore, an individual of rational nature ought not to have a special name besides other individuals in the genus of substance, so that there is thereby a difference between hypostasis and person.

Reply Obj. 3. We should say that, as it is particular to an individual substance to exist of itself, so it is particular that it act of itself, since nothing acts except an actual being. And so, as heat does not exist of itself, it does not act of itself. Rather, a hot thing by its heat warms things. And acting of itself belongs in a more excellent way to substances of a rational nature than to other substances. For only rational substances have mastery over their actions, so that it belongs to them to act or not to act, but other substances are acted upon rather than acting. And so it was fitting that an individual substance of a rational nature had a special name.

Obj. 4. We understand the word *subsistence* from subsisting. But nothing subsists except individuals in the genus of substance, included in which there are accidents and second substances (i.e., genera and species), as Aristotle says in *Categories*. Therefore, only an individual in the genus of substance is a hypostasis or person. Therefore, subsistence is the same as hypostasis and person.

Reply Obj. 4. We should say that, although only an individual substance, which we call a hypostasis, subsists, we do not call it subsistent and a substance by the same aspect, but subsistent inasmuch as it is not in another, and a substance inasmuch as other things are in it. And so, if there were to be a substance that existed intrinsically but was not the subject of any accident, we could properly call it a subsistence but not a substance.

Obj. 6. Boethius says that *ousia*, that is, essence, signifies a composition of matter and form.[5] But this is necessarily an individual, since matter is the source of individuation. Therefore, essence signifies an individual, and so person, hypostasis, essence, and substance are the same.

Reply Obj. 6. We should say that the essence in material substances signifies a composite of matter and form, but common, not individual, matter. For the definition of human being, which signifies the human being's essence, indeed contains flesh and bones, but not particular flesh and bones. But individual matter is included in the meaning of hypostasis and subsistence in material things.

Article 2

What Is a Person?

We should say that we reasonably assign a special name to an individual in the genus of substance, since a substance's own sources individuate it, and an external other thing does not, since a subject individuates an accident. Also, of individual substances, we reasonably give a special name to an individual in a rational nature, since it belongs to such an individual truly and properly to act by itself, as I have said before (A. 1, Reply Obj. 3).

Therefore, as the word *hypostasis*, according to the Greeks, and the term *first substance*, according to the Latins, is a special name of an individual in the genus of substance, so the word *person* is the special name of an individual of rational nature. Therefore, each particularity is included under the name *person*.

And so, in order to show that a person is particularly an individual in the genus of substance, we say that a person is an individual substance, and in order to show that a person is particularly in a rational nature, we say that a person is a substance of rational nature. Therefore, by saying *substance*, we exclude accidents, none of which we can call a person, from the notion of person. By saying *individual*, we exclude genera and species in the genus of substance, which we also cannot call persons. And by saying *of a rational nature*, we exclude nonliving material substances, plants, and irrational animals, which are not persons.

Obj. 1. We do not define anything individual, as Aristotle says in the *Metaphysics*.[6] But person signifies an individual in the genus of substance, as has been said (A. 1). Therefore we cannot define person.

Reply Obj. 1.We should say that there are three things to consider about an individual substance. One is the generic and specific nature existing in individual things. The second is the way of existing of such a nature, since a generic and specific nature exists in an individual substance as proper to that individual and not as common to many. The third is the source that causes such a way of existing. And as a nature, absolutely considered, is common, so also is the nature's way of existing. For example, we find the nature of a human being existing in things only as individuated in a particular individual, since there is no human being who is not a particular human being, except in the opinion of Plato, who posited separate universals. But the source of such a way of existing that is the source of individuation is not common, but one thing is in this one, and another thing in that one, since this matter individuates this individual, and that matter individuates that individual. Therefore, as the word that signifies a nature, such as *human being* or *animal*, is common and definable, so there is a word that signifies a nature with such a way of existing (e.g., *hypostasis* or *person*). But a word that in its signification includes the fixed source of individuation (e.g., *Socrates* or *Plato*) is not common or definable.

Obj. 2. One might say that, although what is a person is something individual, the notion of person is common, and we can to that extent define person. On the contrary, what is common to all individual substances of a rational nature is their singular extension, which is not in the genus of substance. Therefore, we ought not to posit substance in the definition, as if a genus.

Reply Obj. 2. We should say that both singular extension and a generic nature with such a way of existing are common to all individual substances, and the word *hypostasis* in this way signifies the generic nature of substance as individuated, and the word *person* signifies only a rational nature in such a way of existing. And so neither *hypostasis* nor *person* is a word signifying extension, such as singular or individual. They are only the name of a thing, not the name of the thing and its extension simultaneously.

Obj. 5. We do not posit extension in the definition of a thing, nor an accident in the definition of substance. But person is the name of a thing and a substance. Therefore, we improperly posit individual, which is the name of an import or accident, in the definition of person.

Reply Obj. 5. We should say that, since the essential differences of things are often unknown and unnamed, it is sometimes necessary to use accidental differences to designate substantial differences, as Aristotle teaches.[7] We posit individual in this way in the definition of person to designate the individual way of existing.

Obj. 7. We divide substance into first and second substances. But we cannot posit second substance in the definition of person, since there would be a contradiction in terms when one speaks of individual substance, second substance being a universal substance. Likewise, neither can we properly posit first substance in the definition of person, since first substance is individual substance, and then there would be a negation when one adds individual to substance in the definition of person. Therefore, one improperly posits substance in the definition of person.

Reply Obj. 7. We should say that some say that one posits substance in the definition of person to signify hypostasis. But, since individual belongs to the concept of hypostasis, insofar as it is contrary to the commonality of a universal or to a part, inasmuch as we cannot call a universal or a part, such as a hand or foot, a hypostasis, individual also belongs to the concept of person, insofar as it is contrary to the commonality of assumability. For they say that the human nature in Christ is a hypostasis but not a person. And so, to exclude assumability, they add individual in the definition of person.

But this seems contrary to the intention of Boethius in *Two Natures*, who by saying individual excludes the universal from the concept of person. And so it is better to say that we do not posit substance for hypostasis in the definition of person. Rather, we posit substance in the definition for what is common to a first substance, that is, a hypostasis, and to a second substance, and is divided into both. And so we, by adding individual, limit the common thing to a hypostasis, so that it is the same thing to say an individual substance of a rational nature as to say a hypostasis of a rational nature.

Obj. 8. The word *subsistence* seems to be closer to person than substance, since we speak of three subsistences, three Persons, in God, but we speak of only one substance, not three. Therefore, we ought to define person by subsistence rather than substance.

Reply Obj. 8. We should say that the foregoing shows that the argument of this objection is invalid, since we take substance as what is common to every understanding of substance, not as hypostasis. But if one were to take substance as hypostasis, the argument still would not follow, since substance as a hypostasis is more closely related to person than subsistence is, although person refers to something as a subject, like first substance, and not only as subsistent, as subsistence does. But because Latins also relate the word *substance* to signify the divine essence, we, in order to avoid error, do not speak of three substances, as we do of three subsistences. But the Greeks, who distinguish the word *hypostasis* from the word *ousia*, without hesitation profess three hypostases in God.

Obj. 11. Nature is only in moveable things, since it is the source of movement, as the *Physics* says.[8] But essence is in both moveable and immoveable things. Therefore, it was more fitting to posit essence in the definition of person than to posit nature, since we also find persons in both moveable and immoveable things. For human beings, angels, and God are persons.

Reply Obj. 11. We should say that we do not understand nature in the definition of person as it is the source of movement, as Aristotle says,[9] but rather as Boethius defines it:[10] nature is "each thing given form by a specific difference." And because a specific difference completes a definition and puts the thing defined into a species, so the word *nature* belongs in the definition of person, which is specifically in certain substances, more than the word *essence*, which is the most common, does.

Obj. 12. A definition ought to be convertible with the thing defined. But not everything that is an individual substance of rational nature is a person, since the divine essence as such is not a person; otherwise, there would be only one Person in God, as there is only one essence. Therefore, the aforementioned definition improperly defines person.

Reply Obj. 12. We should say that we understand individual in the definition of person as what we predicate of many things, and the divine essence in this respect is not an individual substance in predication, since we predicate the essence of the several Persons, although the essence is in fact individual. But Richard of Saint Victor, correcting the definition of Boethius insofar as we understand a Person in the Godhead, said:[11] "A Person is the incommunicable existence of the divine nature," so that the word *incommunicable* shows that the divine essence is not a Person.

Obj. 13. The human nature in Christ is an individual substance of rational nature, for it is neither an accident nor a universal substance nor the substance of an irrational nature. But the human nature in Christ is not a person, since it would follow that the divine Person that assumed human nature had assumed a human person. And then there would be two persons in Christ, namely, the divine Person assuming and the human person assumed, which is the heresy of Nestorius. Therefore, not every individual substance of rational nature is a person.

Reply Obj. 13. We should say that, since an individual substance is something complete existing intrinsically, we cannot call the human nature in Christ an individual substance, that is, a hypostasis, since it was assumed into a divine person, just like a hand or foot or any of those things that do not intrinsically subsist separate from other things. And so it does not follow that the human nature of Christ is a person.

Article 3

Can There Be Personhood in God?

We should say that, as I have said (A. 2), person signifies a nature with a way of existing. But the nature that person includes in its meaning is the most excellent of all natures, namely, an intellectual nature by its genus. Likewise, the way of existing that person signifies is the most excellent, namely, that something exists intrinsically.

Therefore, since we should attribute to God everything that is most excellent in creatures, we can fittingly attribute the name *person* to God, just like other names that we properly predicate of God.

Obj. 1. As Boethius says,[12] we take the word *person* from impersonating, since people called masked actors persons, as they played a role in comedies and tragedies. But being masked is improper for God, except, perhaps, metaphorically. Therefore, we cannot predicate the word *person* of God, at least according to the aforementioned definition (A. 2).

Reply Obj. 1. We should say that there are two things to consider regarding a word, namely, what we impose the word to signify, and that from which we take it in order to signify. For a word is often taken to signify a thing from an accident or action or effect of that thing, which the word does not chiefly signify but rather signifies the very substance or nature of the thing. For example, we take the word *stone* from the word for hurting the foot,[13] which the word does not signify but rather signifies a material substance in which such an accident often happens. And so hurting the foot pertains to the etymology of the word *stone* more than to its signification.

Therefore, when what a word is imposed to signify is inappropriate for God but is a certain property of his by a certain likeness, we predicate the word of God metaphorically. For example, one calls God a lion because of the strength that one finds in a lion, not because the nature of that animal belongs to God. But when the thing signified by the word belongs to God, such as good, wise, and the like, then we properly predicate the word of God, even though that from which the word is taken sometimes does not belong to God.

Therefore, although impersonating in the way of a masked actor, from which the word *person* was taken, does not belong to God, what the word signifies, namely, subsisting in an intellectual nature, belongs to God, and so we properly understand personhood in the Godhead.

Obj. 3. God is not in a genus, since, inasmuch as he is infinite, he cannot be included within the limits of any genus. But person signifies something in the genus of substance. Therefore, person is unsuitable for God.

Reply Obj. 3. We should say that, although God is not in the genus of substance as a species, he pertains to the genus of substance as its source.

Obj. 4. There is no composition in God. But person signifies something composite, since an individual of human nature is of the greatest composition. Parts of the definition of person demonstrate that person is composite. Therefore, there is no personhood in God.

Reply Obj. 4. We should say that it happens to a person as such to be composite because the complement and perfection required for the nature of a person is not immediately in one simple thing but requires a combination of many things, as is evident in the case of human beings. But in God, the highest perfection accompanies the greatest simplicity, and so there is in him personhood without composition. But the parts posited in the definition of person demonstrate a composition of a person only in the case of material substances, and individual, since it is a negation, does not signify composition by being added to substance. And so there remains in him only the composition of the individual substance, that is, the hypostasis with a nature, which two things in immaterial substances are really altogether the same.

Obj. 5. There is no matter in God. But the source of individuation is matter. Therefore, since a person is an individual substance, it is unsuitable for God.

Reply Obj. 5. We should say that for material things, in which the forms inhere in matter and are not intrinsically subsistent, it is necessary that the source of individuation be from matter. But immaterial forms, since they are intrinsically subsistent, individuate themselves, since, inasmuch as something is subsistent, it has no capacity to be predicated of many things. And so nothing prevents there being an individual substance and a person in immaterial things.

Obj. 6. Every person is a subsistence. But we cannot call God a subsistence, since he is not under anything. Therefore, he is not a person.

Reply Obj. 6. We should say that, although there is no composition in God, so that we can understand anything in him under something else, nevertheless, in our way of understanding, we separately understand his existing and his substance subject to his existing, so that we call his substance subsistent to his existing. Or one should say that, although being subject, from which we take the word *subsisting*, does not belong to God, intrinsically existing, what we impose the word to signify, belongs to him.

Article 4

Does the Word *Person* Signify Something Relative or Something Absolute in the Godhead?

We should say that the word *person* has something common with the names absolutely in the Godhead that we predicate about each Person, nor does it by the name refer to anything else, and in common with the names signifying a relation, which we distinguish and predicate in several ways. And so it seems that both meanings of something relative and something absolute belong to *person*. Different people have assigned how each meaning belongs to the word.

Some say that *person* signifies both but equivocally, for they say that the word as such signifies the essence absolutely, both in the singular and the plural, like the words *God* or *good* or *great*. But because of the insufficiency of words in speaking about God, the holy fathers in the Council of Nicea used the word *person* in such a way that we sometimes understand it, especially in the plural, as something relative. For example, we say that the Father, the Son, and the Holy Spirit are three Persons, or, in a disjunction, that one Person is the Father, another the Son, or that the Son is a different Person than the Father. And when we predicate it absolutely in the singular, it can indifferently signify the essence or the Person, as when we say that the Father is a Person, or that the Son is a Person. This seems to be the opinion of Lombard.[14]

But this does not seem to be adequate, since, not without reason from the very meaning of the word, the holy fathers, inspired by God, used the word to express profession of the true faith, especially because they would have provided an occasion of error by saying three Persons if the word signifies the essence absolutely.

And so others said that it signifies essence and relation at the same time but not equally, the one directly and the other indirectly. Some of them said that it signifies essence directly and relation indirectly, and others said the converse. But neither side resolves the doubt, since, if one signifies essence directly, one should not predicate it in the plural, and if one signifies relation directly, one should not predicate it absolutely or of individual Persons.

And so others said that it signifies both directly. Some of them said that it signifies essence and relation equally. And we consider neither regarding the other. But this is unintelligible, since what does not signify one and the same thing signifies nothing. And so every word signifies one thing in one understanding, as Aristotle says in the *Metaphysics*.[15]

And so some said that we consider a relation about the absolute. But it is difficult to see this, since relations do not determine the essence in the Godhead.

And so some said that it does not signify anything absolute, or the substance that is the essence, but signifies the substance that is a hypostasis, since a relation determines this. This is true, but this statement shows us nothing, since the word *hypostasis* or *subsistence* is less clear to us than the word *person*.

And so, to clarify this question, we should note that, according to Aristotle,[16] the proper definition of a word is the one that the word signifies. And we say that a word presupposes a thing to which we attribute the word if that thing should be directly subsumed under the thing signified by the word, as the determined in the undetermined. But should a thing not be directly subsumed under the thing signified by the word, we say that the word links that thing indirectly to the thing signified. For example, *animal* signifies a living, sensibly perceptible substance, and *white* signifies a color that dilates the organ of sight. But we directly subsume *human being* under the definition of animal as something determined in something undetermined, since a human being is a living, sensibly perceptible substance with a particular kind of soul, namely, a rational soul, but we do not directly subsume *human being* under white, which is outside a human being's essence. And so the word *animal* includes human being, and the word *white* links a human being to white.

And because the inferior that a common word includes is related to the common thing as the determinate to the indeterminate, what was presupposed becomes signified, with the determination applied to the common thing. For example, rational animal signifies a human being.

But we should note that something signifies in two ways: in one way, formally; in the second way, materially. The word signifies formally regarding what it was chiefly imposed to signify, which is the definition of the word. For example, the word *human being* signifies something composed of a body and a rational soul. The word signifies materially that in which such a definition is preserved. For example, the word *human being* signifies something having a heart, a brain, and such like parts, without which there cannot be a body enlivened by a rational soul.

Therefore, we should accordingly say that the word *person*, in the general sense, signifies only an individual substance of a rational nature. And because individual substance (i.e., one incommunicable and distinct from other things) is included in individual substance of a rational nature, both of God, a human being, and an angel, a divine Person necessarily signifies a a distinct subsistent thing in the divine nature, as a human person signifies a distinct subsistent thing in human nature. This is the formal meaning of both a divine Person and a human person.

But because a distinct subsistent thing in human nature is simply a thing individuated by individual matter and distinct from other things, we necessarily signify this materially when we speak of a human person.

But a distinct incommunicable thing in the divine nature is only a relation, since every absolute thing is common and undivided in the Godhead. And a relation in God is really the same thing as his essence. And as the essence in God is the same as the one who has the essence (e.g., divinity and God) so a relation is the same as the one that the relation relates. And so it follows that a relation is the same as what is a distinct subsistent thing in the divine nature.

Therefore, *person*, in the general sense, evidently signifies an individual substance of a rational nature, but *divine Person* formally signifies a distinct subsistent thing in the divine nature. And since this can be only a relation or something relative, it materially signifies the relation or relative thing. And so we can say that it signifies a relation as a substance, that is, a hypostasis, not an essence, just as it signifies a relation as a relative thing, not as a relation (e.g., as the word *Father*, not the word *fatherhood*, signifies a divine Person). For then the signified relation is indirectly included in the meaning of divine person, which is simply a thing subsisting in the divine nature distinguished by a relation.

Obj. 4. Augustine says in *Trinity* that, even though the word *essence* is common to them, namely, the Father, and the Son, and the Holy Spirit, so that we call each the divine essence, the word *person* is common to them.[17] But relation in the Godhead is distinctive, not common. Therefore, person in the Godhead does not signify relation.

Reply Obj. 4. We should say that the essence is really common in the Godhead, but person only conceptually common, just like the word *relation*.

Obj. 5. One might say that person in the Godhead is conceptually, not really, common. On the contrary, there is no universal in the Godhead. And so Augustine in *Trinity* disproves the opinion of those who said that the divine essence is like a genus or species, but person like a species or individual.[18] But what is conceptually, not really, common is common in the way of a universal. Therefore, person is really and not merely conceptually common. And so person cannot signify a relation.

Reply Obj. 5. We should say that nothing in the Godhead is different regarding existing, since there is only one existing in it. But this is contrary to the nature of a universal. And so there is nothing universal in it, although there is one thing in it conceptually, not really.

Obj. 6. No word signifies things of different genera except equivocally. For example, we equivocally predicate acute regarding tastes and angles measuring less than 90 degrees. But person in angels and human beings evidently signifies something absolute, not a relation. Therefore, if person should signify relation in God, it will be predicated equivocally.

Reply Obj. 6. We should say that the fact that person signifies different things in God and human beings pertains to a difference of supposition rather than a different meaning of the common word *person*. But different signification, not different supposition, causes equivocation.

Obj. 15. One might say that Person signifies one distinct thing, and since distinction in the Godhead is by relation, Person signifies relation. On the contrary, we say that the Son and the Holy Spirit are distinguished in the Godhead by their way of origin, since the Son proceeds by way of the intellect as the Word, but the Holy Spirit proceeds by way of the will as Love. Therefore, there is distinction in the Godhead only by relations, and so it is not necessary that Person signify relation.

Reply Obj. 15. We should say that the different way of procession, in which one says that the Son proceeds by way of the intellect, and the Holy Spirit by way of the will, does not suffice to distinguish the Holy Spirit personally from the Son, since the will and the intellect are not personally distinguished in the Godhead. But if one should grant that that suffices for their distinction, both are evidently distinguished from the Father by a relation, as one of them proceeds from the Father by generation, and the other by procession, and these relations constitute their Persons.

Obj. 16. If relation in the Godhead distinguishes, and Person is what is distinguished, not distinguishing, the word *Person* will not signify relation.

Reply Obj. 16. We should say that, as relation signifies as what distinguishes in the Godhead, so what is related is signified as distinct. But in God, relation is not one thing, and what is related another, as neither is his essence one thing, and his existing another. And so neither do what distinguishes and what is distinct differ in God.

Obj. 18. There are four relations in the Godhead, namely, paternity, sonship, common origination of the Spirit, and procession of the Spirit, since being without a source, which is the fifth notion, is not a relation. But the word *person* signifies none of these. For, if it were to signify paternity, it would not be predicated of the Son. If it were to signify sonship, it would not be predicated of the Father, If it were to signify the procession of the Holy Spirit, it would not be predicated of the Father or the Son. And if it were to signify the common

origination of the Spirit, it would not be predicated of the Holy Spirit. Therefore, the word *person* does not signify relation.

Reply Obj. 18. We should say that, although a universal cannot be without
singulars, we can understand it and so signify it. And it follows, because of
this, that, if there is no singular, there is no universal. But it does not follow
that, if we do not understand and signify a singular, we do not understand and
signify a universal. For example, the term *human being* only signifies human
being in general, not an individual human being. Likewise, although the word
Person does not signify paternity or sonship or the common origination and
procession of the Spirit, it signifies relation in general by the way indicated in
the body of the article, just as the word *relation* does in its way.

Article 5
Are There Several Persons in the Godhead?

We should say that the plurality of Persons in the Godhead concerns matters
subject to faith, and natural reason can neither investigate not sufficiently
understand it, although we expect to understand it in heaven, when we will
behold God essentially, with vision replacing faith. But the holy fathers,
because of the urgency to refute those who contradict the faith, were forced to
discuss this and other things that look to faith, but modestly and reverently
without the presumption of understanding them. Nor is such an inquiry useless, since it raises the spirit to capture the part of truth sufficient to exclude
errors. And so Hilary says:[19] "In believing this," namely, the plurality of Persons in the Godhead, "start, run, and persist, and if I should know that you will
not arrive, I shall praise your progress. For one who devotedly pursues infinite
things, although one does not ever attain them, will progress by continuing."

Therefore, to manifest a little about this question, and especially as Augustine manifests it,[20] we should consider that it is necessary to attribute everything perfect in creatures to God as regards what belongs to the nature of the
perfection absolutely, not as it is in this or that particular thing. For goodness
or wisdom is not in God as an accident, as they are in us, although the highest
goodness and wisdom is in him.

But there is nothing more excellent and more perfect in creatures than
understanding, and a sign of this is that intellectual substances are more
excellent than other creatures, and we say that, regarding the intellect, they
have been made in the image of God. Therefore, understanding and all the
things essential to it necessarily belong to God, although they belong to him
in a way different than they belong to creatures.

And it belongs to the nature of understanding that there is the one who understands and the thing understood. What is in itself understood is not the thing of which the intellect has knowledge, since that thing is sometimes only potentially understood and exists outside the one who understands, as when a human being understands material things, such as a stone or an animal or such like. But the understood thing is necessarily in the one who understands and united with the knower. Nor is the thing in itself understood the understood thing's likeness that gives form to the intellect in order that the intellect understand. For the intellect can understand only insofar as this likeness makes the intellect active, as nothing else can act insofar as it is potential but only insofar as a form actualizes it. Therefore, this likeness is disposed in understanding as the source of understanding, as heat is the source of heating action, not as the terminus of understanding.

Therefore, what the intellect conceives within itself about the thing understood, whether it is a definition or statement, as the *De anima* posits the two actions of the intellect,[21] is first and in itself the understood thing. And we call this concept by the intellect the internal word, since it is what the spoken word signifies. For the spoken word does not signify the understood thing, the thing's intelligible form, or the understanding itself, but rather the concept of the intellect by means of which it signifies the thing, as when I say, "human being" or "a human being is an animal." In this regard, it does not matter whether the intellect understands itself or something else, since, as when it understands something other than itself, it forms a concept of the thing signified verbally, so, when it understands itself, it forms a concept of itself, which it also can express verbally.

Therefore, since God is his understanding and, by understanding himself, understands all other things, he necessarily has the intellectual conception that belongs absolutely to the nature of what is his understanding. And if we were to be able to understand what and how God understands, as we understand our understanding, the conception of the divine word would not be beyond reason, as the conception of a human word is not.

But we can know what it is not and understand how it is not, and so we can know the difference between the Word conceived by God and a word conceived by our intellect. For we know first that God has only one understanding, not many acts of understanding, as we have, since there is one act of understanding whereby we understand a stone, and another act whereby we understand a plant, but God has only one act of understanding whereby he understands both himself and all other things. And so our intellect conceives many words, but God conceives only one Word.

Second, our intellect often understands both itself and other things imperfectly, but divine understanding cannot be imperfect. And so the divine Word is perfect, perfectly representing all things, but our word is often imperfect.

Third, in our intellect, it is one thing to understand and another thing to exist, and so a word conceived in our intellect, since it proceeds from the intellect as such, is one with it only in the act of understanding, not in nature. But God's understanding is his existing, and so the Word that proceeds from God inasmuch as he is understanding proceeds from him inasmuch as he is existing. And so the Word conceived has the same essence and nature as the intellect conceiving it. And because we call what receives a nature in living things begotten and a son, we call the divine Word begotten and a Son. But we cannot call our word a son except metaphorically.

The word of our intellect differs from the intellect in two ways, namely, in it being from the intellect and in it being of a different nature. Therefore, we conclude that the only remaining difference after the difference of nature from the divine Word has been taken away, as I have shown (Q. 8, A. 1), is that our word proceeds from something other. Therefore, since difference causes number, we conclude that there is in God only the number of relations. But the relations in the Godhead are not accidents, and each of them is really the divine essence. And so also each of them is subsistent, like the divine essence, and as divinity is the same as God, so fatherhood is the same as the Father, and so the Father is the same as God. Therefore, the number of relations is the number of subsistent things in the divine nature. But the subsistent things in the divine nature are the divine Persons, as A. 4 makes clear. And so we posit several Persons in the Godhead.

Obj. 8. Number is a species of quantity. But there is in no quantity in God, since, if anything signifying quantity came into predication about God, he would be substantially changed, as Boethius says in *Trinity*. Therefore, either there is no number in any way in the Godhead, or it belongs to his substance, which is contrary to faith.

Reply Obj, 8. We should say that the division of a continuum causes the number that is a species of quantity. And so, as a continuous quantity is something mathematical, since it is conceptually but not really separate from sensibly perceptible matter, so also is the number that is a species of quantity, which is also the subject of arithmetic, whose source is the unit that is the first measure of quantity. And so it is evident that this number cannot be in immaterial things, but there is in them a multiplicity that is contrary to the one convertible with being. Formal distinction, which results from certain contrary forms, whether absolute or relative, causes this. And such is the number in the Godhead.

Obj. 10. Every number is finite. Therefore, the infinite cannot be numbered. Therefore, since God is infinite, there cannot be number in him.

Reply Obj. 10. We should say that God is infinite regarding the perfection of magnitude, wisdom, and the like. And so Ps. 147:5 says: "His wisdom is beyond number." But procession in the Godhead, which multiplies the divine Persons, is not endless, since there is no unlimited divine generation, as Augustine says in *Trinity*. And so neither is the number of Persons infinite.

Obj. 13. In every nature that does not differ from its existing individual thing, existing individual things of that nature cannot be multiplied. Accordingly, there can be several human beings in the same human nature, since this particular human being is not the human being's humanity, and so many individuals in the same human nature result from different individual sources, which do not belong to consideration of their common nature. And in immaterial substances, in which the specific nature is a subsistent existing individual, there cannot be several individuals of the same species. But the nature and the existing individual in God are the same, since the divine existing itself, which is the divine nature, is subsistent. Therefore, there cannot be several existing individuals or persons in the divine nature.

Reply Obj. 13. We should say that the sources of individuation in created things have two things: one, that they are the source of subsisting, since common nature of itself subsists only in individual things; second, that the individuating sources distinguish existing subjects of a common nature from one another. But personal properties in the Godhead have only the function of of distinguishing existing individuals of the divine nature but are not the source of the subsisting of the divine essence. For the divine essence as such is subsistent, but, conversely, the personal properties have their subsistence from the essence, since paternity has from it that it is something subsistent, inasmuch as the divine essence, with which it is really the same, is a subsistent thing. Thus it follows that, as the divine essence is God, so paternity is the Father. And it is also because of this that the plurality of the divine essence's existing individuals does not numerically multiply it, as happens in the things here below. For that from which something has subsistence multiplies it. And although the divine essence as such is individuated, so to speak, regarding what is intrinsically subsistent, itself being numerically one, subsisting relations in the Godhead distinguish the several existing individuals from one another.

Obj. 14. Person is the name of a thing. Therefore, where there are not a number of things, there are not a number of persons. But there are not a number of things in God, since Damascene says that, in the Godhead, the Father and the Son and the Holy Spirit are really one thing but differ conceptually and mentally.[22] Therefore, there are not a number of Persons in God.

Reply Obj. 14. We should say that, if the Father, Son, and the Holy Spirit differ only conceptually, not really, nothing prevents one being predicated of the other, as clothing and tunic are predicated of one another, and likewise the Father would be the Son, and the converse, which is the heresy of Sabellius. And so we should say that the Father, Son, and Holy Spirit are things, as Augustine says in *Christian Doctrine*,[23] if we should understand it about something relative, since if we understand it in an absolute sense, then they are one thing, as the same Augustine says.[24] And we should understand in this way that Damascene says that they are really one. And he says this, that we generally explain that they are distinguished only conceptually, that is, relatively. For relation, although it, in contrast to contrary relation, causes a real distinction in the Godhead, differs from the divine essence only conceptually. Moreover, of all genera, relation is a thing in a weaker way.

Obj. 18. Things distinguished by specifically different forms are necessarily specifically different, as a human being and a horse differ specifically as rational and irrational. But paternity and sonship are specifically different relations. Therefore, if only relations distinguish the divine Persons, it is necessary that they differ specifically, and so they will not belong to one and the same nature, which is contrary to faith.

Reply Obj. 18. We should say that, although only paternity and sonship distinguish the Father and the Son from each another, it is not necessary that the Father and the Son differ specifically in the Godhead, as it were, because the relations are specifically different. For these relations are not related to different Persons as giving them form but rather as distinguishing and constituting existing individuals, and what is related to the divine Persons as giving them form is the divine nature, in which the Son is like the Father. For the one begetting generates one like himself in form, not in individual properties. Socrates and Plato, even if only whiteness or blackness, which are specifically different qualities, were to distinguish them individually from one another, would not differ specifically, since what is the species of white and black is not the species of Socrates and Plato. Therefore, just so, neither does it follow that the Father and the Son differ specifically because of the specific difference between paternity and sonship, although one cannot properly say that anything differs specifically in the Godhead, since there is no species or genus in it.

Obj. 19. It is unintelligible that there are different existing individuals belonging to one and the same existing. But there is in the Godhead only one existing. Therefore, it is impossible there that there are several existing individuals or Persons in it.

Reply Obj. 19. We should say that one should altogether concede that there is in the Godhead only one existing, since existing always belongs to the essence, and especially in God, whose existing is his essence. And the relations that distinguish the existing individuals in the Godhead do not add another existing to that of the essence, since they do not cause composition with the essence, as I have said. But every form adding an existing to a substantial existing causes composition with the substance, and this is an accident, such as the existing of white and black. Therefore, diversity as to being results from a plurality of existing individuals, just as different essences in created things do. But neither of them applies to the Godhead.

Obj. 23. When the whole perfection of a species is in one existing individual, there are not several existing individuals of that nature, as Aristotle proves that there is only one world, since it consists of all of its matter.[25] But the whole perfection of the divine nature is in one existing individual. Therefore, there are not several existing individuals or Persons, in one and the same nature.

Reply Obj. 23. We should say that, although the whole and perfect divinity is in each of the three Persons according to its own way of existing, it belongs to the perfection of divinity that there be several ways of existing in the Godhead, namely, that there be in it one from whom another is but proceeds from no one, and one who is from another, since there would not be perfection in every way in the Godhead unless there were to be in it the processions of the Word and Love.

Article 6

Can We Properly Predicate the Word *Person* in the Plural in the Godhead?

We should say that, as Obj. 4 says, nouns derive their number from the form signified, but adjectives derive their number from individual existing things. The reason for this is that nouns signify as substances, and adjectives signify as an accident that its subject individualizes and multiplies, but the substance itself individualizes and multiplies things.

Therefore, since the word *person* is a noun, we need to consider from its signified form whether we can predicate it in the plural. But the word *person* is not a nature absolutely, since then *human being* and *person* would mean the same thing, which is obviously false. Rather, *person* formally signifies the incommunicability or individuality of what subsists in a nature, as what I have said before makes clear (A. 2).

Therefore, since there are several properties that cause distinct and incommunicable existing in the Godhead, we need to predicate *person* in the Godhead in the plural. Just so, we predicate *person* of human beings in the plural because of the plurality of their individuating sources.

Obj. 4. One might say that, although we understand subsisting from essence, we can say that there are three subsistents in the Godhead, and likewise three Persons. On the contrary, we cannot predicate things that signify the essence of several things unless they be adjectives, which take their number from existing individuals, not the form signified, although the contrary is the case with nouns. And so we say that there are the three eternal if we should understand *eternal* adjectively, but if we should understand it substantively, then it is true, as Athanasius says in the Creed, that there is one, not three eternal. But the word *person* is a noun, not an adjective. Therefore, we should not predicate it in the plural.

Reply Obj. 4. We should say that the form signified by the word *Person* is what is the source of incommunicability or individuation, not the essence absolutely. And so one predicates it several times, even if it is a noun. And also, because there are several distinguishing properties in the Godhead, we call them several personalities.

Obj. 6. As God signifies having divinity, so divine Person signifies one subsisting in divinity. But, as we say that there are three subsistents in divinity, so there are three having divinity. Therefore, if one can say by this argument that there are three Persons in the Godhead, one could likewise say that there are three Gods, which is heretical.

Reply Obj. 6. We should say that the word *Person* signifies one subsisting in the divine nature, with difference and incommunicability, but the word *God* signifies one having the divine nature, signifying nothing about difference or incommunicability. Thus it is dissimilar.

Obj. 7. Boethius says that there are not then three Gods, since God does not differ from God in divinity.[26] But divine Person likewise does not differ from divine Person by a difference of personality, as it seems, since what it is to be a Person is common to them. Therefore, we cannot plurally predicate Person in the Godhead.

Reply Obj. 7. We should say that, although God does not differ from God by any difference of divinity, since there is only numerically one divinity, a divine Person differs from a divine Person by a different personality, since a property distinguishing the Persons also belongs to personality in the Godhead.

Article 7

How Do We Predicate Numerical Terms of Divine Persons, Namely, Whether Positively or Only Negatively?

We should say that different things also gave rise to different opinions among philosophers about unity and multiplicity, since we discover that unity is the source of number, and that it is convertible with a being, and likewise that multiplicity belongs to the species of quantity we call number, and also envelops every genus, just like unity, regarding which a multitude seems to be contrary.

Therefore, some of the philosophers did not distinguish between the unity that is convertible with a being and the unity that is the source of number, thinking that unity predicated in either sense would not add anything to substance, and that unity howsoever predicated would signify the substance of a thing. It followed from this that number, which is composed of units, is the substance of all things, according to the opinion of Pythagoras and Plato.

But others, not distinguishing between the unity that is convertible with a being and the unity that is the source of number, conversely believed that the unity howsoever predicated would add an accidental existing to substance, and so every multitude is necssarily an accident belonging to the genus of quantity. This was the position of Avicenna, which all the teachers of antiquity seem to have followed, since they understood by unity and multiplicity only something belonging to the genus of discrete quantity.

Others, noting that there cannot be any quantity in God, held that the terms signifying unity or multiplicity about God do not posit anything but only remove something, since they can posit only what they signify, namely, discrete quantity, which can in no way exist in God. Therefore they predicate one of God in order to remove the multiplicity of discrete quantity. But they predicate terms signifying plurality in order to remove unity, which is the source of discrete quantity.

This seems to have been the position of Lombard in the *Sentences*,[27] and presupposing the basis of this opinion, namely, that every multiplicity signifies discrete quantity, and all unity is the source of that quantity, this seems the most reasonable of all the opinions. Dionysius likewise says that negations are most true about God, but affirmations are loose expressions.[28] For we know that God exists, not what he is, as Damascene says.[29]

And so also Rabbi Moses says that all the things we seem to predicate affirmatively of God are introduced to remove something, not to posit anything. For example, we say that God is living in order to eliminate from him the way of existing that nonliving things have with us, not to posit life in him, since we impose life and all such names to signify particular forms and perfections of creatures that are far distant from him. But this is not at all true, since, as Dionysius says,[30] we do not remove wisdom, life, and other like things from God as if he lacks them, but because he has them more excellently than the human intellect can grasp, or words can signify, and created perfections come from the divine perfection as an imperfect likeness. And so, according to Dionysius,[31] we predicate something of God not only by way of negation and causality but also by way of eminence.

But whatever is the case about spiritual perfections, it is certain that material dispositions are eliminated from God. And so, since quantity is a disposition of matter, if the numerical terms signify only what is in the genus of quantity, it is necessary that we predicate them only to eliminate what they signify, as Lombard held.[32] Nor does his position, in which unity eliminates multiplicity, and multiplicity unity, result in a vicious circle, since we eliminate from God the unity and multiplicity in the genus of quantity, neither of which we predicate of him. And so we do not eliminate the unity predicated of God that removes multiplicity. Rather, we eliminate the other unity, which we cannot predicate of God.

But some did not understand that we can use affirmative names in predication about God in order to eliminate something and considered unity and multiplicity only as what is in the genus of discrete quantity, which they did not dare to posit in God. Accordingly, they said that we predicate numerical terms of God as if authoritative expressions positing something in the Godhead, namely, a distinction in a way incapable of signifying when standing alone, not as if expressions signifying a conceived thing. This is obviously false, since we can obtain no such thing from the meaning of the term.

And so others said that the aforementioned terms posit something positively in God, although they presuppose that unity and multiplicity are only in the genus of quantity. For they say that it is not improper to attribute a species of quantity to God, although the genus is eliminated from him, just as we positively predicate some species of quality, such as wisdom and justice, of God, although quality cannot be in God.

But there is no comparison, as indicated in Obj. 5, since all species of quantity by their specific nature have imperfection, but not all species of quality do. Besides, quantity in the proper sense is a disposition of matter. And so all species of quantity except time and space, which are natural things, are certain mathematical things, which are joined to, and cannot be really separated from, sensibly perceptibly matter. And so it is clear that no species of quantity can befit spiritual things except metaphorically. But quality results from form, and so some qualities are altogether immaterial, and we can attribute them to spiritual things.

Therefore, these opinions proceeded from the supposition that the unity compatible with a being and the unity that is the source of number are the same, and that a multiplicity is only the number that is a species of quantity. But this is evidently false, since, inasmuch as division causes multiplicity, and the absence of division unity, we need to judge about unity and multiplicity by the nature of division.

There is a division that altogether surpasses the genus of quantity, namely, the one that is by formal opposition and concerns no quantity. And so the multiplicity resulting from this division and the unity that lacks this division are necessarily more universal and comprehensive than the genus of quantity.

And there is another division regarding quantity that does not transcend quantity. And so also the multiplicity resulting from this division, and the unity lacking it, belong to the genus of quantity. This unity adds something accidental to the thing of which it is predicated, which has the nature of a measure. Otherwise, the number constituted by the unity would not be anything accidental or the species of any genus. But the unity convertible with a being adds to the being only the negation of division, which signifies not only the being's lack of division but also its substance with the unity, since the unity is the same as the undivided being. Likewise, the corresponding multiplicity adds to many things only their distinction, which we note in that one of them is not the others, and they have this from their own forms, not from anything added.

Therefore, it is evident that the unity convertible with a being posits the being itself and adds only the negation of division. And the multiplicity corresponding to that unity adds to the things we call many that each of them is one, and one of them is not the others, of which the nature of distinction consists. And so, since unity adds to a being a negation, insofar as something is undivided in itself, multiplicity adds two negations, namely, as something in itself is undivided, and as it is divided from anything else. This division consists of one of them not being another.

Therefore, I say that we predicate in the Godhead the unity convertible with a being and the multiplicity corresponding to it, not the unity and multiplicity belonging to the genus of quantity. And so unity and multiplicity posit in the Godhead the things of which we predicate them but add only a distinction or lack thereof. This is to add negations, as I have just explained. And so we grant that, as to what they add to the things of which we predicate them, we understand them in God by way of negation, but insofar as they include in their meaning the things of which we predicate them, we understand them in a positive way. And so we should reply to each set of objections.

Obj. 2. According to Dionysius in *Divine Names*,[33] we predicate something of God in three ways, namely, by negation, eminence, and causality. But in whichever of these ways we were to predicate numerical terms in the Godhead, they necessarily posit something. And this is obvious if we were to predicate them by eminence or causality, and likewise if we were to predicate them negatively. For we do not deny some things of God so that, as the same Dionysius says,[34] as if he altogether lacks them, but because they do not belong to him in the same way as they do to us. Therefore, numerical terms in all three ways necessarily posit something.

Reply Obj. 2. We should say that, although we should also understand in eliminating some things from God the predication of some things about God by eminence or causality, we only deny some things of God and in no way predicate them of him, as when we say: God is not a material substance. And one can in this way say, according to the opinion of Lombard, that we altogether deny numerical quantity of God, and likewise, by what we posit, we altogether deny essential division when we say: the divine essence is one.

Obj. 6. We call four things first beings, namely, being, one, true, and good. But we predicate three of these, namely, being, true, and good, about God positively. Therefore, we also predicate one of God positively, and so multiplicity.

Reply Obj. 6. We should say that, of the four first things, the first most of all is being, and so we necessarily predicate it first, since negation or privation cannot be the first thing conceived by the intellect, inasmuch as what is denied or lacking belongs to understanding negation or privation. And the other three necessarily add something that does not constrict being, since, if they were to constrict being, they would not then be first things. But this cannot be unless they should add something conceptually. This is either negation, which adds one, as I have said, or relation or something produced to be related universally to being. The latter is either the intellect, to which the true signifies a relation, or the appetite, to which the good signifies a relation, since good is what all things desire, as the *Ethics* says.[35]

Obj. 11. There is no privation in God, since every privation pertains to a lack. But we predicate oneness of God. Therefore, it does not signify privation.

Reply Obj. 11. We should say that, as the *Metaphysics* says,[36] we speak of privation in three ways. We speak of it in one way in the proper sense when something lacks what it is designed by nature to have, and at the time when it is, as, for example, lacking sight is a privation of sight in a human being. We speak of it in a second way in a general sense when something is removed from something that it is not by nature destined to have, but it generically is, as if, for example, we should say that there is a privation of sight in a mole. We speak of it most generally in a third way when something is removed from what anything else, not the thing itself or something of its genus, is destined by nature to have, as if, for example, we should say that not having sight is a privation of it in a plant. And the latter privation is in between true privation and pure negation, having something in common with each, with true privation in being a negation in a subject, and so it does not belong completely to negation, and with pure negation in that it does not require a capacity in a subject. And we predicate oneness privatively in this sense, and we can predicate it in this sense in the Godhead, just as we in like manner predicate other things, such as invisible, immense, and such like, in the Godhead.

Obj. 15. If we predicate one by removing multiplicity, one is necessarily contrary to multiplicity, like privation to possession. But possession is by nature prior to privation, and so conceptually, since one can define privation only by possession. Therefore, multiplicity will be prior to one by nature and reason, which seems improper.

Reply Obj. 15. We should say that, according to Aristotle,[37] multiplicity is prior to one according to the senses, as the whole to the parts and the composite to the simple, but one is prior to multiplicity by nature and reason. But this does not seem to suffice to explain the fact that one is contrary to multiplicity privatively. For privation is conceptually posterior, since, in understanding privation, there is its contrary, by which it is defined, unless, perhaps, this is related only to the definition of the word, as the word *one* signifies privatively, and the word *multiplicity* signifies positively, since we impose names insofar as we understand things. And so, in order that a word signify something as privation, it suffices that it is in some way posterior in our knowledge, although this does not suffice that the thing itself be privative unless it should be conceptually posterior.

And so one can better say that division causes multiplicity, and we speak of one privatively regarding division, since it is an undivided being, and not regarding multiplicity. And so division is conceptually prior to one, but multiplicity posterior. This is evident as follows. The first thing that falls into the intellect is being. The second is negation of being. Third, understanding division results from the foregoing two things, since, from the fact that one understands something as a being but not this being, there results in the intellect that the former is distinct from the latter. Fourth, there results in the intellect the concept of one, namely, as one understands that this being is undivided in itself. Fifth, understanding of multiplicity follows, namely, we understand this being as different from another, and that each of them is in itself one. For however much one understands some things as distinct from one another, we understand multiplicity only if we should understand that each of the diverse things is one. And so also it is clear that there will not be circular reasoning in the definition of one and multiplicity.

Counterobj. 9. One might say that substance is not one intrinsically but by a unity accidental to it. But a unity is intrinsically one, since first things denote themselves, as goodness is good, truth is true, and unity is likewise one.

On the contrary, such things denote themselves because of the fact that they are first forms, and second forms do not denote themselves, as, for example, whiteness is not white. But things that are disposed by addition to something else are not the first things. Therefore, unity and goodness are not disposed by addition to substance.

Reply to the Counterobjections. According to the foregoing, it is easy to reply to those who consider in what respect they reach the truth. But we should consider one thing touched upon in the objections, that such first things, namely, essence, unity, truth, and goodness, denote themselves inasmuch as one, true, and good are consequences of being. But since being is the first thing conceived in the intellect, we necessarily understand as being anything that falls into the intellect, and so as one, true, and good. And so, since the intellect understands essence, unity, truth, and goodness in the abstract, we need to predicate being and the three other concrete things of each of these things. And so they denote themselves, but other things inconvertible with being do not.

Article 8

Is There Any Diversity in God?

We should say, as Jerome says, that inordinately expressed words lead to heresy. And so we should speak about the Godhead in such a way that we occasion no error. But there were two errors about the Godhead that those who speak about the unity and the Trinity in it should avoid, namely, the error of Arius, who denied its essential unity, positing one essence of the Father and another of the Son, and the error of Sabellius, who denied the plurality of Persons, saying that the one who is the Son is the same one as the Father.

Therefore, to avoid the error of Arius, we should avoid four things in professing the faith, which we profess by saying that there is one God: (1) diversity, which takes away the essential unity; (2) division, which is incompatible with God's simplicity; (3) inequality, which is contrary to the divine simplicity; and (4) professing that the Son is unrelated to the Father, which takes away likeness.

Likewise, there are, against the error of Sabellius, four things to be avoided: (1) singularity, which takes away the sharing of the divine nature; (2) the words *only one* regarding the Persons, which takes away their real distinction; (3) mingling, which takes away the order in the divine Persons; and (4) isolation, which takes away the community of the divine Persons.

We profess essential unity against diversity, simplicity against division, equality against inequality, likeness against lack of relation, plurality against singularity, distinction against only one, separation against mingling, and harmony and the bond of love against isolation.

Obj. 1. According to Aristotle,[38] one in substance makes things the same, and multiplicity in substance makes things diverse. But there is substantial multiplicity in the Godhead, since Hilary says that The Father and the Son and the Holy Spirit are three in substance and one in harmony.[39] Therefore, there is diversity in the Godhead.

Reply Obj. 1. We should say that substance is there cited for hypostasis, not the essence, whose multiplicity would cause diversity.

Obj. 2. According to Aristotle,[40] we speak of diversity absolutely, and difference relatively. And so every difference is a diversity, but not every diversity is a difference. But there is admittedly a difference in the Godhead, since, as Damascene says:[41] "We acknowledge different Persons in three properties, that is, paternity, sonship, and procession [of the Holy Spirit]." Therefore, there is diversity in the Godhead.

Reply Obj. 2. We should say that, although some doctors of the church use the word *difference* regarding divine things, one should not use it generally or expand the usage, since difference signifies a formal distinction, which cannot be in the Godhead, inasmuch as the form of God is the divine nature, as Augustine says. But one should explain in place of distinction a difference that signifies the least distinction, since we say that relations or only reason distinguish some things. So also we should explain the matter if there should be diversity in the Godhead. As, if we should say that the Person of the Father is diverse from the Person of the Son, we should understand diverse in place of distinct. But we should be more careful about using the word *diversity* than using the word *difference*, since diversity pertains more to essential division. For any multiplicity of forms causes difference, but only substantial forms cause diversity.

Obj. 3. An accidental difference only makes something different, but a substantial difference makes another, that is, diverse, thing. Therefore, since there is a difference in the Godhead, and there could not be an accidental difference in it, and so the difference needs to be substantial, there is necessarily diversity in it.

Reply Obj. 3. We should say that, although there is no accident in the Godhead, there is relation in it, whose contrariness causes distinction but not diversity in the Godhead.

Obj. 5. Sameness and diversity sufficiently distinguish being. But the Father is not the same as the Son, since it is inadmissible that the Father in generating the Son generates God himself. Therefore, the Son is diverse from the Father.

Reply Obj. 5. We should say that the Son is the same God as the Father, but one cannot say that the Father in generating the Son generated God himself, since the word *himself*, as it is reflexive, refers to the same existing individual. But the Father and the Son are two existing individuals in the Godhead.

Article 9

Are There Three, or More or Less, Persons in the Godhead?

We should say that, in the opinion of heretics, one cannot assign a definite number of Persons in the Godhead. For example, Arius understood the Trinity of Persons such that the Son and the Holy Spirit were creatures, and Macedonius held the same opinion about the Holy Spirit. But the progression of creatures from God is not necessarily limited to a fixed number, since divine power has from its infinity to surpass the way, species, and number of a creature. And so, if God, the almighty Father, created two most excellent creatures, whom Arius calls the Son and the Holy Spirit, nothing is taken away from his power to create other creatures equal or even greater than they.

And Sabellius held that the Father and the Son are distinguished only nominally and conceptually, and such things could be multiplied endlessly insofar as our intellect can think about God in an infinite number of ways from his various effects and name him in different ways.

But only the Catholic faith, which holds the unity of the divine essence in three really distinct Persons, can assign the reason for a three fold number in the Godhead. For one simple nature can be in only one as the source. And so Hilary says that one who professes two in the Godhead without a source professes two Gods, since the nature of a God without a source demands that we predicate a God of it.[42]

And so also some philosophers said that there can be plurality in immaterial things only by reason of origin, since one nature can be equally in many things because of the division of matter, which has no place in God.

And so one can posit in the Godhead only one Person without a source, one that does not proceed from another. But if other Persons should proceed from him, an action needs to do this. This action is not one that goes into what is outside the active thing, such as heating and cutting are the actions of fire and a saw, and as creation by God himself, since then the Persons proceeding would be outside the divine nature.

Therefore, we conclude that the procession of the Persons into the one divine nature is only by reason of actions that abide in the one active, not going outside. There are two of these in an intellectual nature, namely, understanding and willing, and something proceeds in each when these actions are perfected. For understanding itself is something perfect only if something is conceived in the mind of the one understanding, which we call the word, since, before there is a conception in our mind, we speak of thinking in order to understand, not understanding. Likewise, the love proceeding from the lover by the will perfects the very act of the will, since love is simply fixing the will in the good willed.

But the word and love in a creature are not subsistent persons in the nature understanding and willing, since a creature's understanding and willing is not its existing. And so a word and love are particular things coming to the creature understanding and willing as particular accidents. But since existing, understanding, and willing in God are the same thing, the Word and Love in God necessarily are not accidents but subsist in the divine nature. And there is only one understanding and one willing in God, since, by understanding his essence, he understands all things, and by willing his goodness, he wills all the things he wills. Therefore, there is only one Word and one Love in the Godhead.

The order of understanding and willing are different in God and in us. For we receive intellectual knowledge from external things, and we by our will tend toward an external thing as an end. And so our understanding is in a way from things to the soul, and our willing in a way from the soul to things. But God does not receive knowledge from things. Rather, he causes things by his knowledge. Nor does he by his will tend toward anything external. Rather, he directs all things toward himself as their end. Therefore, there is in both God and us a circular movement in the actions of the intellect and the will, since the will returns to the source of its understanding. The movement in us ends in what is external, an external good moving our intellect, the intellect moving our will, and the will by desire and love tending toward the external good. But in God, the movement ends in himself, since God, by understanding himself, conceives his Word, which is also the exemplar of all the things understood by him, on which account he understands all things by understanding himself. From this Word, he proceeds to love all things and himself. And so a certain person said that a monad begot a monad and deflected its heat on itself.[43] After the circular movement was concluded, nothing more can be added to it, and so a third procession in the divine nature cannot result, although a further procession into an external nature follows.

Therefore, there are necessarily only one Person not proceeding and only two Persons proceeding, one of which proceeds as Love, the other as Word, and so there is a three fold number of Persons in the Godhead.

And a three fold likeness is evident in creatures. The first is as an effect represents its cause, and what is the first thing in a creature, namely, being in itself a subsistent creature, represents the source of the whole divinity, namely, the Father. The form of any creature represents the Word, since in things produced by an intelligent thing the form produced is derived from the concept of that thing. And Love is represented in the order of a creature, since, by reason of God loving himself, he directs all things to himself in a certain order.

And so we call this likeness vestigial, and it represents a footprint, as an effect represents its cause.

The second way is by reason of the same nature of action, and so it is represented only in a rational creature, which can understand and love itself, just like God, and so produce the word and love of itself. We call this the likeness of a natural image, since things that bear a like form bear the image of other things.

The third way is by the unity of the object, inasmuch as a rational creature understands and loves God, and this is a conformity of union, which we find only in the saints, who understand and love the same thing as God does.

Job 11:7 says of the first likeness: "Will you perhaps understand the footprints of God?" Gen. 1:26 says of the second likeness: "Let us make a human being in our image and likeness." We call this the image of creation. 2 Cor. 3:18 says of the third way: "We, beholding with unveiled face the glory of the Lord, will be transformed into the same image." We call this the image of re-creation.

Obj. 1. Augustine says in his work *Against Maximinus:*[44] "The Son did not beget the creator, not because he could not, but because it was improper." But the actual and the possible do not differ in the Godhead, nor do they in perpetual things.[45] Therefore, the Son begot another Son, and so there are two Sons in the Godhead. And so there are more than three Persons.

Reply Obj. 1. We should say that Augustine says that one should not say that the Son could not generate, but that it was improper, since it is not due to the Son's lack of power that he does not generate, and so one understands the words *could not* privatively and not simply negatively. And the words *it was improper* signify that something unbecoming would result if the Son were to generate another Son in the Godhead. And we can consider the impropriety in four ways.

First, since the Son proceeds as the Word in the Godhead, if the Son were to generate a Son, it would follow that in God a Word would proceed from the Word. But this can only be so in an inquiring and discursive intellect, in which one word proceeds from another as one proceeds from considering one truth to considering another truth. This in no way belongs to the perfection and simplicity of the divine intellect, which sees all things at once in one glance.

Second, what individuates something and makes it incommunicable cannot be common to many things. For example, we cannot understand that by which Socrates is this thing to be present in many things. And so, if sonship were to belong to several Persons in the Godhead, it would not be the sonship constituting the incommunicable person of the Son, and so it would be necessary that something absolute that does not belong to the unity of the divine essence constitute the Son an individual Person.

Third, nothing being specifically one can be multiplied except by reason of matter, and there can be only one essence in the Godhead because the divine essence is altogether immaterial. But if there were several Sons in the Godhead, it would also be necessary that there be several sonships, and so it would be necessary that subject matter multiply them, which does not belong to divine immateriality.

Fourth, we call someone a son because he proceeds by nature, but nature is fixedly disposed to one thing unless several things proceed incidentally from something because of division of matter. And so, where there is an altogether immaterial nature, there is necessarily only one Son.

Obj. 2. One might say that the words "not because he could not" need to be explained, that is, that it was not due to lack of power. On the contrary, the acts of a particular nature belong to each existing subject of that nature except because of its lack of power. But generation is an act belonging to the perfection of the divine nature; otherwise, it would not belong to the Father, in whom there is only what belongs to perfection. Therefore, if the Son does not generate another Son, this will be due to his lack of power.

Reply Obj. 2. We should say that something can belong to a nature in two ways. Something belongs to a nature in one way insofar as one considers it absolutely, and then things that belong to a nature necessarily belong to all the existing individuals of that nature. And so it belongs to the divine nature to be omnipotent, creator, and other such things, which are common to the three Persons. Something belongs to a nature in a second way insofar as we consider it a particular existing individual, and then it is not necessary that what belongs to a nature belong to each existing individual of that nature. A generic nature, for example, has something in one species that does not belong to another species, as certain things regarding sensory nature, such as having a most excellent sense of touch and memory, result in a human being but not in irrational animals. So also something belongs to a specific nature as it is in one individual that does not belong to another individual of the same species, as it is clear that it belongs to the human nature that was in Adam not to be conceived by natural generation, but this is not true of other individuals of human nature. And the power to generate in this way results from the divine nature, as it is in the Person of the Father, and this is evident because the Father is constituted an incommunicable Person only by paternity itself, which belongs to him insofar as he is the one generating. And so it does not follow that the Son, although he is a complete existing individual of the divine nature, can generate.

Obj. 3. If the Son cannot generate, he can be generated. Therefore, he has the power to be generated, not the power to generate. For it is one thing to generate, and another thing to be generated. Therefore, since powers' objects distinguish the powers, there will not be the same power of the Father and the Son, which is heretical.

Reply Obj. 3. We should say that, although the Father can generate, and the Son cannot, it does not follow that the Father has a power that the Son does not have, since the same power belongs to the Father and the Son, the power whereby the Father generates, and the Son is generated, for power is something absolute and so is not distinguished in the Godhead, as goodness or anything so expressed is not. But generating and being generated in the Godhead signify only a relation in the Godhead, not anything absolute. And contrary relations share in one and the same absolute thing in the Godhead and do not divide it, as there is clearly one and the same essence in the Father and the Son. And so we do not distinguish power in the Godhead in regard to generating and being generated, since it is not even necessary in creatures that every distinction of objects distinguish power, but a formal difference of objects in the same genus distinguishes power. For example, we do not distinguish the power of sight by what consists of seeing a human being and what consists of seeing an ass, since this distinction is not sensibly perceptible as such. Likewise, relation does not distinguish the absolute in the Godhead.

Obj. 4. We trace action and being acted upon in things that act and are acted upon to different sources, since something acts by reason of the form in created things but is acted upon by reason of matter. But we signify generation and being generated by way of action and being acted upon. Therefore, they need to be related to different sources. And so there cannot be one and the same power by which the Father generates, and the Son is generated.

Reply Obj. 4. We should say that, in every action that goes from an active thing into an external thing, a source is required in the active thing whereby it is active, and another source in the thing undergoing action whereby it does. And in every action that does not go into an external thing but remains in the active thing, there is required only one source of action, as there is required for willing a source on the part of the one willing, by which the one willing can will. In creatures, generation is by an action going into an external thing, and so an active power needs to be in the one generating and a passive power in the one generated. But we note divine generation by an action that remains within (i.e., the conception of the Word) and does not go into anything external. And so there need not be an active power in the Father and a passive power in the Son.

Obj. 11. One might say that there cannot be several Sons in the Godhead because there can be only one sonship in it, since only division of matter, of which there is none in the Godhead, multiplies the form of one and the same species. On the contrary, nature produces every difference to cause plurality. But there can be a difference between two sonships both due to matter and because this sonship is such-and-such, and that sonship is such-and-such. Therefore, nothing prevents positing several sonships in the Godhead, although there is no matter in it.

Reply Obj. 11. We should say that, since sonship is a relation consequent upon a fixed way of originating, namely, one by way of nature, it is impossible that sonship differ from sonship by a formal difference, except, perhaps, by a difference of natures communicated by generation as we can say that one species of sonship is that whereby this human being is a son, and another that whereby this horse is a son. But in the Godhead, there is only one nature. And so there cannot be several formally different sonships in it. And it is also clear that there cannot be several materially different sonships. And so it follows that there is only one sonship and one Son in it.

Obj. 14. According to Dionysius,[46] good communicates itself. But we appropriate goodness to the Holy Spirit, like power to the Father and wisdom to the Son. Therefore, it seems most properly to belong to the Holy Spirit that he communicate the divine nature to another Person, and so there are more than three Persons in the Godhead.

Reply Obj. 14. We should say that goodness is that in which the activity of a living being terminates, and it abides in the active thing. For we first understand something as true and then desire it as good, and the internal action stops and rests in it as its end. But the process of action on external things begins from this, since, inasmuch as the intellect desires and loves something considered beforehand as good, it begins to act externally regarding it. And so, because we appropriate goodness to the Holy Spirit, we can properly understand that the procession of the divine Persons extends no further. But what follows is the procession of a creature, which is outside the divine nature.

Arguments that there are less than three Persons in the Godhead:

Counterobj. 1. In one and the same nature, there is only one way of communicating the nature. And so, according to Averroes,[47] animals generated by semen do not belong to the same species as animals generated by putrefaction. But the divine nature is especially one. Therefore, it can be shared in only one way. Therefore, there can be only two Persons, one sharing divinity in a particular way, and the other receiving divinity in that way.

Reply Counterobj. 1. We should say that there are in any created nature many ways of procession but not in every one of them a specific nature is communicated, and this is due to the imperfection of a created nature, in which not everything in it subsists. For example, the word of a human being, which proceeds from the human being's intellect, is nothing subsistent, nor is love, which proceeds from the human will. But a son, whom the action of nature generates, is subsistent in human nature, and so he is the only way in which the nature is communicated, although there are many ways of procession in him. But everything in God is subsistent in him, and so any way of procession communicates the nature in the Godhead.

Counterobj. 3. The nature of the will and the intellect in God differ only conceptually. Therefore, the procession by way of nature of both the intellect and the will differ in God only conceptually. Therefore, if we distinguish the Son and the Holy Spirit by the fact that one proceeds by way of nature, or intellect, and the other by way of the will, they will be distinguished only conceptually. Therefore, there will not be two Persons. Since plurality of Persons signifies real plurality.

Reply to Counterobj. 3. We should say that, although the will and intellect differ in God only conceptually, the one who proceeds by way of the intellect is necessarily really distinct from the one who proceeds by way of the will. For the Word, which proceeds by way of the intellect, proceeds from only one, as from a speaker, but the Holy Spirit, who proceeds by the way of love, necessarily proceeds from two things reciprocally loving each other, or from a speaker and the speaker's word, since nothing can be loved whose word the intellect does not conceive beforehand. And so the one who proceeds by way of the will is necessarily from one who proceeds by way of the intellect, and so is distinguished from it.

Arguments that there are only three Persons in the Godhead:

1. 1 Jn. 5:7 says:[48] "There are three who bear witness in heaven." To those who ask: "three what?" the Church answers: "three Persons," as Augustine says.[49] Therefore, there are three Persons in the Godhead.

2. For perfect divine goodness, happiness, and glory, there needs to be true and perfect charity in God, since nothing is better or more perfect than charity, as Richard of St. Victor says in *Trinity*.[50] But there is no happiness without pleasure, which one most possesses through charity. For, as the same work says,[51] "Nothing is sweeter, nothing more pleasant, than charity, and the rational life experiences nothing sweeter than the delights of charity and enjoys no more delectable pleasure." Also, the perfection of glory consists of a magnificence of perfect sharing, which charity causes. But true and perfect charity requires the Trinity of Persons in the Godhead, since the love whereby one loves only oneself is self-love, not true charity. And God cannot love another who is not most loveable, nor is another most loveable who is not supremely good. Therefore, the highest true charity evidently cannot be in God if there should be in him only one Person, nor can there

be perfect charity if there should be only two Persons in him, since perfect charity requires that the lover wish that the beloved equally love what the lover loves. For it is a sign of great weakness to be unable to share one's love, and it is a sign of great perfection to be able to do so. "The greater the pleasure to receive, the greater the desire required," as Richard says.[52] Therefore, if there should be perfect goodness, pleasure, and glory in God, there needs to be a Trinity of Persons in the Godhead.

3. Since goodness shares itself, perfect divine goodness requires that God share his perfection to the highest extent. But if there were only one Person in the Godhead, God would not share his goodness to the highest extent, since he does not share himself with creatures to the highest extent. And if there were only two Persons, the pleasures of mutual charity would not be perfectly shared. Therefore, there needs to be a second Person, with whom divine goodness is perfectly shared, and a third Person, with whom the pleasures of divine charity are perfectly shared.

4. Love requires three things, namely, the lover, the beloved, and love itself, as Augustine says in *Trinity*.[53] The lover and the beloved are the Father and the Son, and the love that is their bond is the Holy Spirit. Therefore, there are three Persons in the Godhead.

5. As Richard says in *Trinity*,[54] you will see in human things that a person proceeds from a person in three ways: sometimes only directly, such as Eve from Adam; sometimes only indirectly, such as Enoch from Adam; sometimes both directly and indirectly, such as Seth from Adam, directly as Seth was Adam's son, and indirectly as Seth was the son of Eve, who proceeded from Adam. But a Person in the Godhead cannot proceed only indirectly, since there would not be in it the highest brotherhood. Therefore, we conclude that there is one Person, namely, the Person of the Father, who does not proceed from another; one Person, namely, the Son, who proceeds only directly; another Person, namely, the Holy Spirit, who proceeds both indirectly from the Father and directly from the Son. Therefore, there needs to be a third Person who both gives and receives the fullness of divinity, and this is the Person of the Son. Therefore, there are three Persons in the Godhead.

6. Giving and receiving the fullness of the Godhead is in between giving and not receiving it, and receiving and not giving it. But giving and not receiving the fullness of divinity belongs to the Person of the Father, and receiving and not giving it belongs to the Person of the Holy Spirit. Therefore, there needs to be a third Person that both gives and receives the fullness of divinity, and this is the Person of the Son. Therefore, there are three Persons in the Godhead.

Question 10

THE PROCESSION OF THE DIVINE PERSONS

Article 1

Is There Procession in the Divine Persons?

We should say that intellectual knowledge in us originates from the imagination and the senses, which do not reach beyond something continuous. And so we transfer words from continuous things to all the things that we grasp intellectually. Just so, this is evident tn the case of distance, which we find first spatially and then transfer to any difference of forms, and so we say that all contrary things, in whatever genus they are, are most distant, although distance first attaches to place, as Aristotle says in the *Metaphysics*.[1]

Likewise, the word *procession* was first used to signify locomotion, whereby something goes progressively from one place to a final place through intermediate points. From this usage, we transfer the word to signify everything in which there is an order of one thing from or after another, and so we use the word *procession* regarding every kind of movement. For example, we say that a material substance proceeds from whiteness to blackness, from a small quantity to a large one, and from nonexisting to existing. Likewise, we use the word *procession* where there is an emanation of one thing from another, as, for example we say that a ray proceeds from the sun, and every action and thing produced proceed from what is active (e.g., the thing produced from a craftsman or one begotten from a begetter). And we universally signify the order of all such things by the word *procession*.

But there are two kinds of action. One is a transition from the active thing into something external, such as heating from fire into a log, and this action perfects the thing acted upon, not the active thing, since the thing heated acquires heat, but fire in causing heat acquires nothing. The second action, such as understanding, willing, and the like, remains in the active thing and does not go into anything external. These actions perfect the active thing, since only actual understanding perfects the intellect. Likewise, only actual sense perception perfects the senses.

The first kind of action is common to the living and the nonliving, but the second kind is proper to the living. And so, if we should understand movement in a broad sense as any action, as Aristotle says in the *De anima*,[2] where he says that sense perception and understanding are movements that are the acts of a perfect thing, not of an imperfect thing, as the *Physics* defines it,[3] then this would seem proper to a living thing. And the explanation seems to consist of the fact that something moves itself. For we say that whatever we find acting by and in itself in whatever way lives, and Plato says in this sense that the first cause of movement moves itself.[4]

We find a procession in creatures in both kinds of action. For we say about the first kind that the begotten proceeds from the begetter, and the product from the producer, and we say about the second kind of action that a word proceeds from a speaker, and that love proceeds from a lover. We attribute both such kinds of action to God. We attribute the kind of action going into another, external thing inasmuch as we say that he creates, preserves, and governs all things. We do not signify that this kind of action adds any perfection to him. Rather, we signify that perfection comes to be in a creature from his perfection.

We attribute the other kind of action to God inasmuch as we call him understanding and willing, whereby we signify his perfection. For he would not be perfect were he not to be actually understanding and willing. And so we profess him to be living.

Therefore, we attribute procession to God in both actions. According to the first kind of action, we say that the divine wisdom or goodness in creatures proceeds from him, as Dionysius says in his *Divine Names*,[5] and also say that creatures proceed from him. According to the second kind of action, we speak of the processions of the Word and Love, and this is the procession of the Son from the Father, whose Word the Son is, and the Holy Spirit, who is the Father's Love and life-giving breath. And so Athanasius in a discourse at the Council of Nicea says that the Arians, holding that the Son is not consubstantial with the Father, seemed as a consequence to say that God is dead and mindless, not living and understanding.[6]

Obj. 3. We understand everything proceeding before its procession, since the thing proceeding is the subject of the procession. But there cannot be in the Godhead anything understood before procession, since the divine essence is not proceeding, nor is it generated. But we do not understand relation before procession, but rather the converse, as has been already said (Q. 8, A. 3). Therefore, there cannot be procession in the Godhead.

Reply Obj. 3. We should say that it is necessary in the procession that is locomotion that we understand the thing proceeding before the procession, since the thing proceeding is the subject of the procession, but in a procession that signifies the proceeding order of origin, the thing proceeding is related to the procession as its terminus. And so, if the thing proceeding is composed of matter and form and brought into existing by way of generation, the matter exists before the procession as its subject, but the form or the composite results conceptually from procession as its terminus, as when fire proceeds from fire by generation. But when what proceeds is not composite but only a form or brought into existing by creation, whose terminus is the whole substance, we in no way understand the thing proceeding before procession, but rather the converse. For example, we do not understand a creature before its creation, nor brilliance before its procession from the sun, nor a word before its procession from a speaker. Likewise, we do not understand the Word before his procession from the Father.

Obj. 8. That from which something comes is necessarily in some way that thing's cause. But one Person cannot cause another, since it cannot be the internal cause of another, namely, a formal or material cause, inasmuch as there is in the Godhead no composition of form and matter, nor an external cause, since one Person is in another. Therefore, there is no procession in the Godhead.

Reply Obj. 8. We should say that Latin teachers rarely or never use the word *cause* to signify the origin of the divine Persons. This is because an effect corresponds to a cause with us, and so in order not to be compelled to call the Son or the Holy Spirit products, we do not call the Father their cause, since the word *cause* with us signifies something essentially distinct, inasmuch as we say that that from which something else results is a cause. And this is also because the word *cause* used by the pagans about God designates his relationship to creatures, since they say that God is the first cause, and that creatures are his effects. And so, lest anyone think that one should posit the Son and the Holy Spirit among creatures essentially diverse from God, we avoid the word *cause* in the Godhead. But the Greeks use the word *cause* more absolutely, signifying only origin by it, and so they use the word *cause* in regard to the divine Persons, since something improperly expressed in the Latin language we can properly express in the Greek language because of the appropriate idiom. And it is not necessary that, if we, following the Greeks, use the word *cause* regarding the Godhead, we understand it in the same way as we say it about creatures, as philosophers distinguish four kinds of causes.

Obj. 9. Everything proceeding comes from something as its source. But we cannot call one Person the source of another, since, inasmuch as we speak of a source in relation to a product, we then necessarily call a Person an effect, which seems to belong only to creatures. Therefore, there is no procession in the Godhead.

Reply Obj. 9. We should say that, of all the things regarding origin, the word *source* most belongs in the Godhead, since, inasmuch as we cannot comprehend divine things, we signify them more suitably by general words that signify something indefinitely than by special words, which definitely express a specific thing. And so we say that the term *He Who Is*, which, according to Damascene,[7] signifies the infinite sea of substance, is the most proper word, as Ex. 3:14 makes clear. And as cause is more general than element, which signifies something first and simple in the genus of material cause, so also source is more common than cause, since we call the first part of a movement or a line its source, not its cause. And it is thereby clear that we can call something that is not essentially distinct, such as the point of a line, a source and not a cause, especially if we are speaking about the cause of origin, which is an efficient cause. And although one says that the Father is the source of the Son and the Holy Spirit, it does not seem proper that we should without qualification say that the Son or the Holy Spirit is an effect, although the Greeks use even this way of speaking, and we can allow it on the part of those who understand it rightly. But we, in order to avoid the error of the Arians, ought to avoid things that signify any inferiority, lest we attribute them to the Son and the Holy Spirit. For example, Hilary, although he concedes that the Father is greater than the Son because of the preeminence of his origin, does not allow that the Son, on whom the Father bestowed equality, is less than the Father.[8] Likewise, one should not apply the word *subordination* or *effect* regarding the Son, although the word *preeminence* or *source* is allowed regarding the Father.

Obj. 15. Whatever has something only insofar as it receives the thing from another, as such lacks it, as air, considered in itself, lacks light, which it receives from another. Therefore, if the Son and the Holy Spirit have existing only because of what they receive from the Father, which we need to say if they proceed from the Father, it is necessary that, if we should consider them in themselves, they are nothing. But what, considered in itself, is nothing, if it should have existing from another, necessarily comes from nothing, and so that it is a creature. Therefore, if the Son and the Holy Spirit proceed from the Father, they are necessarily creatures, which is the impiety of the Arians. Therefore, there is no procession in the divine Persons.

Reply Obj. 15. We should say that we consider the Son, considered in himself according to what he has absolutely, which is the essence of the Father.

Accordingly, he is not nothing but one with the Father. But insofar as he is related to the Father, we consider him as receiving existing from the Father. And so he is also in this way not nothing. And so the Son is in no way nothing. But considered in himself, he would be nothing if there were something absolute in him from the Father, as is the case in creatures.

Article 2

Are There One or More Processions in the Godhead?

We should say that the things pressed by heretics forced the ancient teachers of the faith to weigh things belonging to faith.

For example, Arius thought that existing from another would be contrary to the divine nature, and so he held that the Son and the Holy Spirit, who Holy Scripture says are from another, are creatures. To refute this error, it was necessary for the holy fathers to show that something proceeding from the Father can be consubstantial with him, inasmuch as ir receives from him the same nature that he has.

But because we say that the Son, since he receives the nature of the Father from the Father, is born or begotten of the Father, and because Scripture does not say that the Holy Spirit, although from God, is born or begotten, Macedonius thought that the Holy Spirit is one of the Father's creatures, not consubstantial with him. For he did not believe that one can receive the nature of another from the other unless one were to be born of the other and be the other's son. And so he thought it unerringly to follow that, if the Holy Spirit receives the Father's nature and essence, he is begotten and a Son. And so, in order to exclude this error, it was necessary for our teachers to show that the divine nature can be shared by two kinds of procession, one generation or begetting, the other not. And this is to seek the difference between the processions in the Godhead.

Therefore, some said that the processions in the Godhead distinguished one another by themselves. The reason for holding this position was because they held that the relations do not distinguish the divine hypostases but only manifest their distinction. They thought that the relations in the Godhead were like the individual properties in created things, which properties only manifest, not cause, the distinction between individual things. Therefore, they say that only origin distinguishes the hypostases in the Godhead. And because the things whereby particular things first differ necessarily distinguish themselves one from another, as contrary specific differences distinguish themselves one from another, lest there be an infinite regression, so they say that the processions in the Godhead are distinguished from one from another by themselves.

But this cannot be true, since that whereby each has its species specifically distinguishes one from another, and what individuates it distinguishes it numerically. And the divine processions necessarily differ both as things numerically different and as things specifically different, since one is generation, and the other not. Therefore, we conclude that that whereby the divine processions have their species distinguish them. But no procession or action or movement has its species from itself. Rather, its goal or its source allots its species. And so it is useless to say that any processions distinguished themselves from one another by themselves. Rather, their sources or their termini distinguish them one from another.

And so some said the divine processions' sources distinguish them one from another, in that, I say, one procession is in the way of nature or the intellect, and the other in the way of the will, since the words *intellect* and *will* seem to signify particular sources of the actions and processions.

But if one should diligently consider the matter, one can easily see that this does not suffice to distinguish the divine processions unless something else is added. For we need to find in the thing proceeding a likeness of what is the source of the procession, as, in created things, a likeness of the form of a begetter needs to be in the thing begotten. Therefore, if the processions in the Godhead are distinguished by the fact that the source of one is nature or the intellect, and the source of the other is the will, it is necessary that only what belongs to nature or the intellect is in the one proceeding in one procession, and only what belongs to the will is in the other one. This is clearly false, since, in one procession, that of the Son from the Father, the Father communicates to the Son whatever he has, both nature, intellect, power, will, and whatever we predicate of him absolutely. Therefore, as the Son is the Word, that is, wisdom begotten, so we can call him nature, will, or power begotten, that is, received by generation, or, rather, receiving such things by generation.

And so it is clear that, since all the essential attributes come together in the one procession of the Son, we cannot find the difference of the processions by reason of different attributes, so that we note the communication of one attribute by one procession, and the communication of another attribute by the other procession. And since the terminus of a procession is having, inasmuch as a divine person proceeds in order to have what he receives by proceeding, and the termini of the processions distinguish them, one proceeding is necessarily distinguished in the Godhead in the same way as one who has is. But one who has is not distinguished from another who has by the fact that this one has these attributes, and that one has other attributes. Rather, one having is distinguished from another having by the fact that one has the same things from another, since the Son has all the things that the Father has but is distinguished from the Father because he has them from the Father.

Therefore, one proceeding is distinguished from another proceeding because one of them receives from the other, not because one has these things by proceeding. Therefore, whatever is in a divine procession that we can immediately understand in a procession, with no other procession presupposed, belongs only to one procession. But there can be another procession where the same things that were received by the first procession are again drawn into another procession.

And so only the order of processions that we note by the origin of the processions multiplies them in the Godhead. And so those who held that one procession is by way of nature and the intellect, and the other by way of the will spoke well as to the fact that the procession by nature or the intellect does not presuppose another procession, but the procession by way of the will does. And love of anything can proceed from the will only if we presuppose that the word conceived of that thing has proceeded from the intellect, since an understood good is the object of the will.

Obj. 4. One might say that processions are distinguished in the Godhead because one, the procession of the Son, is by way of nature, and the other, namely, the procession of the Holy Spirit, by way of the will. On the contrary, what comes naturally proceeds by way of nature. But the Holy Spirit proceeds naturally from the Father, since Athanasius says that he is the natural Spirit of the Father.[9] Therefore, the Holy Spirit proceeds by way of nature.

Reply Obj. 4. We should say that nothing prevents something proceeding naturally from the will, since the will by nature tends toward a final end, just as any other power by nature acts for its object. And so a human being by nature desires happiness. In the same way, God by nature loves his goodness, just as he by nature understands his truth. Therefore, as the Son proceeds by nature from the Father as the Word, so the Holy Spirit proceeds by nature from him as Love. But the Holy Spirit does not proceed by way of nature, since we call proceeding in the Godhead by way of nature what proceeds like things produced in creatures by nature, not the will. Therefore, being produced by nature and being produced by way of nature differ, since we say that nature produces something because of the natural relationship that it has to its source, but we say that it is produced by the way of nature if the source producing it does so in the way nature does.

Obj. 5. The will is free. Therefore, what comes by way of the will proceeds by way of freedom. Therefore, if the Holy Spirit proceeds by way of the will, it necessarily proceeds by way of freedom. But what proceeds by way of freedom can proceed or not proceed, and can proceed so much or not so much, since things done freely are not determined to one thing. Therefore, the Father could produce or not produce the Holy Spirit, and give to him whatever measure of magnitude he willed. Therefore, it follows that the Holy Spirit is a possible being and not an intrinsically necessary being. And so he will not belong to the divine nature, which is the heresy of Macedonius.

Reply Obj. 5. We should say that the natural necessity whereby we say that the will necessarily wills something, such as happiness, is not contrary to the freedom of the will, as Augustine teaches.[10] For freedom of the will is contrary to violence or force, and there is no violence or force in the order of something's nature moving it. Rather, there is violence or force in natural movement being prevented, as when a heavy object is prevented from falling toward the earth's center. And so the will freely seeks happiness, although it necessarily desired it. And so also God by his will freely loves himself, although he does so necessarily. And he necessarily loves himself as much as he is good, as he understands himself as much as he exists. Therefore, the Holy Spirit freely proceeds from the Father necessarily, not possibly. Nor was it possible that he proceed as less than the Father, but it was necessary that he be equal to the Father, just like the Son, who is the Word of the Father.

Obj. 7. Nature and will differ in God only conceptually. Therefore, if we should distinguish the processions of the Son and the Holy Spirit by one being by way of nature, and the other by way of the will, it follows that the processions of the Son and the Holy Spirit differ only conceptually, and so the Son and the Holy Spirit are not personally distinguished.

Reply Obj. 7. We should say that, although nature and the will differ in God only conceptually, not really, the one who proceeds by way of the will necessarily really differs from the one who proceeds by way of nature, and one procession really differs from the other. For I have said that we understand procession by way of nature when something proceeds from something as something proceeds from nature, and we likewise understand procession by way of the will when something proceeds as something proceeds from the will, since the will always produces something with a procession presupposed. For the will tends to something only by a preexisting production of the intellect conceiving something, since the understood good moves the will. And a procession from a natural active thing presupposes another procession only incidentally, namely, insofar as a natural active thing depends on another active thing. But that does not belong to the aspect of nature as such. And so we understand the procession by way of nature in the Godhead that presupposes no other, and the procession by way of the will takes its source from a presupposed procession. And so there is necessarily procession from a procession, and a Person proceeding from a Person proceeding, and this causes a real distinction in the Godhead.

Obj. 11. The will in the Godhead does not differ from nature more than the intellect does. But there is no procession in the Godhead by way of the intellect other than the one by way of nature. Therefore, neither is there another power by way of the will besides one by way of nature.

Reply Obj. 11. We should say that we do not distinguish in the Godhead the procession by way of the intellect from the procession by way of nature, but we distinguish the procession by way of the will from both. We do so for three reasons.

First, as the procession by way of nature does not require another procession beforehand, so neither does the procession by way of the intellect, and the procession by way of the will necessarily requires beforehand the procession by way of the intellect.

Second, as nature produces something into likeness of itself, so also does the intellect both within and without, as the form of the intellect is brought into the product of a craft. But the will does not produce its likeness, either within or without. It does not produce its likeness internally, since love, which is the internal procession of the will, is not a likeness of the will or the thing willed. Rather, it is an impression from the will on the thing willed, or a union of one thing with the other. The will does not produce its likeness externally, since the will imposes on the product of a craft a form conceptually understood before it was willed. And so it is chiefly a likeness of the intellect, although secondarily a likeness of the will.

Third, the procession of nature is only from one thing as the active thing if it should be a perfect active thing. Nor is it an objection that two things in animals, namely, the father and the mother, generate something, since only the father is the active thing in generation, and the mother passive. Likewise, the procession of the intellect is only from one thing, but friendship, which is mutual love, proceeds from two persons loving each other.

Obj. 12. One might say that the procession of the Holy Spirit differs from the procession of the Son because the procession of the Son is only from one who does not proceed, namely, the Father, and the procession of the Holy Spirit is from one who does not proceed and one who does, namely, the Father and the Son, and simultaneously. On the contrary, if we should posit two processions in the Godhead, they differ only numerically, or specifically. If only numerically, it follows that we should call each procession a generation or birth, and we ought to call each one proceeding a Son. But if they should differ specifically, the nature communicated by a procession necessarily differs specifically. For example, the procession of a human being and that of a horse from its source

differ specifically, but not the procession of Socrates and that of Plato. Therefore, since there is only one divine nature, there cannot be several specifically
different processions, one being from one who proceeds, and the other not.

Reply Obj. 12. We should say that, although we do not properly speak of
genus and species, or the universal and the particular, in the Godhead, yet,
as we speak about the Godhead according to the likeness of creatures, we
distinguish the Father, the Son, and the Holy Spirit as several individuals of
the same species, as Damascene also says.[11] But we should note that we can
consider species in any individual in the genus of substance in two ways: in
one way the species of the hypostasis itself; in the other way the species of
the individual property. For, given that Socrates is white, and Plato black, and
supposing that whiteness and blackness are properties individuating
Socrates and Plato, it will be true to say that Socrates and Plato are specifically the same, and that the hypostases are included in that species. They are
one in humanity but differ in their specific property, since whiteness and
blackness differ specifically. It is likewise in the Father and the Son, since we
consider them as one in the species of which they are existing individuals,
inasmuch as they are one in the divine nature. But they differ by their specific property, since paternity and sonship are specifically different relations.
We should also note that generation in created things is intrinsically ordered
to species. For example, nature strives to generate a human being. And so
also generation in created things multiplies a specific nature. But procession
in the Godhead is to multiply hypostases, in which the divine nature is numerically one. And so the processions in the Godhead are, as it were, specifically
different because of the different personal properties, although there is one
common nature in the Persons proceeding.

Arguments that there are more than two processions in the Godhead:

Counterobj. 2. One might say that there is one and the same procession in
the Godhead by way of nature and by way of the intellect, since there is the
same Son and Word. On the contrary, the processions of creatures are imita-
tions of the processions of the divine Persons. And so Eph. 3:15 says of God
the Father that "every paternity in heaven and earth takes its name from him."
But in creatures, there is a procession of nature, in which a human being
generates a human being, and another procession of the intellect, in which
the intellect produces a word. Therefore, in the Godhead, there is not one and
the same procession by way of the intellect and by way of nature.

Reply Counterobj. 2. We should say that human nature is material, that is,
composed of matter and form, and so the procession by way of nature in
human beings can be only by a natural transformation. But the procession by
way of the intellect is always immaterial, insofar as the intellect is immaterial.

And so there cannot be in human beings one and the same procession by way of nature and by way of the intellect. But it is one and the same in the Godhead, since the divine nature is immaterial.

Counterobj. 3. According to Dionysius,[12] it belongs to the divine goodness to proceed. But the Father is supremely good. Therefore, he proceeds. Therefore, there are three processions in the Godhead: one whereby the Father proceeds, the second whereby the Son proceeds, and the third whereby the Holy Spirit proceeds.

Reply Counterobj. 3. We should say that it is one thing to proceed into another, and another thing to proceed from another, since proceeding into another is to communicate one's likeness to another, and we should in this way understand the procession of divine goodness into creatures, according to Dionysius. But to proceed from another is to have existing from another, and so we are speaking here of such procession, in which way it is evident that proceeding does not belong to the Father.

Article 3

What Is the Order of Procession to Relation in the Godhead?

We should say that there is no order without distinction. And so, when there is only a distinction according to our way of understanding, not really, then there can be only an order according to our way of understanding. But there is real distinction in the Godhead only of the Persons to one another and of the opposite relations. And so there is in the Godhead a real order only regarding the Persons, among whom there is an order of nature, according to Augustine,[13] as one thing is from another, not one prior to another.

But we distinguish processions and relations in the Godhead only by our way of understanding, not really. And so also Augustine says that it is proper to the Father to beget the Son.[14] In this, we are given to understand that begetting the Son is a property of the Father, nor is there a property of his other than fatherhood, which we say is his personal property. Therefore, between procession and relation in the Godhead, we should look for an order only according to our way of understanding, not a real order.

As relation and procession in the Godhead are really the same thing and differ only conceptually, so also the very relation, although really one and the same, is multiple according to our way of understanding. For we understand the relation as constituting the Person, which it does not have as a relation. This is evident by the fact that relations in human affairs do not constitute persons, since relations are accidents, but a person is something subsistent in the genus of substance, and we cannot consider a person as an accident. But a relation in the Godhead has the capacity to constitute a Person inasmuch as it is a divine relation, since it is thereby identical with the divine essence, as there cannot be any accident in God. For a relation, being really the divine nature itself, can constitute a divine hypostasis. Therefore, there is one way of understanding a relation as constituting a divine Person and another way of understanding a relation as such. And so nothing prevents a relation as to one way of understanding from presupposing procession, and the converse as to the other way of understanding.

Therefore, we should say that, if one should consider a relation as such, it presupposes an understanding of procession, but if one should consider it as constituting a Person, then the relation that constitutes the Person from whom there is a procession is conceptually prior to the procession. For example, paternity as constituting the Father as a Person is conceptually prior to him begetting. But the relation that constitutes the Person proceeding, even as being such, is conceptually subsequent to procession, as sonship is subsequent to being begotten, and this is because we understand the Person proceeding as the terminus of the procession.

Obj. 4. We say everything is relative in reference to something else. But there cannot be anything else where there is no distinction. Therefore, relation presupposes distinction. But distinction in the divine Persons is by origin, namely, as one person proceeds from another. Therefore, the processions in the Godhead precede the relations conceptually.

Reply Obj. 4. We should say that it is necessary in things in which relations are accidents that relation presupposes distinction, but relations in the Godhead constitute three distinct Persons.

Obj. 5. Every procession conceptually precedes the terminus of the procession. But the sonship that is the relation of the Son is the terminus of birth, which is the procession of the same Son. Therefore, the procession of the Son precedes sonship. But sonship and paternity are simultaneous not only by nature and time but also conceptually, since one relative thing concerns understanding of the other. Therefore, the birth of the Son conceptually precedes paternity, and far more does generation, which is the activity of the Father. Therefore, the processions absolutely precede the relations in the Godhead conceptually.

Reply Obj. 5. We should say that paternity concerns sonship, and vice versa, insofar as we consider each as a relation. And we say in this sense that the relations are subsequent to the processions conceptually.

Article 4
Does the Holy Spirit Proceed from the Son?

We should say that, according to things determined before, the Holy Spirit necessarily proceeds from the Son, since, if the Son and the Holy Spirit are two Persons, there is necessarily one procession of one and another procession of the other. But I have shown before (A. 2) that there can be two processions in the Godhead only in an order of processions, namely, a second procession from the one proceeding in the first procession. Therefore, the Holy Spirit is necessarily from the Son.

Besides this argument, other arguments conclusively prove that the Holy Spirit is from the Son. Every difference between two things necessarily results from the primary basis of their distinction, unless, per chance, the difference should be accidental, as, for example, walking differs from sitting. This is because everything intrinsically in something either belongs to its essence or results from its essential sources, from which the primary basis of the distinction between things arises. But there cannot be in the Godhead anything by accident, since everything in something by accident, as extraneous to the thing's nature, necessarily belongs to it from an external cause, and we cannot say this about the Godhead.

Therefore, every difference between the divine Persons necessarily results from the primary basis of their distinction. But the primary basis of the distinction between the Father and the Son is by reason of paternity and sonship. Therefore, every distinction between the Father and the Son results from the fact that one is the Father, and the other is the Son. But being the source of the Holy Spirit does not belong to the Father as such by reason of his paternity, since he is in this way only related to the Son, and so it would follow that the Holy Spirit was the Son.

Likewise, this is not contrary to the nature of sonship, since sonship is only a relationship to the Father. Therefore, there cannot be a difference between the Father and the Son in that the Father and not the Son is the source of the Holy Spirit.

Also, as the book *Councils* says,[15] it belongs to a creature that God by his will produced it, and Hilary proves this by the fact that a creature exists as God willed it to be, not as God exists. But because the Son exists as the Father does, we say that the Father begot the Son by nature. And by the same reasoning, the Holy Spirit is from the Father by nature, since the Spirit is like and equal to the Father, inasmuch as nature produces its like. But a creature, which is from the Father by the Father's will is necessarily also from the Son, since there is the same will of the Father and the Son. Likewise, there is the same nature of both.

Therefore, as the Holy Spirit is necessarily from the Father, so is he necessarily from the Son. But it does not follow that the Son or the Holy Spirit is from the Holy Spirit, although the Spirit also has the same nature as the Father, because of the contradiction that would follow if were to say that the Holy Spirit is from himself, or if we were to say that the Son, who is the source of the Spirit, is from the Spirit (It does follow that a creature is from the Spirit inasmuch as the Spirit has the same will as the Father.)

This is evident in another way, since there can be a distinction in the divine Persons only by relations. For things that we predicate absolutely in the Godhead, such as goodness, wisdom, and the like, signify the essence and are common. But different relations can cause distinction only by reason of their contrariness, since one thing can have different relations to the same thing. For example, it is evident that one and the same thing can be related to another and same thing as son, disciple, equal, and any other relations that do not include contrariness.

The Son is clearly distinguished from the Father by being related to him by a particular relationship, and the Holy Spirit is likewise clearly distinguished from the Father because of a particular relationship. Therefore, however disparate these relations seem, they could in no way distinguish the Holy Spirit from the Son unless they are contraries. But there can be contrariness in the Godhead only by reason of origin, namely, as one is from another. Therefore, the fact that the Son and the Holy Spirit are each related to the Father could in no way distinguish them unless one of them is related to the other as existing from him.

But it is evident that the Son is not from the Holy Spirit, since it belongs to the nature of a son to be related only to a father, as existing from him. Therefore, we necessarily conclude that the Holy Spirit is from the Son.

But because one can say that both arguments and authorities confirm the things of faith, it remains to show by the authorities of sacred Scripture that the Holy Spirit is from the Son. For many texts of sacred Scripture hold that Holy Spirit is of the Son. For example, Rom. 8:9 says: "One who does not have the Spirit of Christ does not belong to Christ." And Gal. 4:6 says: "God sent the Spirit of his Son into your hearts." And Acts 16:7 says: "They tried to go to Bithynia, and the Spirit of Jesus did not permit it." For we cannot understand that the Holy Spirit is the Spirit of Christ only regarding Christ's humanity, as if filling him, since the Holy Spirit belongs to a human being as one who possesses the Spirit, not one who gives the Spirit. But the Holy Spirit belongs to the Son as one who gives the Spirit, as 1 Jn. 4:13 says: "We know that we remain in him, and he in us, because he has given us of his Spirit." And Acts 5:32 says that he gave the Holy Spirit to those who obey him.

Therefore, we need to say that the Holy Spirit belongs to the Son as a divine Person. Therefore, we say either that the Spirit is absolutely Christ's, or that the Spirit is Christ's as his spirit. But if absolutely, then the Son necessarily has authority over the Holy Spirit. For we can say that one who does not have authority over another belongs to another in a limited way, as when we say that Peter is a companion of John, but we can say that Peter belongs to John absolutely only if Peter should be John's possession, as we say that a slave, the very thing that he is, belongs to his master. But there can be in the Godhead no slavery or subjection, although we understand preeminence in it only by reason of origin. Therefore, the Holy Spirit necessarily originates from the Son.

The same thing follows if we should say that the Holy Spirit belongs to the Son as the Son's spirit, since the Spirit as a personal name signifies a relation of origin to the one originating him, as the Son does to the one begetting him. Likewise, we find in the Scripture, as I have said before, that the Son sends the Holy Spirit, and the one sending always seems to have authority over the one sent. But authority in the Godhead is only by reason of origin, as I have said. And so it follows that the Holy Spirit originates from the Son.

And sacred Scripture holds that the Holy Spirit configures us to the Son, as Rom. 8:15 says: "You receive the Spirit of adoption as sons." And Gal. 4:6 says: "Because you are sons, God sent the Spirit of his Son into your hearts." But nothing is configured to something except by the thing's proper characteristic. In created natures, what conforms something to something is from the source, as, for example, a man's semen is likened to the man from which it is, not to a horse. And the Holy Spirit is from the Son as the Son's proper characteristic. And so 2 Cor. 1:21–22 says: "Who sealed us, anointed us, and planted the pledge of the Spirit in our hearts." More explicitly, Christ says of the Holy Spirit in Jn. 16:14: "He will glorify me, since he will receive of what is mine." It is evident that the Holy Spirit from eternity receives from the Son, nor could he receive anything that is not eternally the Son's essence. Therefore, the Holy Spirit receives his essence from the Son.

The Son himself adds in Jn. 16:15 the reason that the Holy Spirit received from the Son, saying: "Everything the Father has is mine. Therefore, he will receive of what is mine." This is as if he were to say that, since the essence of the Father and what is mine are the same, the Holy Spirit cannot be of the Father's essence without being of my essence. For sacred Scripture transmits that the Son acts through the Spirit, as Rom. 15:18 holds, "Christ works through me," namely, miracles and other good things, "in the Holy Spirit," that is, by the Holy Spirit. And Hebr. 9:14 says that "he offered himself by the Holy Spirit." Whenever we say that one acts through someone, either the one acting gives active power to the one through whom the one acting acts, as we say that a king acts through a commander or an officer, or, conversely, as when we say that an officer acts through a king.

Therefore, if the Son acts through the Holy Spirit, it is necessary that the Holy Spirit give active power to the Son, or the converse, and so that one gives its essence to the other, since the active power of each is simply its essence. But it is evident that the Holy Spirit does not give his essence to the Son, since the Son is the Son only of the Father. Therefore, we conclude that the Holy Spirit is from the Son.

Therefore, we can maintain the same thing by the following argument from the things the Greeks profess. They profess that the Holy Spirit is from the Father through the Son, and that the Father originates the Holy Spirit through the Son. But that whereby something is produced is always the source of what is produced. Therefore, the Son is necessarily the source of the Holy Spirit. But if they should refuse to profess that the Holy Spirit is from the Son, since the Son is from another and so not the primary basis for the Holy Spirit's origin, they clearly object in vain. For no one refuses to say that a stick moves a stone, although a hand moves the stick, or that Jacob is from Isaac, although Isaac is from Abraham. Still less should we refuse to say this in the matter at hand, since there is one and the same power of the Father and the Son, which is not the case regarding created causes of movements and actions.

And so, as we should profess that creatures are from the Son, although the Son is from the Father, so we should profess that the Holy Spirit is from the Son, although the Son is from the Father. Therefore, it is clear that those who say that the Holy Spirit is through the Son but not from him do not know what they are saying, as Aristotle says of Anaxagoras.[16] And 1 Tim. 1:7 says: "Those wishing to be teachers of the Law do not understand of what they are speaking or of what they are affirming."

Obj. 7. Anything in the Godhead is either common or proper. But emitting the Holy Spirit is not common to the whole Trinity, since it does belong to the Holy Spirit. Therefore, it is proper to the Father and so does not belong to the Son.

Reply Obj. 7. We should say that everything in the Godhead is common or proper. But we speak of proper in two senses: in one way, simply and absolutely, which belongs to only one thing, as a sense of humor to a human being; in the second way, we speak of something in relation to something else, not absolutely, as if one should say that rational is proper to a human being in relation to a horse, although rational also belongs to something else, namely, an angel. Therefore, there is something common in the Godhead that belongs to the three Persons, such as to be God and the like, something proper absolutely, which belongs to only one person, and something proper in relation to something, as originating the Holy Spirit is proper to the Father and the Son in relation to the Holy Spirit. For we need to posit such a property in the Godhead even if the Holy Spirit does not proceed from the Son, since being from another still remains proper to the Son and the Holy Spirit in relation to the Father.

Obj. 12. Dionysius says:[17] "We should absolutely not dare to say, or even to think, anything about the more than substantial hidden divinity except things that have been divinely revealed to us by sacred oracles." But sacred Scripture says only that the Holy Spirit proceeds from the Father, not from the Son, as Jn. 15:26 says: "When the Paraclete has come, the one that I shall send to you from the Father, the Spirit of truth, who proceeds from the Father." Therefore, we should not say or think that the Holy Spirit proceeds from the Son.

Reply Obj. 12. We should say that we find regularly in sacred Scripture that we need to understand about the Son what we say about the Father, and to understand about the Holy Spirit what we say about both or either of them, even if it should use an exclusive expression, excepting only things that distinguish the divine Persons from one another. For example, Jn. 17:3 says: "This is divine life, that they know you, the only true God, and the one whom you sent, Jesus Christ." For one cannot say that it does not belong to the Son to be true God, which the Son attributes only to the Father, since, inasmuch as the Father and the Son are one thing, although not one Person, we need to understand what we say of the Father also about the Son. Nor, because there is no mention there of the Holy Spirit, should one deny that eternal life consists of knowing the Holy Spirit, since there is one and the same knowledge of the three Persons. Likewise, we should not take away knowledge of the Father and the Son from the Holy Spirit, although Mt. 11:127 says: "No one knows the Son except the Father, nor one who knows the Father except the Son." And so, since having the Holy Spirit proceeding from oneself does not belong to the nature of paternity or sonship, which distinguish the Father and the Son, we need to understand when the Gospel says that the Holy Spirit proceeds from the Father that he proceeds from the Son.

Obj. 13.[18] The Acts of the First Council of Ephesus [the Third Ecumenical] say that, after the accomplishment of the Nicene Creed, the Holy Council decreed: "No one may profess, write, or devise any faith other than what the holy fathers assembled at Nicea in union with the Holy Spirit defined. And if they presume either to devise, teach, or profess another faith to those willing to be converted from paganism, Judaism, or any heresy, let them, if they should be bishops or clerics, be expelled as bishops from the episcopate and as clerics from the clerical state, and if they were monks or lay persons, let them be excommunicated." Likewise, the Acts of the Council of Chalcedon, after reciting the decisions of other Councils, adds: "Let those who dared to devise another faith, or to profess, teach, or transmit another Creed to those willing to be converted from paganism to knowledge of the truth, from Judaism, or from any heresy be expelled from the episcopate or clerical state if they were bishops or clerics, and excommunicated if they were monks or lay persons." And the foregoing decision of the Council maintains only that the Holy Spirit proceeds from the Father, not that he proceeds from the Son. We also read in the Constantinopolitan Creed: "We believe in the Holy Spirit, the Lord and giver of life, proceeding from the Father, to be adored and glorified with the Father and the Son." Therefore, we ought in no way add in the creed of faith that the Holy Spirit proceeds from the Son.

Reply Obj. 13. We should say that the Nicene Creed adequately transmits the teaching of the Catholic faith. And so the holy fathers in succeeding Councils did not intend to add anything, but because of rising heresies endeavored to explain what it implicitly contained. And so it is stated in the decision of the Council of Calcedon: "This holy, great, and universal Council, teaches the doctrine held from the beginning, and the Council of 318 holy fathers, namely, those assembled in Nicea, chiefly defined the doctrine to be the unalterable faith. Because of those who contend against the Holy Spirit, it strengthened the doctrine handed down later by the 150 fathers assembled at Constantinople. They made this doctrine known to all, not as if anything were less relevant in previous decisions, but declaring their understanding about the Holy Spirit by the witnesses of Scripture against those who strove to belittle his power."

And we should in this way say that the Constantinopolitan Creed implicitly contains the procession of the Holy Spirit from the Son, inasmuch as it contains that the Spirit proceeds from the Father, since we need to understand about the Son what we understand about the Father. For they differ in nothing except that one is the Son, and the other is the Father. But because of the rising errors of those who denied that the Spirit is from the Son, it was suitable to be posited in the Creed, not as if something added, but something explicitly interpreted that was implicitly contained. For example, if a heresy were to arise that denied that the Holy Spirit made the heavens and the earth, we would need to posit it expressly, since the aforementioned Creed says this only about the Father. And as a later Council has the power to interpret the Creed established by a prior Council and to posit things to explain it, as is clear from what I have said before, so also the Roman Pontiff can do this by his authority, whose authority alone can convoke a Council, and who confirms the decisions of the Council, and the appeals from the Council come to him. All of these things are evident from the Acts of the Council of Calcedon.

Nor is it necessary that, in order to authorize an explanation of this, a universal Council be assembled, since the discord of war prevents this from happening, as we read regarding the Sixth Council [the Third of Constantinople] that Constantine Augustus said that he could not assemble all of the bishops because of threatening wars, but those who did convene resolved some questions about the faith, following the opinion of Pope Agatho, namely, that there are in Christ two wills and two actions. Likewise, the fathers assembled at the Council of Calcedon followed the opinion of Pope Leo, who decreed that Christ is in two natures after the incarnation.

But one should note that the decision of the chief Councils maintains that the Holy Spirit proceeds from the Son, since the Council of Calcedon, as expressed in its decrees, received the synodal letters of blessed Cyril, head of the church of Alexandria, to Nestorius and others throughout the East. We read in one of the four: "Because Christ, in order to demonstrate his divinity, used his Spirit for many actions, he said that the Spirit glorified him, as if one should say of those who have their own strength, learning, or whatever that they will glorify that one. Thus it is also in the particular subsistence of the Spirit, or we certainly understood it as such, insofar as the Spirit is not the Son but not different from him, since we call him the Spirit of truth, which he is, and he flows from the Son as well as from the Father." Nor is it an obstacle that he says *flows*, not *proceeds*, since, as is evident from what I said before, the word *proceeds* is the most general of words relating to origin. And so it follows that whaever is emitted or flows or arises in any way proceeds. It is also maintained in the decision of the Fifth Council, at Constantinople: "We follow in all things the holy fathers and teachers of the Church: Athanasius, Hilary, Basil, Gregory the theologian, Gregory of Nyssa, Ambrose, Augustine, Theophilus, John of Constantinople, William, Leo, and Proclus And we receive all the things that they explained about the true faith in order to condemn heretics." And it is plain that many of them transmitted in the teaching of faith that the Holy Spirit proceeds from the Son, and no one of them denied it. And so it is consonant with, not contrary to, the Council, to say that the Holy Spirit proceeds from the Son.

Obj. 14. If we say that the Holy Spirit proceeds from the Son, we say this either because of a scriptural authority or because of some reason. No authority of sacred Scripture seems sufficient to demonstrate this. Sacred Scripture indeed maintains that the Holy Spirit belongs to the Son, as Gal. 4:6 maintains: "God sent the Spirit of his Son into our hearts." And Rom. 8:9 says: "If anyone does not have the Spirit of Christ, such a one does not belong to him." Sacred Scripture also holds that the Son sent the Holy Spirit, since Christ says in Jn. 16:7: "If I have not gone away, the Paraclete will not come to you, but if I go, I shall send him to you." But it does not follow that the Holy Spirit proceeds from the Son because he is the Spirit of the Son, inasmuch as we, according to Aristotle, express the genitive in many senses. Likewise, it does not follow from the fact that we say that the Holy Spirit sent the Son, since, even if the Son does not proceed from the Holy Spirit, we say that the Holy Spirit sent him, according to Is. 48:16 in the mouth of Christ: "Now the Lord God and his Spirit sent me"; and Is. 61:1: "The Spirit of the Lord is upon me; he sent me to preach to the meek." This says that Christ is complete in himself.

Likewise, reason cannot effectively prove that the Holy Spirit proceeds from the Son, since, even so, they will still, as it seems, remain distinct from one another, inasmuch as they differ by their personal properties. Therefore, nothing seems to compel us to say that the Holy Spirit proceeds from the Son.

Reply Obj. 14. We should say that, although we express the genitive case of a demonstrative pronoun in many ways, we can understand it in the Godhead only by the relationship of origin. And we should note regarding the mission that all the teachers agree that no Person is sent except one that is from another, and so it is completely inappropriate for the Father, who is from no one, to be sent. But regarding the Person who sends another, there are different opinions of the teachers.

Athanasius[19] and some others say that no Person is sent in time except by the one from whom he proceeded eternally, as the Father sends in time the Son who proceeded from him eternally, and we can accordingly conclude unerringly that, if the Son sends the Holy Spirit, the Spirit exists eternally from him. But we should understand the saying about the Holy Spirit sending the Son about the Son in his human nature, whom the Holy Spirit sent to preach. And so Is. 61:1 says plainly: "He sent me to preach to the poor." And Ambrose so explains this,[20] although Hilary explains that we understand by the spirit the Father, insofar as one understands *spirit* in the Godhead essentially.[21]

But Augustine holds that even the Person from whom another Person does not proceed eternally sends temporally the Person proceeding.[22] For, inasmuch as we understand the mission of a divine Person by an effect in a creature, which is from the whole Trinity, the whole Trinity sends the Person sent, so that we understand causality in a mission in relation to the effect, by which one says that a Person is sent, not the authority of a sender in relation to the person sent.

But the fact that their properties distinguish them does not refute the argument proving that the Holy Spirit proceeds from the Son because of their distinction from each other, since those properties are relative and can distinguish only if they are contrary to each other, as is clear from what I have said before (Q. 8, AA. 3 and 4).

Obj. 24. Damascene says that we say that the Holy Spirit is of the Son but not proceeding from the Son.[23]

Reply Obj. 24. We should say that the position of the Nestorians was that the Holy Spirit did not proceed from the Son, and so one of them said in a creed condemned at the First Council of Ephesus [the Third Ecumenical]: "We hold that the Holy Spirit is neither the Son nor receives his essence by the Son." On this account, Cyril in the aforementioned letter held against Nestorius that the Holy Spirit is from the Son.[24] And Theodorus in a letter to John of Antioch says the following: "The Holy Spirit is not from the Son nor has his substance by the Son but proceeds from the Father. He is called the Spirit of the Son because he is consubstantial with him." Theodorus attributes these word to Cyril, as if they were said in the letter written to John of Antioch, although we do not read this in that letter. Rather, Cyril says in it: "The Spirit of God the Father proceeds from himself and from the Son, the Father being the same with the Son by reason of the same essence." And Damscene later followed this opinion of Theodorus, although the teachings of the same Theodorus were condemned in the Fifth Council. And so we should not agree to the opinion of Damascene in this.

Article 5

Would the Holy Spirit Still Be from the Son if He Were Not to Proceed from Him?

We should say that, if one should correctly consider the statements of the Greeks, they differ from us in words rather than in content. For they do not grant that the Holy Spirit proceeds from the Son, whether because of ignorance, boldness, artifice, or any other cause, but they do grant that the Holy Spirit is the Spirit of the Son and from the Father through the Son, which they could not say if the procession of the Holy Spirit were to be altogether without the Son. And so this gives us to understand that even the Greeks themselves understand that the procession of the Holy Spirit has a relationship to the Son.

But I say that if the Holy Spirit should not be from the Son, or the Son in no way the source of the procession of the Holy Spirit, the Holy Spirit cannot be distinguished personally from the Son, or the procession of the Holy Spirit differ from the generation of the Son. This is clear if one should consider the things whereby some manifest the distinction of the divine persons. For some speak of the distinction of persons by their relations, and others by their way of origin, and still others by their relationship to essential attributes.

Therefore, if we should consider the way of distinguishing the Persons by relations, it is clearly evident that we cannot personally distinguish the Holy Spirit from the Son if the former should not proceed from the latter. First, we can distinguish particular things from one another only because of a material or quantitative, or a formal, division. We find the distinction by material and quantitative division in material things, in which there are many individuals of the same species because a specific form is in different parts of matter by quantitative division. And so, if something undivided consists of the totality of matter, in which there can be a specific form, there cannot be several individuals of that species, as Aristotle proves about the world in the beginning of the *De coelo*.[25] But this way of distinction is altogether absent from the Godhead, since there is in God no matter or material quantity. And regarding a formal distinction, there can be one between particular things having the same nature at least generically only by reason of a contrariety. And so all generic distinctions are contraries.

And so there can be a distinction in the divine nature, and we can understand one, only by contrariety, since the divine nature is the same both generically and numerically. And so, since the Persons in the Godhead are distinct, this needs to be by relative contrariety, since there cannot be another contrariety in the Godhead. This is clearly evident, since, howsoever much things like essential attributes are conceptually different, they do not distinguish the Persons, since the Persons are contrary to one another. So also are there several notions in one divine Person because they do not have contrariety to one another, as in the Father, namely, being without a source, fatherhood, and originating the Holy Spirit. For there is distinction when relative contrariety first occurs, as in the case of being the Father and the Son. Therefore, when there is no relative contrariety in the Godhead, there can be no real distinction, that is, a personal distinction.

But if the Holy Spirit does not proceed from the Son, there will be no contrariety between the Son and the Holy Spirit, and so the Holy Spirit is not personally distinguished from the Son. Nor can one say that the contrariety between affirming and denying suffices to make such a distinction. For such contrariety results from the distinction and does not cause it, since something inhering substantially or accidentally distinguishes what comes from another, and one thing is not another because they are different. Likewise, the truth of any negative proposition about things existing is clearly based on the truth of an affirmative proposition. For example, the truth of the negative proposition, *An Ethiopian is not white*, is based on the truth of the affirmative proposition, *An Ethiopian is black*. And so we need to trace every difference by the contrariety of affirming and denying to the difference of an affirmative contrariety. And so the primary reason for the distinction between the Son and the Holy Spirit cannot be because the Son is begotten, not originated as the Spirit, the other originated as the Spirit, not begotten, unless one understands beforehand the distinction between generation and originating as the Spirit, and between Son and Holy Spirit, by a contrariety of the two affirmations.

Second, according to Augustine in his work *Trinity*,[26] what we predicate absolutely in the Godhead is common to the three Persons. And so we conclude that there can be a distinction of the divine Persons only by what we predicate relatively, since these are two categories in the Godhead. And the first distinction in the Godhead relatively is between one from another and one from no one. But if we need to subdivide one of these, namely, what is from another, it is necessary that things of the same character distinguish it. For, as Aristotle teaches,[27] if one in subdividing should use incidental, not intrinsic, things, this violates the right order of division. This is as if we were to say that one kind of animal is rational, and the other irrational, and that one kind of irrational animals is white, and the other black, since, inasmuch as incidental things do not constitute one thing absolutely, the last species, constituted of many differences, would not be one thing absolutely.

Therefore, if we should distinguish or subdivide one who is from another in the Godhead, this is necessarily by differences of the same character, namely, as of things from another, one being from the other. And this signifies the different processions that we signify when we say that one is by generation, and the other by originating as the Spirit. And so Richard of St. Victor distinguishes proceeding from another in that one has another proceeding from him, and the other does not.[28]

Third, although there are two relations in the Father, namely, paternity and active origination of the Spirit, only paternity constitutes the Person of the Father, and so we call it a property or personal relation. But active origination of the Spirit is not the personal relation of a Person but a relation adding to a Person already constituted, as it were. It is evident from this that, according to our order of understanding, the origination of the Spirit presupposes active generation, that is, paternity. Therefore, it is likewise necessary that the passive origination of the Spirit, that is, the procession of the Holy Spirit, sequentially presupposes sonship, which corresponds to paternity by contrariety. Or it is therefore necessary in such a way that we understand the passive origination of the Spirit to add to sonship in the same Person, as active origination of the Spirit adds to paternity, and so the same Person will be originated and born, as the same Person generates and originates the Spirit. Or it is necessary that sonship has some other order to passive origination of the Spirit. But there is only an order of nature in the Godhead, as one Person is from another, as Augustine says.[29] And so we conclude that either there is one Person of the Son and the originated Holy Spirit, or that the Holy Spirit is from the Son.

If one should consider the distinction of the divine Persons by their origin, not by the relations of origin, one reaches the same conclusion, as will be evident as follows. First, if one should consider the property of the divine nature, there cannot be plurality of Persons in God except because one does not originate from another, and in no way because two originate from one. This is evident if one should consider how there is distinction in different things. For example, in material things, in which there can be multiplicity by the division of matter and quantity, as I have said, two individuals of the same species can be equally disposed, just as two quantitative parts can be equally disposed. But where the primary difference regards form, two things cannot be in any way equally disposed, since, as Aristotle says,[30] the forms of things are like numbers, in which species differ by adding or subtracting a unit, and the formal differences of things consist of an order of perfection. For example, a plant specifically differs from a stone in adding life, an irrational animal from a plant in adding sense perception, and a human being from an irrational animal in adding reason. And so, in immaterial things, in which there cannot be multiplicity by the division of matter, there can be plurality only with an order. In created spiritual substances, there is an order of perfection insofar as one angel has a higher nature than another. And because some philosophers believed that a more perfect nature created every imperfect nature, they said that there can be multiplicity in separate substances only by cause and effect. But the true faith does not hold this, since we believe that the order of divine wisdom produced the different ranks of spiritual substances.

And since there cannot be an order of perfection in the Godhead, as the Arians held, saying that the Father is greater than the Son, and that both are greater than the Holy Spirit, we conclude there can be, and we can understand, plurality in the divine Persons only by the order of origin, namely, that the Son is from the Father, and the Holy Spirit from the Son. For, if the Holy Spirit were not to be from the Son, the Spirit would equally with the Son relate to the Father as to origin. And so either they would not be two Persons, or the order of perfection between them would be as the Arians said, or there would be a material division between them. But this is impossible. Hilary, following this argument, says that positing in the Godhead two who are not begotten, that is, not existing from anyone, is to posit the two as Gods, since, if there should not be multiplicity by the order of origin, it would necessarily be by the order of natures.[31] And so the argument is the same if one does not presuppose the order of origin between the Son and the Holy Spirit.

Second, what proceeds by nature from one thing is necessarily itself one thing, since nature is always related to one thing, but things proceeding from something by an act of the will can be many, although they are from one thing, as different creatures proceed from one God by his will. But it is evident that the Son proceeds from the Father by nature, not by his will, as the Arians said. This is why Hilary says:[32] "What proceeds by nature from something is just like the thing from which it proceeds, but what proceeds from something by an act of the will is not of the same nature as that from which it proceeds but is as the one willing wishes it to be." And the Son is just like the Father, but creatures are as God willed them to be. And so the Son is from the Father by nature, but creatures are from him by the will. Likewise, the Holy Spirit is of the same nature as the Father, since he is not a creature, as Arius and Macedonius said. And so he necessarily proceeds from the Father, and this is why Athanasius and other saints say that he is the natural Spirit of the Father and the Son. Therefore, the Son and the Holy Spirit can proceed from the Father only such that only one, namely, the Son, proceeds only from the Father, and one, the Holy Spirit, proceeds from the Father and the Son in unison.

Third, as Richard of Saint Victor proves,[33] there cannot be an indirect procession in the Godhead, since each divine person, inasmuch as each is in the other, is of necessity directly ordered to the other. But if the Son and the Holy Spirit were to be from the Father without the Holy Spirit being from the Son, there would not be a direct order of the Holy Spirit to the Son, since each would be ordered to the other only by means of the one from whom they exist, like two brothers begotten by the same Father. And so the Son and the Holy Spirit cannot be from the Father in this way, as two distinct Persons, one of them not being from the other.

And if one should consider the distinction of the Persons by their order to essential attributes, it is also evident that the same conclusion results. First, we say by this that the Son proceeds by way of nature, and the Holy Spirit by way of the will, since the procession of nature is always the source and origin of any other procession, as all the things done by skill and the will or intellect proceed from things that are by nature. And so Richard of Saint Victor says that, of all the ways of proceeding, evidently holding the first place and more important than other ways is the way of the Son from the Father.[34] For, unless the Father preceded the others, no one of the others will have room to exist at all.

Second, this is clear if we should say that the Son proceeds by an intellectual procession as the Word, and the Holy Spirit by a procession of the will as Love. For it cannot be, nor can we understand, that love belongs to anything not preconceived in the intellect. And so every love is from a word, if we are speaking about love in an intellectual nature.

Third, the same thing is evident if we say that the Holy Spirit is a life-giving breath of the Godhead, as Athanasius says, since the intellect directs every vital movement and action unless something contrary from an imperfection of nature occurs.

And so all the aforementioned things give us to understand that the Holy Spirit would not be different from the Son were the Spirit not to proceed from the Son, nor would the origination of the Spirit be different from generation.

Obj. 2. Anselm says:[35] "The Son and the Holy Spirit have existing from the Father, but in different ways, since the former is by being born, and the latter by proceeding, so that they are thereby distinct from each other." And he adds afterward: "For, if the Son and the Holy Spirit were several Persons for no other reason, this alone would differentiate them." Therefore, even if the Holy Spirit were not to proceed from the Son, he would remain personally distinct from the Son because of his different way of originating.

Reply Obj. 2. We should say that what Anselm says, that only the fact that the Son and the Holy Spirit proceed in different ways distinguishes them from each other, is altogether true, but, as I have shown, they could not proceed in different ways unless the Holy Spirit proceeded from the Son. And so, without the Holy Spirit being from the Son, the distinction of the Holy Spirit is altogether eliminated. And the intention of Anselm is first to posit things in which we agree with those who deny that the Holy Spirit proceeds from the Son but say that the Holy Spirit is distinguished from the Son. And so Anselm introduced the aforementioned words as a argumentative supposition rather than a definition of truth.

Obj. 5. Eternal relations in the Godhead are subsistent Persons, not accidents or assistants. Therefore, whatever results in a plurality of relations in the Godhead suffices to distinguish the Persons. But specifically different actions suffice for different relations. For example, the relation of lordship results from the action of governance, and another relation (i.e., paternity) results from the action of generation. Just so, different relations result in specifically different quantities. The relation *double* results from the number two, and the relation *triple* from the number three. But we signify processions in the Godhead by way of actions. Therefore, if there are two processions, there are necessarily two relations resulting from the processions. Therefore, there are necessarily two Persons, and so the Holy Spirit would remain personally distinct from the Son even if the Spirit were not to proceed from the Son.

Reply Obj. 5. We should say that it is not necessary that there be as many subsistent Persons in the Godhead as there are relations, since there are two relations in the one Person of the Father, namely, paternity, by which he is related to the Son, and the common originating of the Spirit, by which he is related to the Holy Spirit. For the relation of paternity constitutes the subsistent Person, but the common originating of the Spirit is a relation inhering in a subsistent Person, not the property constituting the Person. And so it does not follow that, if two relations result from generation and procession, there are thereby only two subsistent Persons. One can also reply that there are two processions only if one of those proceeding proceeds from the other, as I have said.

Obj. 11. When something subsequent has been removed, something prior is not necessarily eliminated. For example, when we eliminate human being, we do not eliminate animal. And we predicate three things of the divine Persons, namely, procession, sharing, and kinship. And the nature of procession precedes the nature of sharing and the nature of kinship. But there would be no sharing or kinship unless there was the plurality of Persons, whom procession multiplies. Therefore, when sharing and kinship in the Godhead have been eliminated, there still remains procession. Therefore, even if there is no sharing of the Father and the Son in originating the Holy Spirit, nor kinship of the Holy Spirit with the Son in that the Holy Spirit proceeds from the Son, the procession of the Holy Spirit from the Father still remains, and so three distinct Persons remain, namely, two Persons proceeding and one from whom they proceed.

Reply Obj. 11. We should say that, although procession is conceptually prior to sharing, as the common is prior to the proper, such procession, namely, of the Holy Spirit, who proceeds, so to speak, as Love and sharing and the bond of the Father and the Son, is not conceptually prior to sharing. And so it is not necessary that, when sharing has been eliminated, procession remains. Just so, animal is conceptually prior to human being, but rational animal is not.

Obj. 12. We speak of properties, relations, and notions in the Godhead. But the nature of property is prior to the nature of relation or notion, since understanding the persons constituted by the personal properties is prior to the fact that they are related to one another and are notional. With the relations also eliminated, the properties constituting the Persons still remain. Therefore, even though the Holy Spirit is not related to the Son as being from him, the Son and the Holy Spirit will still be distinct Persons by their properties.

Reply Obj. 12. We should say that properties, relations, and notions are really the same in the Godhead, except that there are only three properties, namely, paternity, sonship, and procession, and four relations, with the common origination of the Spirit added to the aforementioned properties. (The latter relation is not a property, since it belongs to two Persons, not one.) There are five notions, with the addition of being without a source, which is not a relation but a notion, since the Father is known by it. It is also a property, since it belongs to the Father alone, but not a personal property, since it does not constitute the Person of the Father.

Therefore, as to reality, the properties, relations, and notions cannot have an order, since the same thing is included in the three. And if we seek their order regarding their own nature, notion is prior to relation in the order in which we call something prior in relation to us, and relation and property are prior in the order in which something is really prior. And if we should seek the order between relation and property, one can assign no order between them in created things. For some but not every property is a relation. Likewise, some but not every relation is a property. But if we should understand property by something absolute, then property is first in the order in which the absolute is prior to the relative. And it is necessary in the divine Persons that the nature of relation precedes the nature of property, since, inasmuch as the proper is what belongs to only one person, the nature of property presupposes distinction. And there can be something distinct in the Godhead only by what is in relation to something. And so relation, which is the source of distinction in the Godhead, is conceptually prior to property.

But we should note that neither property nor relation as such has the nature of constituting a Person. For, inasmuch as a person is an individual substance of a rational nature, what is external to substance cannot constitute a person. And so, in created things, properties and relations do not constitute persons but come to constituted persons. But in the Godhead, the very relation, which is also a property, is the divine essence, and so what it constitutes is a Person, since, unless paternity were the divine essence, the word *Father* would in no way signify a Person but only the relative accident of a Person, as is evident in the case of human persons. Therefore, paternity, insofar as it is the divine essence, constitutes the subsistent hypostasis in the divine nature, but insofar as it is relation, paternity distinguishes, and insofar as it is property, it belongs to one Person and not another, and insofar as it is a notion, it is the source of knowing the Person. Therefore, the first thing conceptually is what is constituting the Person, the second what is distinguishing it, the third what is the property, and the fourth what is the notion.

Obj. 14. Many held that the Holy Spirit does not proceed from the Son but held three Persons in the Godhead, as is evident in the case of the Greeks. Therefore, even though the Holy Spirit does not proceed from the Son, he still remains distinct from the Son.

Reply Obj. 14. We should say that, although the Greeks do not profess that the Holy Spirit proceeds from the Son, they do profess that the Son is in some way the source of the origin of the Holy Spirit. And this is evident because they say that the Holy Spirit proceeds from the Father through the Son, and that the Holy Spirit is of the Son. Nevertheless, nothing prevents an ignorant person from explicitly granting what implicitly involves a contradiction. And so an ignorant person can say that the Holy Spirit does not proceed from the Son, although the Spirit is distinct from the Son.

Notes

QUESTION 1

1. A transitively active thing is an efficient cause.
2. *Physics* III, 4.
3. *De interpretatione* I.
4. *Topics* IV, 5.
5. *Metaphysics* IX, 1.
6. Ibid., XII, 10.
7. *Physics* VIII, 10.
8. *Commentary of the Physics* VIII, comm. 79.
9. *Metaphysics* V, 12.
10. Ibid., X, 4.
11. *Commentary on the De coelo* III, comm. 20.
12. Letter 22, to Eustochius.
13. Against Faustus XXVI, 5.
14. *Ethics* V, 2.
15. *Metaphysics* IV, 3.
16. Ibid., IX, 1 and 7.
17. *Physics* VIII.
18. *Generation of Animals* II, 1.
19. *Metaphysics* V, 12.
20. *Grace and Free Decision* 21.
21. Aristotle, *Metaphysics* IX, 2 and 5.

QUESTION 2

1. *Trinity* I.
2. *Sleep and Waking* 1.

3. Notion in the Trinitarian context is the property of a Divine Person, in this case of the Father.

4. *Ethics* I, 1.

5. *Metaphysics* IX, 6.

6. *Councils.*

7. *Metaphysics* VIII, 4.

8. *Councils.*

9. *Trinity* IX, 8.

10. *Similitudes* 2. The reference is to philosophical fragments by Anselm, not one of his major works.

11. *Physics* VIII, 5.

12. Ibid., II, 4.

13. *Monologion* 32.

14. *Trinity* VII, 1.

15. *Monologion* 60.

16. *Faith,* hom. 15.

17. *Orthodox Faith* II, 27.

18. *Physics* II, 4 and 5.

19. *De anima* II, 4.

QUESTION 3

1. *Liber de causis,* prop. 18.

2. Ibid., prop. 3.

3. *Metaphysics* V, 12,

4. Ibid., VII, 13.

5. *Monologion* 5 and 8.

6. *Metaphysics* III.

7. Ibid., V, 15,

8. *Sentences* IV, dist. 30.

9. *Metaphysics* III, 10.

10. *Literal Commentary on Genesis* VIII, 12.

11. *Liber de causis,* prop. 10.

12. *Metaphysics* IX, 4.

13. *Orthodox Faith* II, 2.

14. *Sentences* IV, dist. 5.

15. *Trinity* III, 8.

16. *Liber de causis,* prop. 19.

17. *Sentences* IV, dist. 5.

18. *Liber de causis,* props. 19 and 20.

19. *Physics* IV

20. *Metaphysics* VII, 8 and 9.

21. *City of God* VIII, 4.

22. *Metaphysics* II, 1.
23. Ibid., VIII, 7, and IX, 4.
24. *Liber de causis*, prop. 4.
25. Aristotle, *Physics* I, 4.
26. Aristotle, *Metaphysics* I, 4.
27. Aristotle, *Physics* I, 2.
28. *Divine Names* 4.
29. *Metaphysics* XII, 10.
30. Aristotle, *Physics* II, 5.
31. Aristotle, *Topics* II, 6.
32. *Categories* 10.
33. Aristotle, *Metaphysics* X, 4.
34. *Physics* I, 9.
35. *Two Natures.*
36. Moses Maimonides, a celebrated Jewish medieval theologian and philosopher, wrote the treatise *Guide of the Perplexed.*
37. Aristotle, *Physics* VI, 10.
38. Aristotle, *De coelo* IV, 2.
39. Aristotle, *Physic* IV.
40. *Liber de causis*, prop. 9.
41. Ibid., prop. 1.
42. *Physics* I, 4.
43. Aristotle, *Metaphysics* VII, 2.
44. Ibid., VII, 8.
45. *Trinity* II, 8.
46. *Literal Commentary on Genesis* X, 21 and 23.
47. Cf. Henry Denziger and Adolph Schoenmetzer, *Enchiridion Symbolorum* (Freiberg in Breislau: Herder, 1965), nn. 360 and 403.
48. Gennadius, *Church Dogmas* 13.
49. *Generation of Animals* I, 18.
50. *Literal Commentary on Genesis* XII, 16.
51. *Generation of Animals* II, 3.
52. Aristotle, *Metaphysics* VII, 7.
53. *Generation of Animals* XVI, 2.
54. *Physics* II, 7.
55. Actually, Nemesius, *Human Nature.*
56. *De anima* II, 1.
57. Aristotle, *Generation of Animals* I, 19.
58. Gennadius, *Church Dogmas* 15.
59. Aristotle, *Physics* I.
60. *Generation of Animals* II, 3.
61. Aristotle, *De anima* III, 8.
62. Ibid., III, 5.

63. *De coelo* I, 2.

64. *Consolation of Philosophy*, prose 10.

65. *De anima* II, 1.

66. Dream of Scipio I.

67. *Laws* V.

68. *Metaphysics* VII, 8.

69. Aristotle, *Physics* VII, 2.

70. *Generation of Animals* I, 18 and 19.

71. Ibid., II, 3.

72. *Physics* V, 2.

73. *Creation of Human Beings* 16.

74. *Generation of Animals* I, 18.

75. *Metaphysics* V, 12.

76. *Literal Commentary on Genesis* VIII, 23.

77. *Consolation of Philosophy* V.

78. *Physics* IV, 11.

79. *Literal Commentary on Genesis* VIII, 23.

80. *Monologion* 8.

81. Aristotle, *Physics* II, 4.

82. The text of John is inaccurate. It actually reads: "Nothing created was created without him. In him was life."

83. *Metaphysics* IX.

84. *Christian Doctrines* I, 32.

85. Aristotle, *De interpretatione* II, 3.

86. *Metaphysics* IX, 4.

87. *Peri archon* I, 7 and 8.

88. Aristotle, *Metaphysics* X, 3.

89. *Physics* II, 3.

90. *Monologion* 8.

91. See note 82, supra.

92. *Physics* VIII, 1.

93. Ibid.

94. *Literal Commentary on Genesis* VIII, 22.

95. Aristotle, *Physics* IV, 12.

96. *Proslogion* 19 and 20.

97. *City of God* XI, 23.

98. Basil, *Hexameron*, hom. 1.

99. *Literal Commentary on Genesis* II, 8, on Gen. 1:1.

100. *Glossa ordinaria*, on Gen. 1:1. The gloss is incorrectly attributed to Walafrid Strabo.

101. *Literal Commentary on Genesis* I, 9.

102. Ibid., I, 5.

103. *Generation of Animals* III, 4.
104. *Commentary on the Metaphysics* XI, comm. 44.
105. *Confessions* XI, 15.
106. *Trinity.*
107. *Physics* II.
108. Aristotle, *Physics* IV, 3.
109. Ibid., IV, 4.
110. *Trinity* III, 4.

QUESTION 4

1. *Confessions* XII.
2. Ibid., X.
3. *Literal Commentary on Genesis* I.
4. Ibid.
5. Ibid., I, 15.
6. It was a common opinion of medieval theologians that Plato had a primitive revelation of creation.
7. *De coelo* I.
8. Basil, *Hexameron*, hom. 2.
9. *Sixty-Five Dialogues*, Q. 21.
10. Aristotle, *De coelo* IV.
11. *Literal Commentary on Genesis* II, 4 and 5.
12. Ibid., II, 1.
13. Basil, *Hexameron*, hom. 3.
14. *Literal Commentary on Genesis* II, 5.
15. *Hexameron*, hom. 4.
16. *Sixty-Five Dialogues*, Q. 21.
17. *Timaeus.*
18. *De coelo* I.
19. *Literal Commentary on Genesis* I, 9.
20. *Confessions* XII.
21. *Literal Commentary on Genesis* II, 1.
22. Ibid., II, 11.
23. Aristotle, *De coelo* III.
24. *Sixty-Five Dialogues*, Q. 21.
25. *Literal Commentary on Genesis* II, 7 and 8.
26. Ibid., II, 11.
27. Ibid., I, 12.
28. Ibid., VI, 6.
29. Basil, *Hexameron*, hom. 4.
30. *Commentary on the De coelo* III, comm. 20.

31. *Physics* VIII.

32. *Literal Commentary on Genesis* I.

33. Ibid., IV.

34. *Sixty-Five Dialogues*, Q. 24.

35. *Literal Commentary on Genesis* I, 17.

36. *Against Faustus* XXII, 11.

37. *Divine Names* 4.

38. *Literal Commentary on Genesis* IV, 34.

39. Ibid., IV, 15.

40. Ibid., II, 7 and 8.

41. *Sixty-Five Dialogues*, Q. 26; *Literal Commentary on Genesis* II, 3 and 8.

42. *Sixty-Five Dialogues*, Q. 26.

43. *Literal Commentary on Genesis* VII, 24 and 25.

44. Ibid., V, 12 and 14.

45. *De anima* II.

46. *Literal Commentary on Genesis* X, 17.

47. Ibid., II, 8.

48. Gennadius, *Church Dogmas*.

49. *Letter to Peter, on Faith*. Actually, Fulgentius is the author.

50. *Ethics* I, 10.

51. *Confessions* V, 4.

52. *Heavenly Hierarchies* 4.

53. Aristotle, *Metaphysics* I, 2.

54. *Confessions* XII, 8.

55. *Literal Commentary on Genesis* III, 11.

56. *Divine Names* 4.

QUESTION 5

1. Aristotle, *Metaphysics* III, 2

2. Hebr. 1:3; Augustine, *Literal Commentary on Genesis* IV, 12; Gregory the Great, *Morals* VI, 18; *Liber de causis*, prop. 9.

3. *Literal Commentary on Genesis* X.

4. Ibid., IV, 12.

5. *Metaphysics* VII, 8.

6. *Metaphysics* IX, 4 and 5.

7. *Literal Commentary on Genesis* VIII, 12.

8. *Sentences* V, 4.

9. *Metaphysics* VIII, 6.

10. *Commentary on the Metaphysics* XI; *Substance of the Heavens*.

11. Aristotle, *Metaphysics* V.

12. *Christian Doctrine* I, 32.

13. *Commentary on the Metaphysics* XI, comm. 41. Actually, the commentary is on Book 12.
14. Aristotle, *Physics* VIII.
15. *Commentary on the Metaphysics* XI, comm. 41. See note 13, supra.
16. *De coelo* I.
17. Aristotle, *De anima* III, 7; *Physics* III.
18. Aristotle, *Metaphysics* II.
19. Aristotle, *De coelo* I.
20. Aristotle, *Ethics* I.
21. Aristotle, *Metaphysics* IX; *Ethics* I, 1.
22. *Physics* II.
23. Aristotle, ibid.
24. *Commentary on Metaphysics* II and *Substance of the Heavens.*
25. *Letter 80, to Hesychius.*
26. *De coelo* I.
27. *City of God* XX, 16.
28. *De coelo* II.
29. *Commentary on the Physics* II.
30. *Literal Commentary on Genesis* II.
31. Ibid., III, 10.
32. *Physics* II.
33. *Politics* I, 5.
34. *De coelo* I.
35. *City of God* XXII, 26.
36. *Literal Commentary on Genesis* XII, 35.
37. *De anima* 10.

QUESTION 6

1. Aristotle, *Metaphysics* II.
2. *De coelo* II.
3. *Trinity* III, 11 and 12.
4. Ibid., III, 4.
5. *Liber de causis*, prop. 4.
6. Aristotle, *Metaphysics* IV.
7. *Ethics* VI, 2.
8. Aristotle, *Physics* III.
9. *Commentary on the Metaphysics* IX.
10. *Metaphysics* I, 2.
11. According to Augustine in his *Commentary on John* VIII and *Trinity* III, 5, a miracle is "something difficult and unusual above the capacity of nature and apparently beyond the expectation of the one wondering."

12. *Trinity* II, 10.

13. *Metaphysics* VII, 8.

14. *Physics* VIII.

15. Aristotle, ibid., VI.

16. *Trinity* III, 8 and 9.

17. *Literal Commentary on Genesis* IX, 17.

18. *Physics* II.

19. *Trinity* III, 4.

20. Gregory the Great, *Dialogues* IV, 6.

21. *City of God* XVIII, 18.

22. Ibid., XXII, 7.

23. Gregory the Great, *Dialogues* II, 30.

24. Ibid.

25. *Homilies on Ezekiel*, hom. 1.

26. *Trinity* III, 9.

27. *City of God* X, 26.

28. *Confessions.*

29. *Physics* VIII.

30. *Metaphysics* XIII.

31. *City of God* IV, 31.

32. *Physics* VIII.

33. *Metaphysics* XI.

34. Aristotle, *Physics* VII.

35. *Dream of Scipio* I.

36. *City of God* VIII, 16.

37. *De anima* I.

38. Aristotle, *Physics* VII.

39. *Literal Commentary on Genesis* II, last chapter.

40. Comment on Eccl. 1:6: "The spirit passing roundabout all things."

41. *Peri archon* I, 7.

42. *Enchiridion* 58.

43. *Heavenly Hierarchies* 14.

44. Aristotle, *Physics* I.

45. Aristotle, ibid., VIII.

46. *Trinity* III, 11 and 12.

47. *Literal Commentary on Genesis* XI, 7 and 24.

48. *Trinity* III, 11 and 12.

49. Ibid.

50. Ibid., III, 8 and 9.

51. Gregory the Great, *Dialogues* II, 30.

52. Augustine, *Commentary on John* XLIV.

53. He gives the following definition of miracle in *City of God* IV, 1: "something difficult and unusual, appearing above the capacity of nature and contrary to the expectation of the one wondering."

54. Augustine, *City of God* VIII, 16.

55. Ibid.

56. Ibid., XXI, 6.

QUESTION 7

1. Aristotle, *Physics* II.

2. *Metaphysics* XI.

3. *Trinity* 7.

4. *Generation* II.

5. *Heavenly Hierarchies* 11.

6. *Commentary on the Metaphysics* XI, comm. 18.

7. *Metaphysics* V.

8. *Christian Doctrine* I, 5.

9. *Liber de causis*, prop. 9.

10. *Orthodox Faith* I, 1 and 3.

11. Aristotle, *Metaphysics* X.

12. *Liber de causis*, prop. 4.

13. Ibid., prop. 20. Thomas here erroneously attributes the *Liber* to Aristotle, although he elsewhere challenged the attribution.

14. *De interpretatione* I.

15. *Divine Names* 5.

16. *Metaphysics* III, 6.

17. Aristotle, ibid., V.

18. *Orthodox Faith* III, 4.

19. *Metaphysics* X.

20. *Metaphysics* III, 8.

21. *Metaphysics* III, 6.

22. *Trinity*.

23. *Metaphysics* VIII.

24. *Metaphysics* V, 5.

25. *De hebdomatibus*.

26. *Orthodox Faith* I.

27. *Trinity* V, 1.

28. *Predicables*, chapter on accidents.

29. *De hebdomatibus*.

30. *Divine Names* 12.

31. *Orthodox Faith* I, 12.

32. *Divine Names* 1.
33. Aristotle, *Metaphysics* V.
34. *Commentary on the Metaphysics* V.
35. *Heavenly Hierarchies* 2.
36. *Mystical Theology* 1; *Heavenly Hierarchies* 2; *Divine Names* 2 and 3.
37. *Mystical Theology* 1.
38. *De interpretatione* I.
39. *Commentary on the Metaphysics* XI.
40. *Christian Doctrine* II, 32.
41. *Orthodox Faith* I, 11.
42. *Divine Names* 9.
43. *Trinity*.
44. *Physics* V.
45. *Categories* V.
46. Ibid.
47. Aristotle, *Metaphysics* IV.
48. *Commentary on the Metaphysics* XI.
49. The second things understood are the logical modes of predication, the most general of which are the predicables: genus, species, specific difference, property, and accident.
50. Aristotle, *Metaphysics* V.
51. Ibid., X.
52. Ibid., V.
53. Ibid., VII.
54. Aristotle, *Metaphysics* IV.
55. Ibid.
56. *Metaphysics* VII, 7.
57. *Metaphysics* V.
58. *Divine Names* 1.
59. *Faith* I, 2.
60. Aristotle, *Metaphysics* V.
61. *Preface of Porphyry on the Predicables*.
62. Aristotle, *Metaphysics* V.

QUESTION 8

1. *Divine Names* 11.
2. *Trinity* V, 16.
3. Ibid., V, 1.
4. *Trinity*.
5. *Metaphysics* V.

6. *Trinity* V, 4 and 5, cited in Objs. 5 and 13 in this article.

7. *Commentary on the Metaphysics* XI, comm. 19.

8. *Topics* I.

9. *Physics* III, 3.

10. *Trinity* VII, 1.

11. Aristotle, *Metaphysics* V.

QUESTION 9

1. *Metaphysics* V.

2. Ibid., VII.

3. *Trinity* VII, 3.

4. Ibid., VII, 4.

5. *Commentary on the Categories.*

6. *Metaphysics* VII.

7. Ibid., VIII.

8. Aristotle, *Physics* II, 1.

9. Ibid.

10. *Two Natures.*

11. *Trinity* IV, 18 and 23.

12. *Two Natures.*

13. Thomas erroneously derives the Latin word for stone (*lapis*) from the Latin word for hurting the foot (*laesio*).

14. *Sentences* I, dist. 25.

15. *Metaphysics* IV.

16. Ibid.

17. *Trinity* VII, 4.

18. Ibid., VII, 6.

19. *Trinity* II.

20. Actually, Anselm, *Monologion* 14.

21. Aristotle, *De anima* III.

22. *Orthodox Faith* I, 11.

23. *Christian Doctrine* I, 5.

24. *Orthodox Faith* I, 11.

25. *De coelo* I.

26. *Trinity.*

27. *Sentences* I, dist. 24.

28. *Heavenly Hierarchies* 2.

29. *Orthodox Faith* I, 4.

30. *Divine Names* 12.

31. *Mystical Theology* 1; *Heavenly Hierarchies* 2; *Divine Names* 1 and 2.

32. *Sentences* I, dist. 24.
33. Actually, *Mystical Theology* 1.
34. *Heavenly Hierarchies* 2; *Divine Names* 4 and 11.
35. Aristotle, *Ethics* I, 1.
36. Aristotle, *Metaphysics* V.
37. Ibid., X.
38. Ibid., V.
39. *Councils.*
40. *Metaphysics* X.
41. *Orthodox Faith* III.
42. *Councils.*
43. Trimegistus.
44. *Against Maximus* III, 11.
45. Cf. *Physics* III.
46. *Divine Names* 4.
47. *Commentary on the Physic* VIII.
48. This text of 1 Jn. 5:7 does not correspond to the Greek text or the best attested Vulgate text.
49. *Trinity* VII, 4.
50. *Trinity* III, 2.
51. Ibid., III, 5.
52. Ibid., III.
53. *Trinity* IX, 1 and 2.
54. *Trinity* V, 6.

QUESTION 10

1. *Metaphysics* X.
2. *De anima* III.
3. Aristotle, *Physics* III.
4. *Timaeus.*
5. *Divine Names* 9.
6. Letter against those who say that the Holy Spirit is a creature.
7. *Orthodox Faith* I, 9.
8. *Trinity* VII.
9. See note 6, supra.
10. *City of God* V, 10.
11. *Orthodox Faith* III, 4.
12. *Divine Names* 2.
13. *Against Maximus* IV.
14. Actually, Fulgentius, *On Faith, to Peter* 2.
15. Hilary, *Councils.*

16. *Physics* VIII, 1.
17. *Divine Names* 1.
18. The first six Ecumenical Councils, in which both the Western Catholic and Eastern Orthodox Churches participated, resolved fundamental Trinitarian and Christological questions. Thomas cites these Councils in this objection and reply, and elsewhere. For the decrees of the Councils, consult *Enchiridion Symbolorum*. For summary data on the Councils and the meaning of key theological terms, see F. L. Cross and E. A. Livingstone, *Oxford Dictionary of the Christian Church*, 3rd ed. (Oxford: Oxford University Press, 1997).
19. See note 6, supra.
20. *Holy Spirit* III, 1.
21. *Trinity* VIII.
22. *Trinity and Unity* 10.
23. *Orthodox Faith* I.
24. Reply Obj. 13.
25. *De coelo* I.
26. *Trinity* VI, 2.
27. *Metaphysics* VIII.
28. *Trinity* V, 10.
29. *Trinity and Unity* 13.
30. *Metaphysics* VIII.
31. *Councils.*
32. Ibid.
33. *Trinity* V, 9.
34. Ibid., VI, 17.
35. Procession of the Holy Spirit II.

Bibliography

For a comprehensive bibliography on the life and works of Thomas and commentaries on his thought, see Brian Davies, *Aquinas* (London: Continuum, 2002), pp. xi–xxii. Among more recent books, the following are noteworthy.

Thomas Aquinas, *The Cardinal Virtues*, translated and edited by Richard J. Regan (Indianapolis: Hackett, 2005).

———. *The Compendium of Theology*, translated and edited by Richard J. Regan (New-York: Oxford University. Press, 2009).

———. *On Creation [Quaestiones Disputatae de Potentia Dei, Q. 3]*, translated, with notes, by Susan C. Selner-Wright (Washington: Catholic University. of America Press, 2011).

———. *A Summary of Philosophy*, translated and edited by Richard J. Regan (Indianapolis: Hackett, 2003).

Etienne Gilson, *Thomism: The Philosophy of Thomas Aquinas*, 6th final and substantially revised edition (Toronto: Pontifical Institute of Medieval Studies, 2002).

Fergus Kerr, editor, *Contemplating Aquinas* (London: SCM Press, 2003).

Herbert McCabe, *Aquinas* (London: Continuum, 2005).

Rik van Nieuwenhove and Joseph Wawrykow, editors, *The Theology of Thomas Aquinas* (Notre Dame: University of Notre Dame Press, 2005).

The SCM Press A to Z of Thomas Aquinas (London: SCM Press, 2005).

Eleanore Stump, *Aquinas* (London: Routledge, 2003).

Rudi A. te Velde, *Aquinas on God* (Aldershot, England: Ashgate, 2007).

Index

Alexander of Aphrodisius, 169, 189–190
Anaxagoras, 60, 85, 90, 91, 177
Algazel, 43
Ambrose, 295
Angels
  and bodies, 176–185
  creation of, 94–98
  and miracles, 172–174
Annihilation of creatures, 14–19, 138–141
Anselm, 301
Aristotle, 48, 49, 91, 102, 165, 168, 176
Arius, 27, 77, 266 268, 277
Athanasius, 277, 294, 295
Augustine
  on angels and creation, 94, 117–127,
    174, 183
  on Father missioning the Son, 295
  on goodness of God as final cause of
    creation, 211
  on miracles, 166
  on perfect vision of God after the
    resurrection, 159
  and power of devils, 174, 190
  on the power of elements to act and
    be acted upon, 154–156
  on procession of the Word, 23
  and qualities of elements at the end
    of the world, 151–156

  on the seventh day after creation, 116
  on the six days of creation, 110, 113
  on spiritual creatures, 167
  on spiritual substances united to
    heavenly bodies, 176–177
  on unformed matter in the Genesis
    account, 100, 102, 104, 106–107,
    109
Averroes, 138, 273
Avicenna, 42, 49, 69, 81, 85–86, 138,
  168

Basil, 102, 104–105, 107
Boethius, 68

Church doctrine, 62–63, 66, 79
Creation
  of angels, 94–98
  difference from change, 39–41
  and eternal existing, 76–81, 89–94
  by free decision of God, 81–84
  of formed matter, 109–131
  and multiplicity from one thing,
    84–89
  and natural action, 59–62
  and possible creatures, 14–19
  power of God regarding, 36–39, 48,
    54

Creation (*continued*)
  power of incommunicable to a
    creature, 41–48
  of rational soul, 62–71
  as real relation in creature, 41–43
  and sensory and vegetative souls,
    71–74
  of unformed matter, 100–109
Cyril of Alexandria, 294, 296

Damascene, 212
Democritus, 81, 90
Devils
  and bodies, 176–185
  and wondrous works, 174–176
Dionysius, 200, 206, 208, 228, 277,
    292

Ecumenical Councils and procession of
    the Holy Spirit, 277, 292–294, 296
Empedocles, 90
End of World
  elements at, 151–154
  heavenly motion at, 144–149
  human bodies at, 158–160
  natural action at, 154–156
  time of, 149–151

Generation of the Son
  in comparison with creation, 34–35
  as included in omnipotence, 32–34
  as necessary, 27–30
  of only one Son, 30–32
  power of in the Godhead, 21–24
  as property (notion) of the Father,
    25–27
Gilbert de la Porreé, 232
God
  identity of essence and existing in,
    196–199
  not in a genus, 200–202

predications about, 202–216.
    See also Predications of
    God, Wise, Just about God
  relations between creatures and,
    216–226. *See also* Relations
  relations in the Godhead, 227–234
  simplicity of, 193–196
  See also Generation, Power of God,
    Procession of the divine Persons
Gregory the Great, 128, 175, 182
Greek theologians
  on equivalence of hypostasis to
    person, 243, 244
  on procession of the Holy Spirit, 291,
    303–304

Hilary, 295
Human embryo, life in, 64–68

Lombard, 44, 295

Macedonius, 268
Macrobius, 70
Manicheans, 50–51, 86
Miracles
  by angels and human beings,
    172–174
  and attribution to faith, 187–189
  and devils, 174–176, 189–190
  and God, 161–167
  and spiritual creatures, 167–176
Moses Maimonides
  on apparitions of angels, 182
  on disposition of creatures by God's
    will, 89–90
  on Genesis account of creation, 103
  on Islam and natural causality, 54
  on predications about God, 206, 214,
    261

Nestorians, 296

Origen, 86, 94, 103

Person
    as absolute in God, 248–250
    meaning of the word, 244–248
    as relation in Godhead, 250–254
Persons in the Trinity
    and diversity in God, 266–267
    predicating numerical terms of,
        260–266
    properties (notions) of, 25–27
    relation of to essence, substance, and
        hypostasis, 242–244
    as several, 254–260
    as three, 268–275
Plato, 48, 69, 86, 102, 177–178, 277
Power of God
    absolutely, 3–20
    to create, 36–99. *See also* Creation
    to generate, 21–35. *See also*
        Generation
Possibility of things, 9–14
Predication of *good, wise,* and *just* about
        God
    not as accidents, 202–205
    as not synonymous, 210–213
    as not univocal or purely equivocal in
        predication about God and
        creatures, 213–219
    as signifying the divine substance,
        205–209

Preservation of creatures
    and annihilation, 14–19, 138–144
    and end of world, 144–160. *See also*
        End of world
    in general, 132–137
Procession of the divine Persons,
        276–280
    of the Holy Spirit from the Son,
        288–304
    number, 280–286
    order of, 286–288

Rational Soul
    creation of, 62–68
    creation in each human body, 68–71
Relations
    of creatures to God, 41–43, 216–222
    distinguishing Persons, 234–238
    of God to creatures, 216–219, 222–226
    in Godhead, 227–234
    and hypostases, 238–241
Richard of St. Victor, 274–275, 298, 300

Sabellius, 4, 227, 266, 268
Sensory and vegetative souls
    not produced or transmitted by
        semen, 71–74
    not in semen at moment of emission,
        74–76

Theodorus, 296

Printed in the USA/Agawam, MA
September 6, 2012